Dogs Are People, Too

A Collection of Cartoons to Make Your Tail Wag

WELL, THAT'S EMBARRASSING.

DAVE COVERLY

Christy Ottaviano Books

Henry Holt and Company 🐾 New York

Belly rubs to Christy Ottaviano, April Ward, Jack Newcombe,
Pete Kaminski, Jessica Burtch, Ira Yoffe, Henrik Werdelin,
Chris & Alayna & Simone, Cathy, Patrick McDonnell, and Dave Barry . . .
and anyone who's ever rescued, helped, sheltered, or loved a dog.

Henry Holt and Company, LLC
Publishers since 1866
175 Fifth Avenue
New York, New York 10010
mackids.com

Henry Holt® is a registered trademark of Henry Holt and Company, LLC.
Compilation copyright © 2015 by Dave Coverly
All Speed Bump cartoons courtesy of Creators (creators.com); cartoons on pages 6, 60, 94,
100, and 127 courtesy of *Parade* magazine; all doodles courtesy of BarkBox (barkbox.com).

Library of Congress Catalog Card Number: 2014942564
ISBN 978-1-62779-042-0

Henry Holt books may be purchased for business or promotional use. For information on
bulk purchases, please contact Macmillan Corporate and Premium Sales Department at
(800) 221-7945 x5442 or by e-mail at specialmarkets@macmillan.com.

First Edition—2015 / Designed by April Ward
Printed in China by Toppan Leefung Printing Ltd., Dongguan City, Guangdong Province

3 5 7 9 10 8 6 4 2

A PEEK INSIDE THE MIND OF A YAPPY DOG

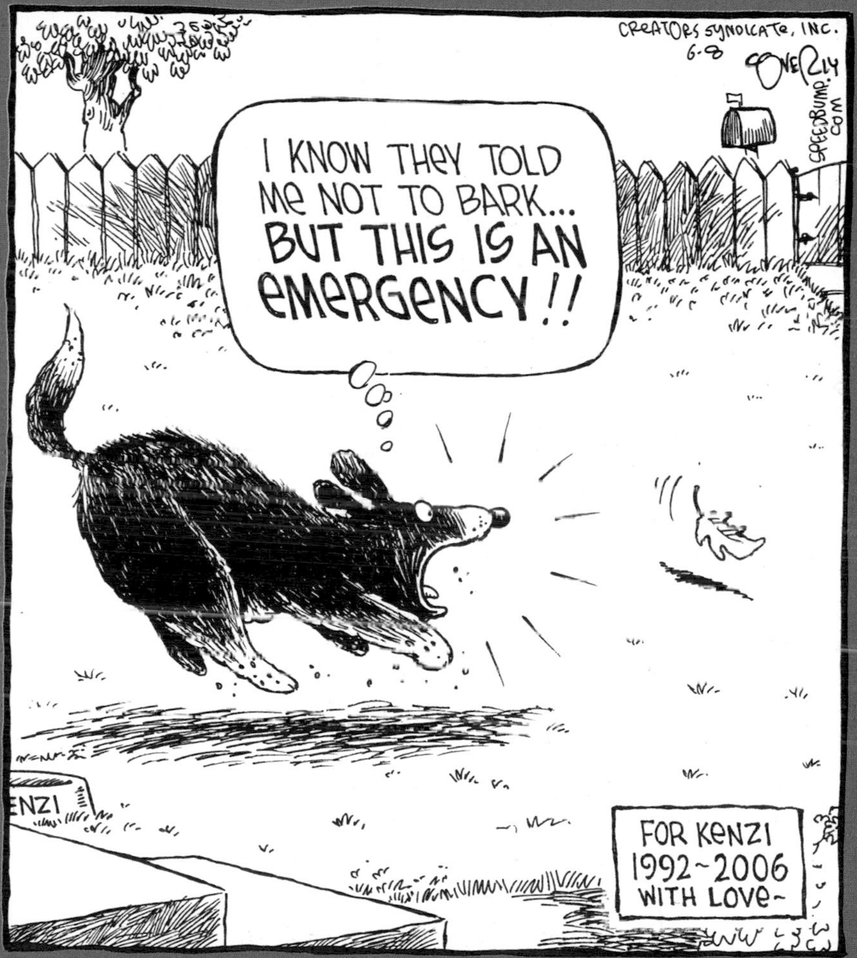
CREATORS SYNDICATE, INC.
6-8
COVERLY
SPEEDBUMP.COM
I KNOW THEY TOLD ME NOT TO BARK... BUT THIS IS AN EMERGENCY!!
ENZI
FOR KENZI
1992~2006
WITH LOVE~

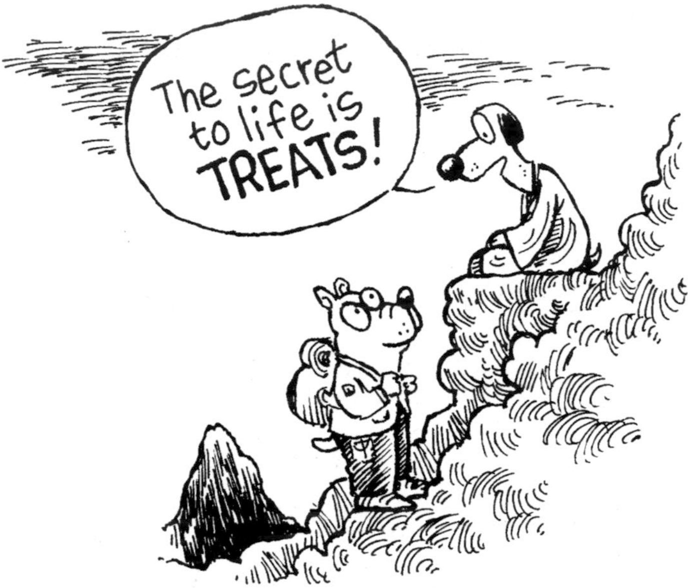
The secret to life is TREATS!

Dogs do speak, but only to those who know how to listen.

—ORHAN PAMUK, *MY NAME IS RED*

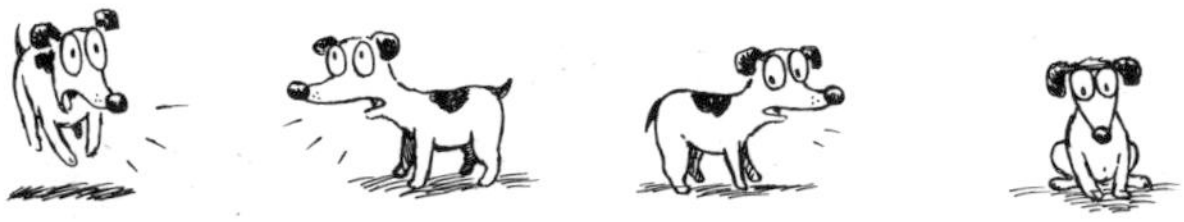

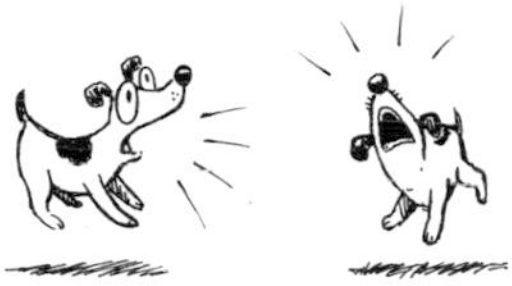

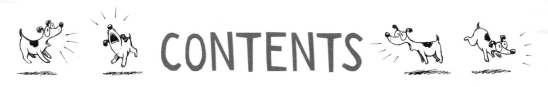

CONTENTS

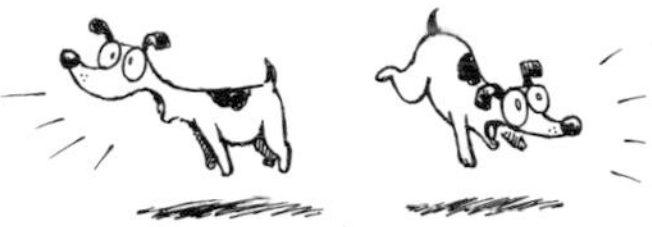

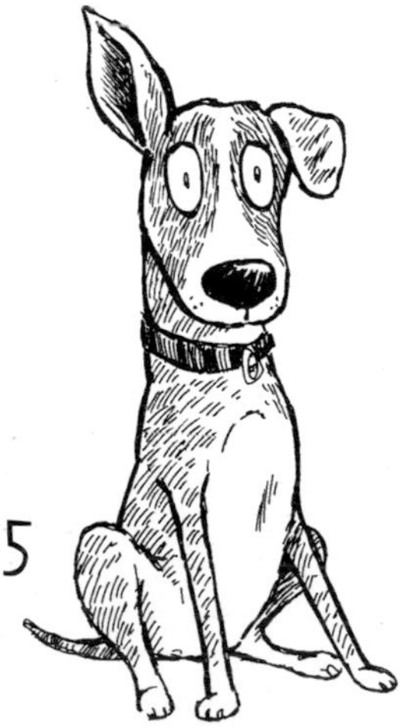

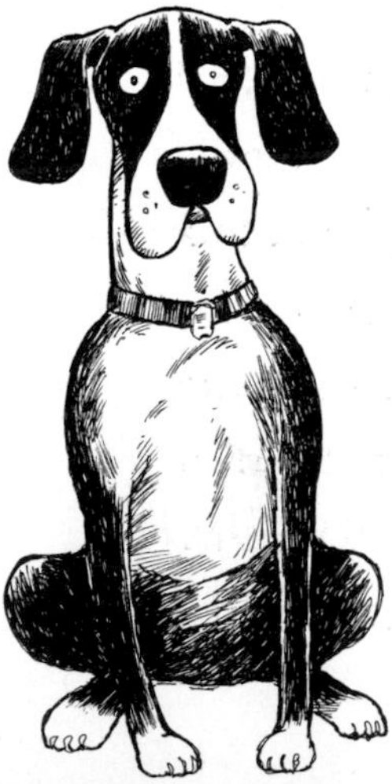

INTRODUCTION

Dave and Teddy (hiding), 1968.

I fell in love with dogs at the same time and in the same place that I fell in love with cartoons. It was in Southfield, Michigan, a suburb fifteen miles northwest of Detroit, where my Grandma and Grandpa Doehring lived when I was little. They had a wonderful, smallish collie named Teddy who would greet us at the door when we visited. In hindsight, his happiness at our arrival may have been because he knew my grandparents would let my sister, Cathy, and me give him a treat the minute we got inside.

In his mind, 2 Little People = 2 Big Milk-Bones. To this day, I love the smell of Milk-Bone dog biscuits. Of course, like most kids, Cathy and I even tried eating one. If you've never had one, they're not as bad as you might think.

My grandparents subscribed to a huge, thick newspaper (yes, in ancient times, newspapers were big) called the *Detroit Free Press*, which had a glorious Sunday Comics section. They carried cartoons I'd never seen before, including my favorite at the time, *Frank and Ernest*. As much as I loved *Peanuts* and *BC* and *Hagar the Horrible*, *Frank and Ernest* dazzled my little brain because the whole joke was in one panel. The creator, Bob Thaves, played on words I'd heard of and concepts I found familiar even at my young age. It was a mini-revelation. Kinda like the taste of Milk-Bones.

This book is about dogs and cartoons, two things that are practically a part of my DNA. So kick back, grab a bowl of water and a Milk-Bone, and take a cartoon peek inside the canine mind with me.

DAVE COVERLY

Belfry Studio
Ann Arbor, Michigan

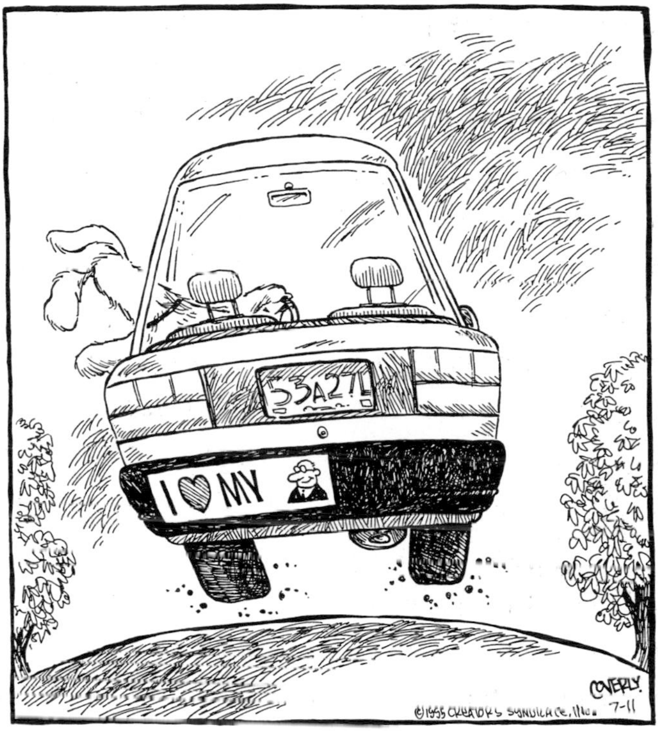
53A27
I ♥ MY
COVERLY
©1995 CREATORS SYNDICATE, INC. 7-11

All his life he tried to be a good person.
Many times, however, he failed.
For after all, he was only human.
He wasn't a dog.

—CHARLES M. SCHULZ

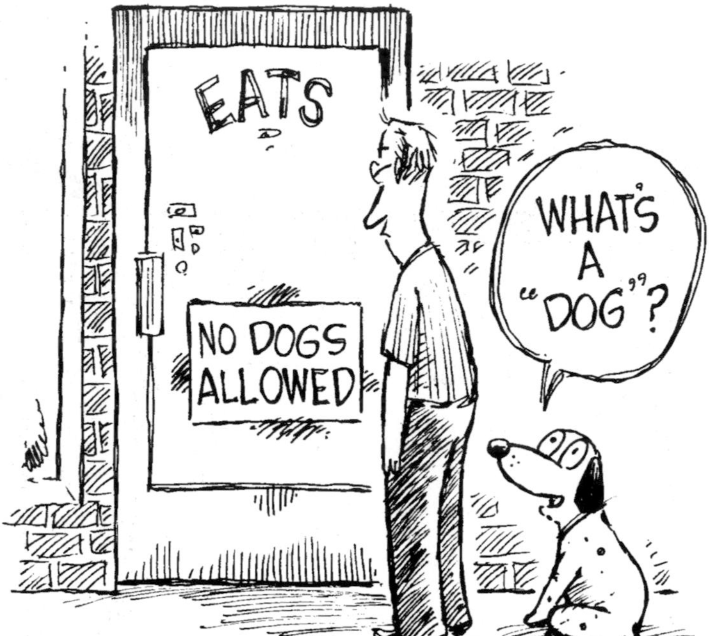
EATS
NO DOGS ALLOWED
WHAT'S A "DOG"?

CHAPTER 1

SNIFFING, BARKING, EATING, POOPING

(You Know, Stuff Dogs Are Good At)

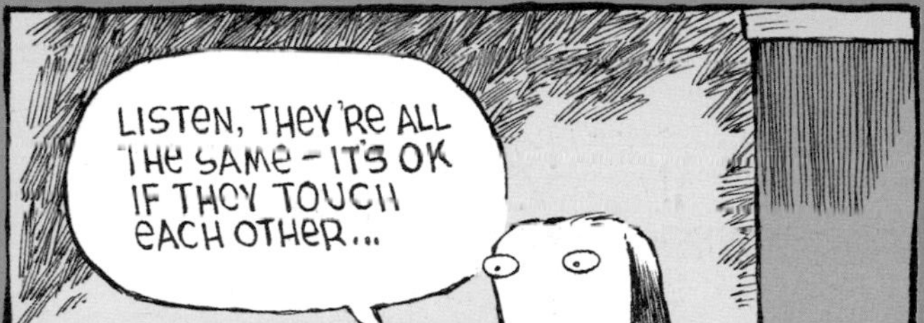
LISTEN, THEY'RE ALL THE SAME – IT'S OK IF THEY TOUCH EACH OTHER...
6-12
©2009 COVERLY
SPEEDBUMP.com
DIST. BY CREATORS SYND.

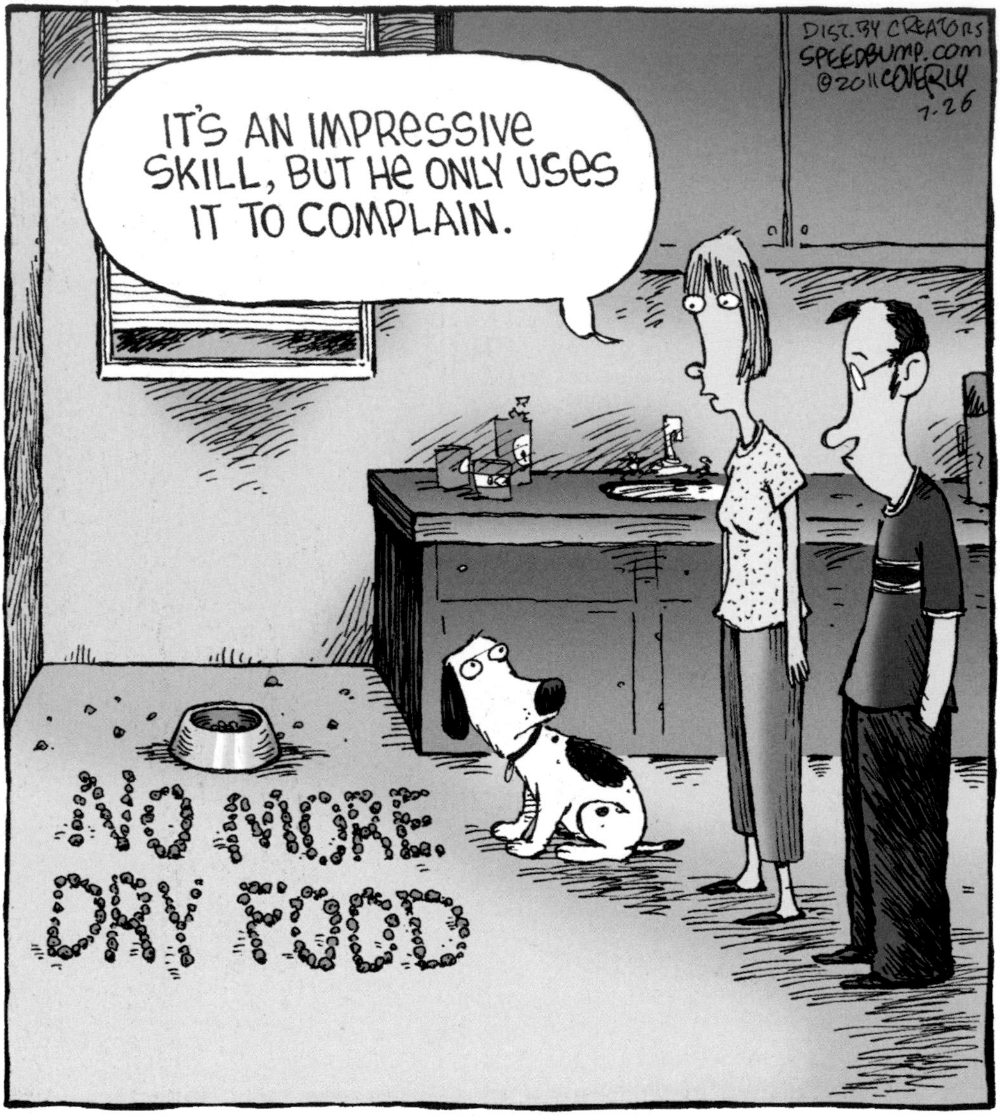
DIST. BY CREATORS
SPEEDBUMP.COM
©2011 COVERLY
7-26
IT'S AN IMPRESSIVE SKILL, BUT HE ONLY USES IT TO COMPLAIN.
NO MORE DRY FOOD

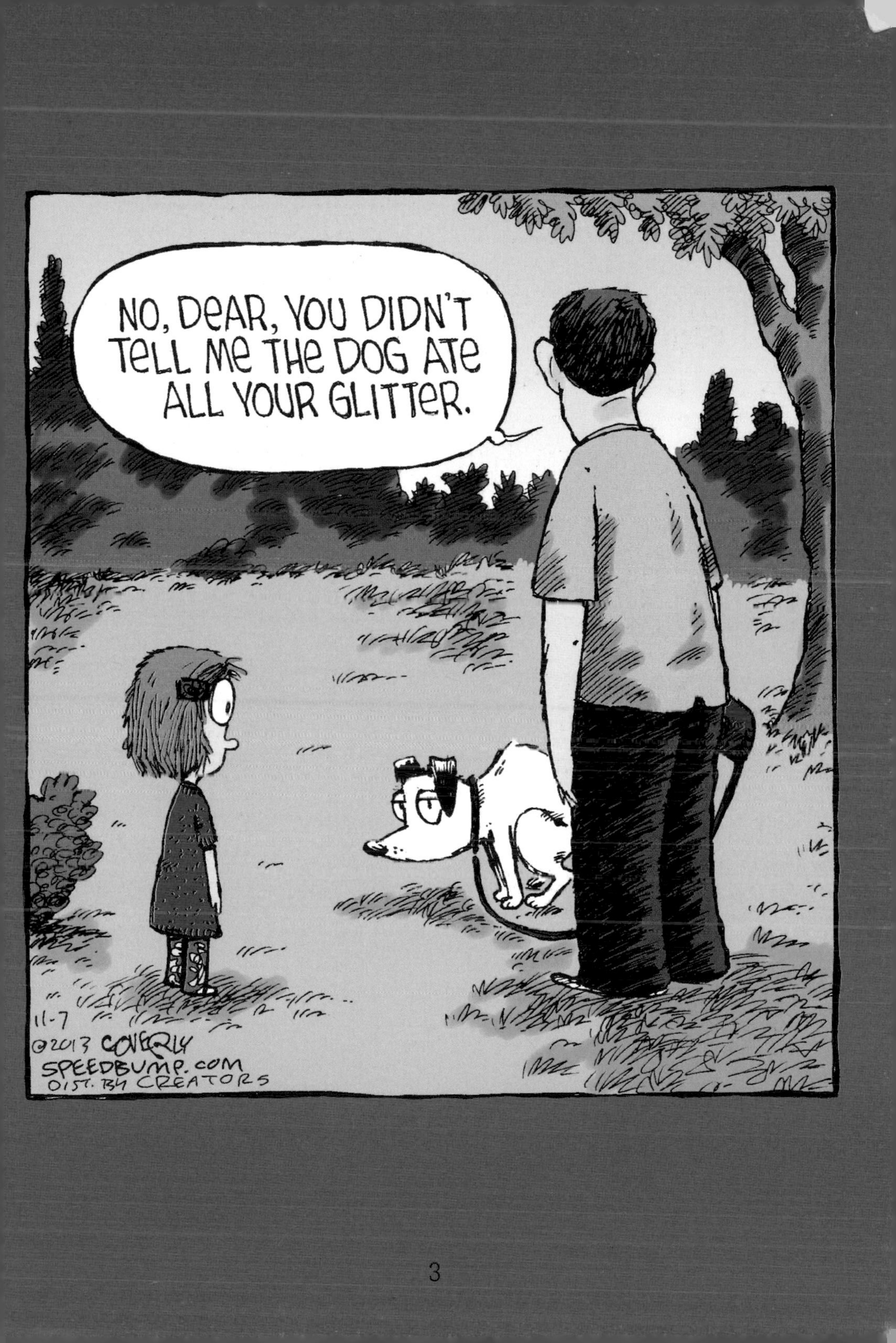
NO, DeAR, YOU DIDN'T TeLL Me THe DOG ATe ALL YOUR GLITTeR.
11-7
©2013 COVERLY
SPEEDBUMP.COM
DIST. BY CREATORS

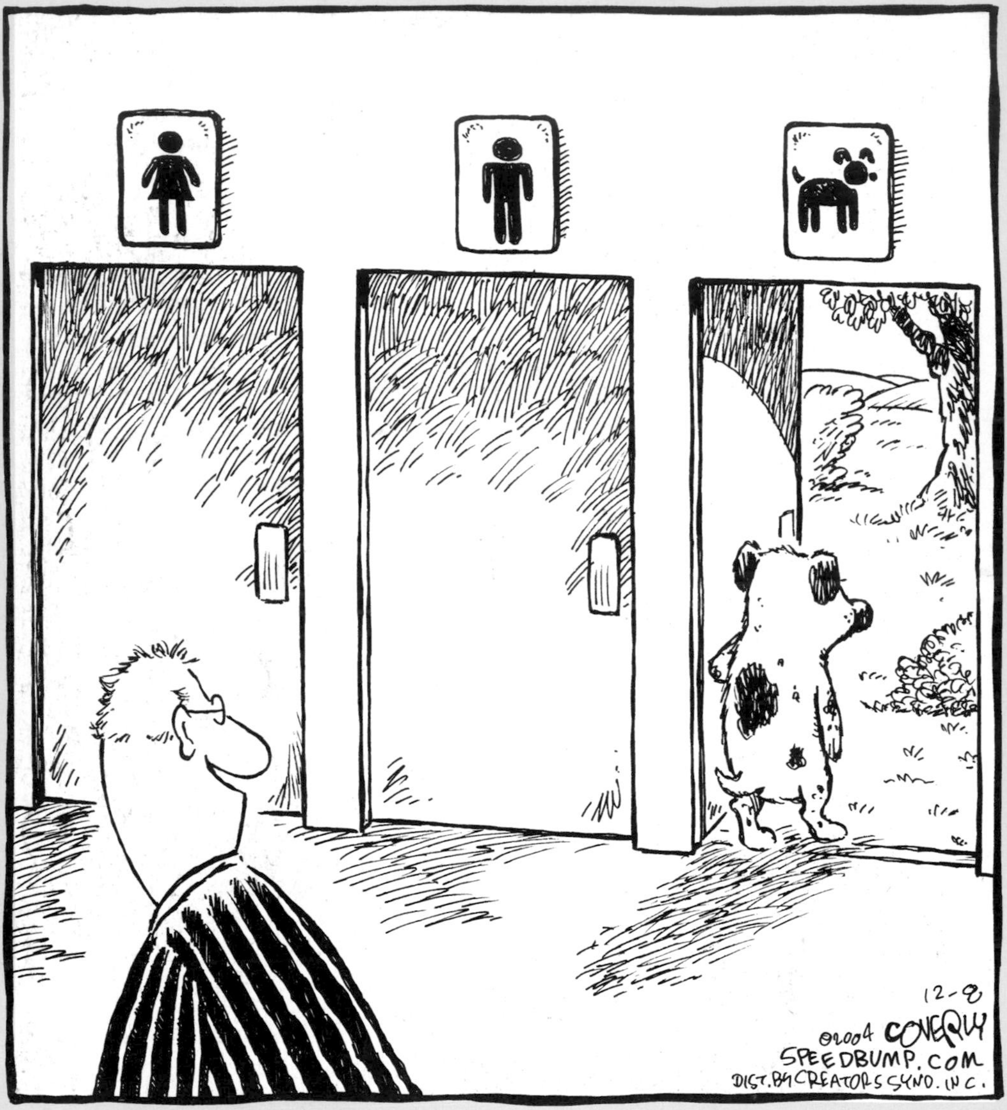
12-8
©2004 COVERLY
SPEEDBUMP.COM
DIST. BY CREATORS SYND. INC.

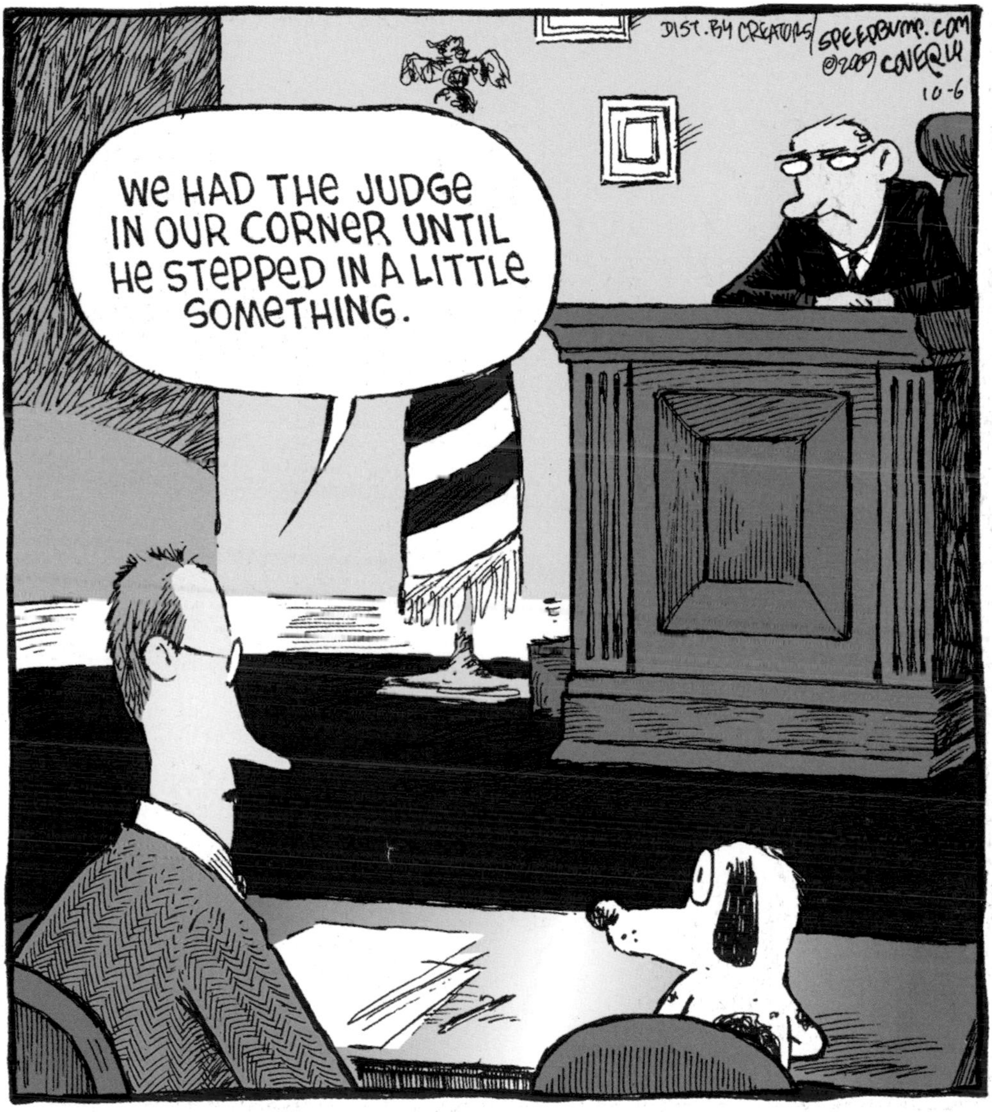
DIST. BY CREATORS/ SPEEDBUMP.COM ©2009 COVERLY 10-6
WE HAD THE JUDGE IN OUR CORNER UNTIL HE STEPPED IN A LITTLE SOMETHING.

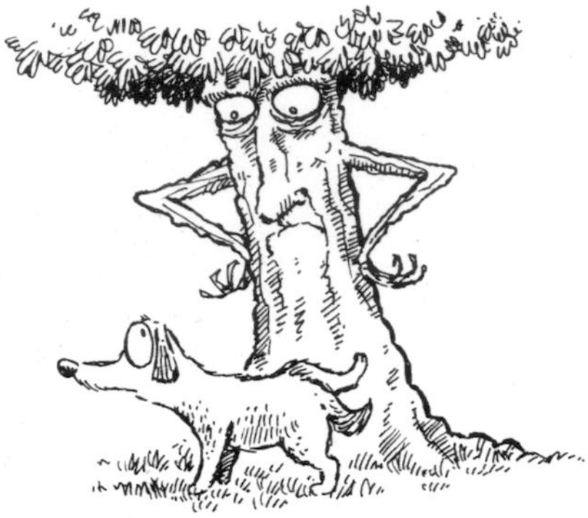

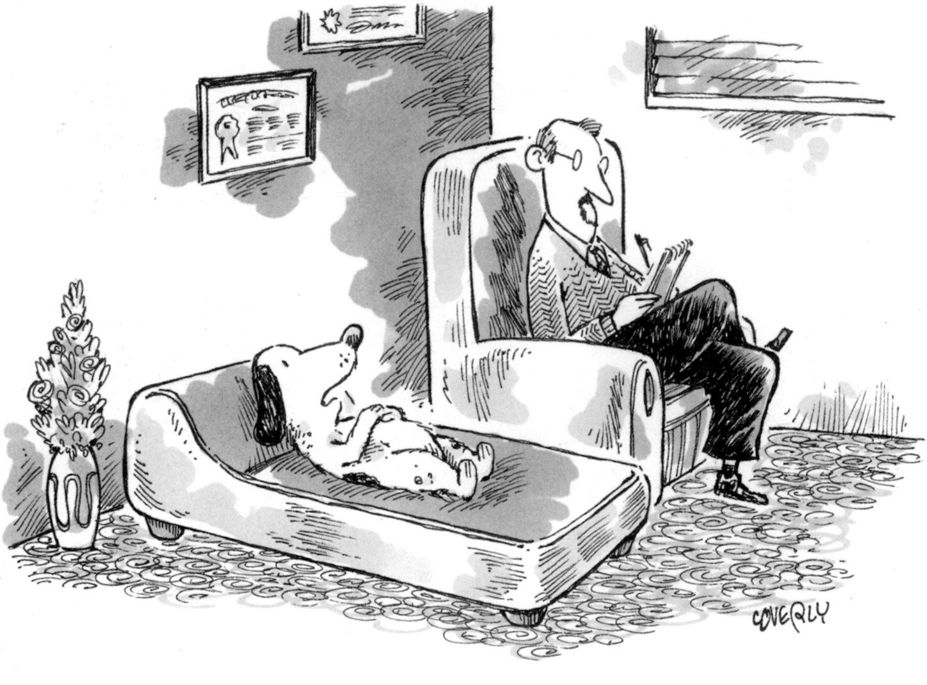
COVERLY

“If I’m being honest with myself, they’re not really ‘accidents.’”

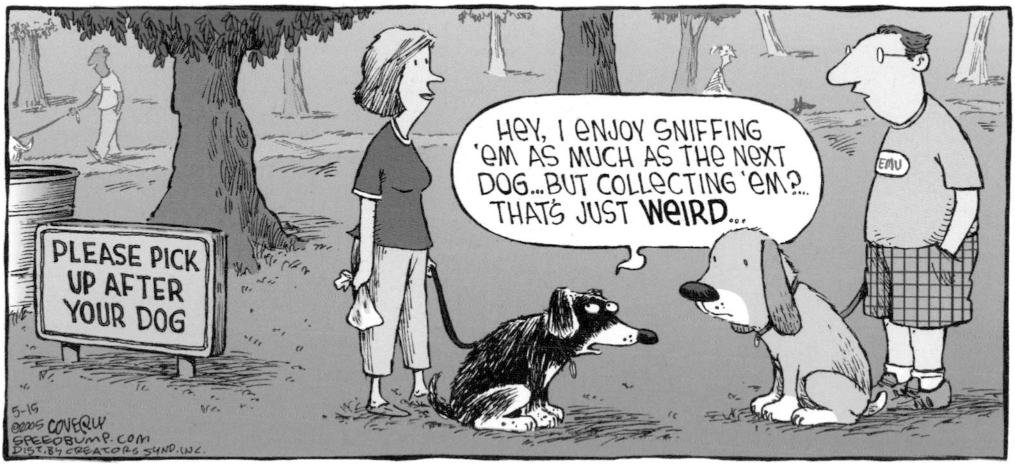
PLEASE PICK UP AFTER YOUR DOG
HEY, I ENJOY SNIFFING 'EM AS MUCH AS THE NEXT DOG...BUT COLLECTING 'EM?... THAT'S JUST **WEIRD**...
EMU
5-15
©2005 COVERLY
SPEEDBUMP.COM
DIST. BY CREATORS SYND. INC.

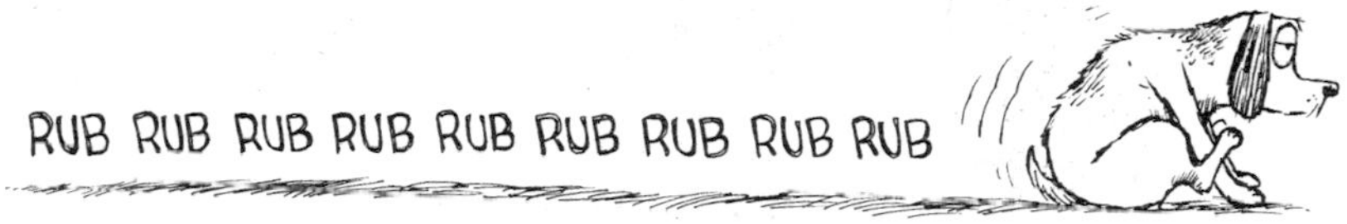
RUB RUB RUB RUB RUB RUB RUB RUB RUB

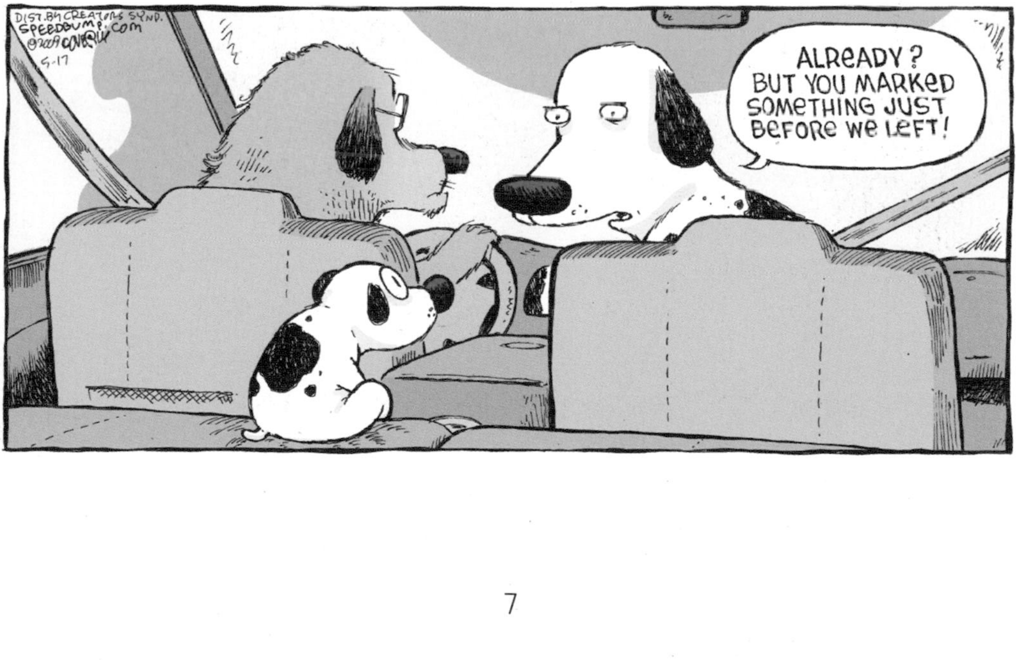
DIST. BY CREATORS SYND.
SPEEDBUMP.COM
©2009 COVERLY
5-17
ALREADY? BUT YOU MARKED SOMETHING JUST BEFORE WE LEFT!

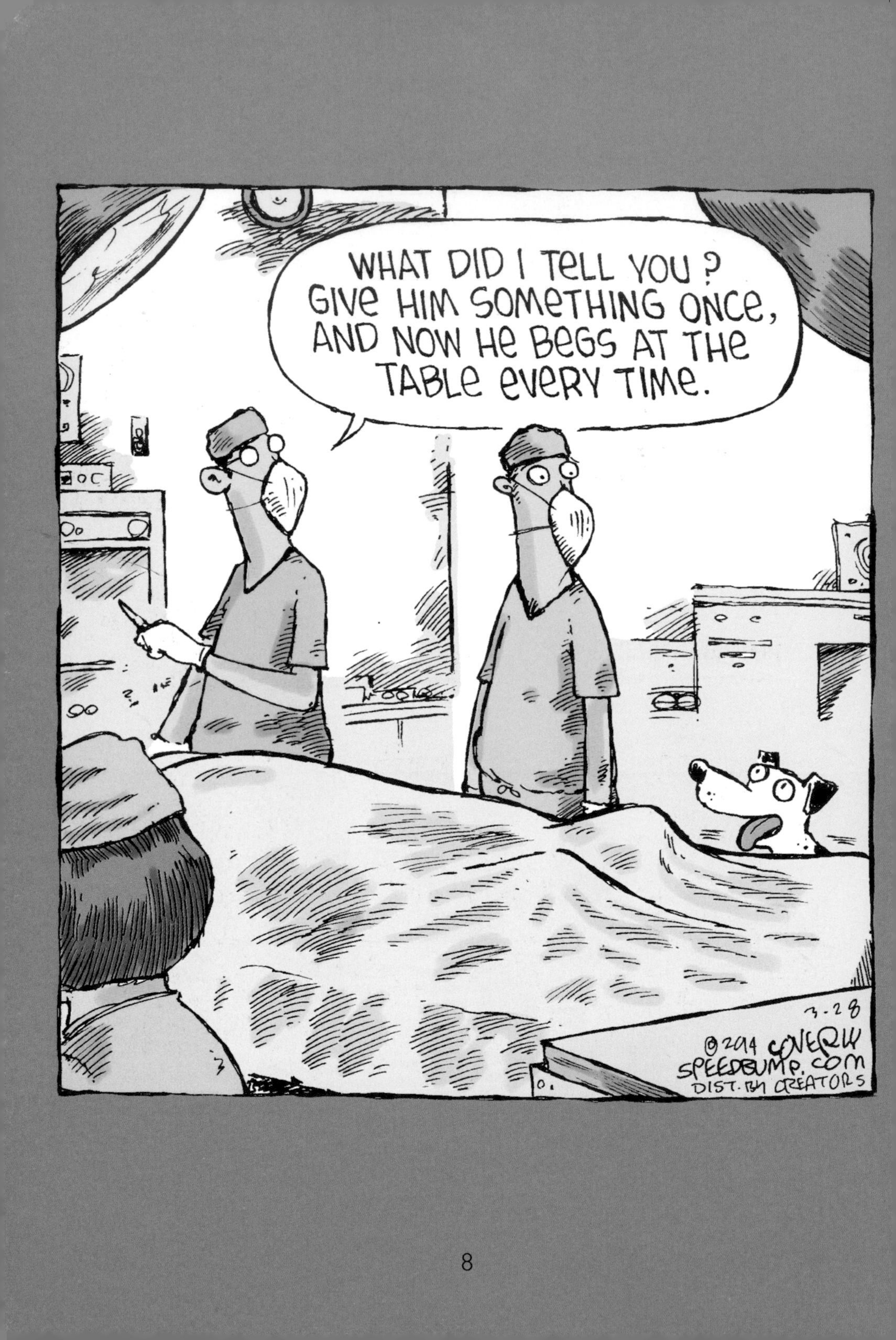
WHAT DID I TELL YOU? GIVE HIM SOMETHING ONCE, AND NOW HE BEGS AT THE TABLE EVERY TIME.
3-28
©2014 COVERLY
SPEEDBUMP.COM
DIST. BY CREATORS

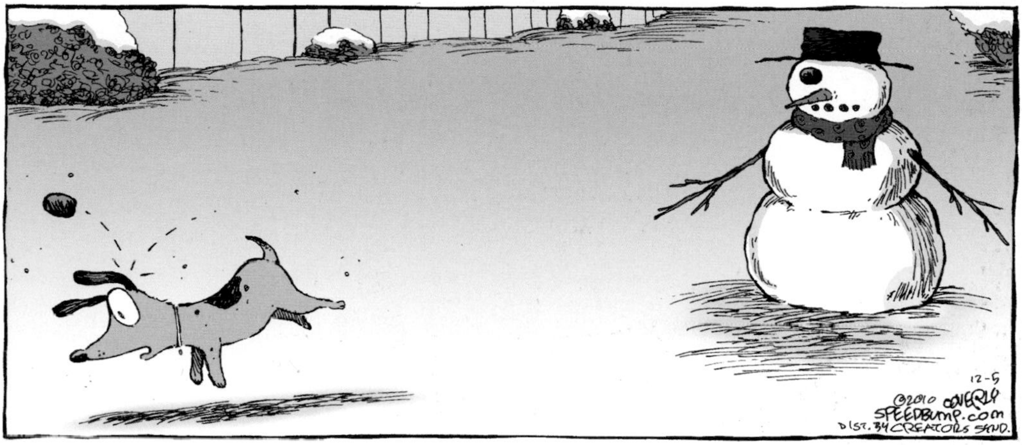
12-5
©2010 COVERLY
SPEEDBUMP.com
DIST. BY CREATORS SYND.

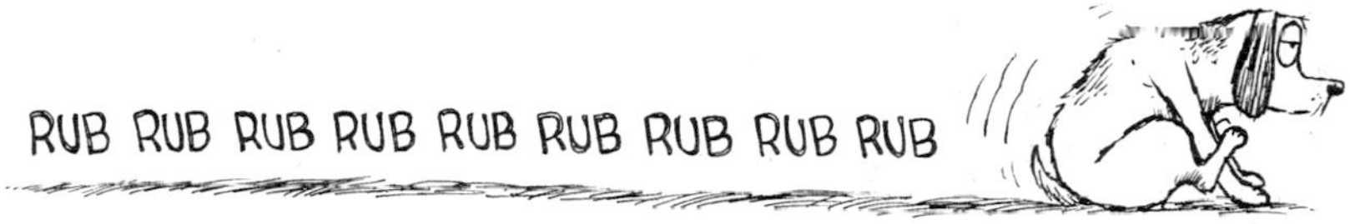
RUB RUB RUB RUB RUB RUB RUB RUB RUB

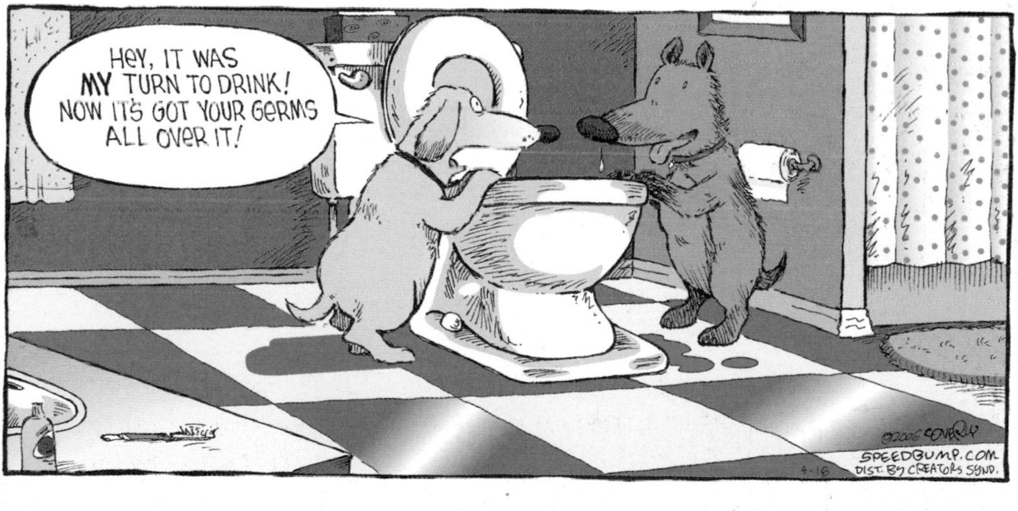
HEY, IT WAS **MY** TURN TO DRINK! NOW IT'S GOT YOUR GERMS ALL OVER IT!
4-16
©2006 COVERLY
SPEEDBUMP.COM
DIST. BY CREATORS SYND.

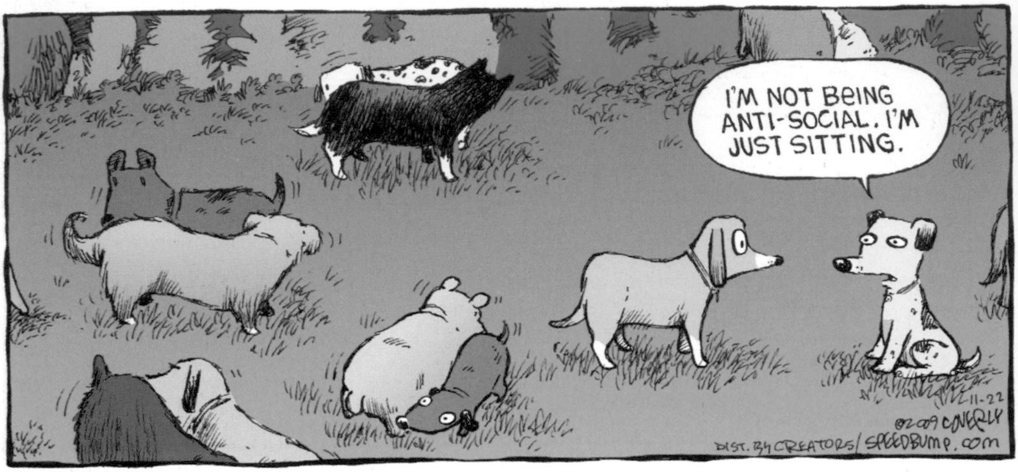
I'M NOT BEING ANTI-SOCIAL. I'M JUST SITTING.
11-22
©2009 COVERLY
DIST. BY CREATORS/ SPEEDBUMP.com

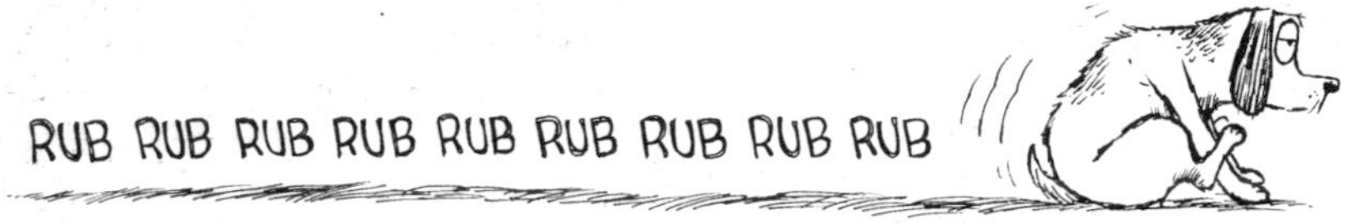
RUB RUB RUB RUB RUB RUB RUB RUB RUB

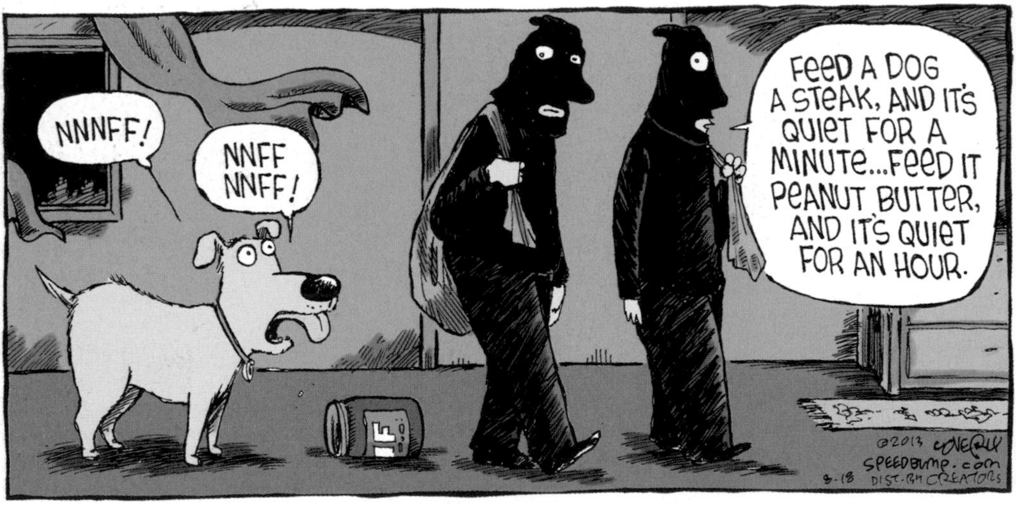
NNNFF!
NNFF NNFF!
FEED A DOG A STEAK, AND IT'S QUIET FOR A MINUTE...FEED IT PEANUT BUTTER, AND IT'S QUIET FOR AN HOUR.
©2013 COVERLY
SPEEDBUMP.com
8-18 DIST. BY CREATORS

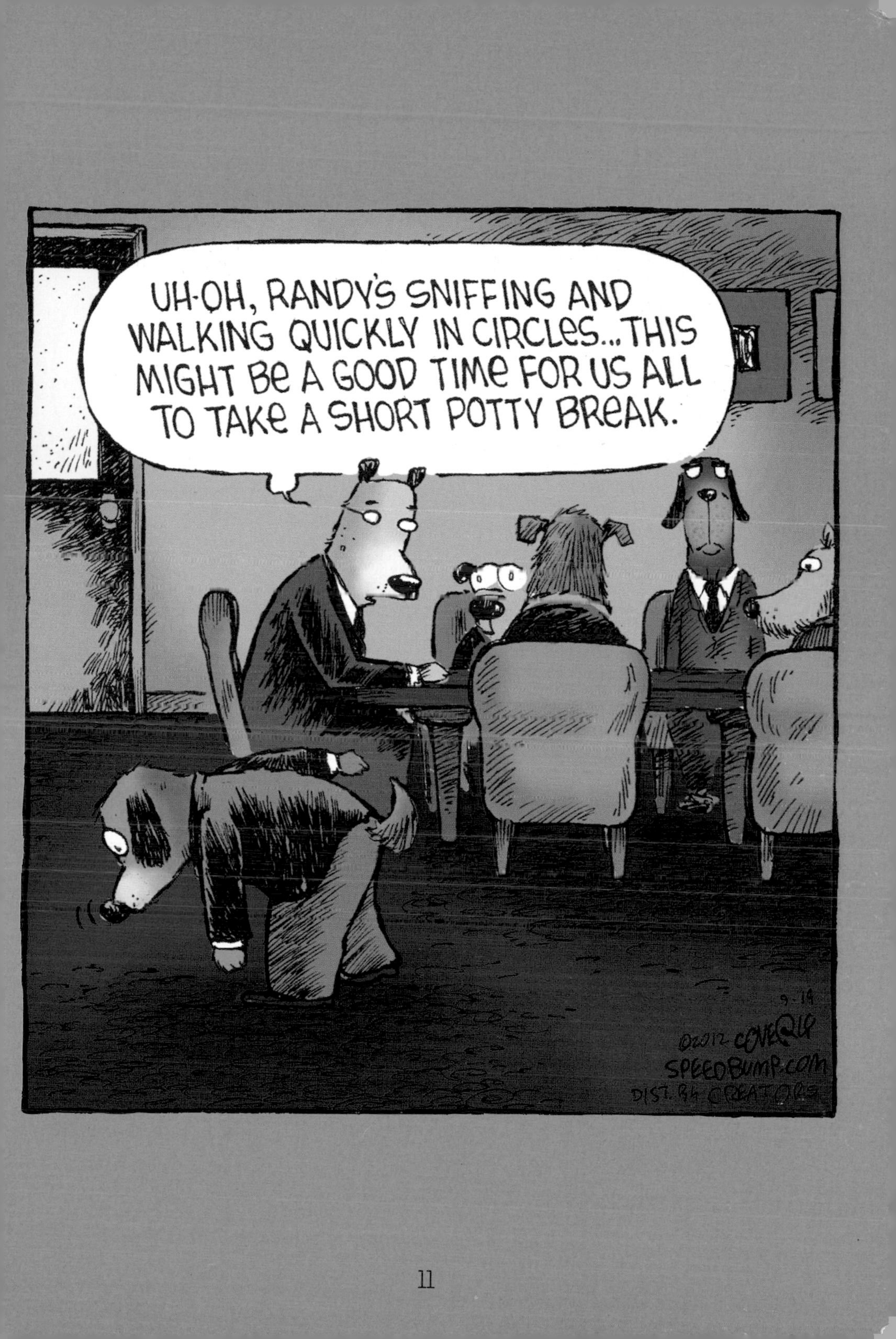
UH-OH, RANDY'S SNIFFING AND WALKING QUICKLY IN CIRCLES... THIS MIGHT BE A GOOD TIME FOR US ALL TO TAKE A SHORT POTTY BREAK.
9-19
©2012 COVERLY
SPEEDBUMP.COM
DIST. BY CREATORS

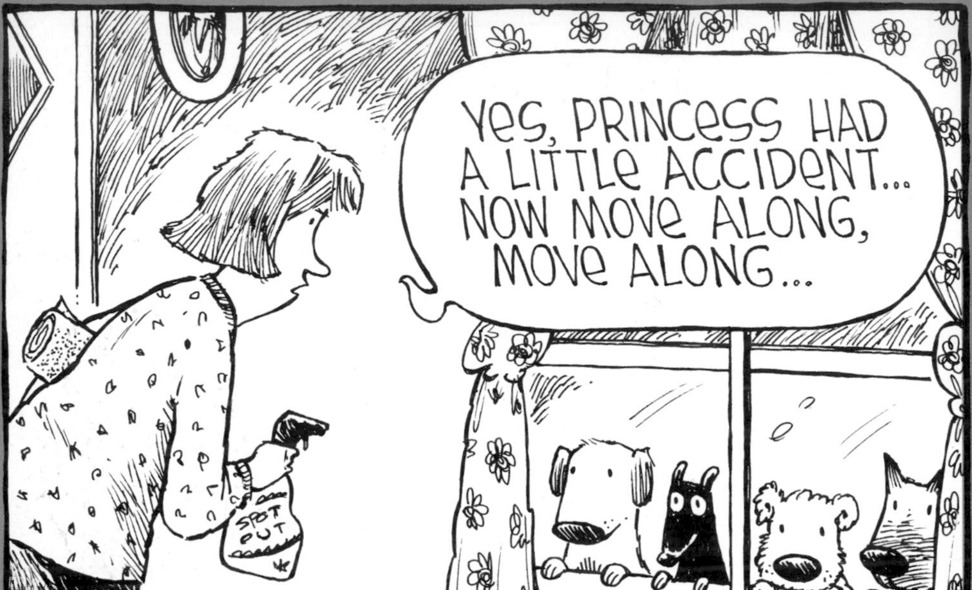
YES, PRINCESS HAD A LITTLE ACCIDENT... NOW MOVE ALONG, MOVE ALONG...
SPOT OUT
DOG GAWKERS
1-8 ©2003 DIST. BY CREATORS SYND. INC.
COVERLY

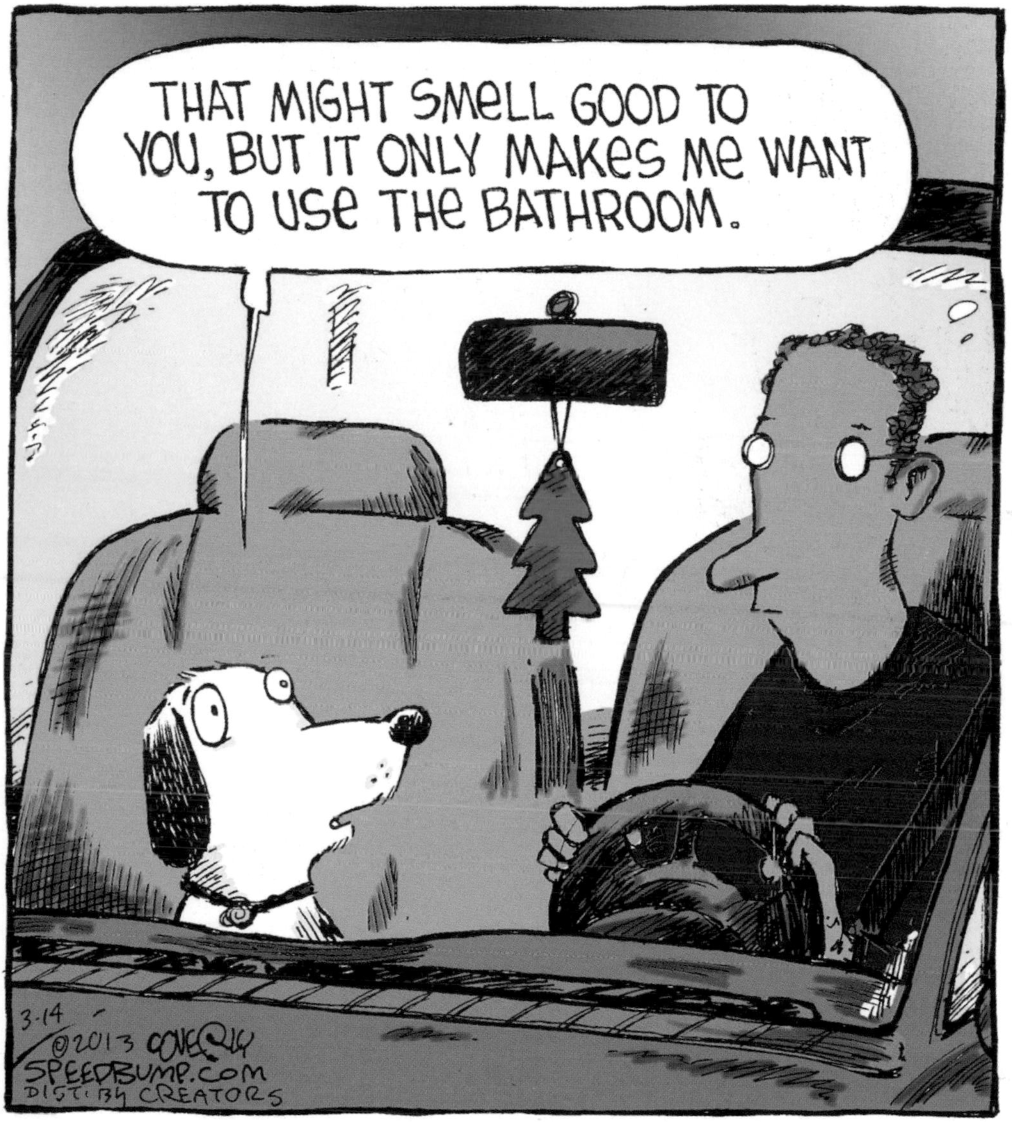
THAT MIGHT SMELL GOOD TO YOU, BUT IT ONLY MAKES ME WANT TO USE THE BATHROOM.
3-14
©2013 COVERLY
SPEEDBUMP.COM
DIST. BY CREATORS

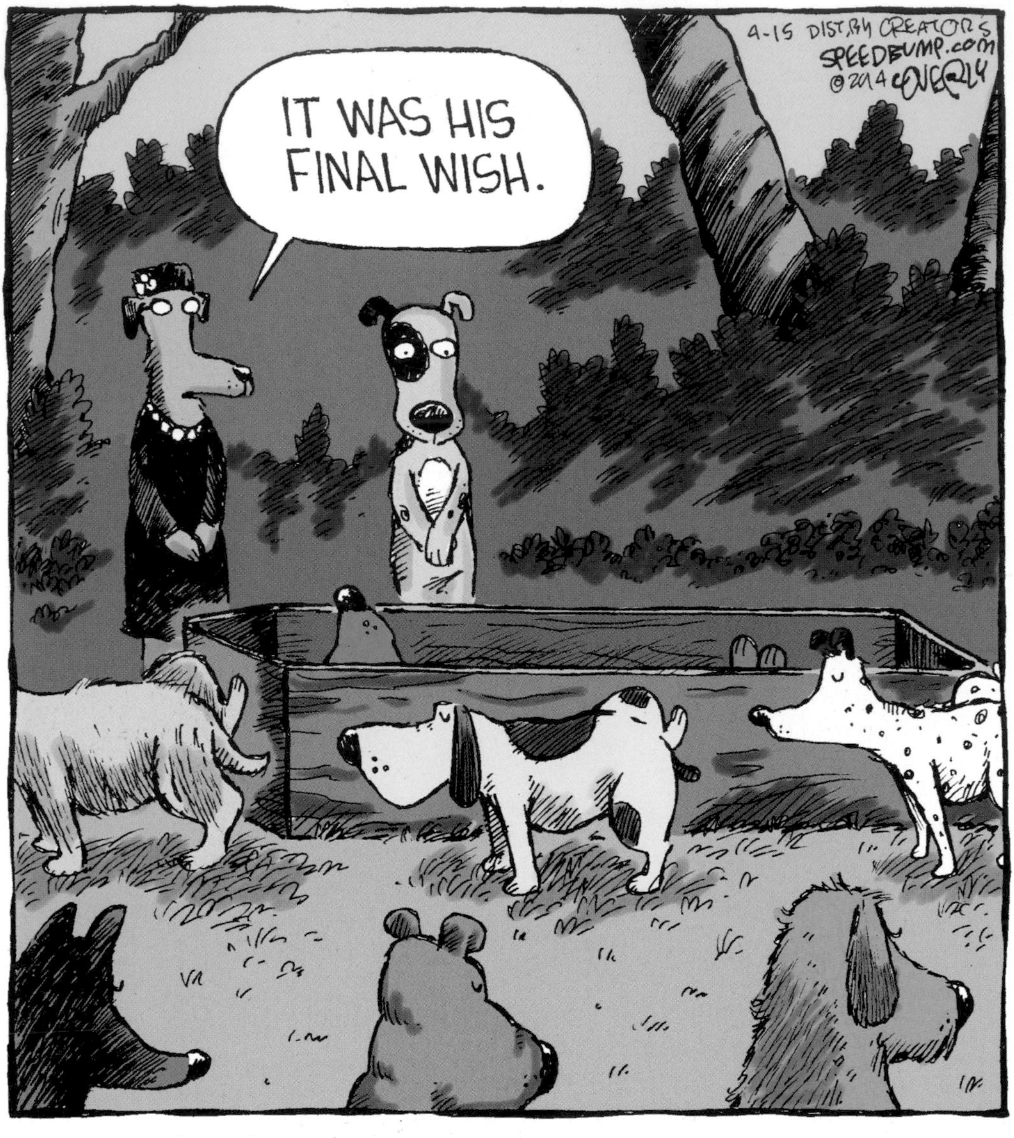
4-15 DIST. BY CREATORS
SPEEDBUMP.com
©2014 COVERLY
IT WAS HIS FINAL WISH.

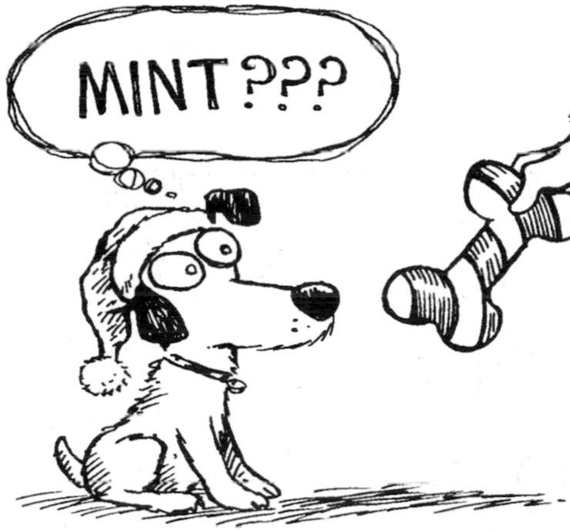
MINT???

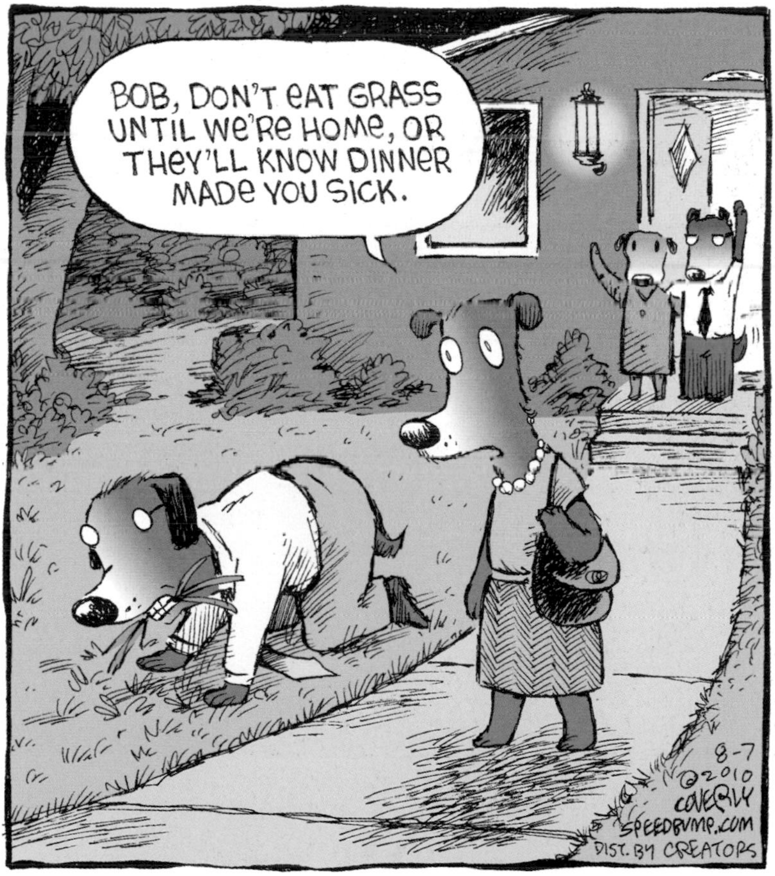
BOB, DON'T EAT GRASS UNTIL WE'RE HOME, OR THEY'LL KNOW DINNER MADE YOU SICK.
8-7
©2010
COVERLY
SPEEDBUMP.COM
DIST. BY CREATORS

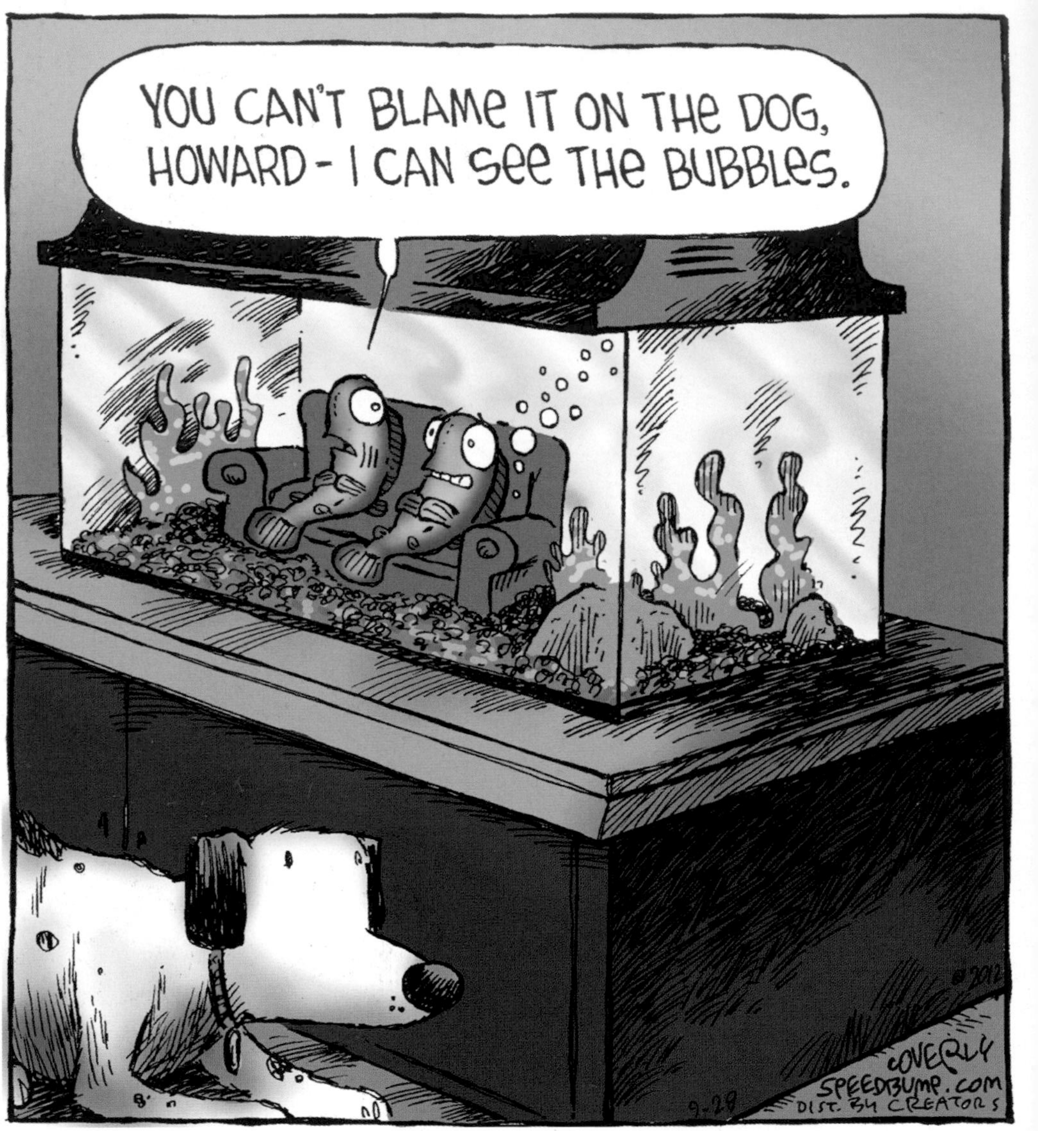
YOU CAN'T BLAME IT ON THE DOG, HOWARD - I CAN SEE THE BUBBLES.
©2012
COVERLY
SPEEDBUMP.COM
DIST. BY CREATORS
9-28

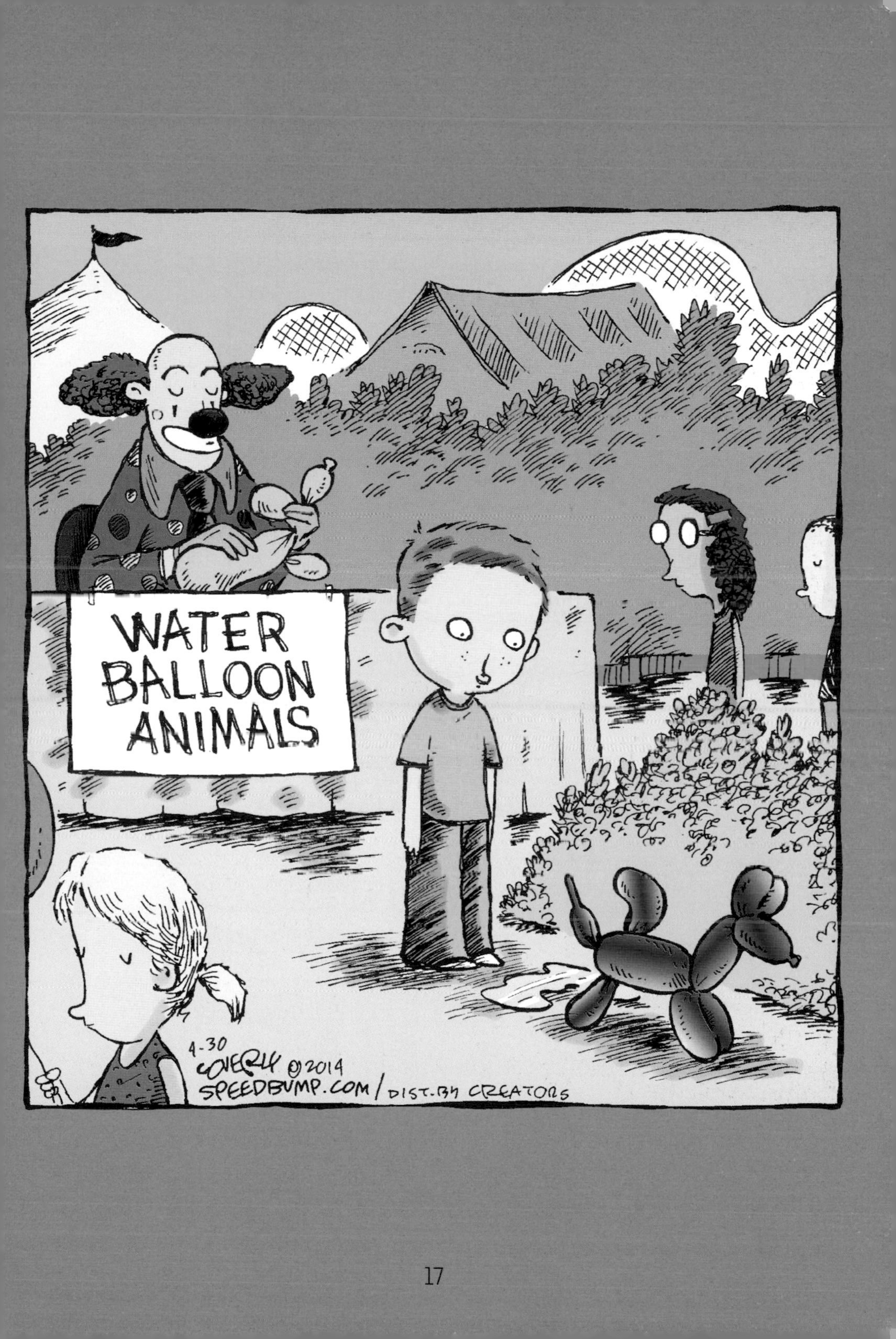
WATER
BALLOON
ANIMALS
4-30
COVERLY ©2014
SPEEDBUMP.COM / DIST. BY CREATORS

I INSTALLED IT BECAUSE HE'S TOO SHORT TO REACH INSIDE THE BOWL.
©2012 SPEEDBUMP.COM / DIST. BY CREATORS 7-30

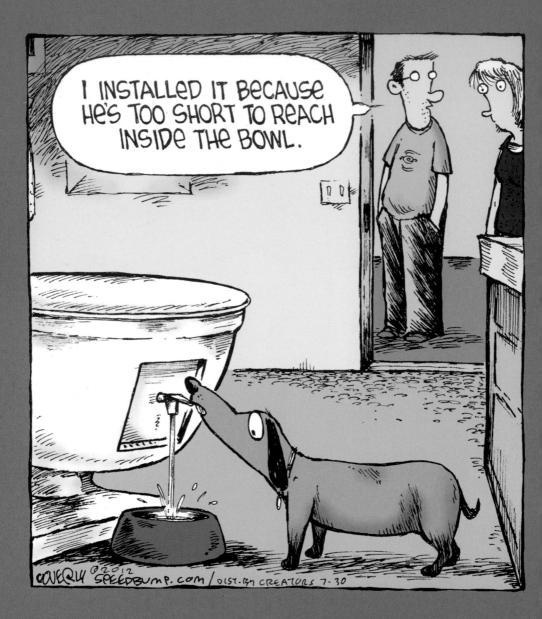

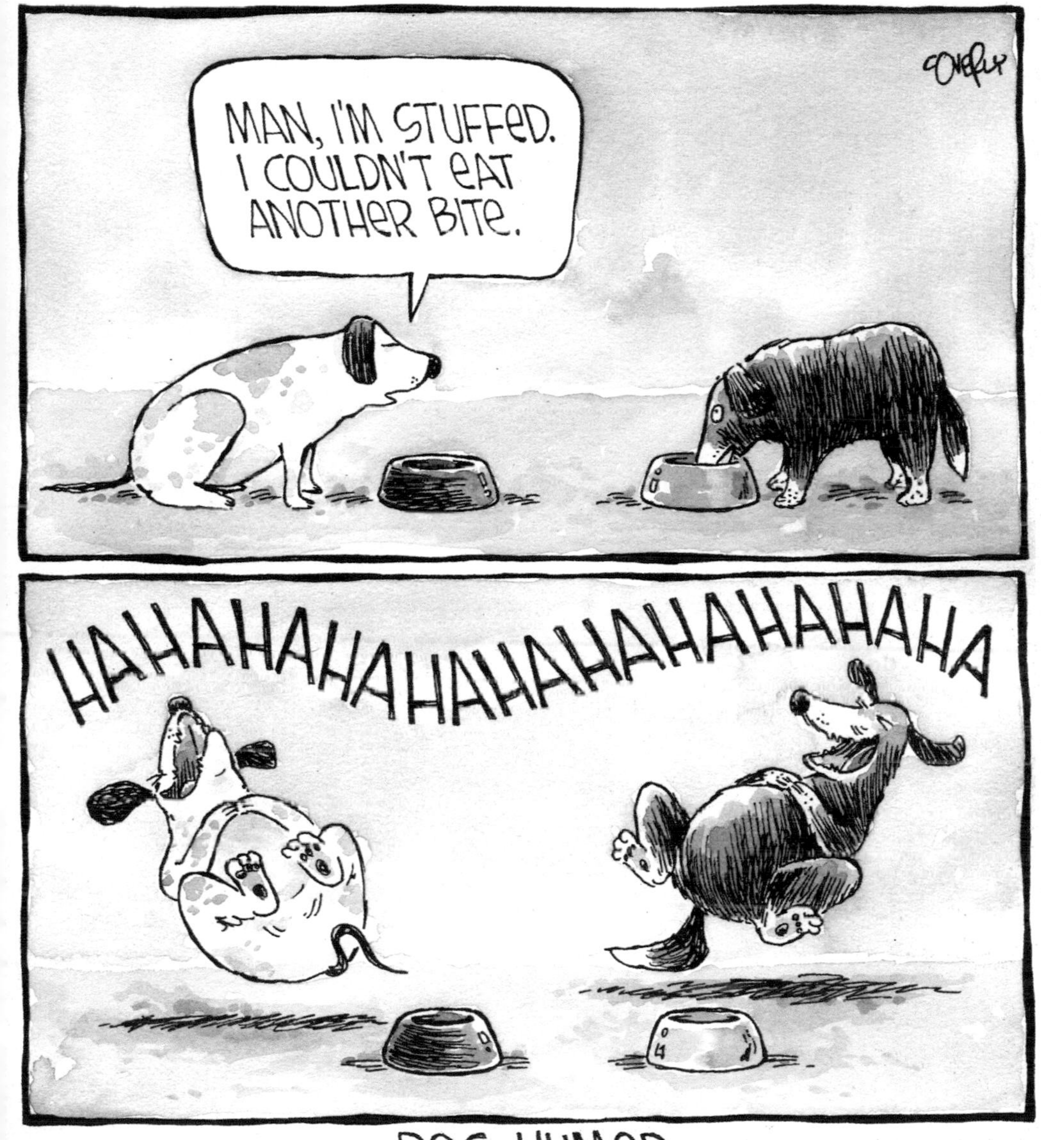
MAN, I'M STUFFED. I COULDN'T EAT ANOTHER BITE.
HAHAHAHAHAHAHAHAHAHAHAHA

DOG HUMOR

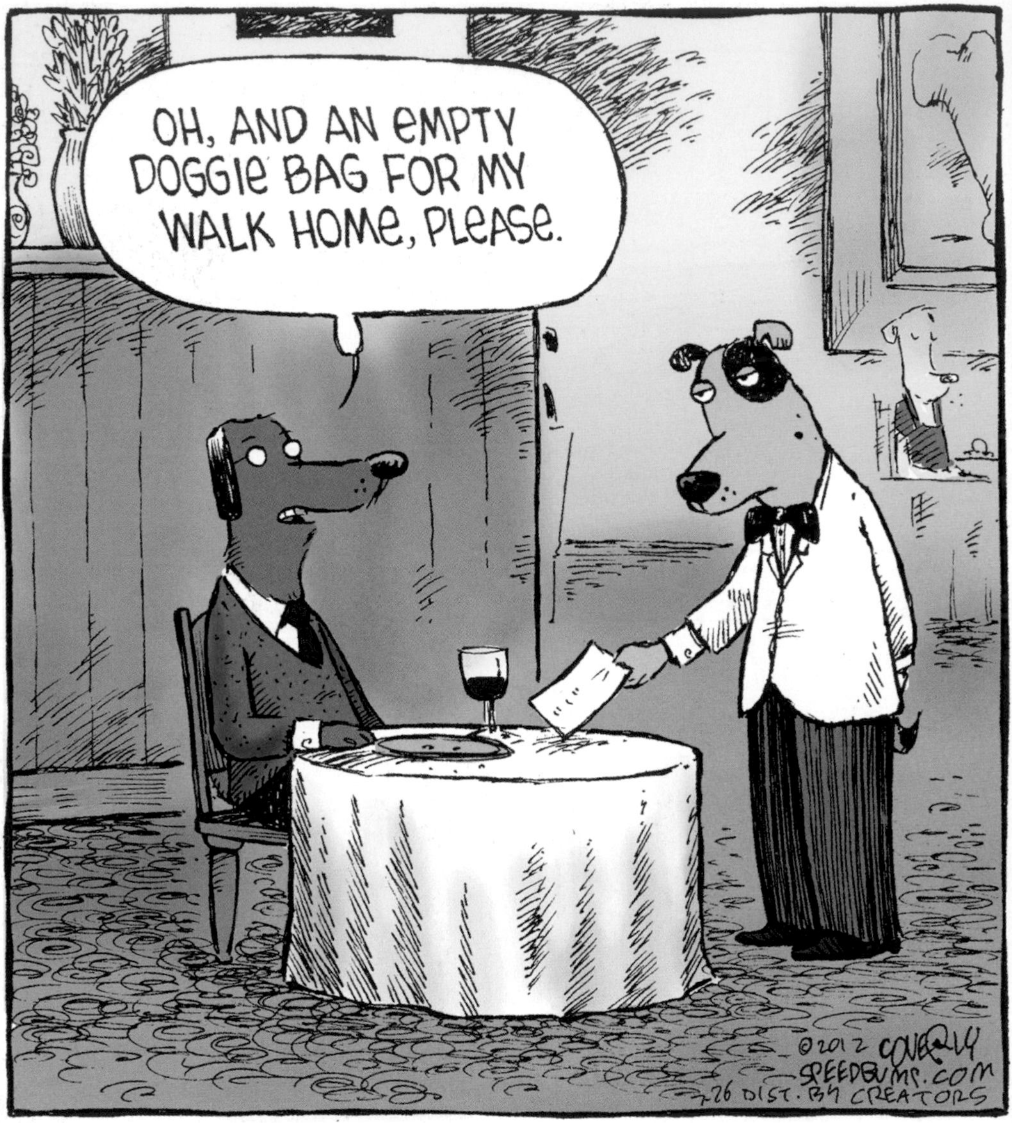
OH, AND AN EMPTY DOGGIE BAG FOR MY WALK HOME, PLEASE.
©2012 COVERLY
SPEEDBUMPS.COM
7-26 DIST. BY CREATORS

WELL, THIS IS AWKWARD...WHAT, HE COULDN'T USE THE NEXT TREE OVER?
4.4
©2012 COVERLY
SPEEDBUMP.COM
DIST. BY CREATORS

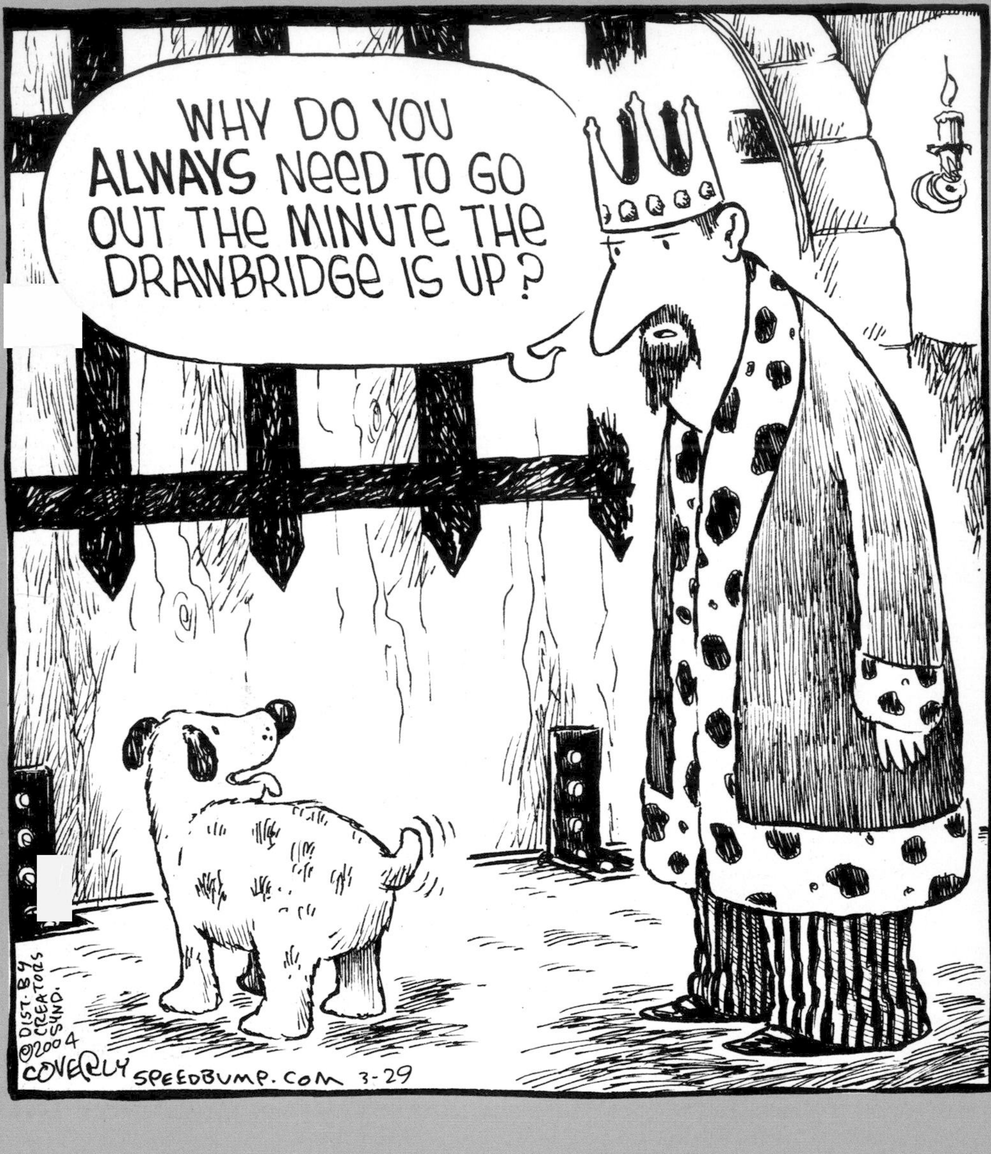
WHY DO YOU ALWAYS NEED TO GO OUT THE MINUTE THE DRAWBRIDGE IS UP?
DIST. BY CREATORS SYND. ©2004
COVERLY SPEEDBUMP.COM 3-29

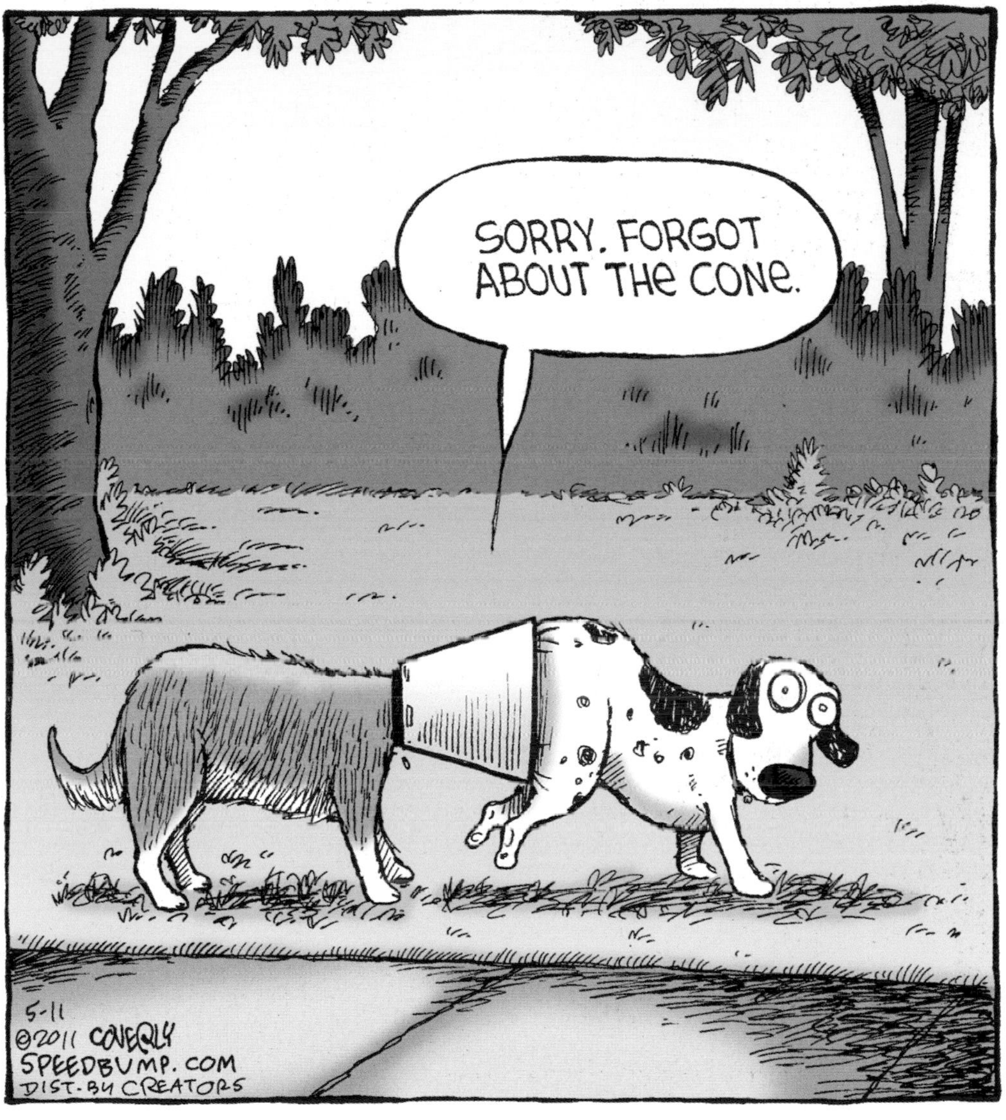
SORRY. FORGOT ABOUT THE CONE.
5-11
©2011 COVERLY
SPEEDBUMP.COM
DIST. BY CREATORS

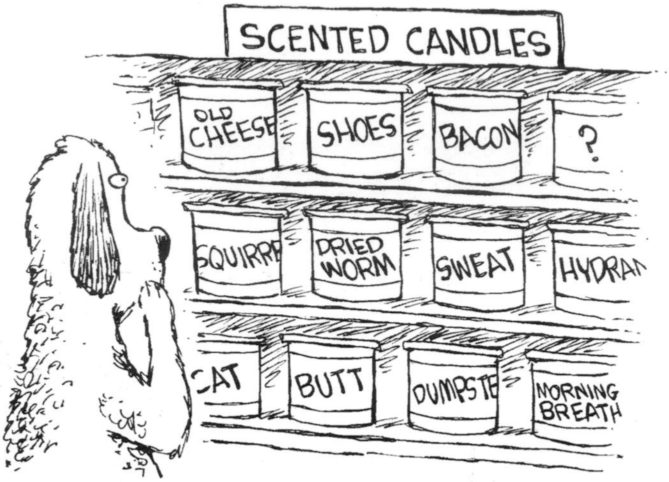
SCENTED CANDLES
OLD CHEESE
SHOES
BACON
?
SQUIRRE
DRIED WORM
SWEAT
HYDRA
CAT
BUTT
DUMPSTE
MORNING BREATH

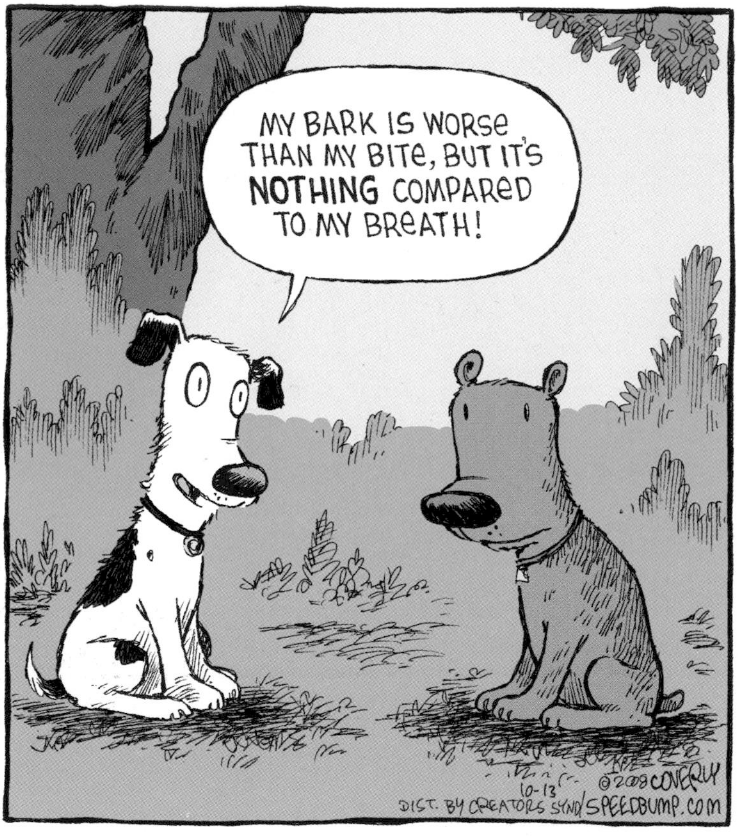
MY BARK IS WORSE THAN MY BITE, BUT IT'S **NOTHING** COMPARED TO MY BREATH!
10-13 ©2008 COVERLY
DIST. BY CREATORS SYND/SPEEDBUMP.COM

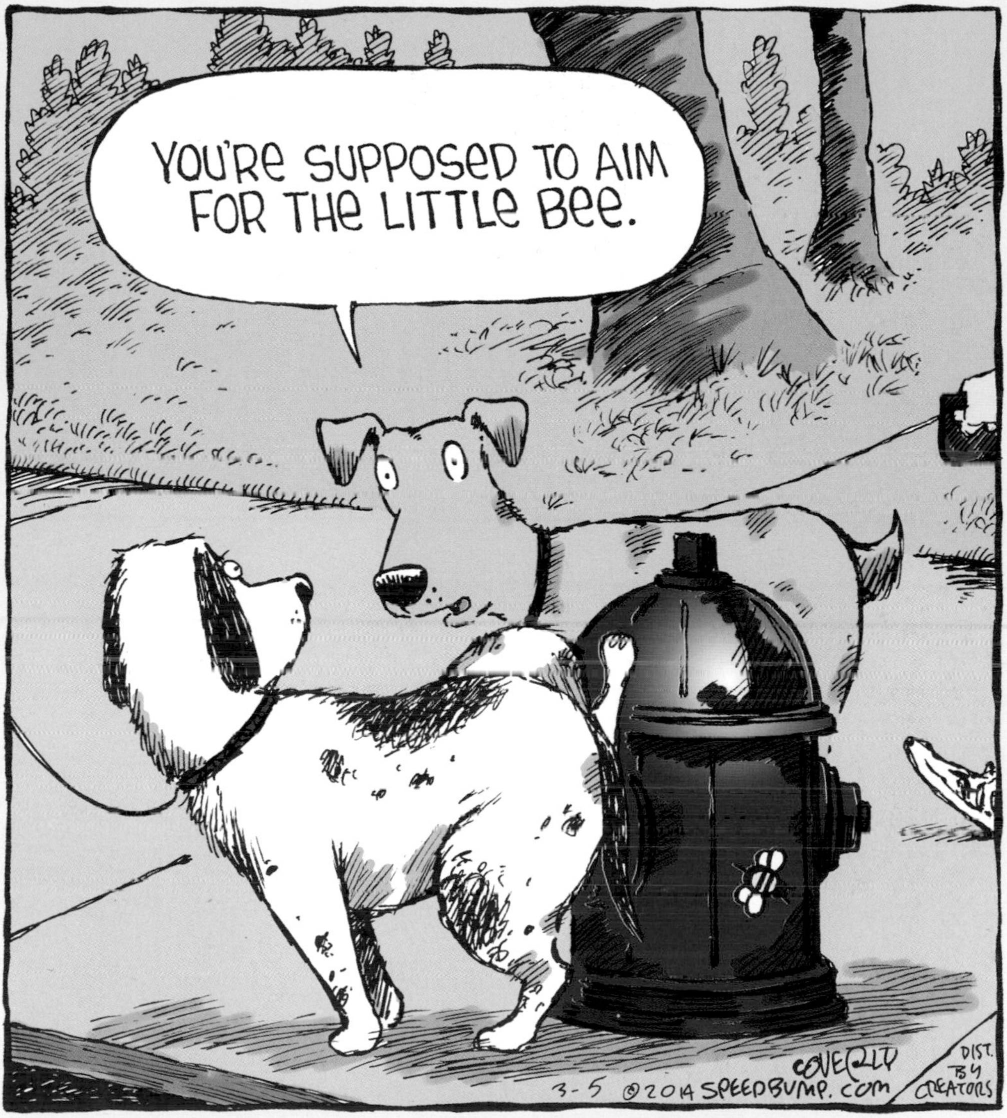
YOU'RE SUPPOSED TO AIM FOR THE LITTLE BEE.
3-5 ©2014 SPEEDBUMP.COM
DIST. BY CREATORS

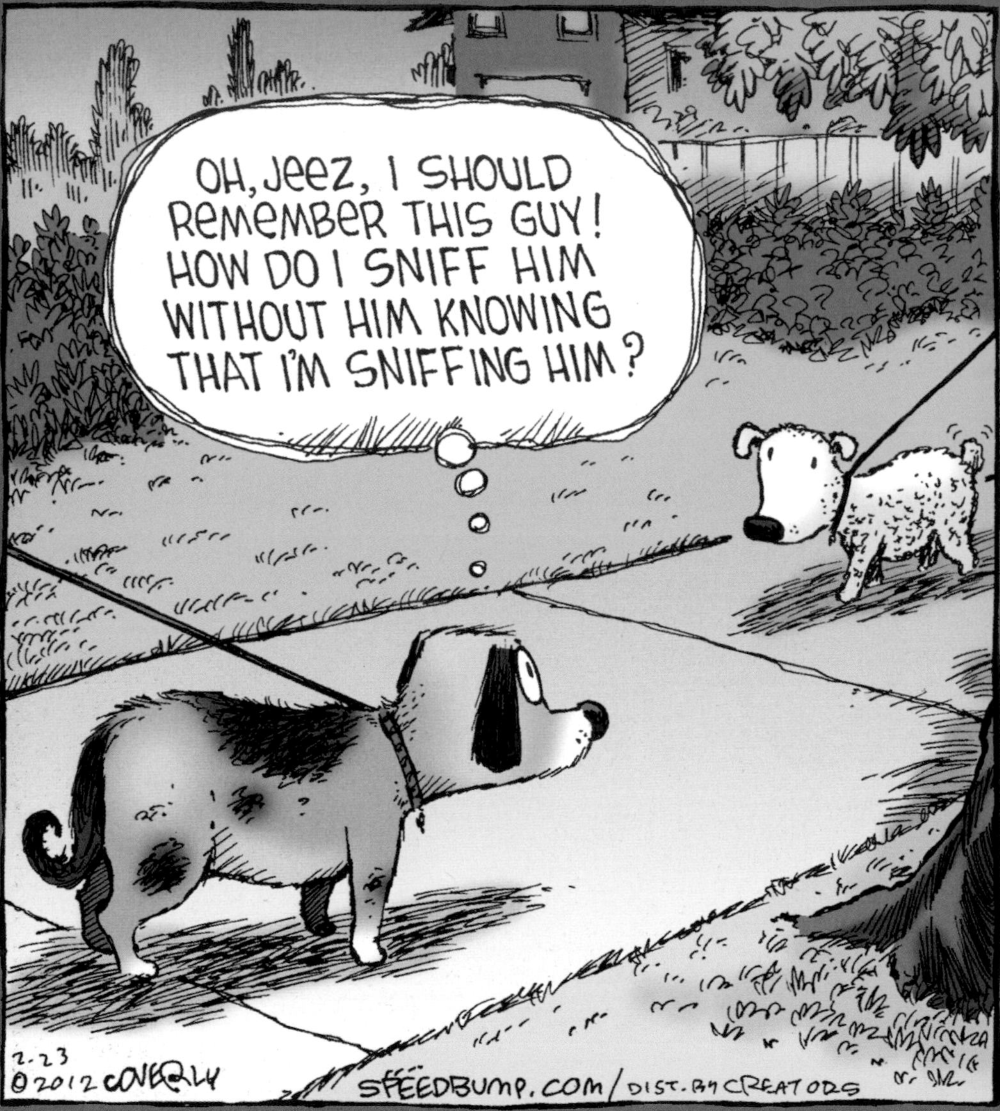
OH, JEEZ, I SHOULD REMEMBER THIS GUY! HOW DO I SNIFF HIM WITHOUT HIM KNOWING THAT I'M SNIFFING HIM?
2-23
©2012 COVERLY
SPEEDBUMP.COM/DIST. BY CREATORS

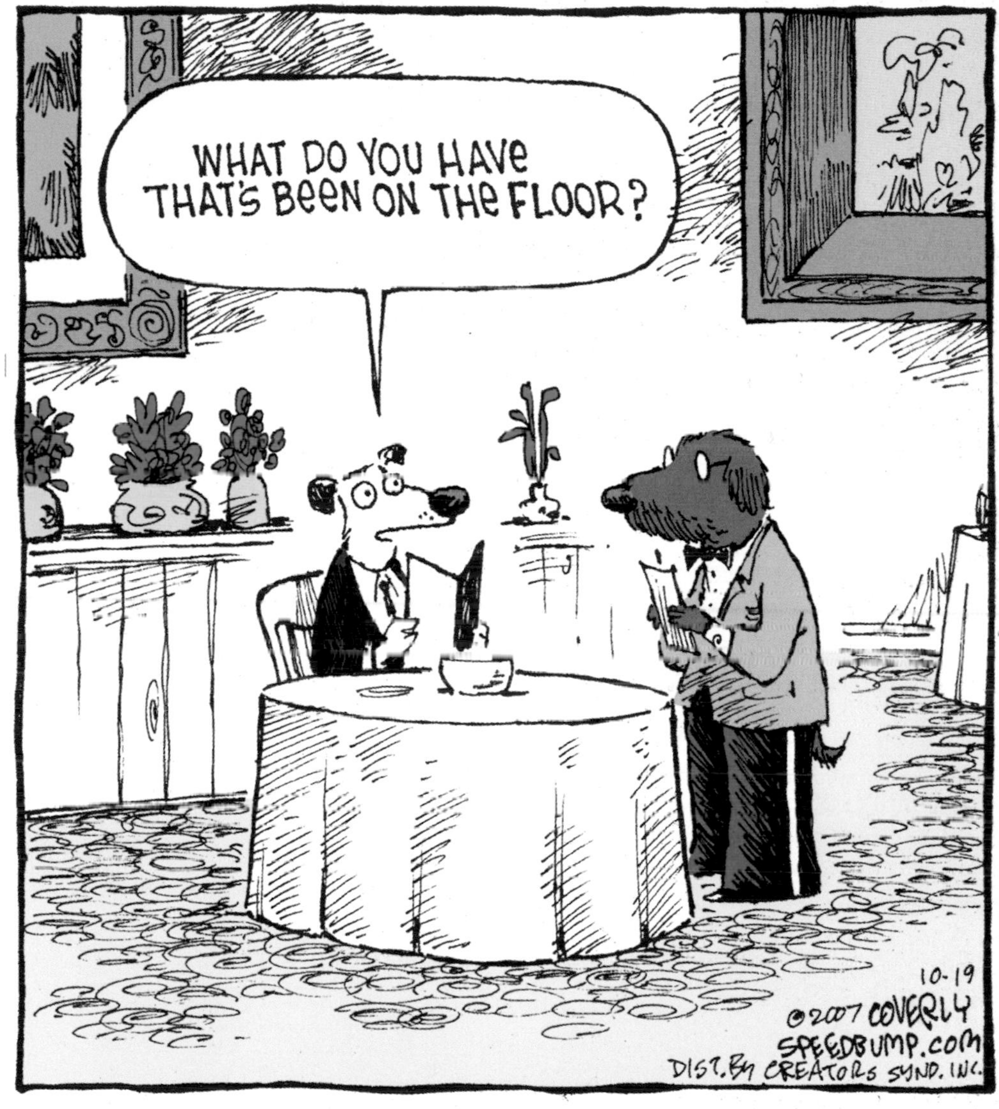
WHAT DO YOU HAVE THAT'S BEEN ON THE FLOOR?
10-19
©2007 COVERLY
SPEEDBUMP.COM
DIST. BY CREATORS SYND. INC.

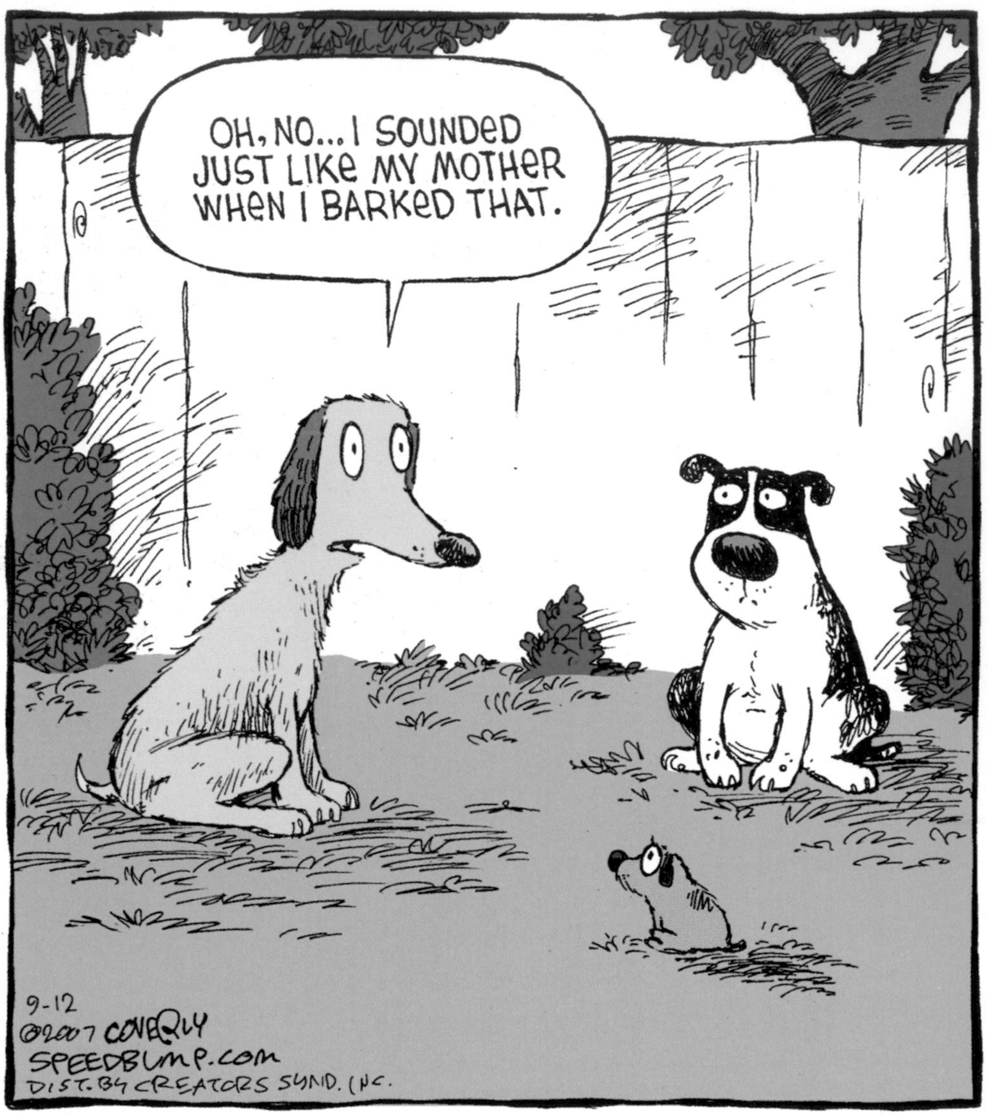
OH, NO... I SOUNDED JUST LIKE MY MOTHER WHEN I BARKED THAT.
9-12
©2007 COVERLY
SPEEDBUMP.COM
DIST. BY CREATORS SYND. INC.

IT'S THE AGE-OLD QUESTION: DO WE CHOOSE NOT TO PIDDLE ON THE RUG, OR ARE WE TRULY HOUSEBROKEN?
12-31 ©2009
COVERLY SPEEDBUMP.COM/ DIST. BY CREATORS

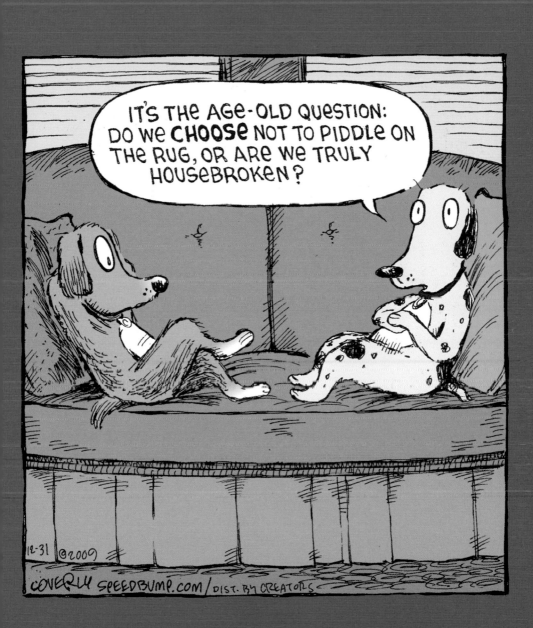

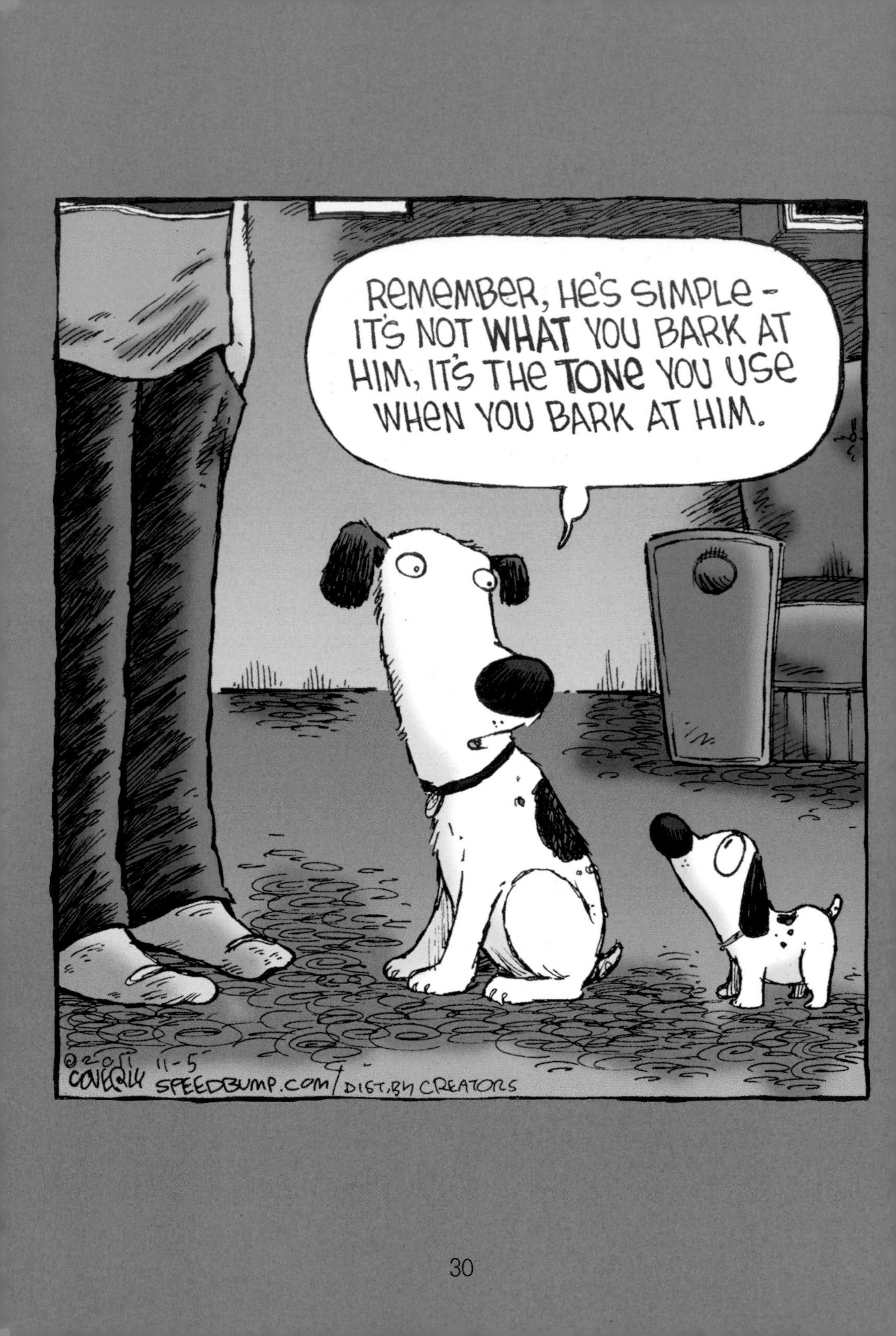
REMEMBER, HE'S SIMPLE - IT'S NOT WHAT YOU BARK AT HIM, IT'S THE TONE YOU USE WHEN YOU BARK AT HIM.
©2011 COVERLY 11-5 SPEEDBUMP.COM/DIST.BY CREATORS

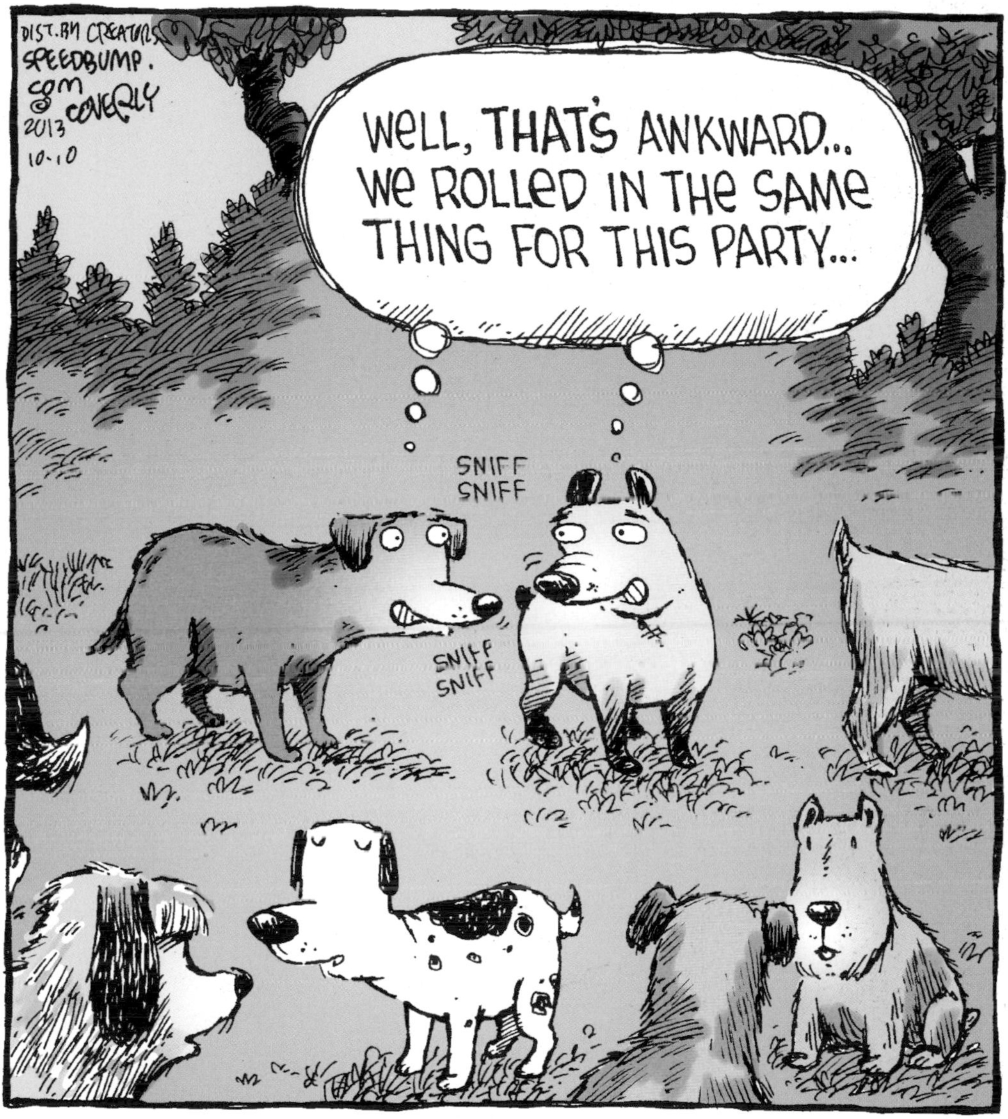
DIST. BY CREATORS
SPEEDBUMP.
COM
COVERLY
2013
10-10
WELL, THAT'S AWKWARD... WE ROLLED IN THE SAME THING FOR THIS PARTY...
SNIFF SNIFF
SNIFF SNIFF

SHAG

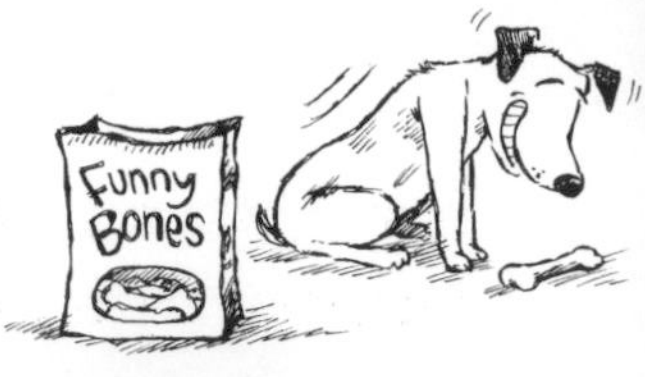
Funny Bones

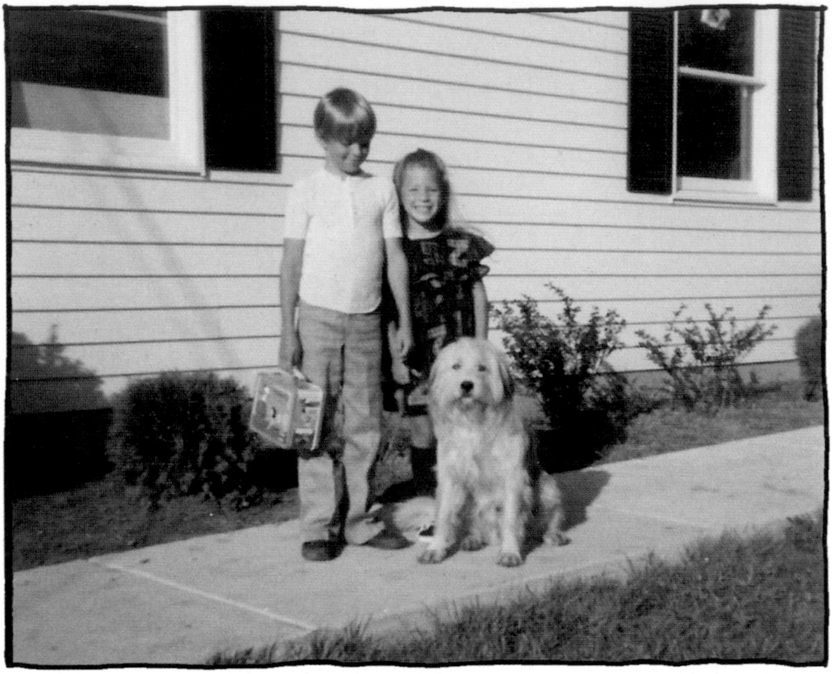

Dave (holding Peanuts lunch box) with sister Cathy and Shag, 1973.

We got Shag when I was in third grade, which would have been 1972. While I don't think my parents named him after the type of carpet that covered the floors of our entire house, his crazy, shaggy fur was definitely the reason for his name. Every day was a bad hair day for Shag. His wild looks suited his personality perfectly, though, because he was a stray my grandfather found on the dicey streets of Detroit. This dog was pretty feral and a little too streetwise to be trained (at least by non-professionals like us), but he was surprisingly gentle and loving toward people. My parents attempted to make him an indoor dog. That lasted less than a week; everything that either looked or smelled like wood was immediately assumed by Shag to be a tree, and so needed to be peed on. And on. And on. He stayed in our garage at night but had a warm bed and got tons of attention from Cathy and me.

During the day he was on a long chain that was attached to a post next to the garage, which I know isn't ideal, but he couldn't stay inside and he'd have run away otherwise. It was the only solution. There were, in fact, a few times he did run away by pulling the chain right off the post—one time he even took the whole post with him—but since our house backed up to some woods, he wouldn't get far before the chain got stuck on something. It never took long to find him, which was good for us and good for him, because if a neighbor dog saw him out there with his chain wrapped around a tree stump, it would be, you know, *awkward*.

When he did break loose of his chain entirely, it didn't matter if you were right there or not. He was fast. Sometimes too fast. Sometimes he ran so fast that his front legs would come off the ground, gradually, like the lifting of landing gear on an airplane, and the next thing we'd know he'd be running on only his hind legs. I can't even imagine how viral that would have gone if we'd taped it and had YouTube back then.

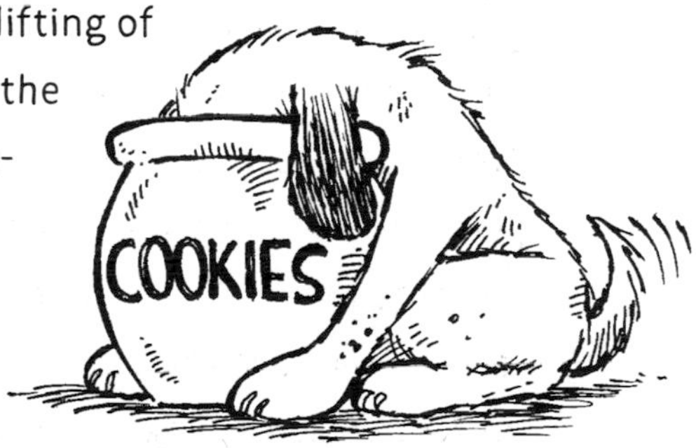
COOKIES

In those days, my parents had this pretty cool car—a Cutlass convertible with a gray body and a black canvas top. The first night Shag stayed in the garage, he managed to leap up onto the trunk, then onto the top of the car, where he apparently slept all night. The next morning, my dad went into the garage and found scratches on the trunk and holes in the roof from the dog's nails (Shag wasn't exactly manicured). My dad got angry. Very, very angry. There was lots of yelling, lots of swearing, then he pulled Shag down and gave him a swat on the butt. The next night it happened again. And the night after that. My dad had private discussions with my mom about getting rid of Shag, but he couldn't bring himself to do it. The fourth morning was the same, except this time my dad just looked at Shag on top of the car and said, "OK, Shag, you win. No more yelling." He took him down gently, petted him, and walked away.

The next morning, Shag was under the car. He never slept on top of the car again. There was a wise old soul in that dog. And my dad still talks about the lesson he learned from Shag.

On a fateful day the summer after Shag arrived, I was running around the neighborhood with my friends when another kid came by on his bike and said, "Hey, I just saw your dog with Tooker's dog in their yard!" We cut through the woods to Tooker's house, and sure enough, Shag was there with Tooker's pure white dog, Queenie. He seemed strangely proud and happy to see me, and I took him home.

A couple months later, Queenie had puppies. One of them was a little bundle of white fur with blond spots. And so we took home dog #2, Shag's son, Tigger.

CHAPTER 2

DOGS ARE (SMARTER THAN) PEOPLE, TOO

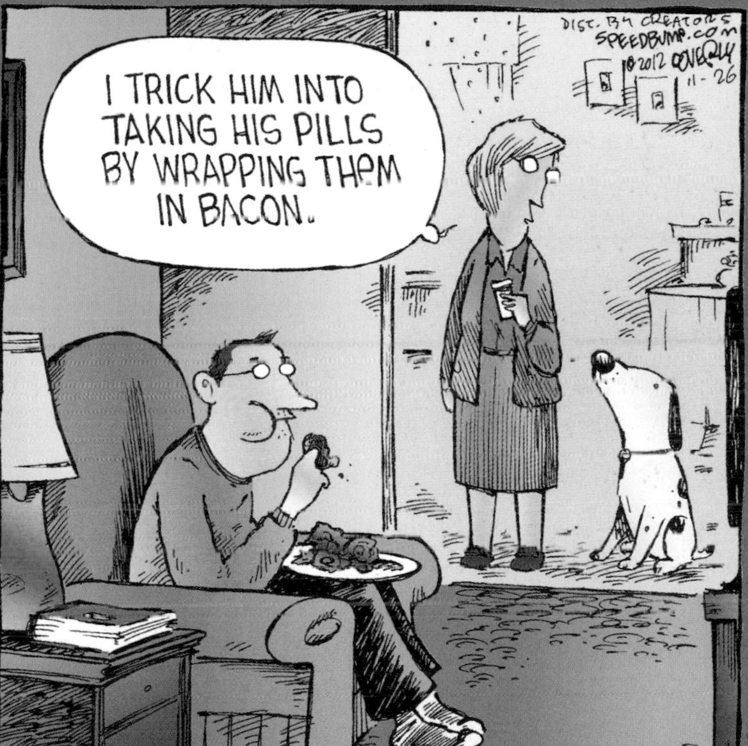
I TRICK HIM INTO TAKING HIS PILLS BY WRAPPING THEM IN BACON.
DIST. BY CREATORS
SPEEDBUMP.COM
©2012 COVERLY
11-26

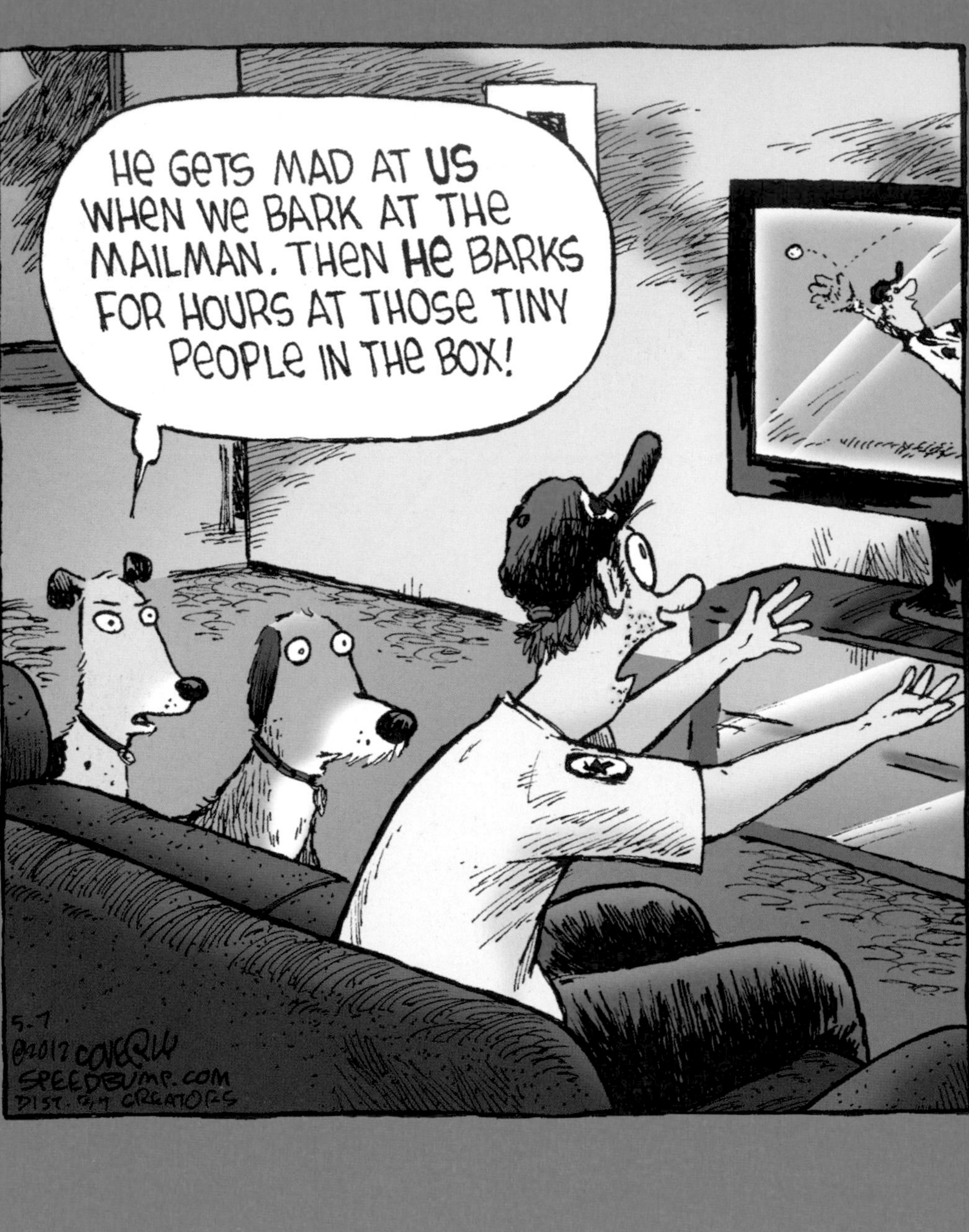
HE GETS MAD AT US WHEN WE BARK AT THE MAILMAN. THEN HE BARKS FOR HOURS AT THOSE TINY PEOPLE IN THE BOX!
5-7
©2012 COVERLY
SPEEDBUMP.COM
DIST. BY CREATORS

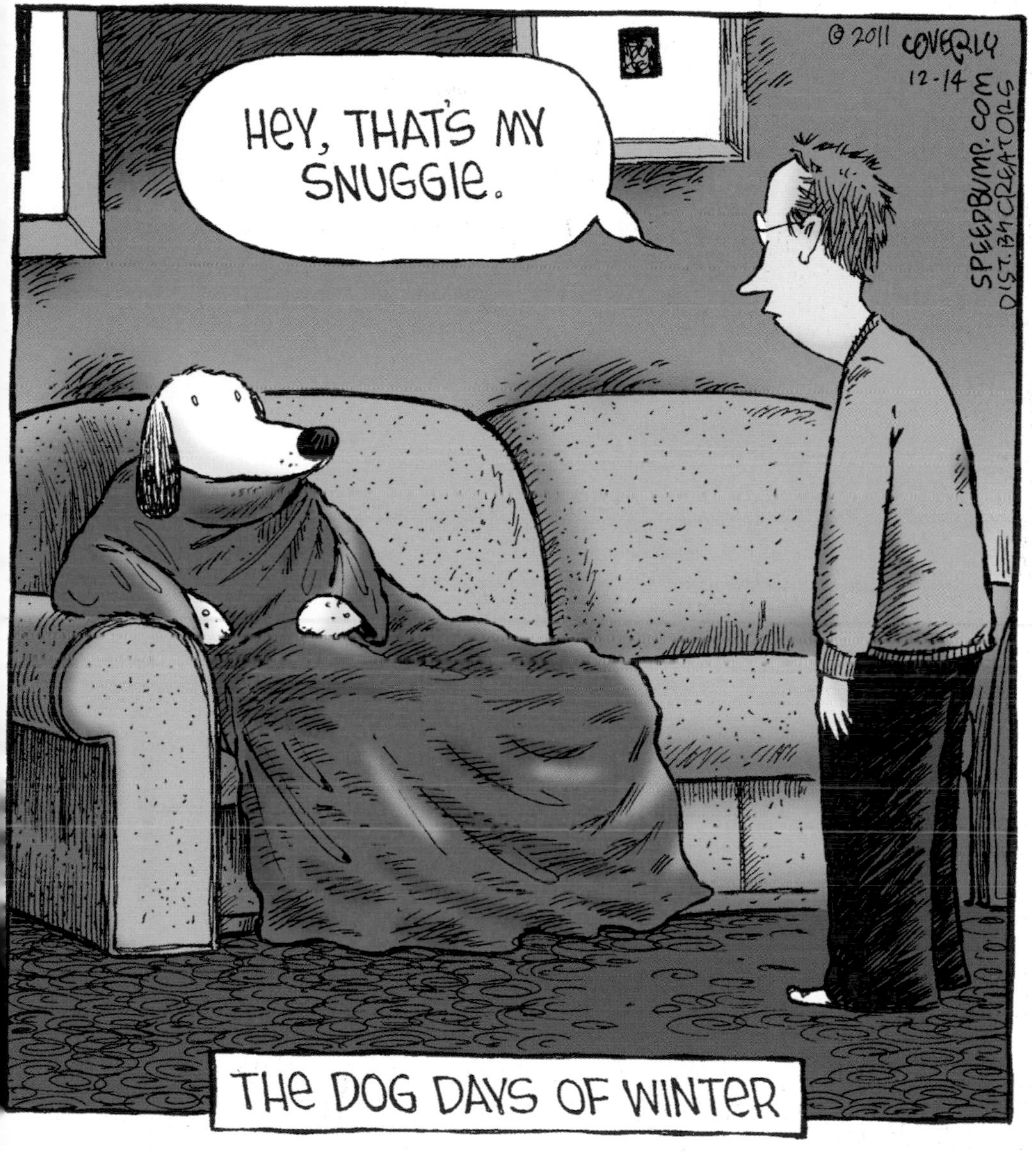
© 2011 COVERLY 12-14
SPEEDBUMP.COM DIST. BY CREATORS
HEY, THAT'S MY SNUGGIE.
THE DOG DAYS OF WINTER

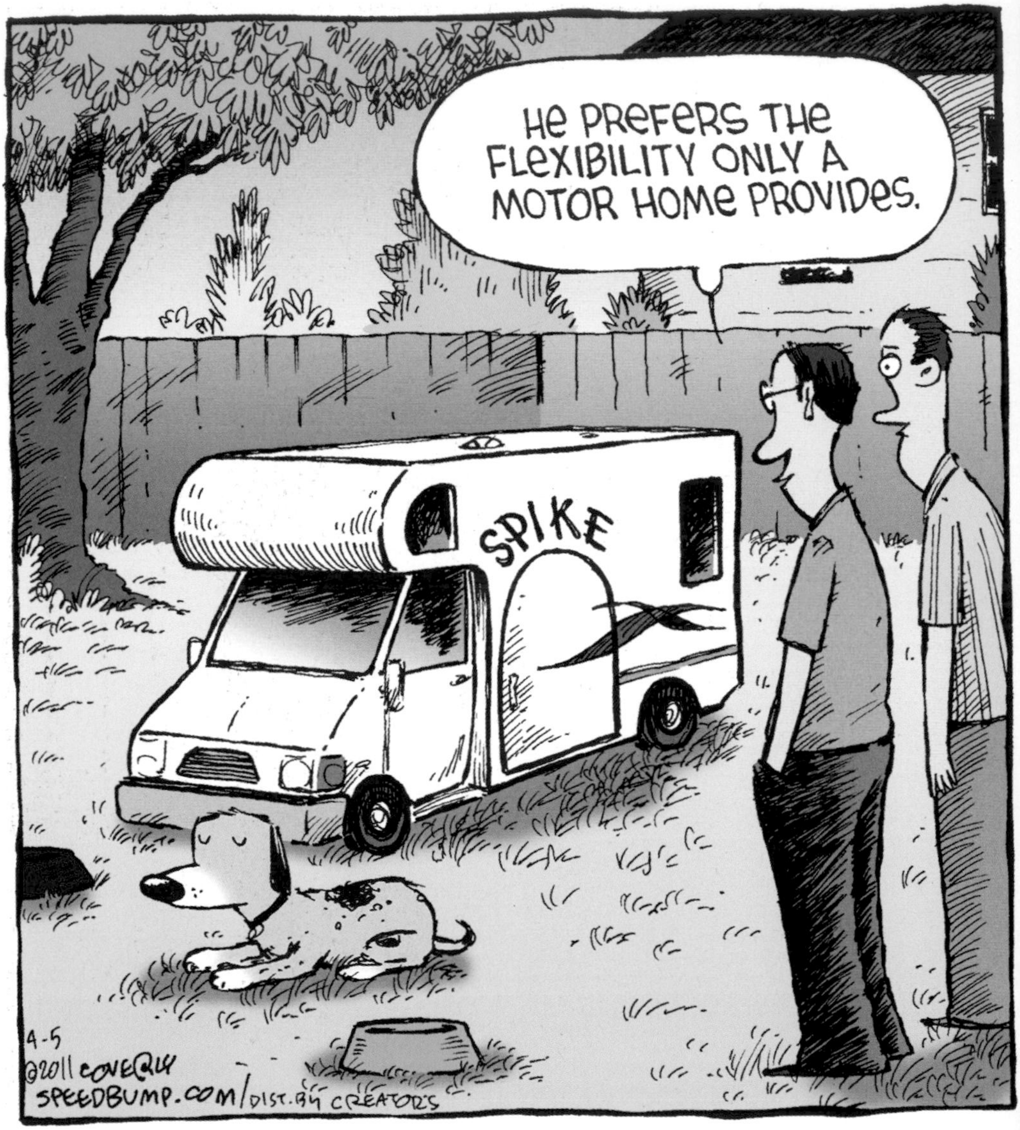
HE PREFERS THE FLEXIBILITY ONLY A MOTOR HOME PROVIDES.
SPIKE
4-5
©2011 COVERLY
SPEEDBUMP.COM/DIST. BY CREATORS

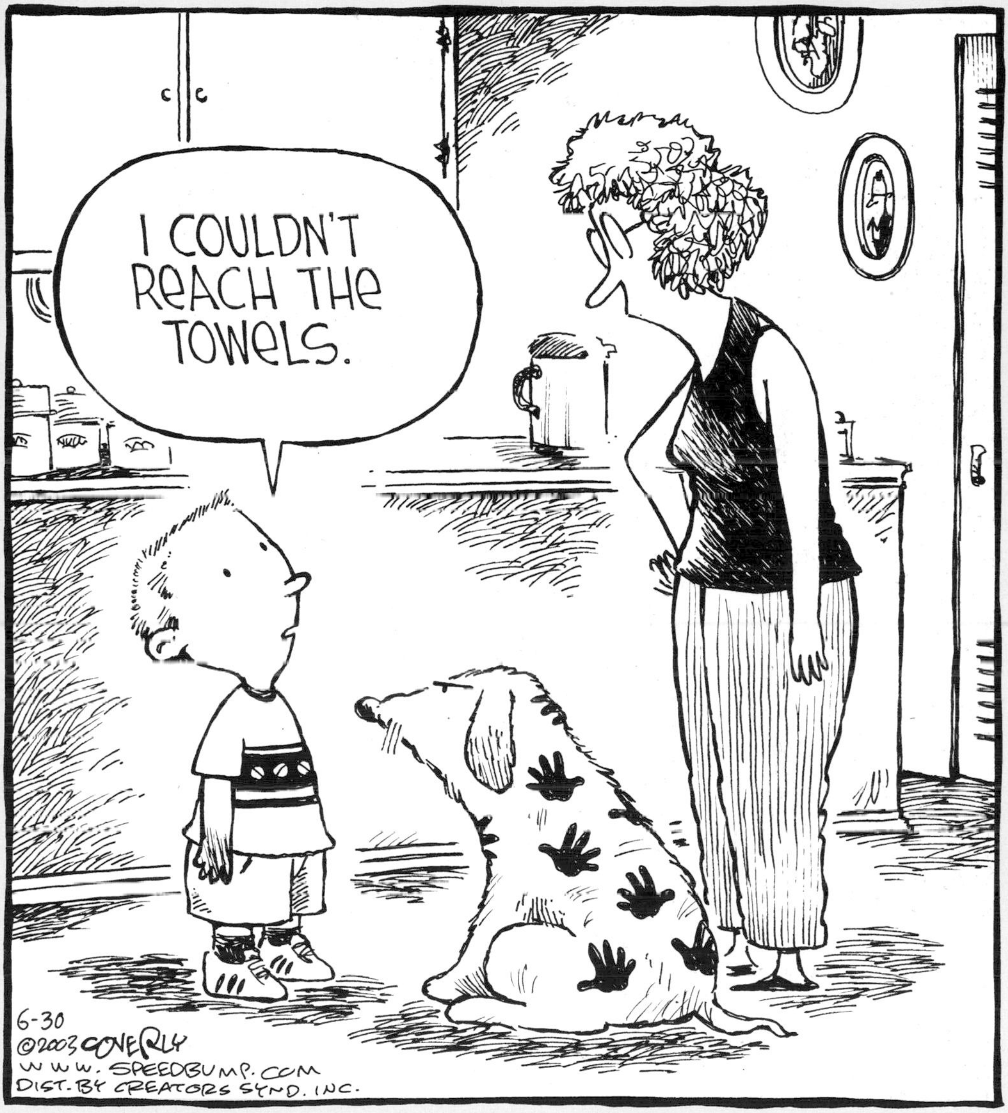
I COULDN'T REACH THE TOWELS.
6-30
©2003 COVERLY
WWW.SPEEDBUMP.COM
DIST. BY CREATORS SYND. INC.

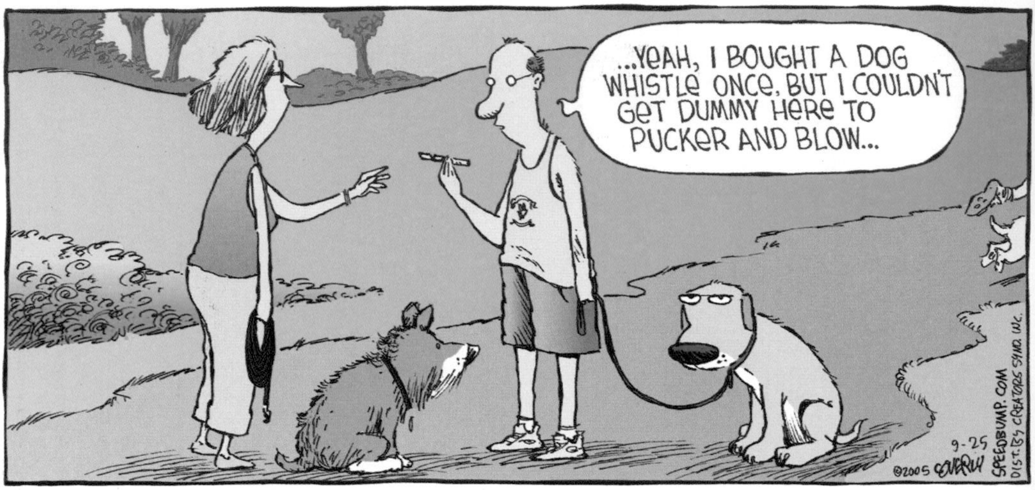
...YEAH, I BOUGHT A DOG WHISTLE ONCE, BUT I COULDN'T GET DUMMY HERE TO PUCKER AND BLOW...
9-25
©2005 COVERLY
SPEEDBUMP.COM
DIST. BY CREATORS SYND. INC.

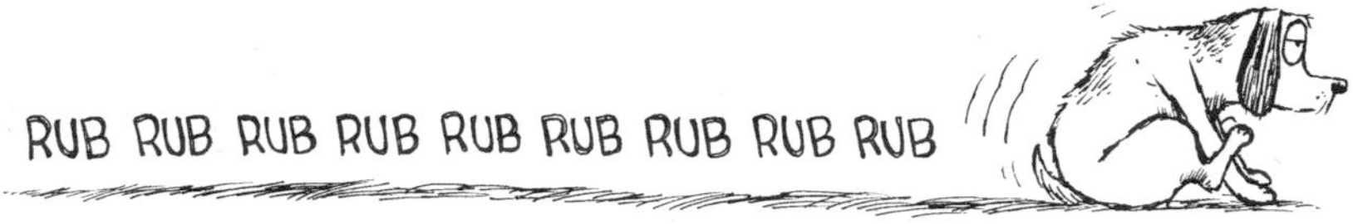
RUB RUB RUB RUB RUB RUB RUB RUB RUB

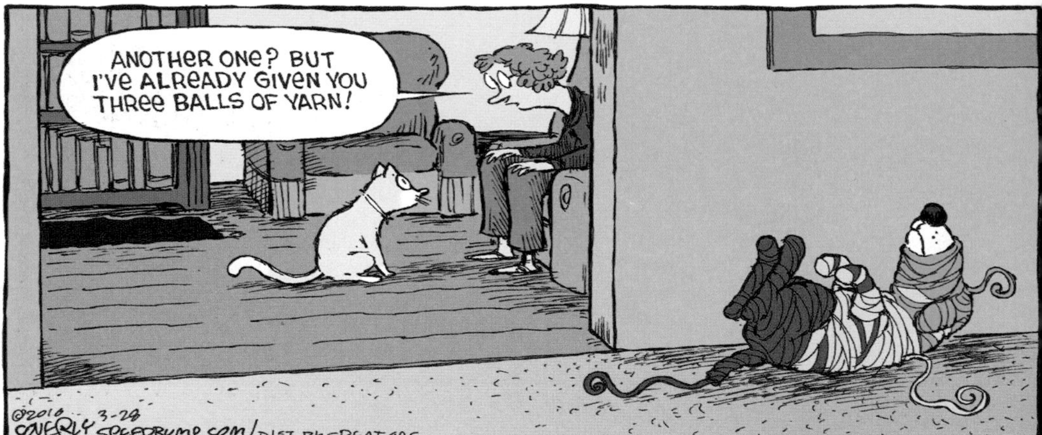
ANOTHER ONE? BUT I'VE ALREADY GIVEN YOU THREE BALLS OF YARN!
©2010 3-28
COVERLY SPEEDBUMP.COM/DIST. BY CREATORS

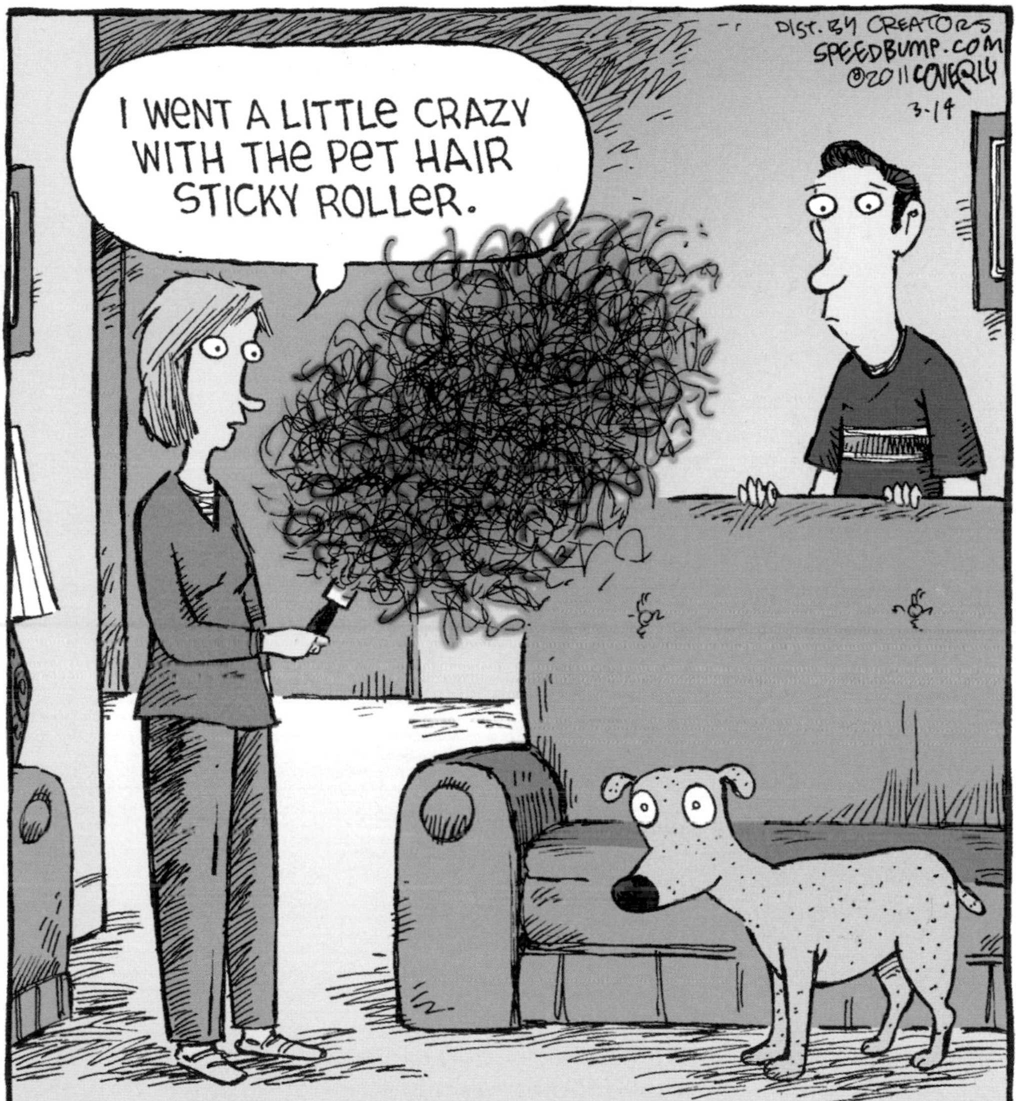
DIST. BY CREATORS
SPEEDBUMP.COM
©2011 COVERLY
3-14
I WENT A LITTLE CRAZY WITH THE PET HAIR STICKY ROLLER.

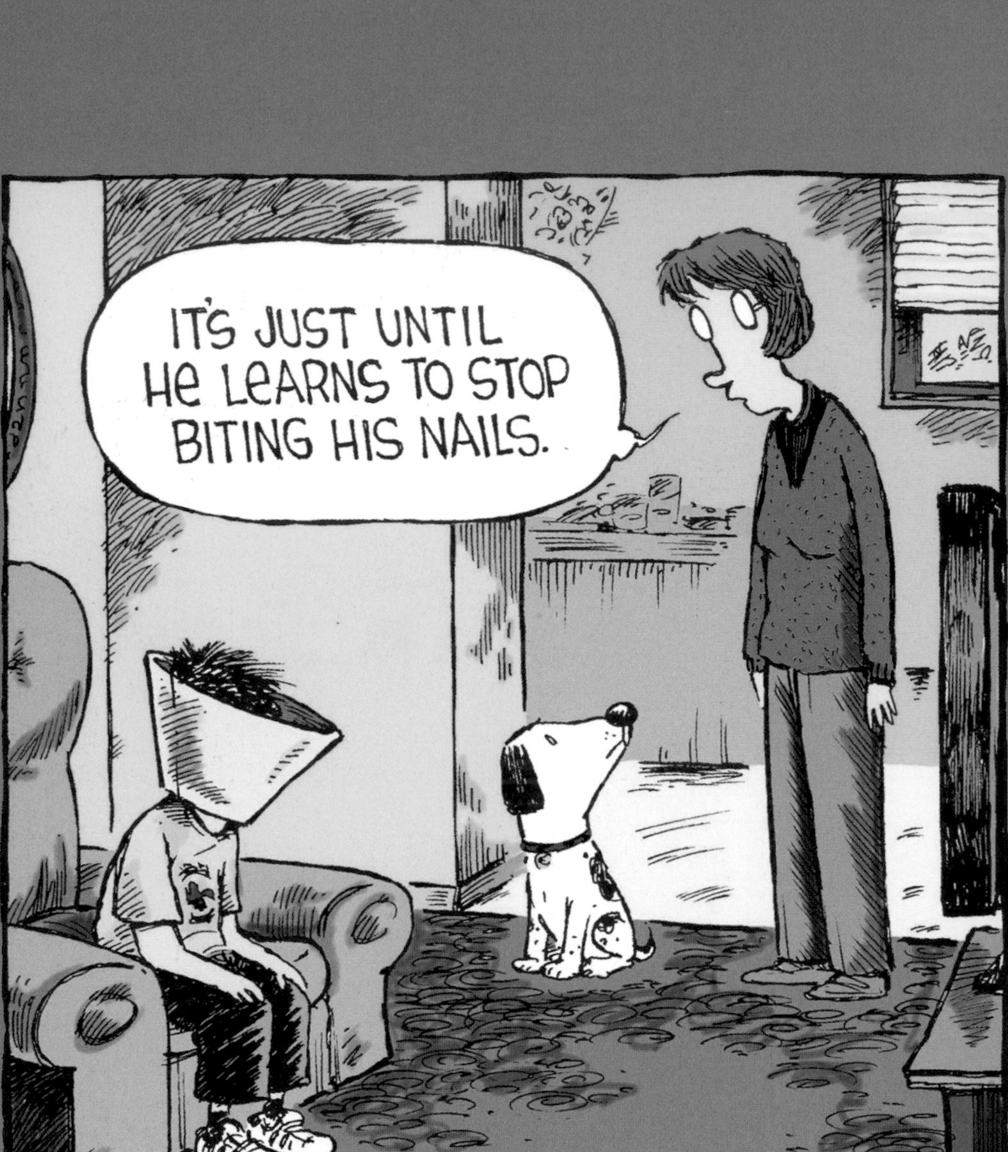
IT'S JUST UNTIL HE LEARNS TO STOP BITING HIS NAILS.
3-1 SPEEDBUMP.com
DIST. BY CREATORS ©2013 COVERLY

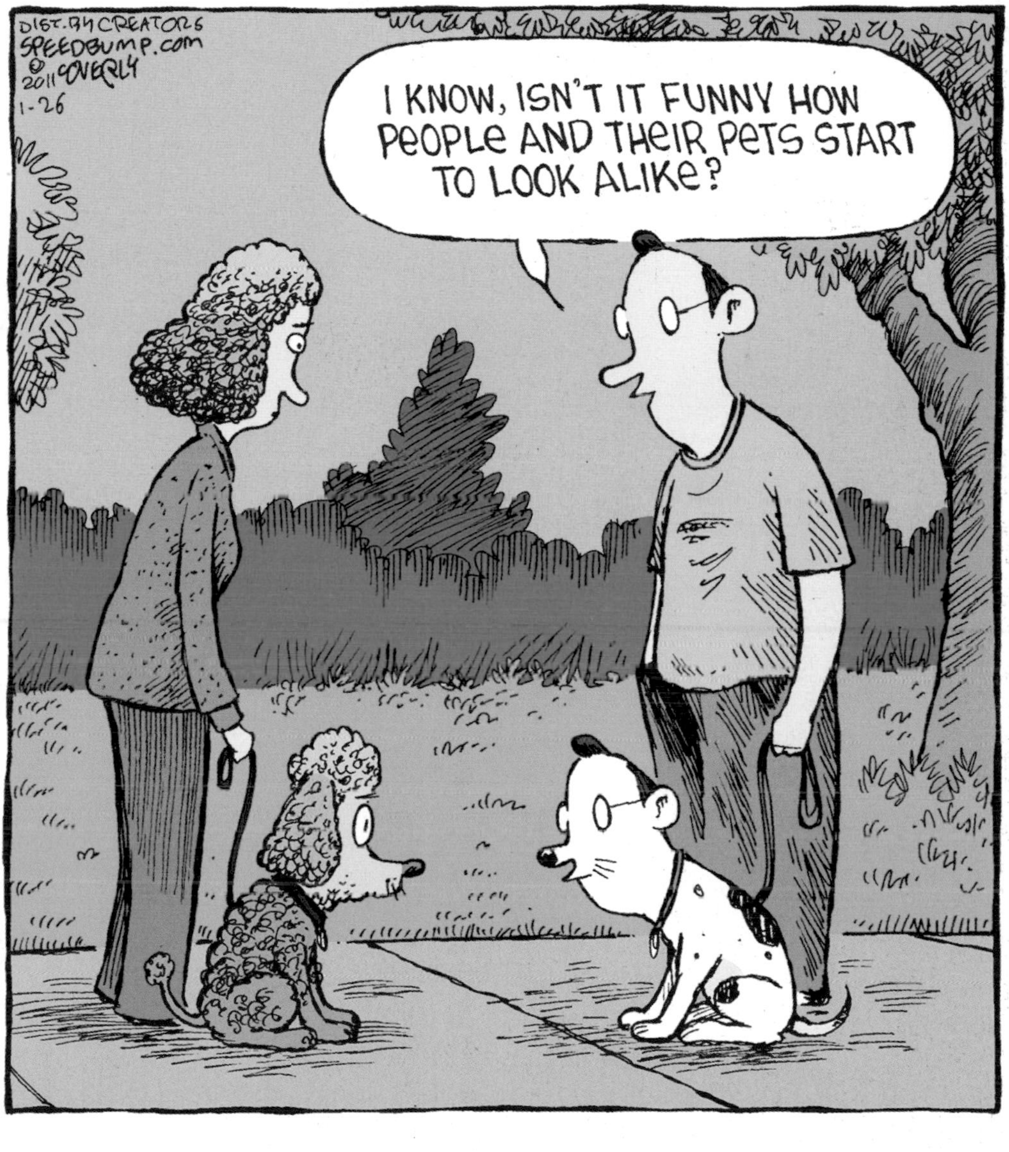
DIST. BY CREATORS
SPEEDBUMP.COM
© 2011 COVERLY
1-26
I KNOW, ISN'T IT FUNNY HOW PEOPLE AND THEIR PETS START TO LOOK ALIKE?

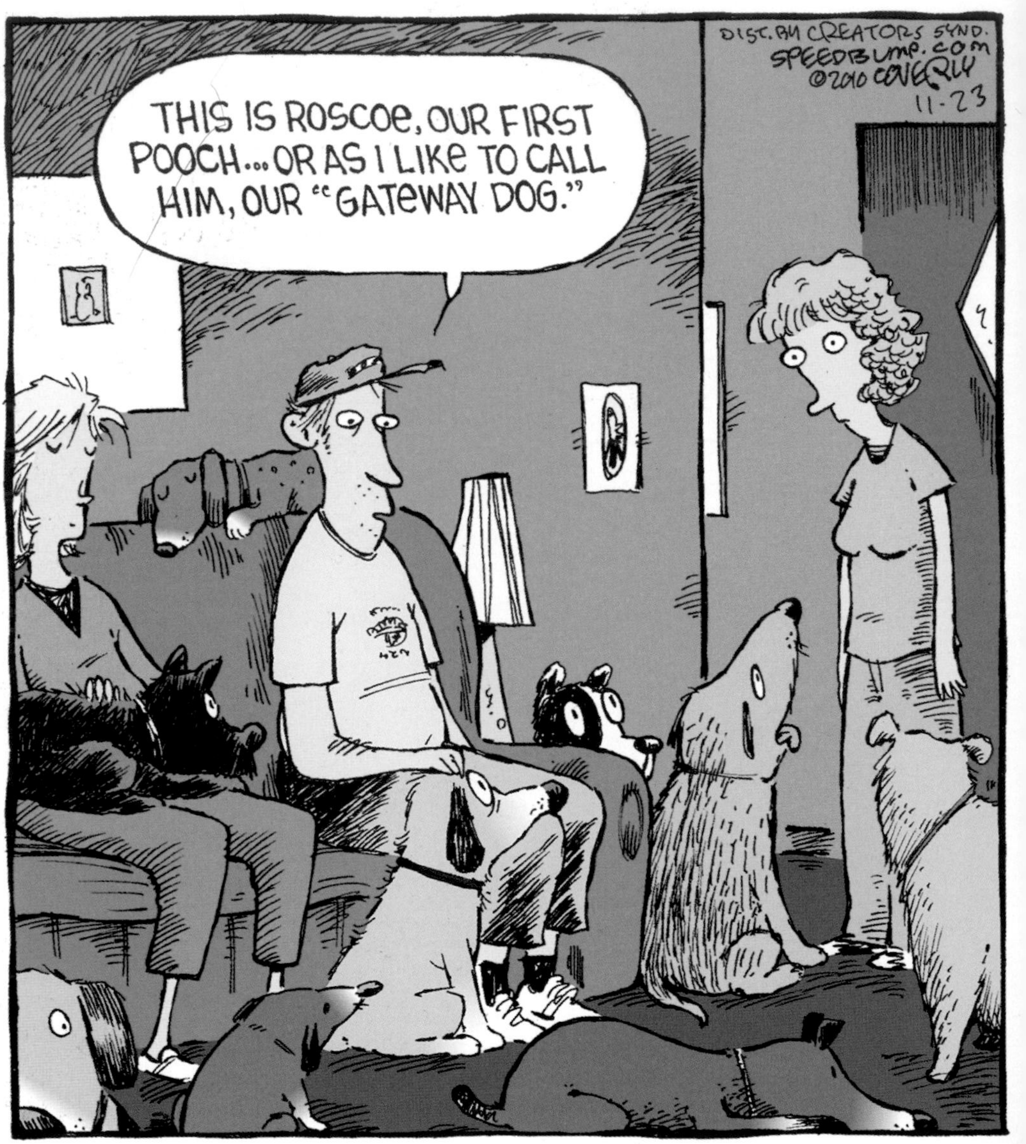
THIS IS ROSCOE, OUR FIRST POOCH... OR AS I LIKE TO CALL HIM, OUR "GATEWAY DOG."
DIST. BY CREATORS SYND.
SPEEDBUMP.COM
©2010 COVERLY
11-23

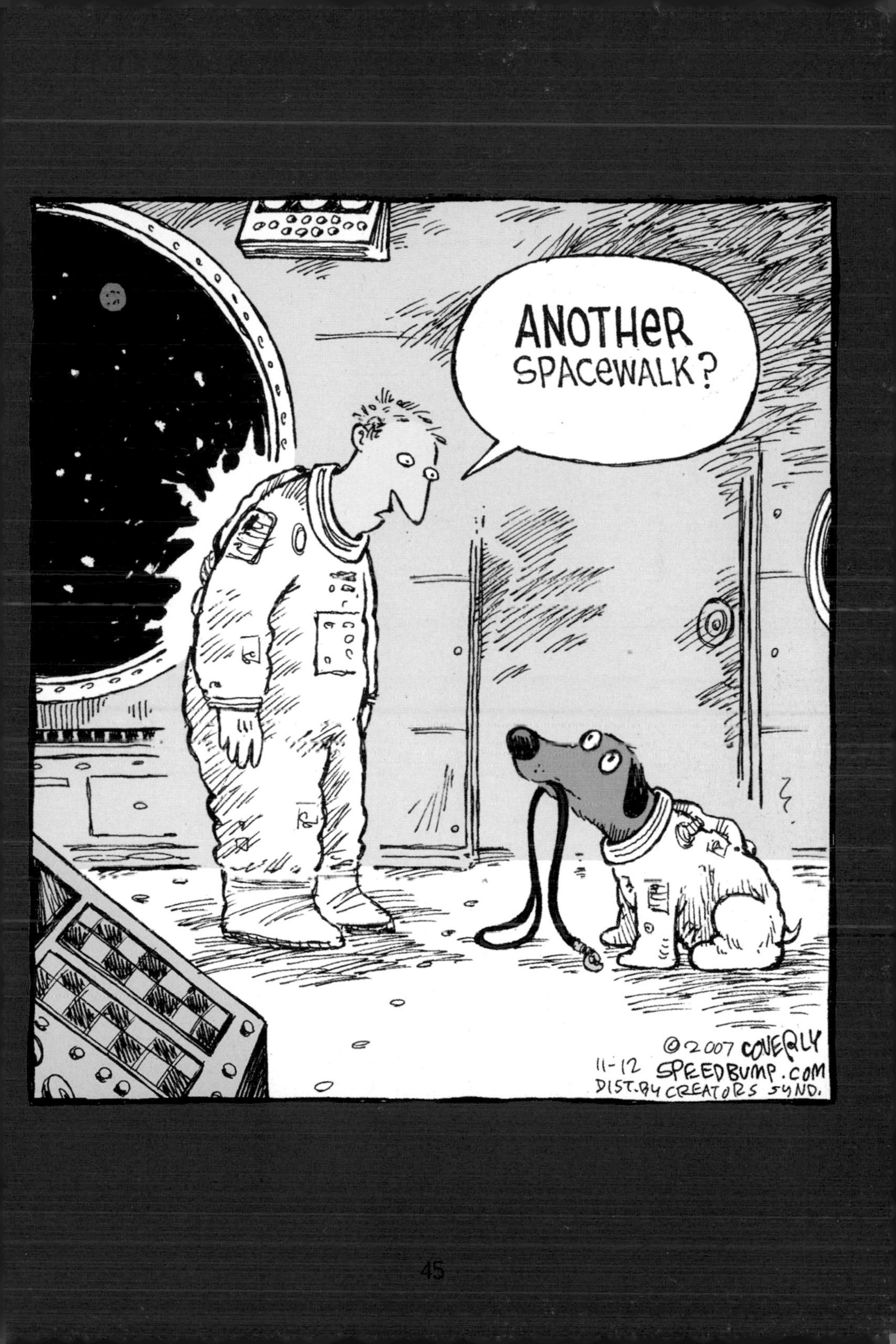
ANOTHER SPACEWALK?
©2007 COVERLY
11-12 SPEEDBUMP.COM
DIST. BY CREATORS SYND.

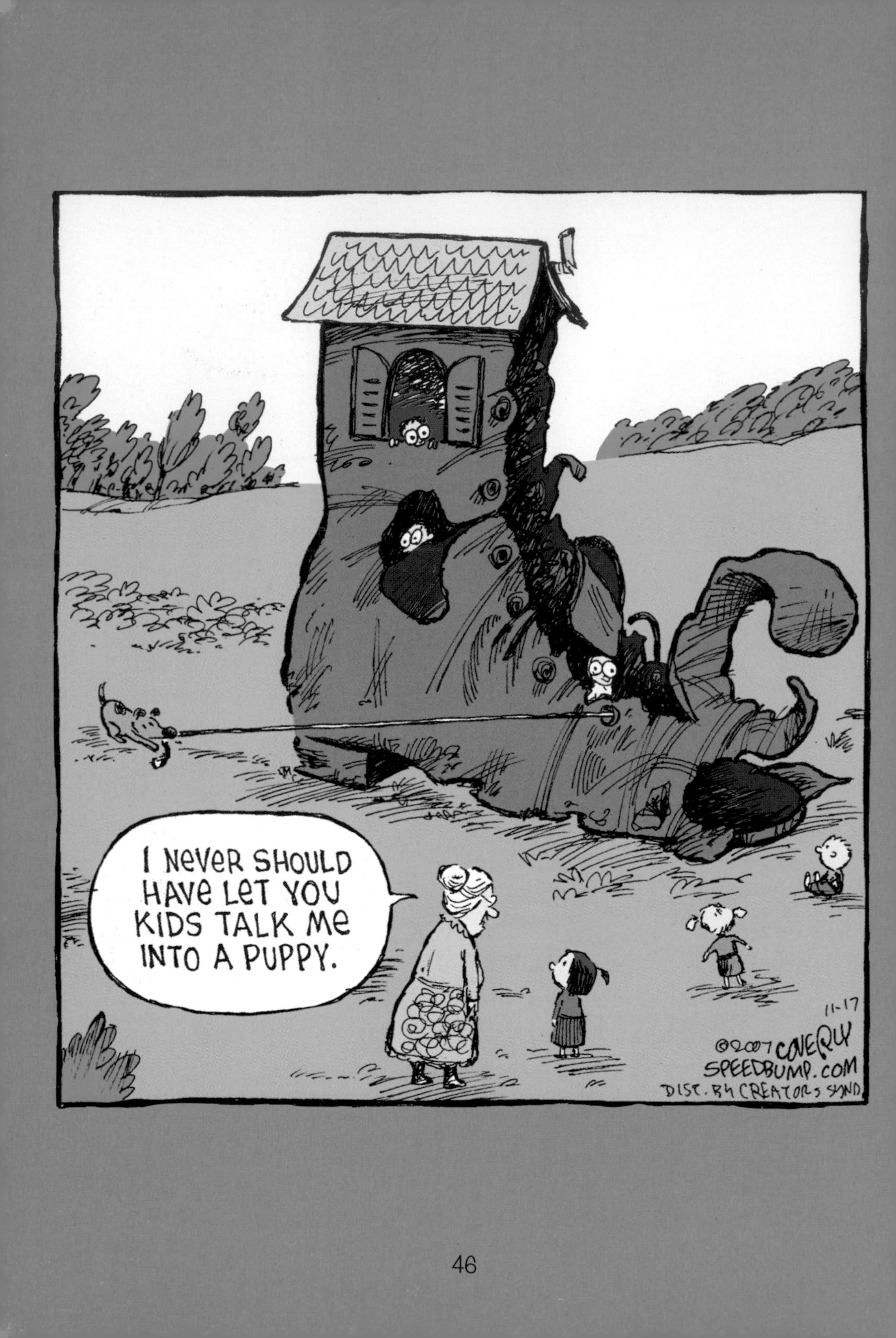
I NEVER SHOULD HAVE LET YOU KIDS TALK ME INTO A PUPPY.
11-17
©2007 COVERLY
SPEEDBUMP.COM
DIST. BY CREATORS SYND.

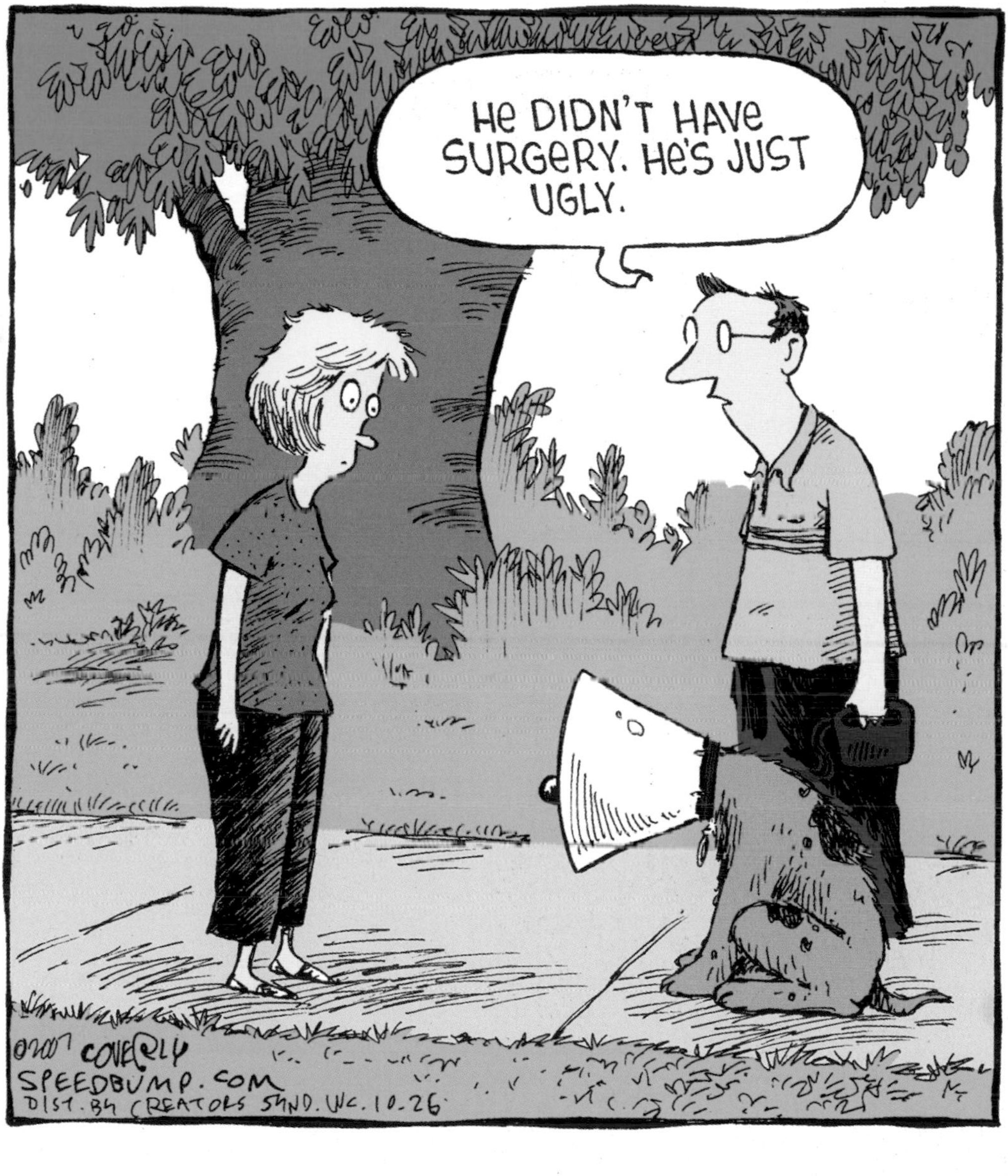
HE DIDN'T HAVE SURGERY. HE'S JUST UGLY.
©2007 COVERLY
SPEEDBUMP.COM
DIST. BY CREATORS SYND. INC. 10.26

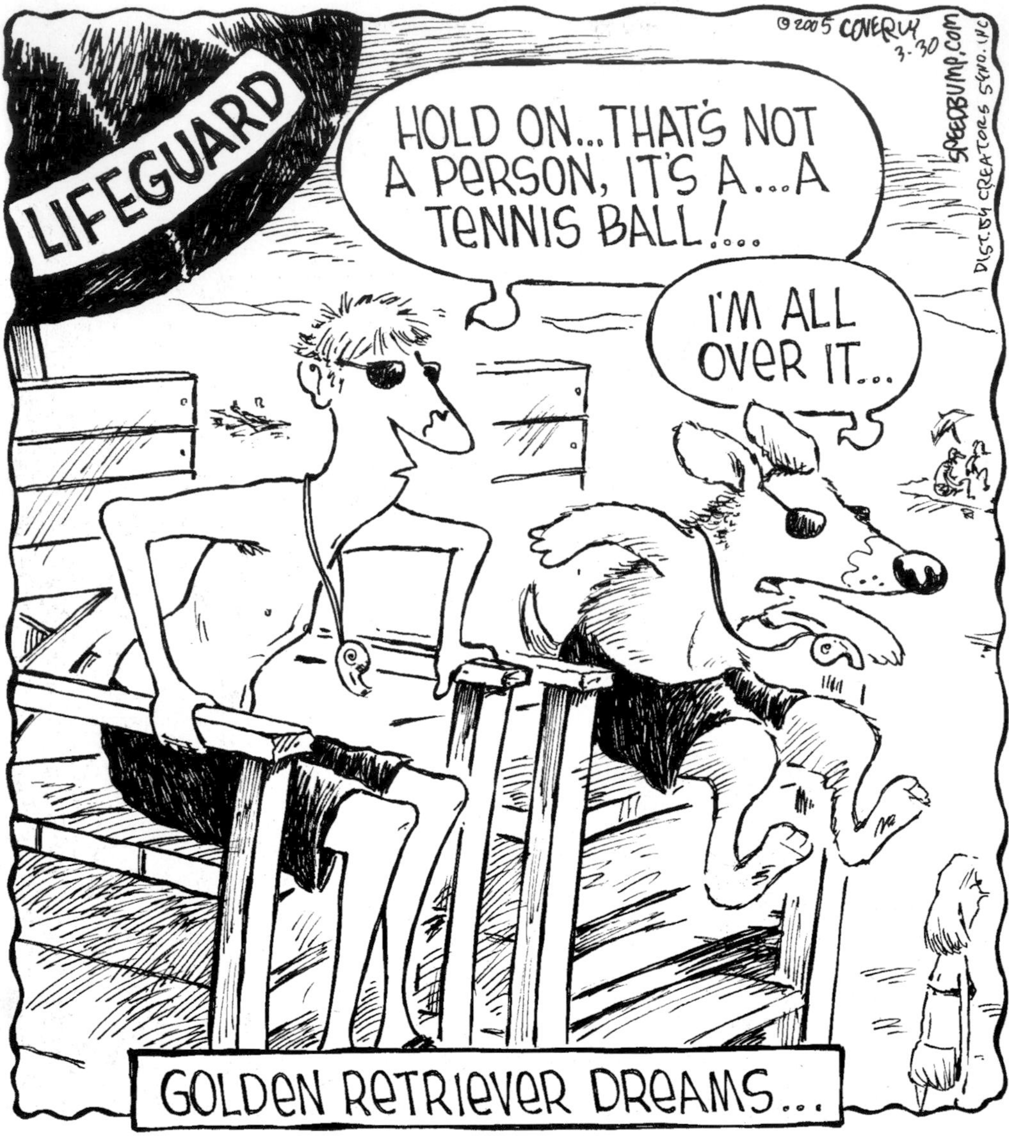
LIFEGUARD
HOLD ON...THAT'S NOT A PERSON, IT'S A...A TENNIS BALL!...
I'M ALL OVER IT...
GOLDEN RETRIEVER DREAMS...
©2005 COVERLY 3-30
SPEEDBUMP.COM
DIST. BY CREATORS SYND. INC

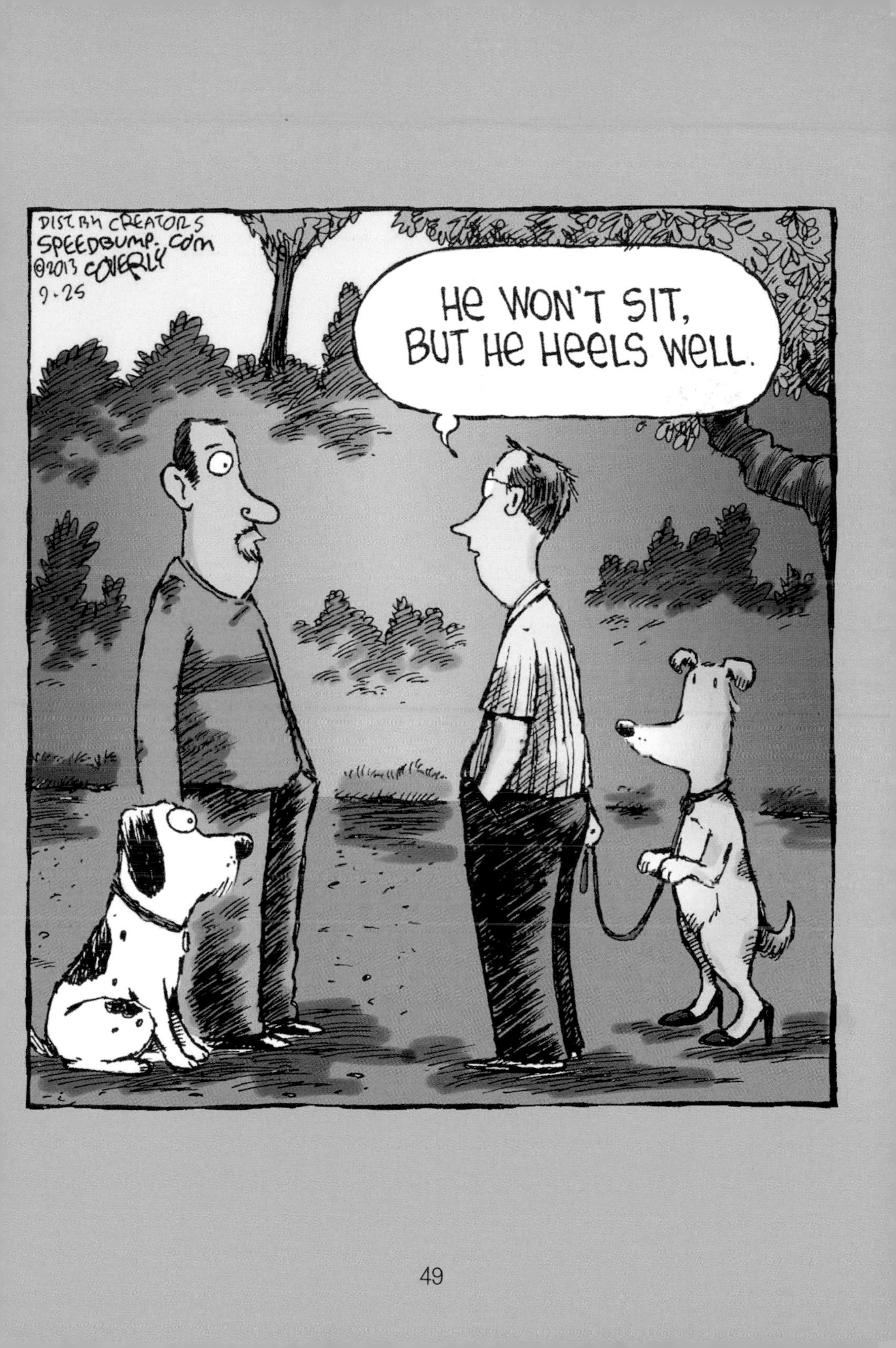
DIST. BY CREATORS
SPEEDBUMP.COM
©2013 COVERLY
9-25
HE WON'T SIT,
BUT HE HEELS WELL.

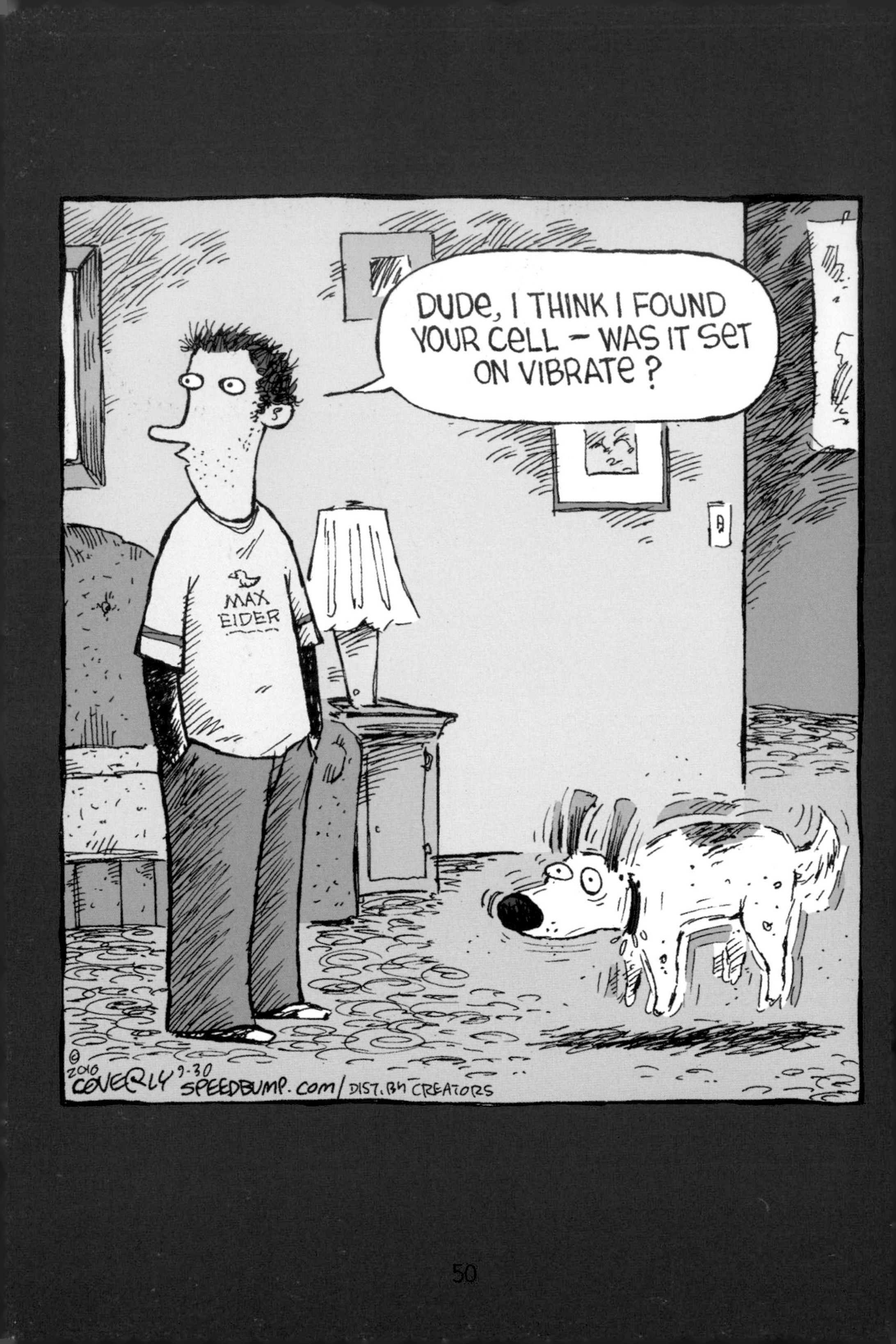
DUDE, I THINK I FOUND YOUR CELL - WAS IT SET ON VIBRATE?
MAX EIDER
© 2010 COVERLY 9-30 SPEEDBUMP.COM / DIST. BY CREATORS

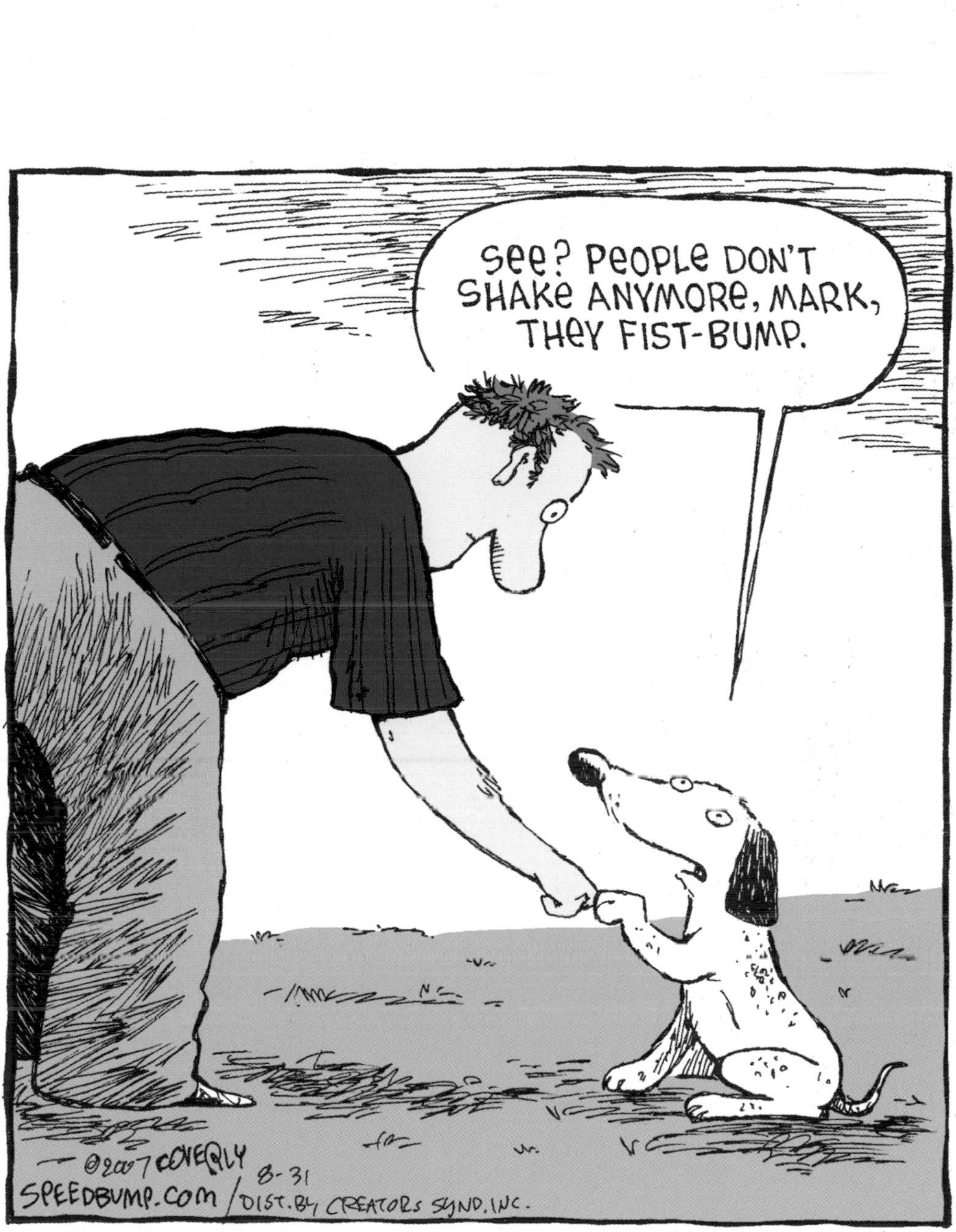
SEE? PEOPLE DON'T SHAKE ANYMORE, MARK, THEY FIST-BUMP.
©2007 COVERLY
8-31
SPEEDBUMP.COM / DIST. BY CREATORS SYND. INC.

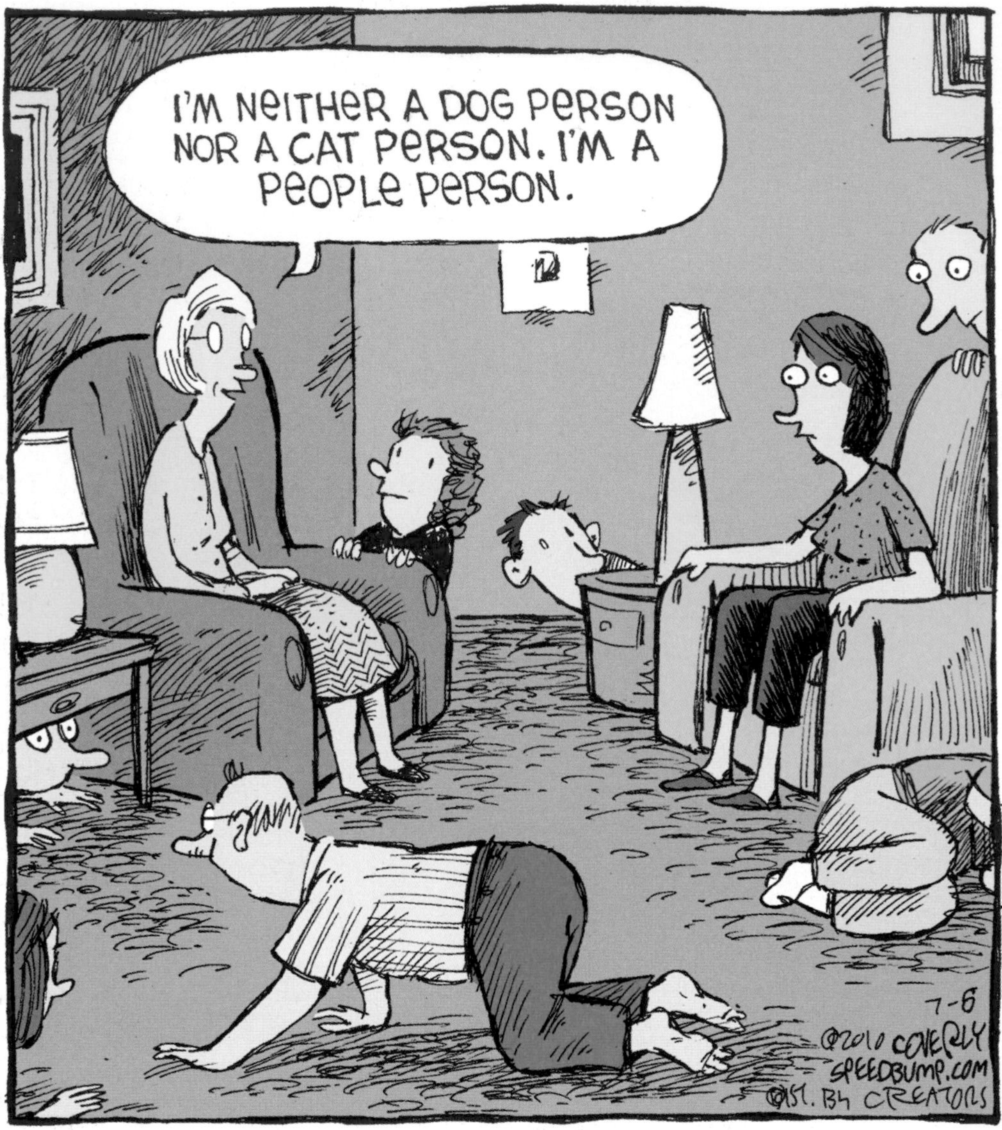
I'M NEITHER A DOG PERSON NOR A CAT PERSON. I'M A PEOPLE PERSON.
7-6
©2010 COVERLY
SPEEDBUMP.COM
DIST. BY CREATORS

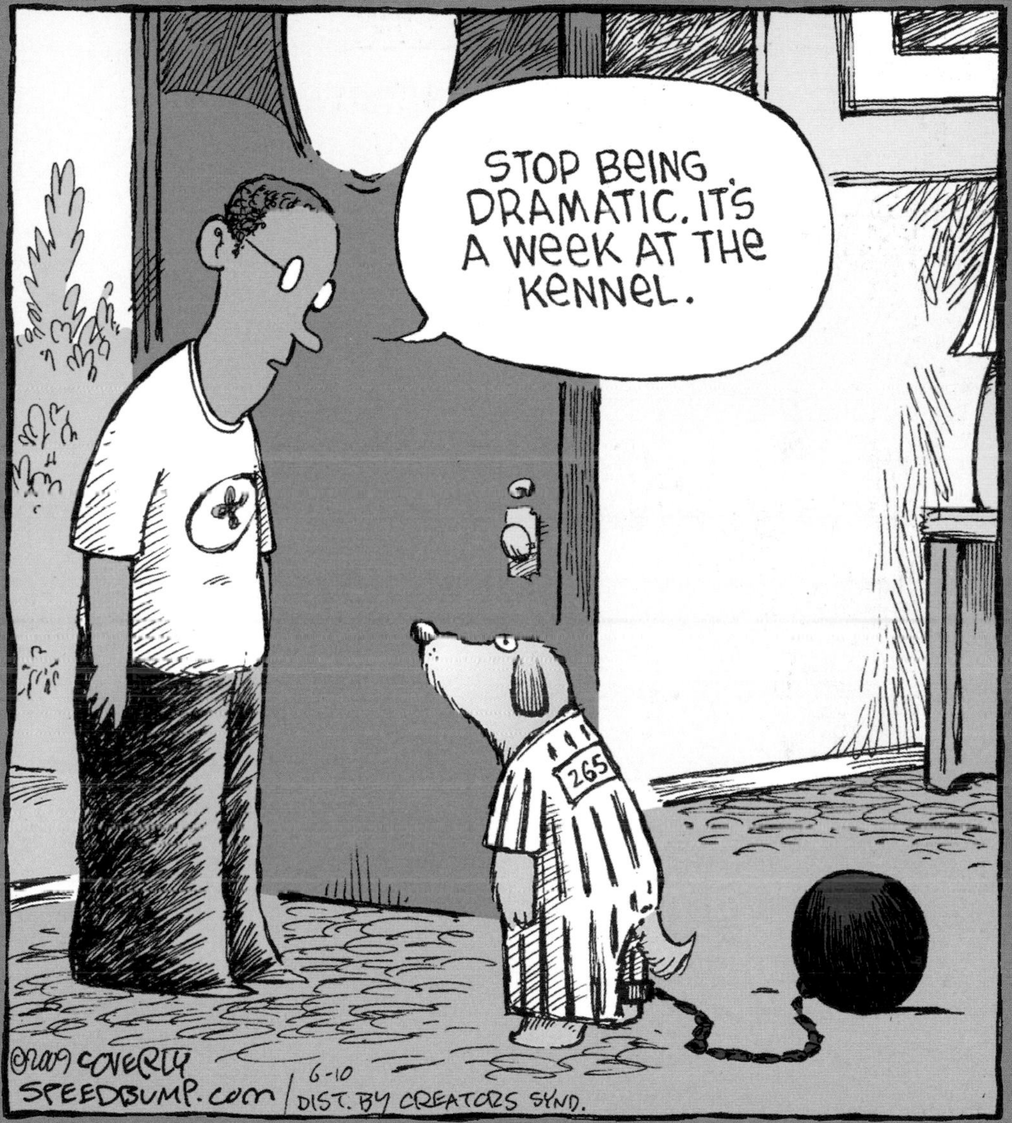
STOP BEING DRAMATIC. IT'S A WEEK AT THE KENNEL.
265
©2009 COVERLY SPEEDBUMP.com
6-10
DIST. BY CREATORS SYND.

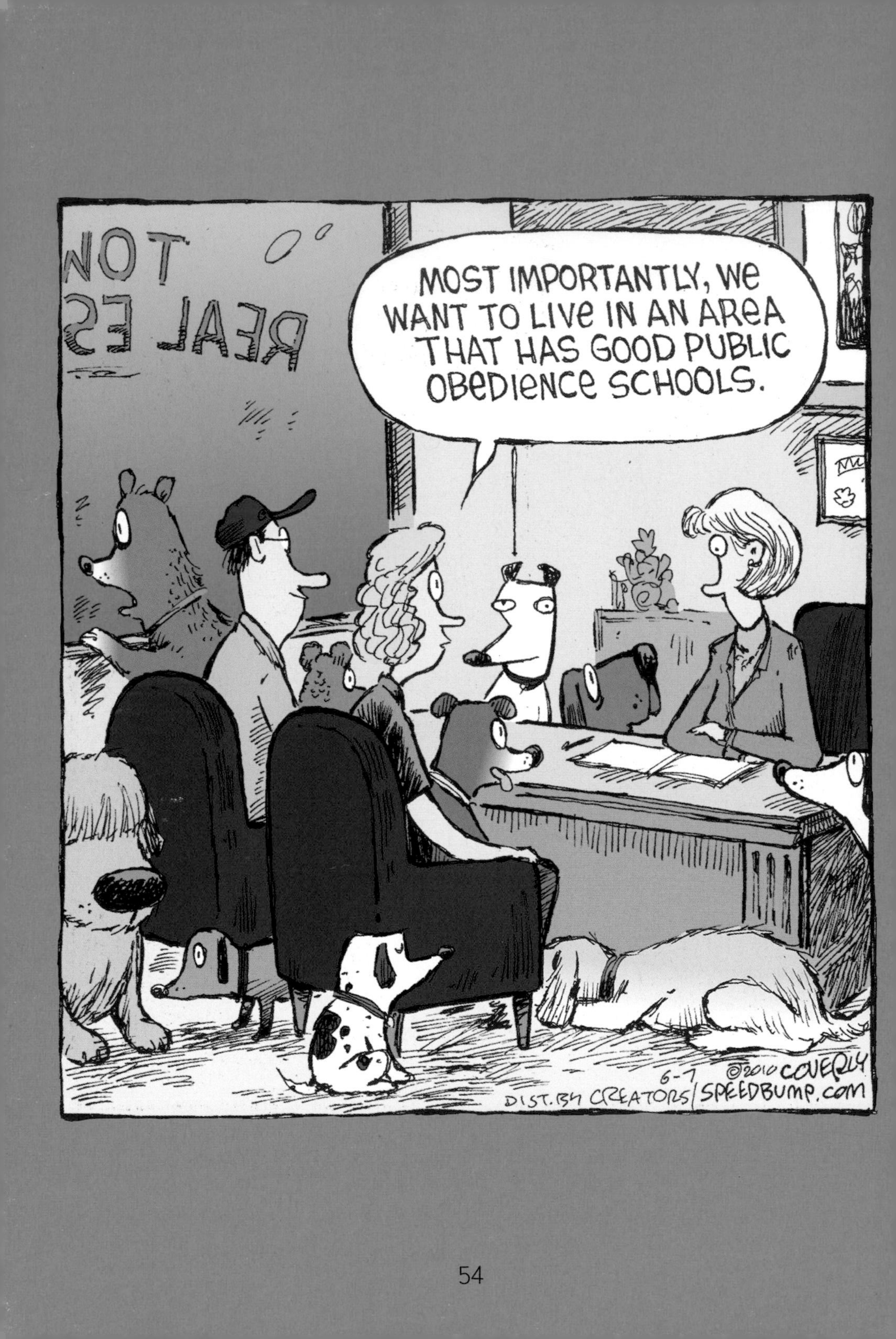
MOST IMPORTANTLY, WE WANT TO LIVE IN AN AREA THAT HAS GOOD PUBLIC OBEDIENCE SCHOOLS.
6-7
©2010 COVERLY
DIST. BY CREATORS | SPEEDBUMP.com

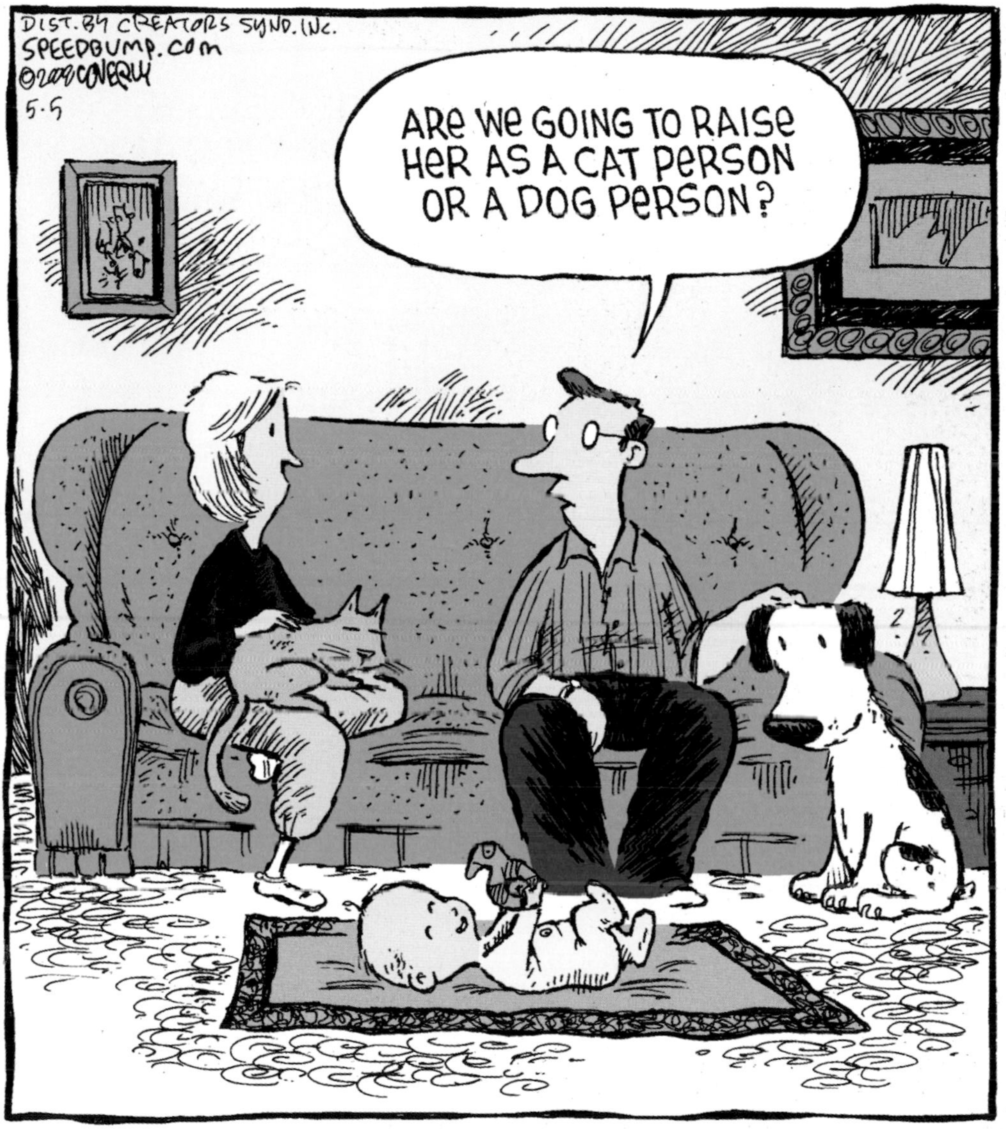
DIST. BY CREATORS SYND. INC.
SPEEDBUMP.COM
ARE WE GOING TO RAISE HER AS A CAT PERSON OR A DOG PERSON?

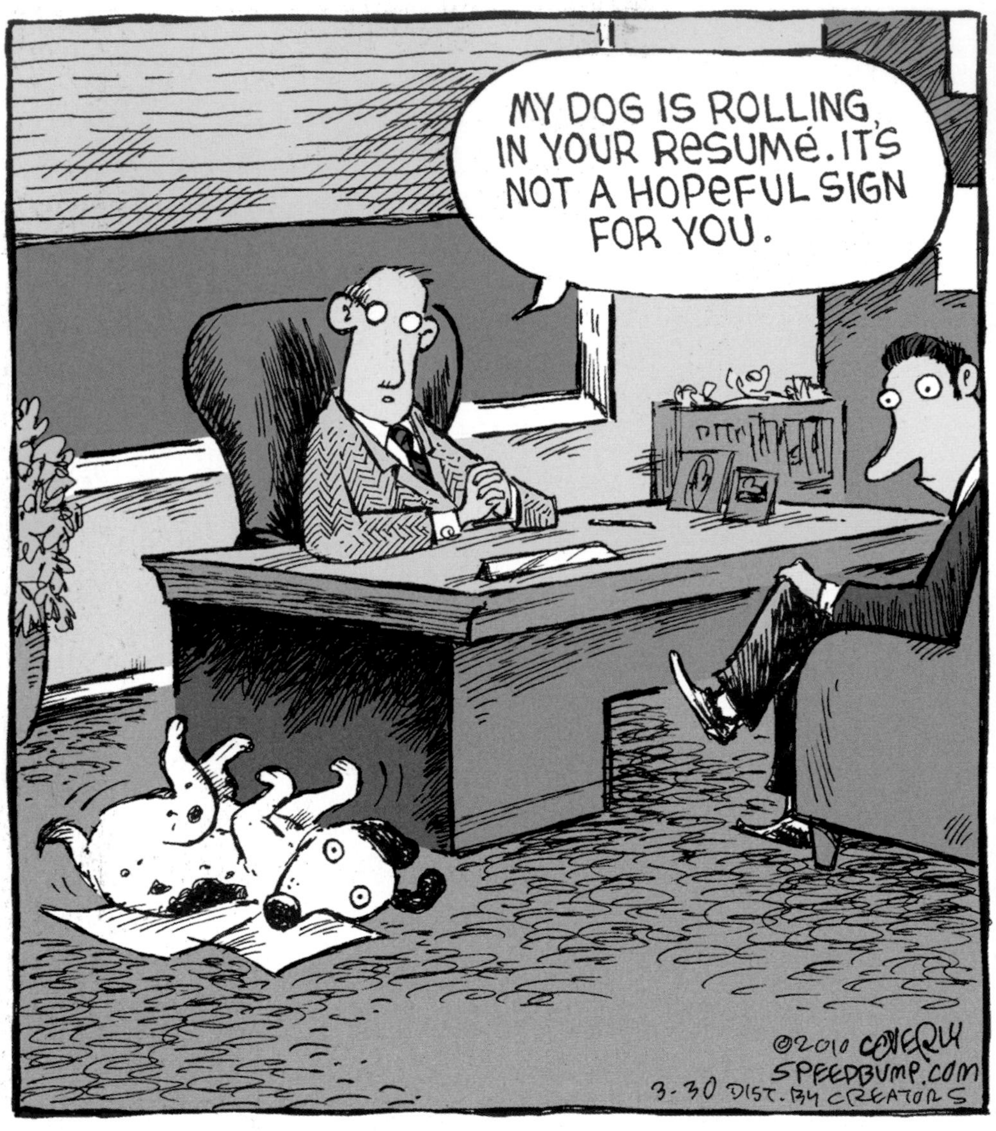
MY DOG IS ROLLING IN YOUR RESUMÉ. IT'S NOT A HOPEFUL SIGN FOR YOU.
©2010 COVERLY SPEEDBUMP.COM
3-30 DIST. BY CREATORS

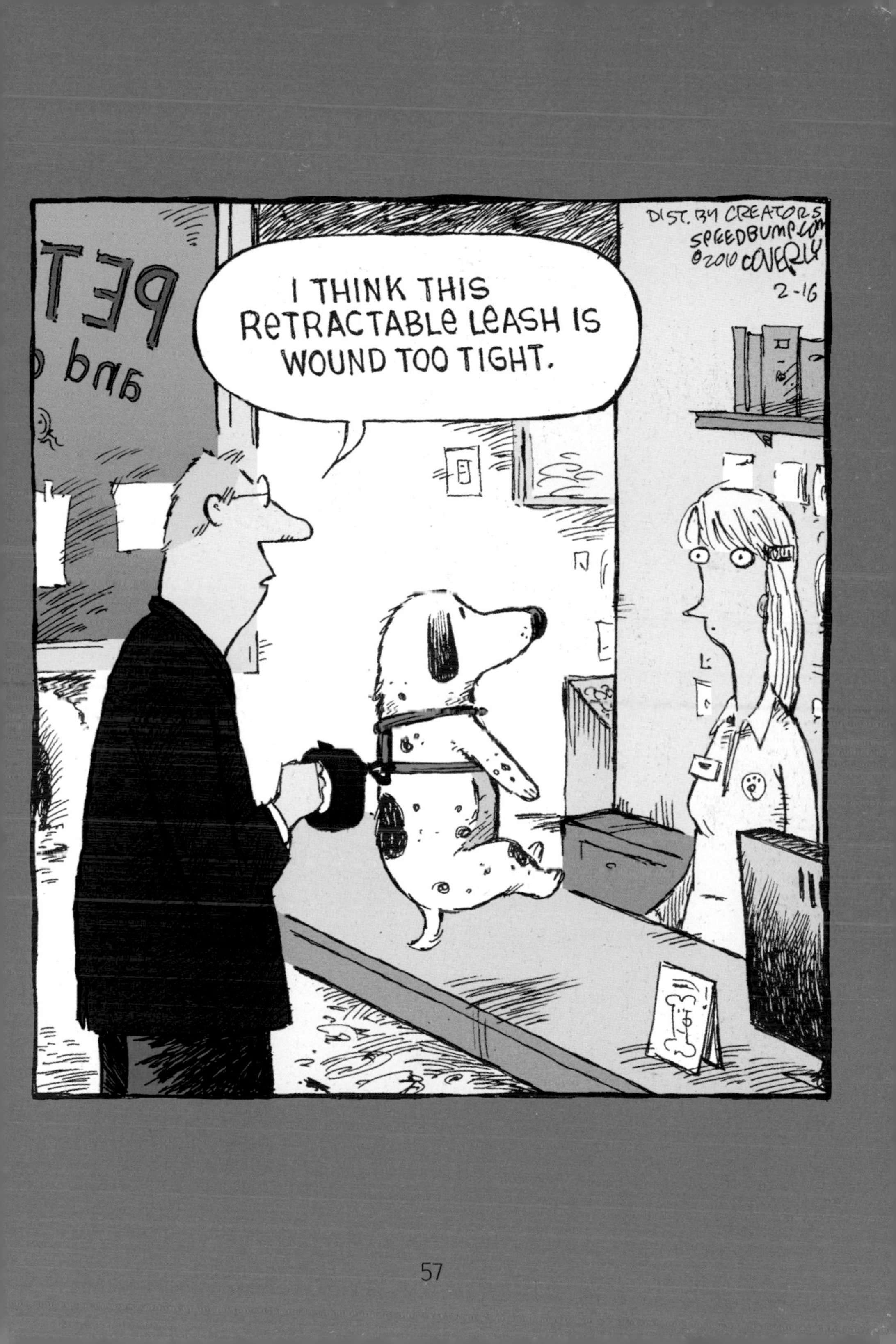
I THINK THIS RETRACTABLE LEASH IS WOUND TOO TIGHT.
DIST. BY CREATORS
SPEEDBUMP.COM
©2010 COVERLY
2-16

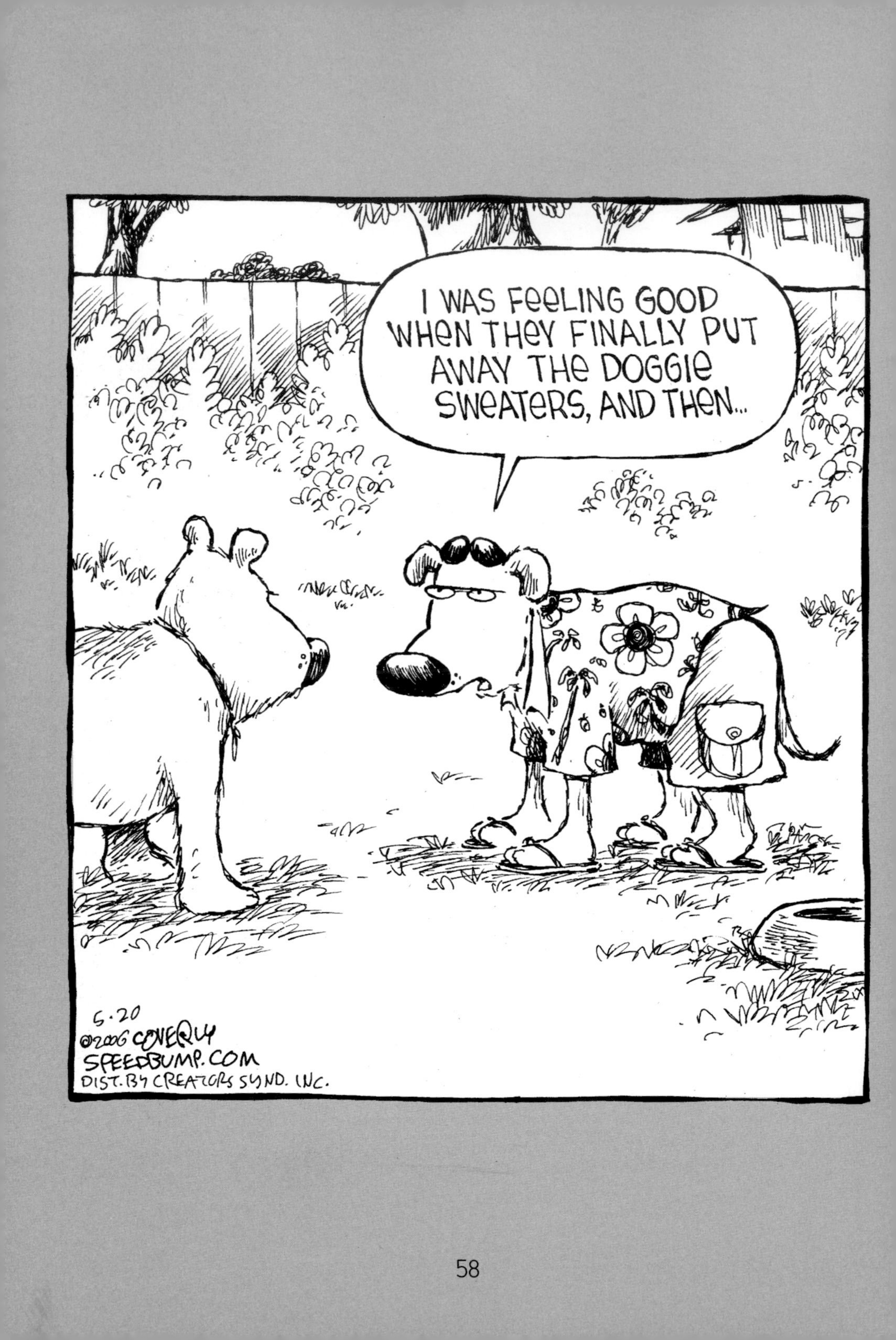
I WAS FEELING GOOD WHEN THEY FINALLY PUT AWAY THE DOGGIE SWEATERS, AND THEN...
5.20
©2006 COVERLY
SPEEDBUMP.COM
DIST. BY CREATORS SYND. INC.

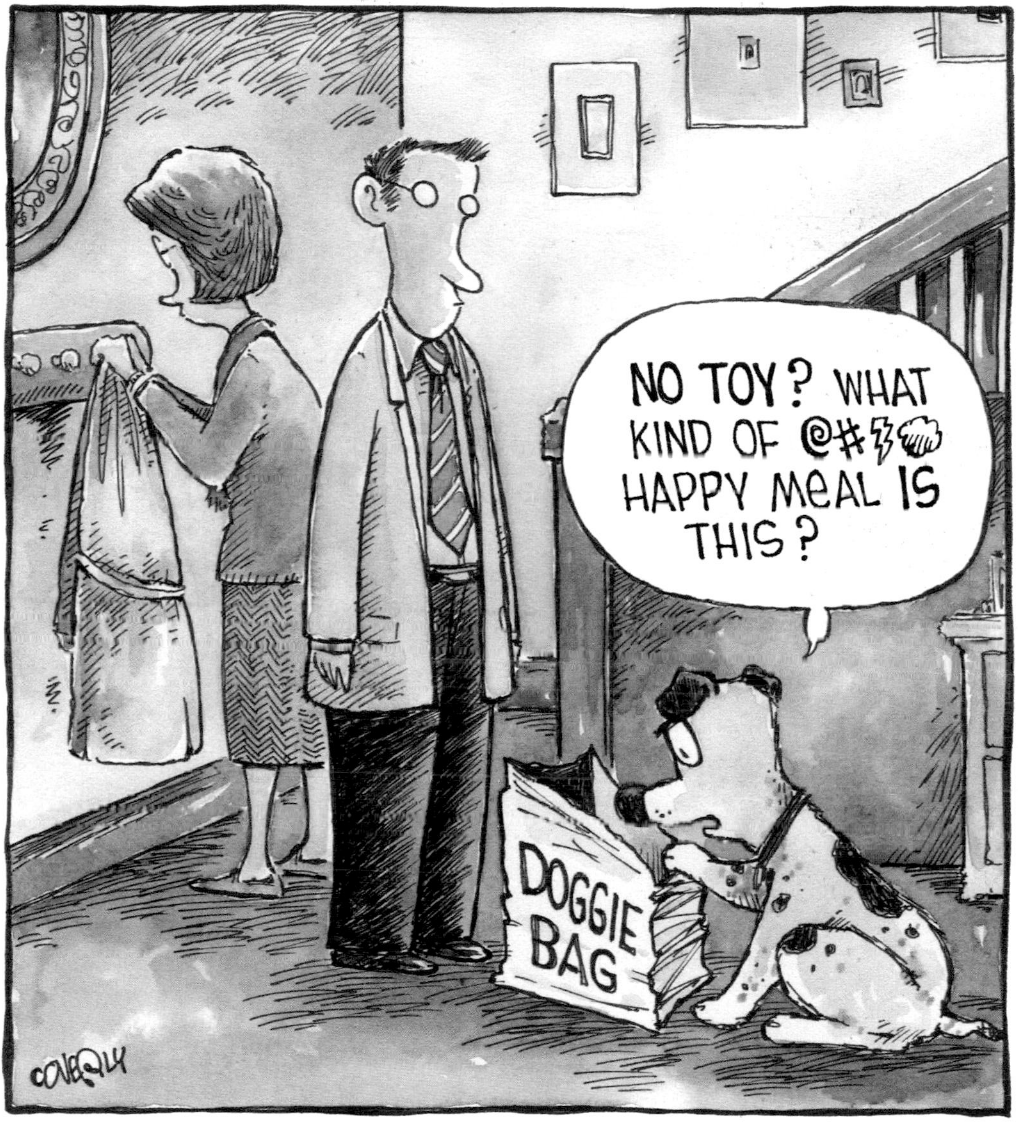
NO TOY? WHAT KIND OF @#%* HAPPY MEAL IS THIS?
DOGGIE BAG
CONCOLLY

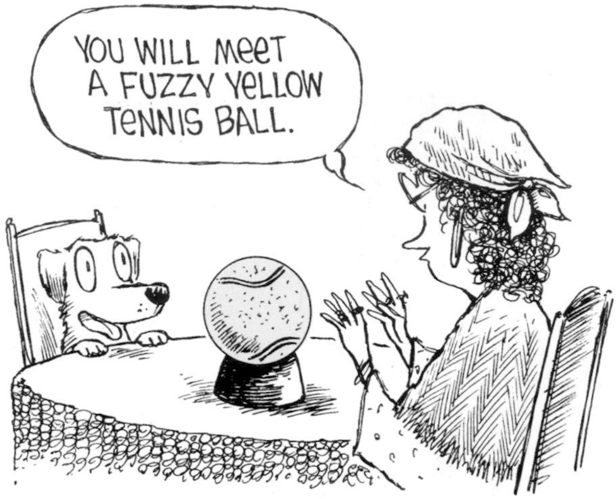
YOU WILL MEET A FUZZY YELLOW TENNIS BALL.

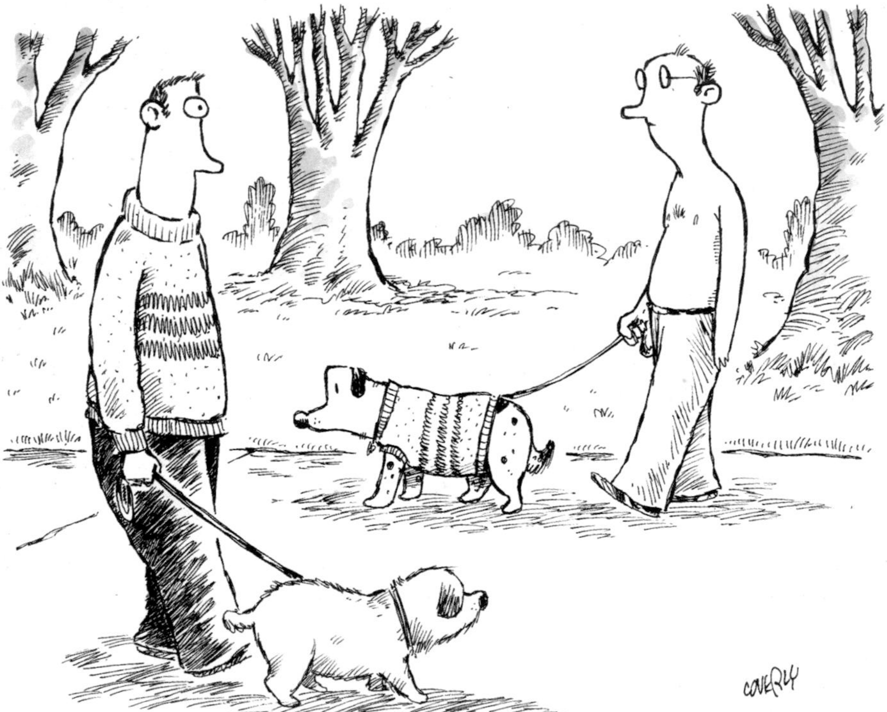
COVERLY

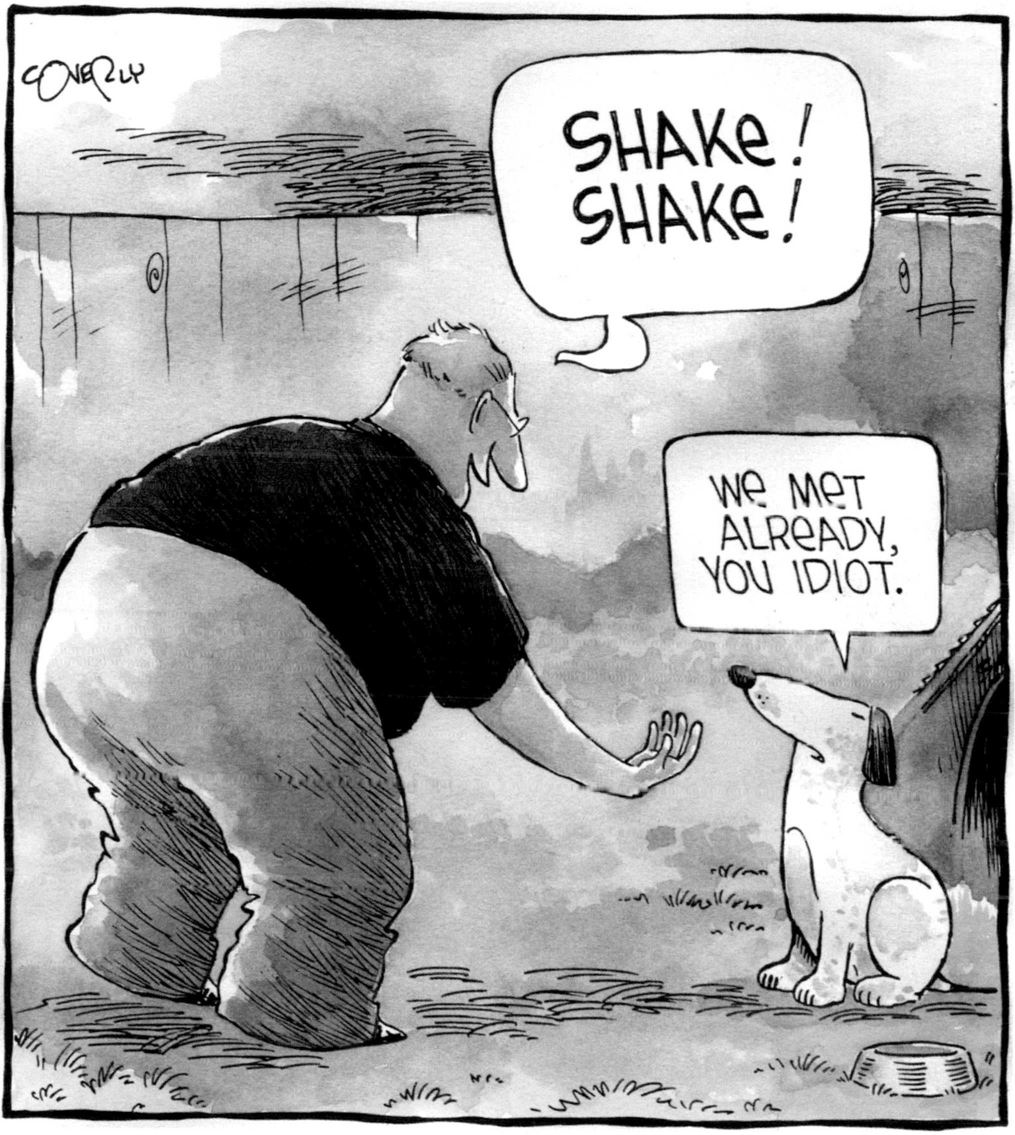
SHAKE! SHAKE!
WE MET ALREADY, YOU IDIOT.

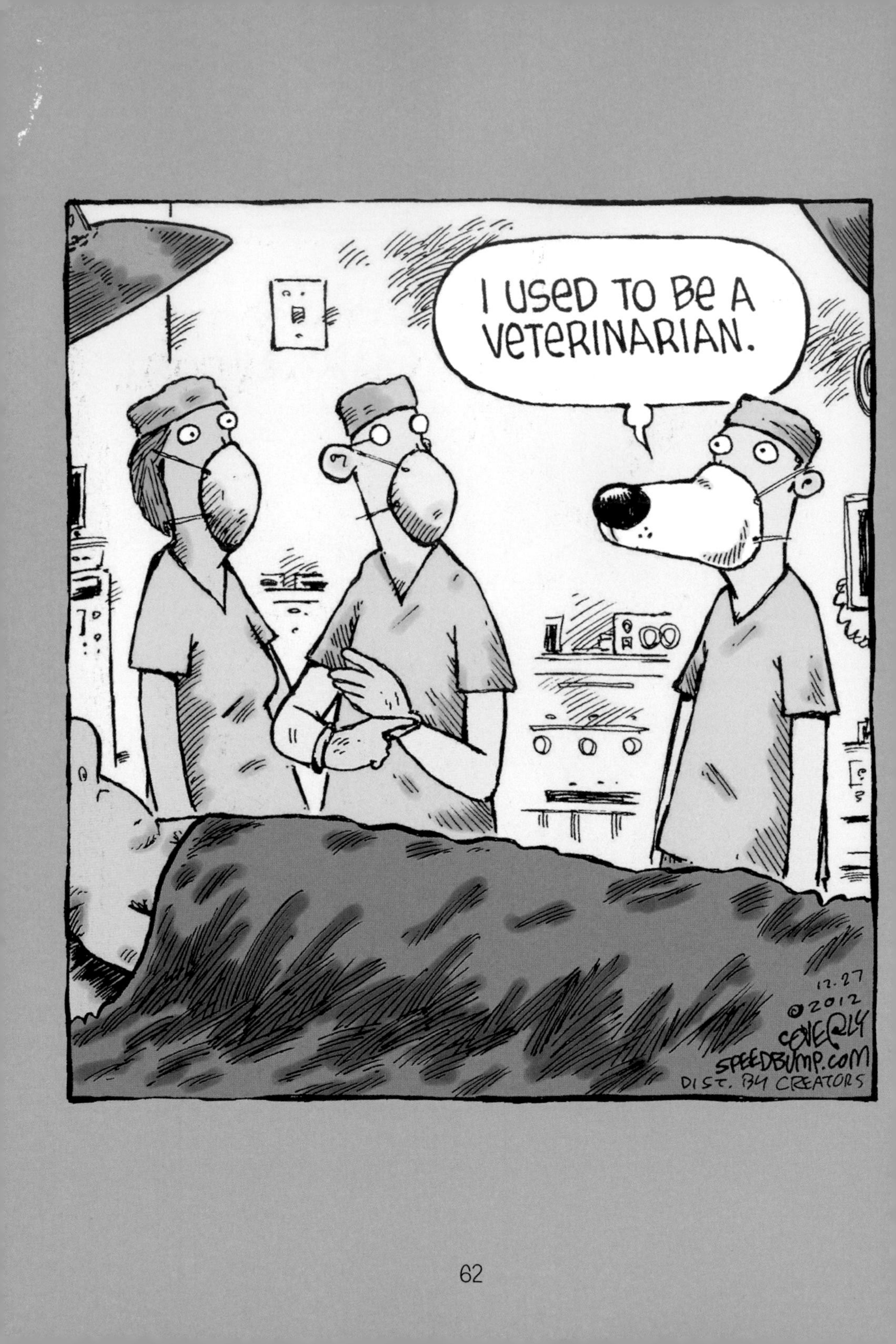
I USED TO BE A VETERINARIAN.
12.27
©2012
COVERLY
SPEEDBUMP.COM
DIST. BY CREATORS

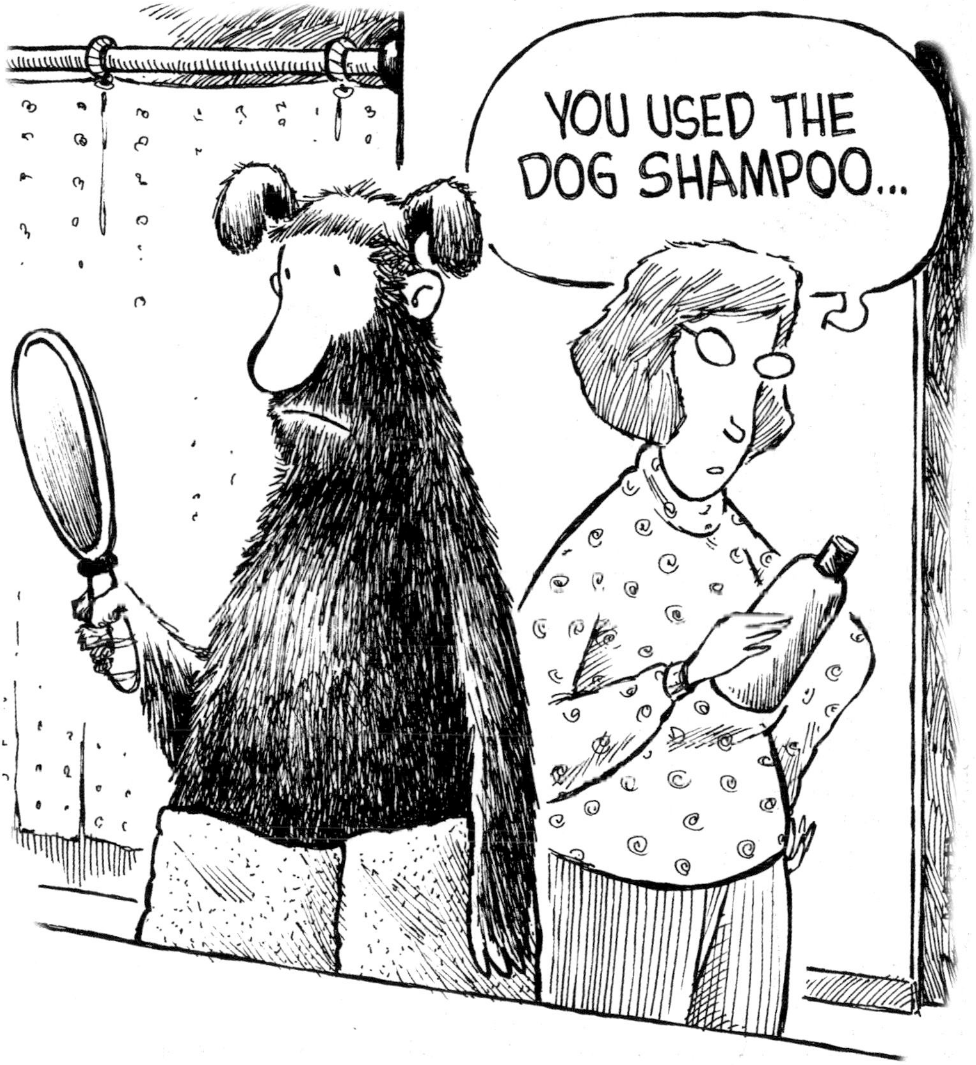
YOU USED THE DOG SHAMPOO...

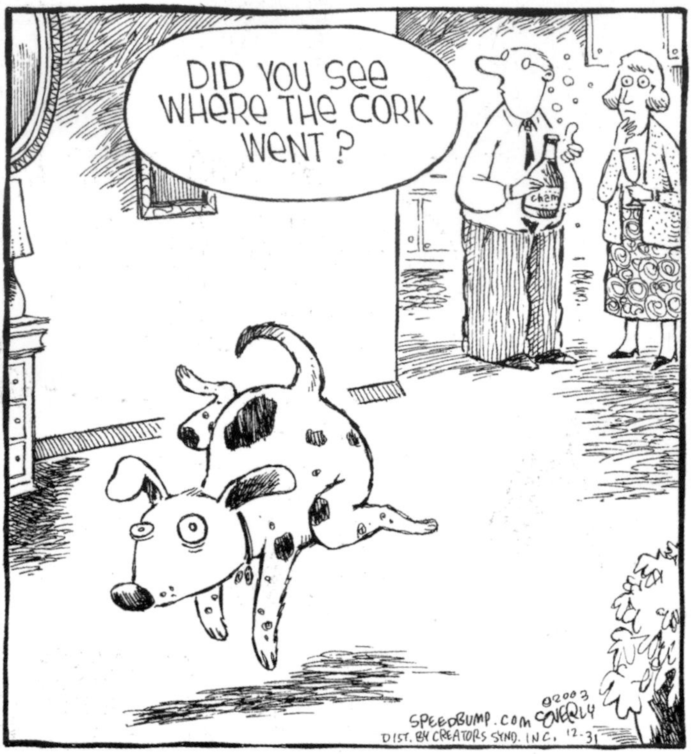
DID YOU SEE WHERE THE CORK WENT ?
SPEEDBUMP.COM ©2003 COVERLY
DIST. BY CREATORS SYND. INC. 12-31

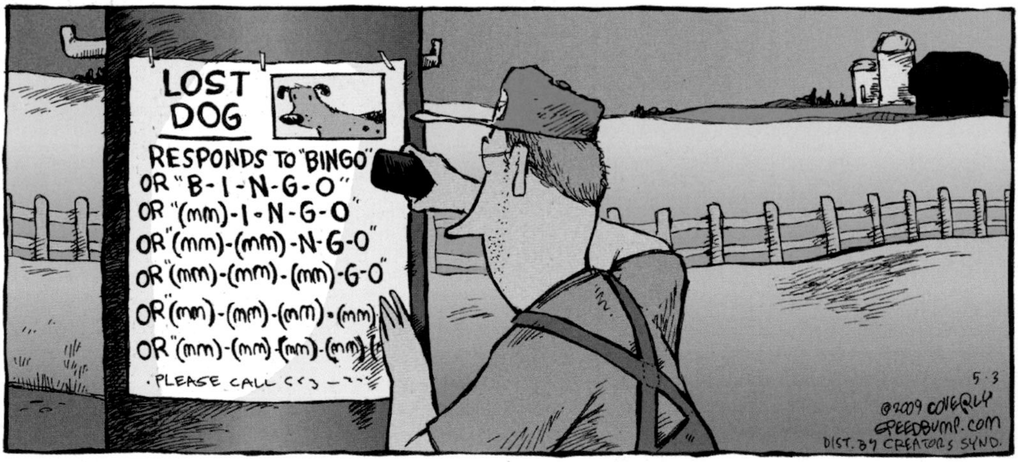
LOST DOG
RESPONDS TO "BINGO"
OR "B-I-N-G-O"
OR "(mm)-I-N-G-O"
OR "(mm)-(mm)-N-G-O"
OR "(mm)-(mm)-(mm)-G-O"
5-3
©2009 COVERLY
SPEEDBUMP.COM
DIST. BY CREATORS SYND.

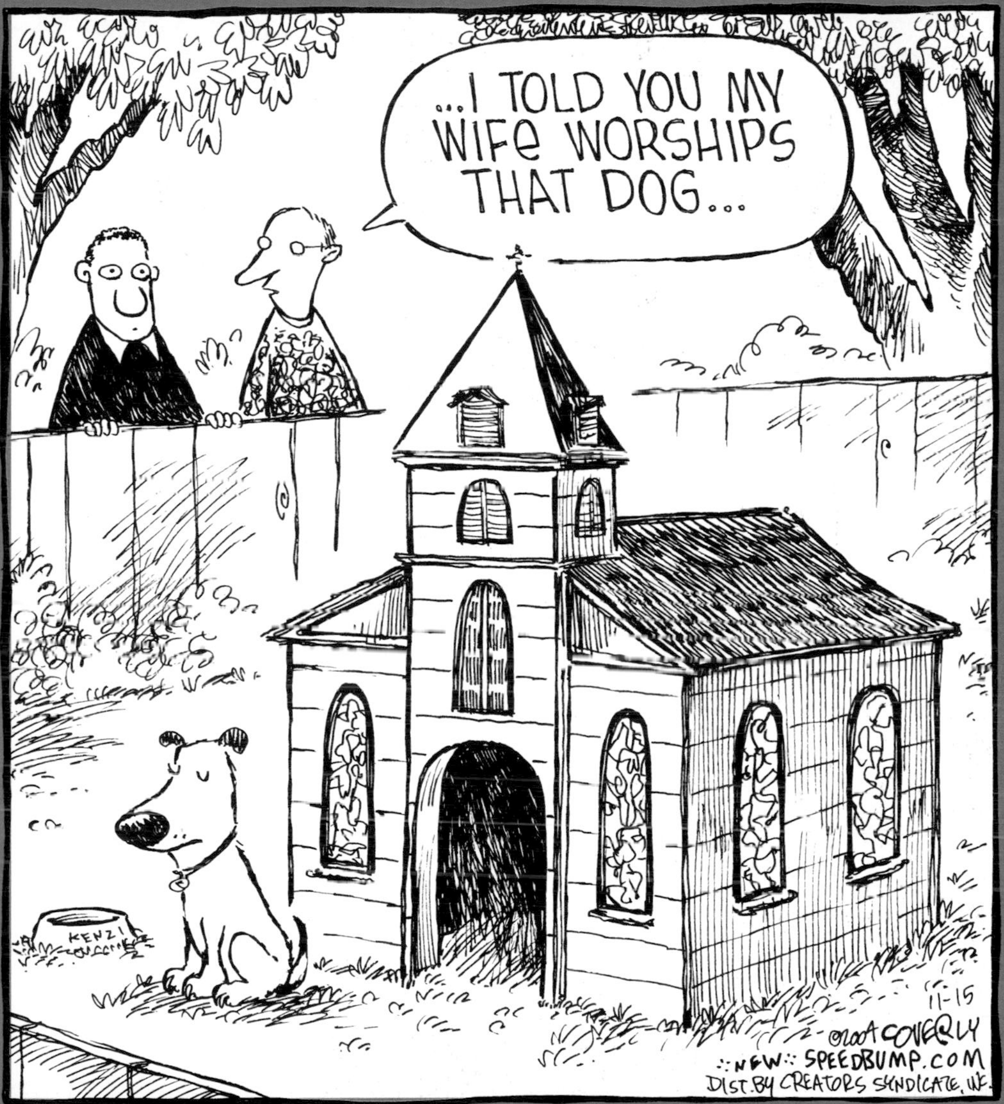
...I TOLD YOU MY WIFE WORSHIPS THAT DOG...
KENZI
11-15
©2007 COVERLY
NEW SPEEDBUMP.COM
DIST. BY CREATORS SYNDICATE, INC.

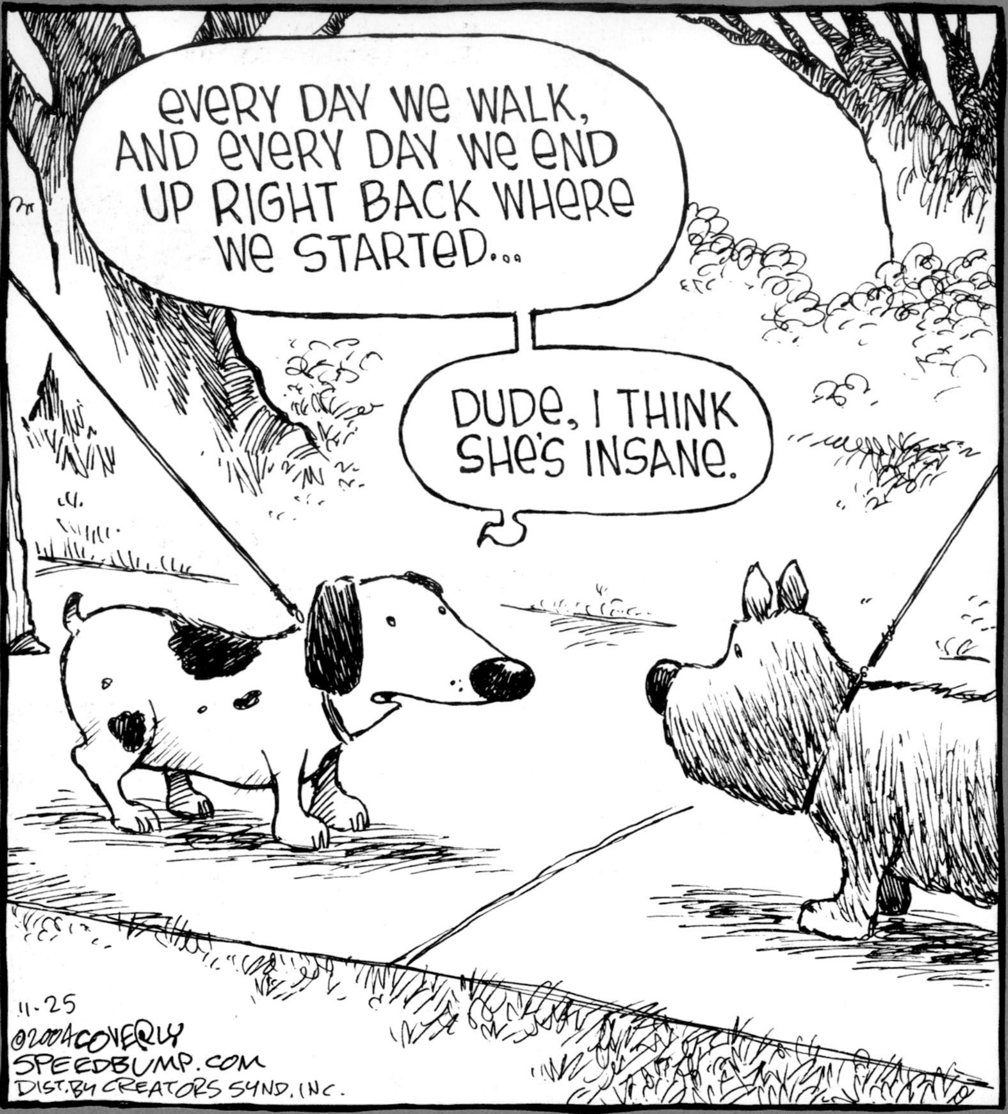
EVERY DAY WE WALK, AND EVERY DAY WE END UP RIGHT BACK WHERE WE STARTED...
DUDE, I THINK SHE'S INSANE.
11-25
©2004 COVERLY
SPEEDBUMP.COM
DIST. BY CREATORS SYND. INC.

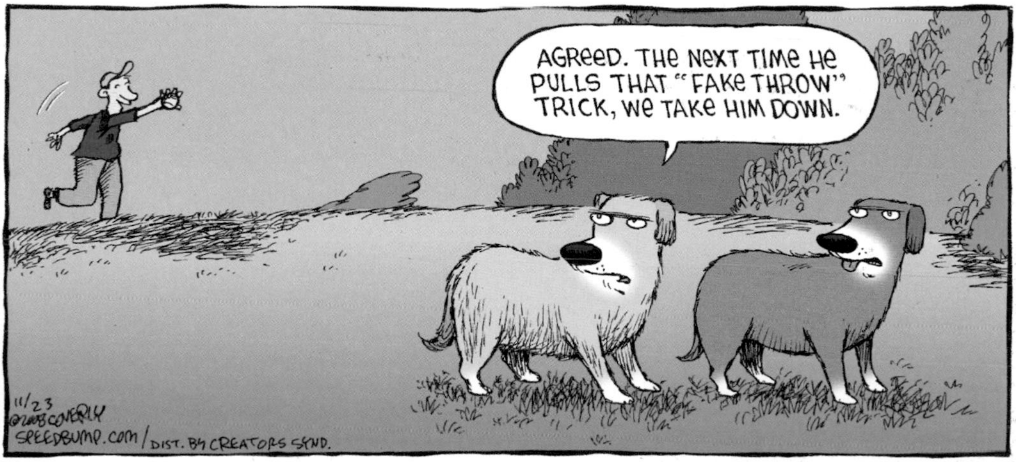
AGREED. THE NEXT TIME HE PULLS THAT "FAKE THROW" TRICK, WE TAKE HIM DOWN.
SPEEDBUMP.COM / DIST. BY CREATORS SYND.

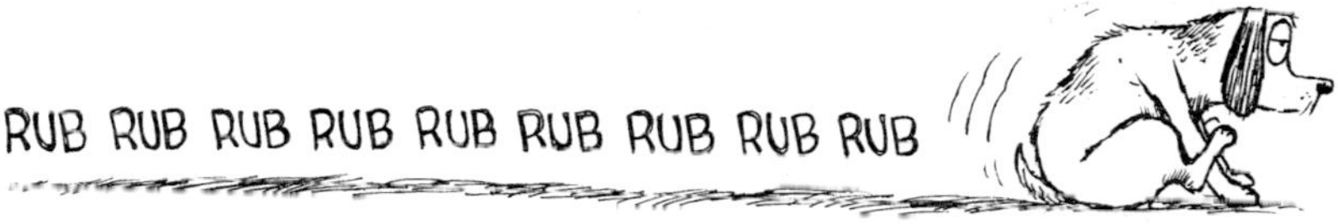
RUB RUB RUB RUB RUB RUB RUB RUB RUB

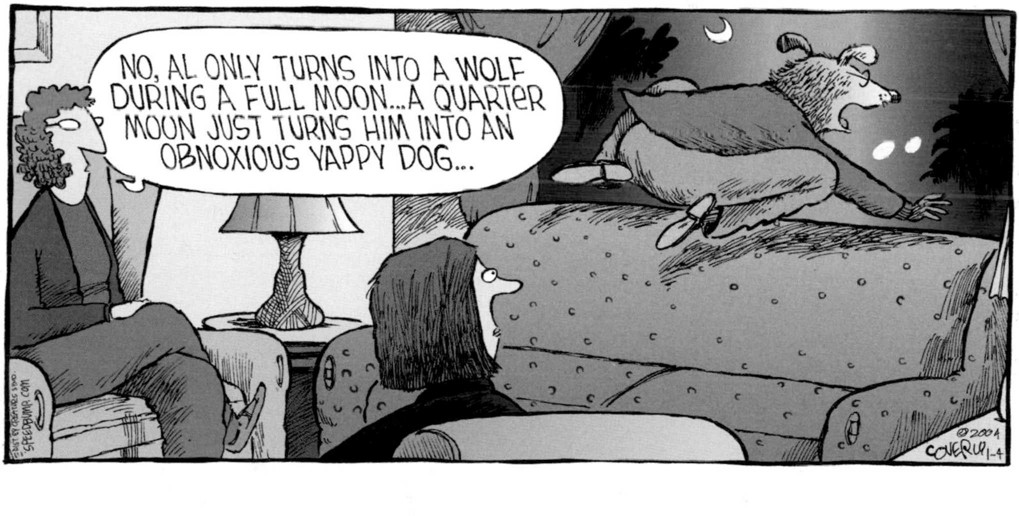
NO, AL ONLY TURNS INTO A WOLF DURING A FULL MOON...A QUARTER MOON JUST TURNS HIM INTO AN OBNOXIOUS YAPPY DOG...
©2004 COVERLY 1-4

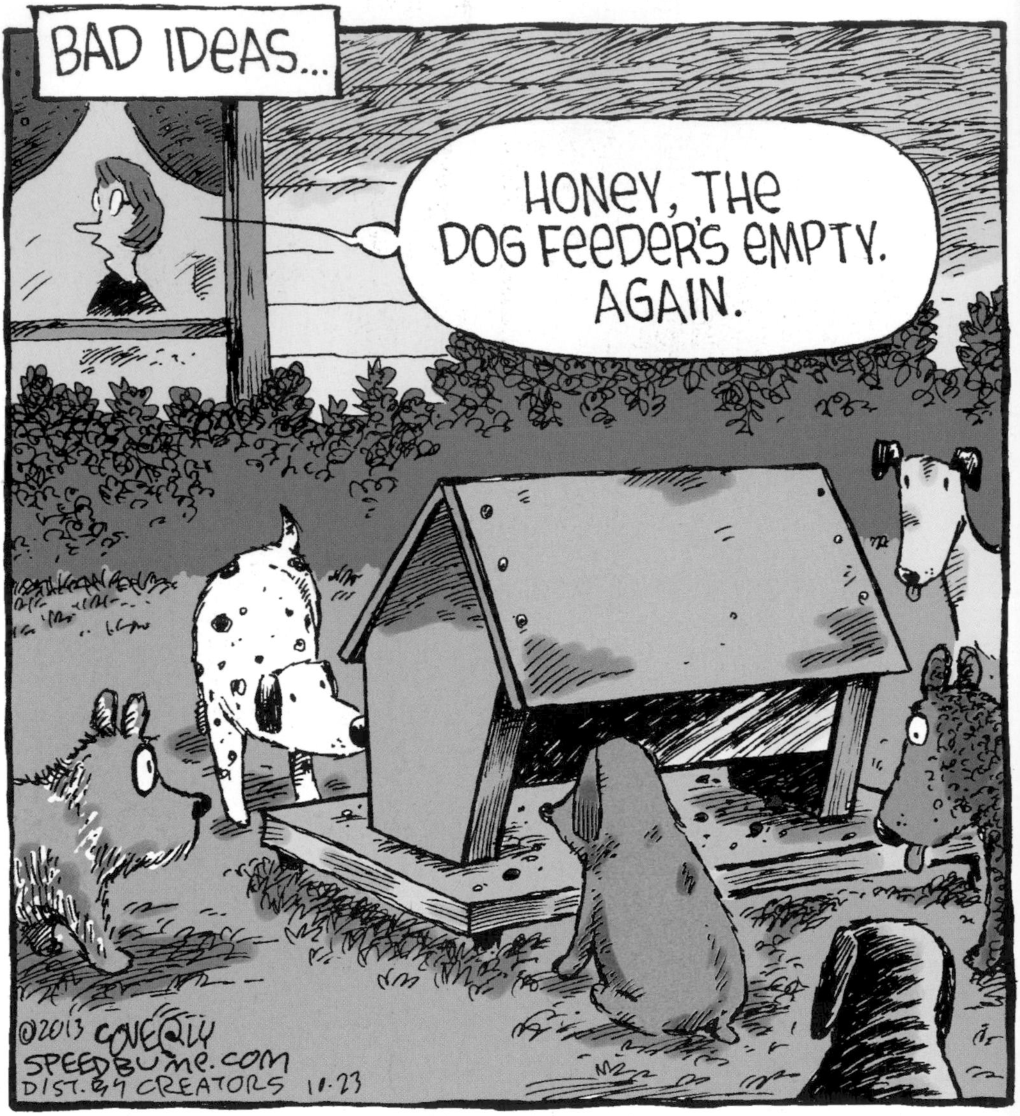
BAD IDEAS...
HONEY, THE DOG FEEDER'S EMPTY. AGAIN.
©2013 COVERLY
SPEEDBUMP.COM
DIST. BY CREATORS 10-23

TIGGER

Cathy, Dave, and Tigger, 1974.

Tigger, Shag's son, had a long and happy life, but it started on a down note. The first time I picked him up, when he was only six weeks old, he wiggled out of my arms and I dropped him on his head on the Tookers' concrete garage floor. I can still recall the glares from the Tooker children, and most of all, from my sister. During the subsequent years of Tigger's life, anytime he did anything remotely dopey—which, if I'm being honest, was quite often—it was because Dave had dropped him on his head.

The truth is that Tigger was a simple, happy-go-lucky dog,

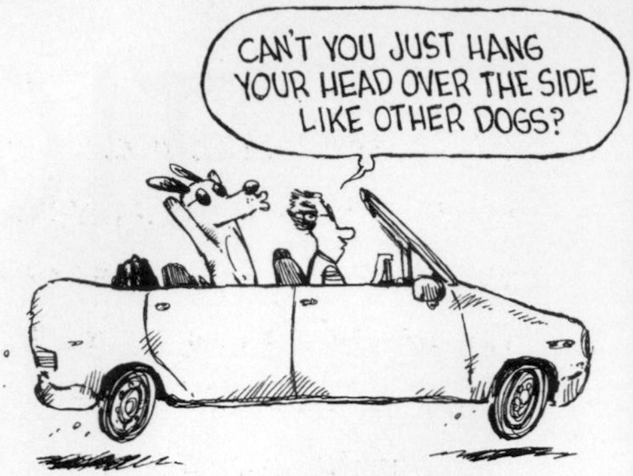
CAN'T YOU JUST HANG YOUR HEAD OVER THE SIDE LIKE OTHER DOGS?

even by dog standards. If he had been a person, he'd have been the agreeable sort of fellow who just wanted to do whatever you wanted to do and never complained about it.

He also had a bad habit of trying to hump Shag, which was hilarious to Cathy and me, but all sorts of wrong; I'm sure ancient Greek dogs even had a name for this sort of complex.

Although Tigger was trained to be an indoor dog, he had a chain from the garage to the yard. He preferred to be outside, actually. Since both dogs' chains needed to be long enough to reach the yard, they were also long enough to reach each other. Somehow, on a daily basis, they'd invariably end up tangled, and we'd find them knotted and looking forlorn, since it meant neither one could move. If you've ever tried untangling a necklace chain, try doing that with a dog at each end pulling in opposite directions.

In the spring of 1977, when I was in seventh grade, Tigger's chain snapped from his collar and he took off. At the time, our small lake neighborhood was still being developed, and the winding roads weren't busy, so the worry wasn't that he'd get hit by a car. The worry was that he'd just keep running, disappear into the woods, or just plain get lost ("because Dave dropped him on his head!"). The worry became more legitimate with each passing day; by Day 3, I could hardly concentrate in school and had to excuse myself from math class because I knew I was about to cry. What I didn't know was, almost at that very moment, Tigger was being rescued and would be waiting for me and barking at me from our driveway as I got off the school bus that afternoon.

I got the story from my mom. As it turned out, Tigger hadn't run very far at all. He'd gone up the hill, around two bends, up another hill, and then chased something into a drainage pipe that ran perpendicular under a neighbor's driveway. The opposite end of the pipe, however, was clogged nearly shut with hard dirt and washed-up gravel. And so he was stuck. There are two important facts to note here about dogs in general: One, they won't pee where they're lying, and two, they won't crawl backward.

It was three days before he was discovered. Some kids waiting for the bus heard whining coming from under their feet. Adults were summoned. They tried coaxing him out with treats, but, of course, he wouldn't back up ("probably because Dave dropped . . ."—well, you know). They tried digging out the dirt themselves, but it was too hard and too far inside the pipe. So they called the fire department.

After some discussion and a few more vain attempts to get Tigger dislodged, it was decided that the only way to save him was their last-resort option: blast through the dirt

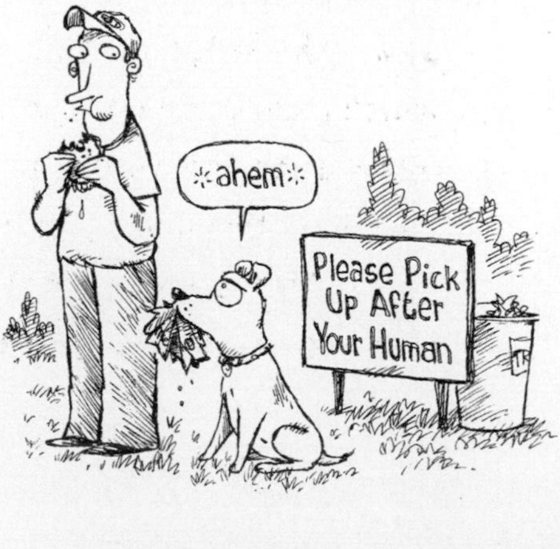
ahem
Please Pick Up After Your Human

and rock with a fire hose. It was risky because a direct hit on his face could maim or kill him.

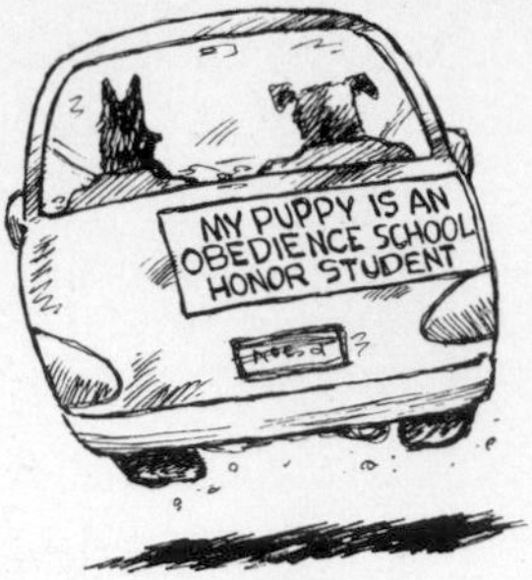
MY PUPPY IS AN
OBEDIENCE SCHOOL
HONOR STUDENT

When the mist cleared and the dust settled, there was a long pause—long enough to worry everyone there—and then a mud-covered Tigger burst out of the pipe like it was a circus cannon, ran to the nearest shrub, and peed. And peed. And peed.

That dog's head may have been soft, but his bladder was world-class.

Both dogs lived long, healthy, and happy lives, and both are buried in my parents' backyard. They're running around somewhere now where there are no chains to get knotted up, and where every drainpipe is open ended.

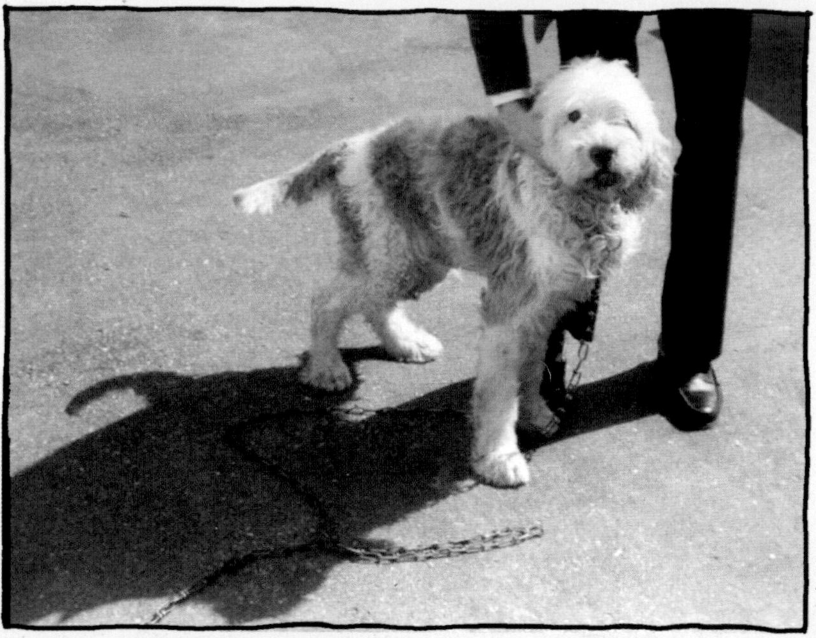

Tigger, 1987.

CHAPTER 3

WORKING LIKE A DOG

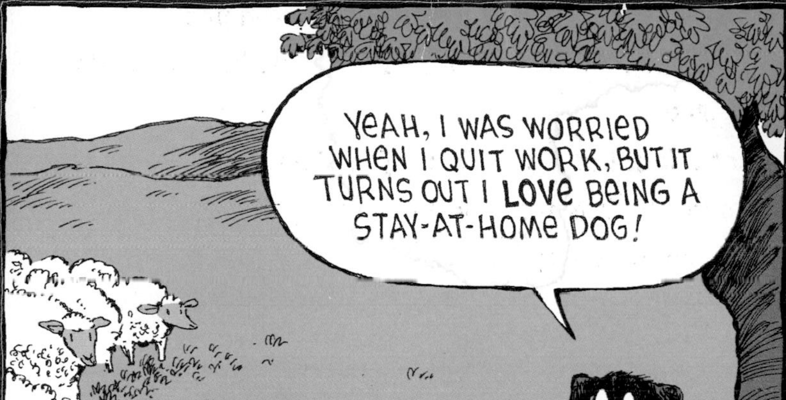
YEAH, I WAS WORRIED WHEN I QUIT WORK, BUT IT TURNS OUT I LOVE BEING A STAY-AT-HOME DOG!
7-29
COVERLY
SPEEDBUMP.COM
DIST. BY CREATORS SYND.

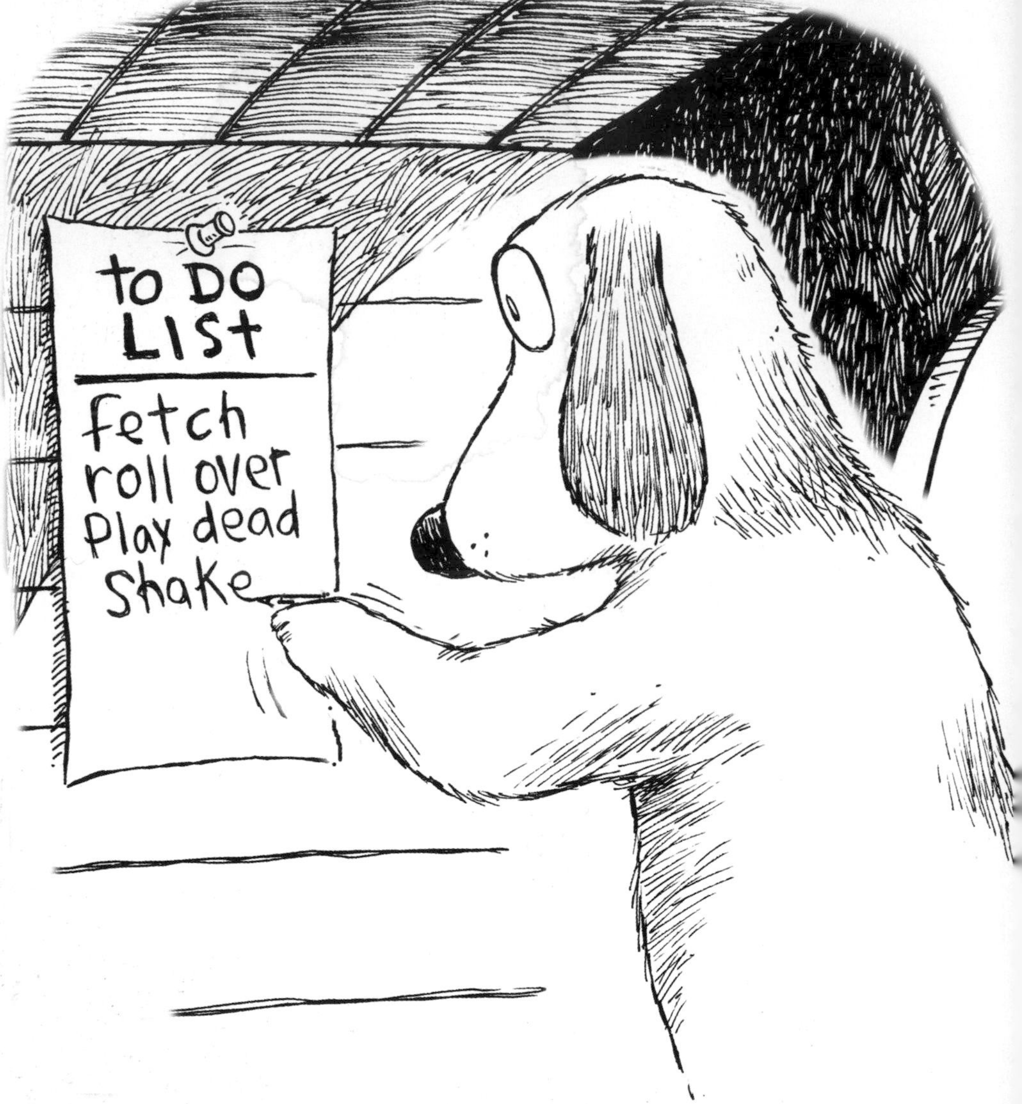
to DO
LIST
fetch
roll over
Play dead
Shake

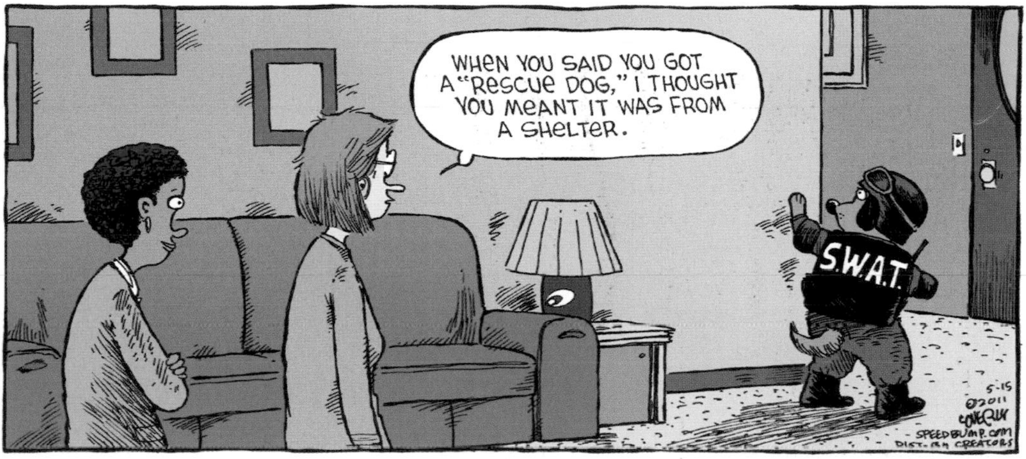
WHEN YOU SAID YOU GOT A "RESCUE DOG," I THOUGHT YOU MEANT IT WAS FROM A SHELTER.
S.W.A.T.
5-15
©2011
COVERLY
SPEEDBUMP.COM
DIST. BY CREATORS

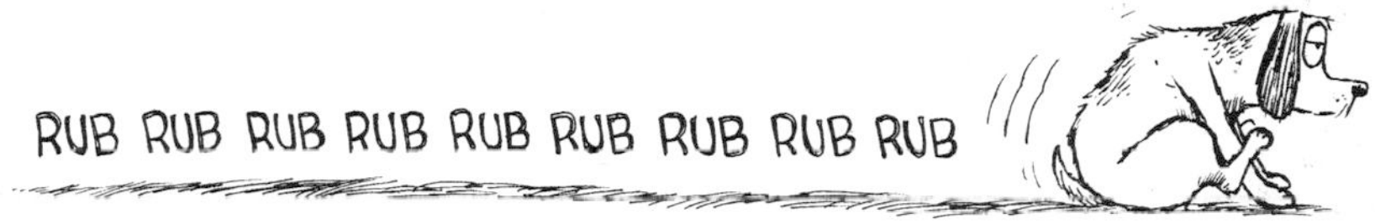
RUB RUB RUB RUB RUB RUB RUB RUB RUB

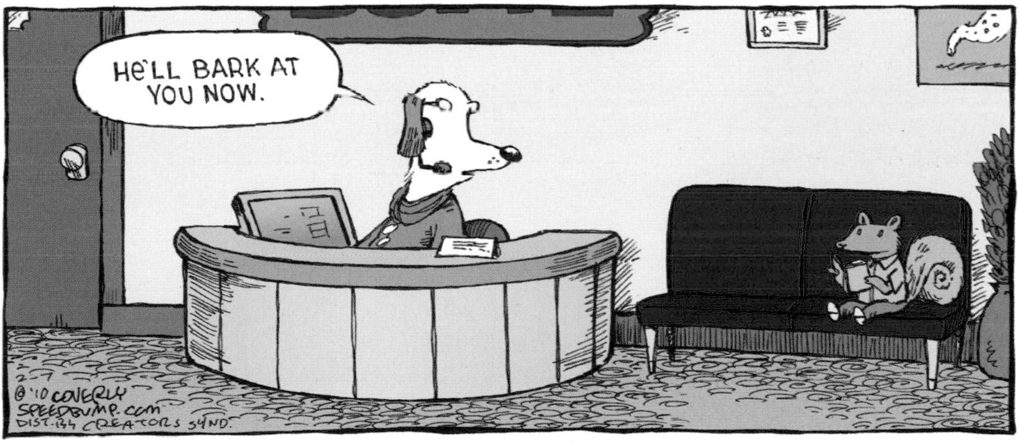
HE'LL BARK AT YOU NOW.
2-7
©'10 COVERLY
SPEEDBUMP.COM
DIST. BY CREATORS SYND.

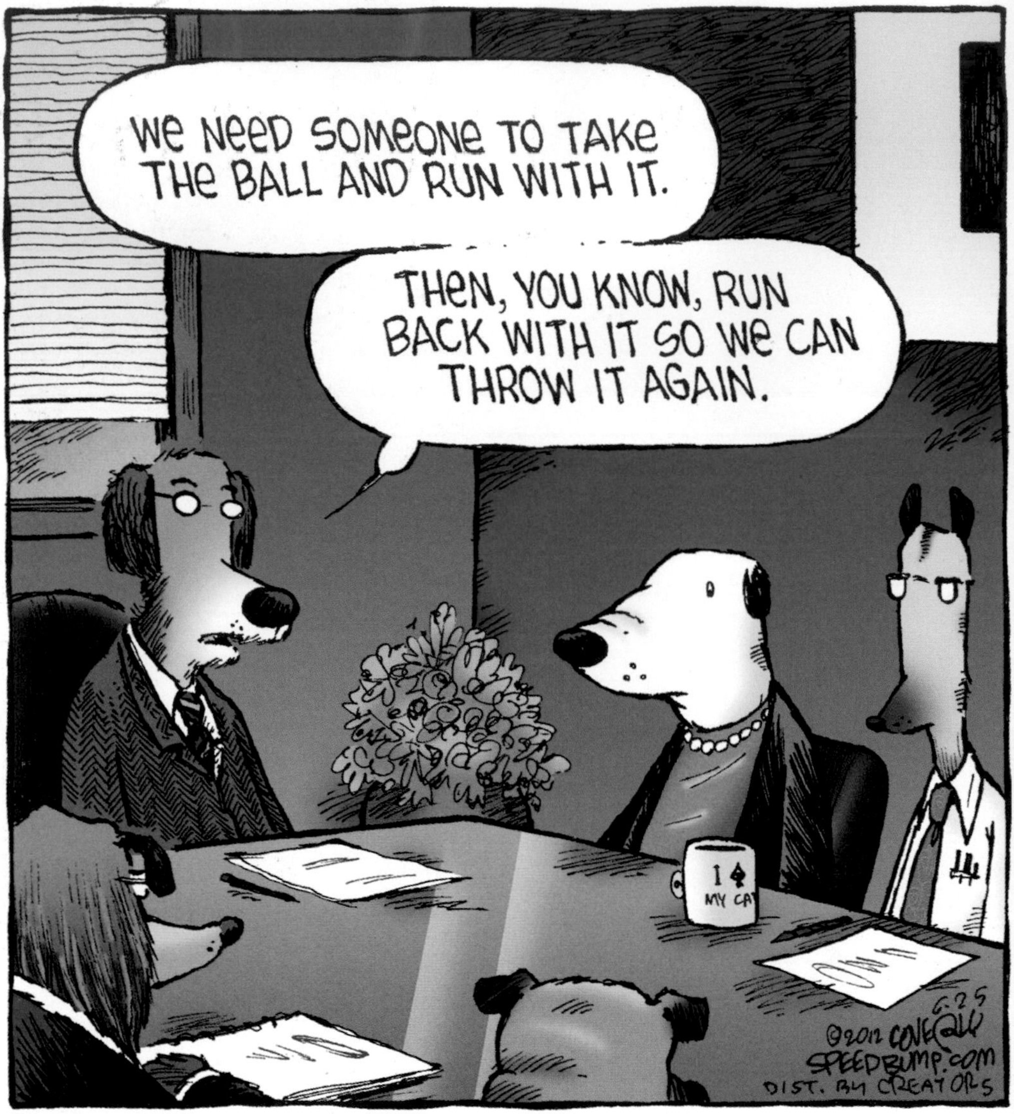
WE NEED SOMEONE TO TAKE THE BALL AND RUN WITH IT.
THEN, YOU KNOW, RUN BACK WITH IT SO WE CAN THROW IT AGAIN.
I ♠ MY CA
6.25
©2012 CONE@LK
SPEEDBUMP.com
DIST. BY CREATORS

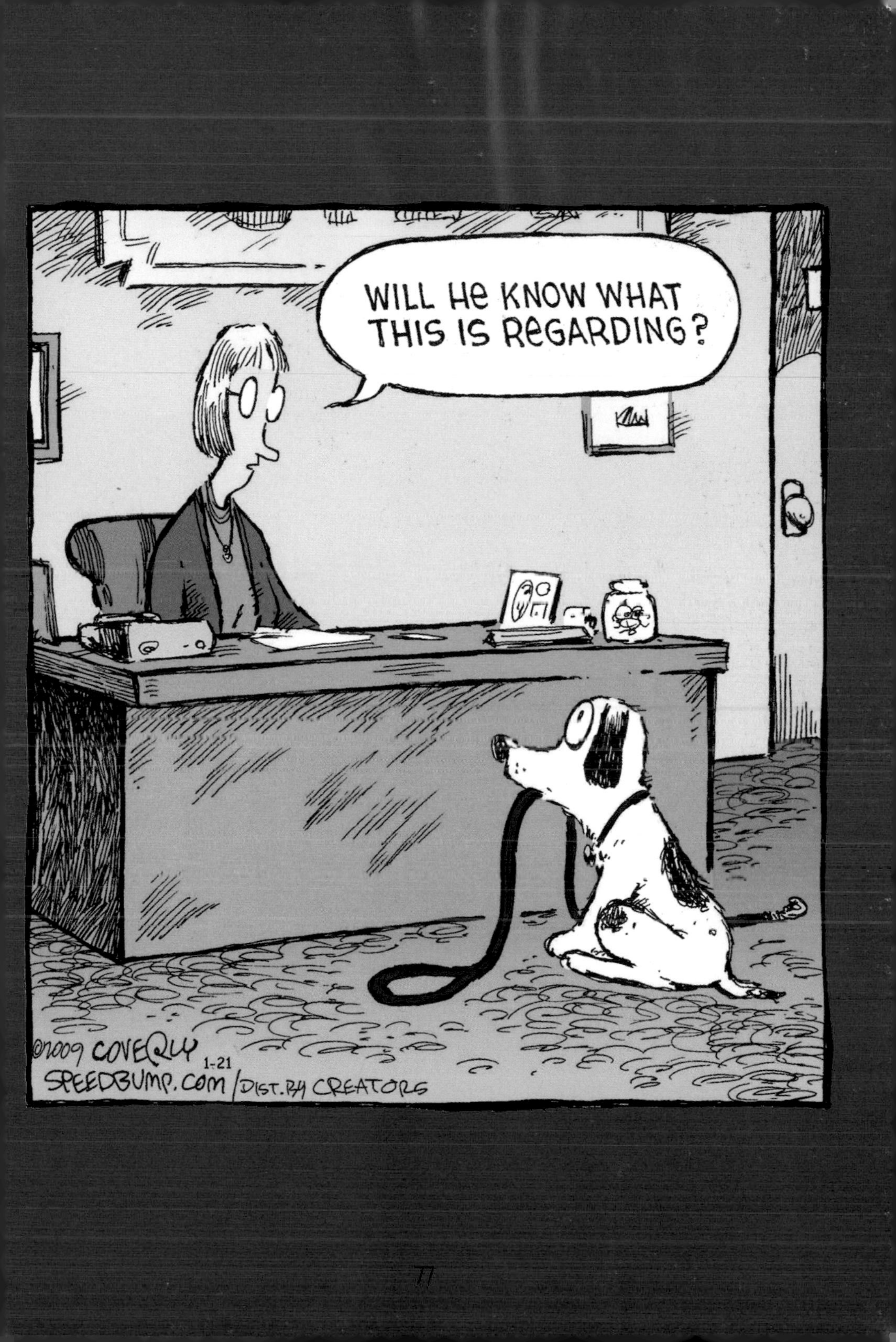
WILL He KNOW WHAT THIS IS ReGARDING?
©2009 COVERLY 1-21
SPEEDBUMP.COM/DIST.BY CREATORS

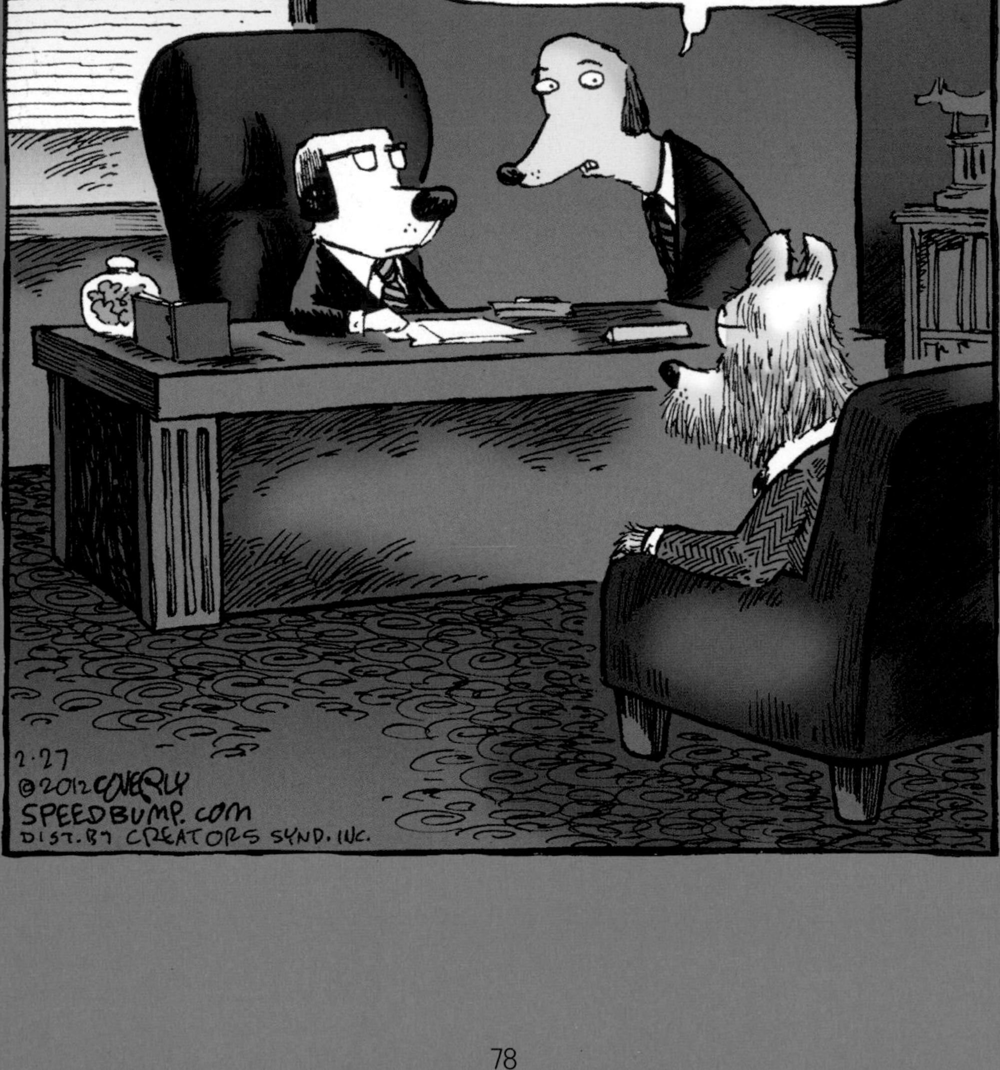
YOU CAN'T FIRE HIM, SIR- HE KNOWS WHERE ALL THE BONES ARE BURIED.
2·27
©2012 COVERLY
SPEEDBUMP.COM
DIST. BY CREATORS SYND. INC.

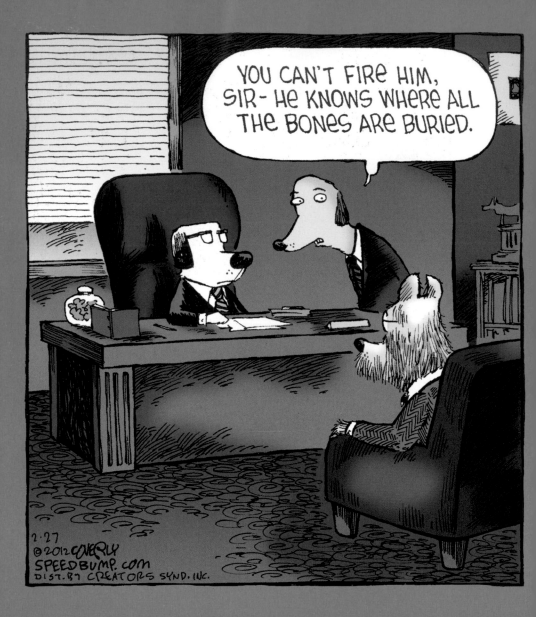

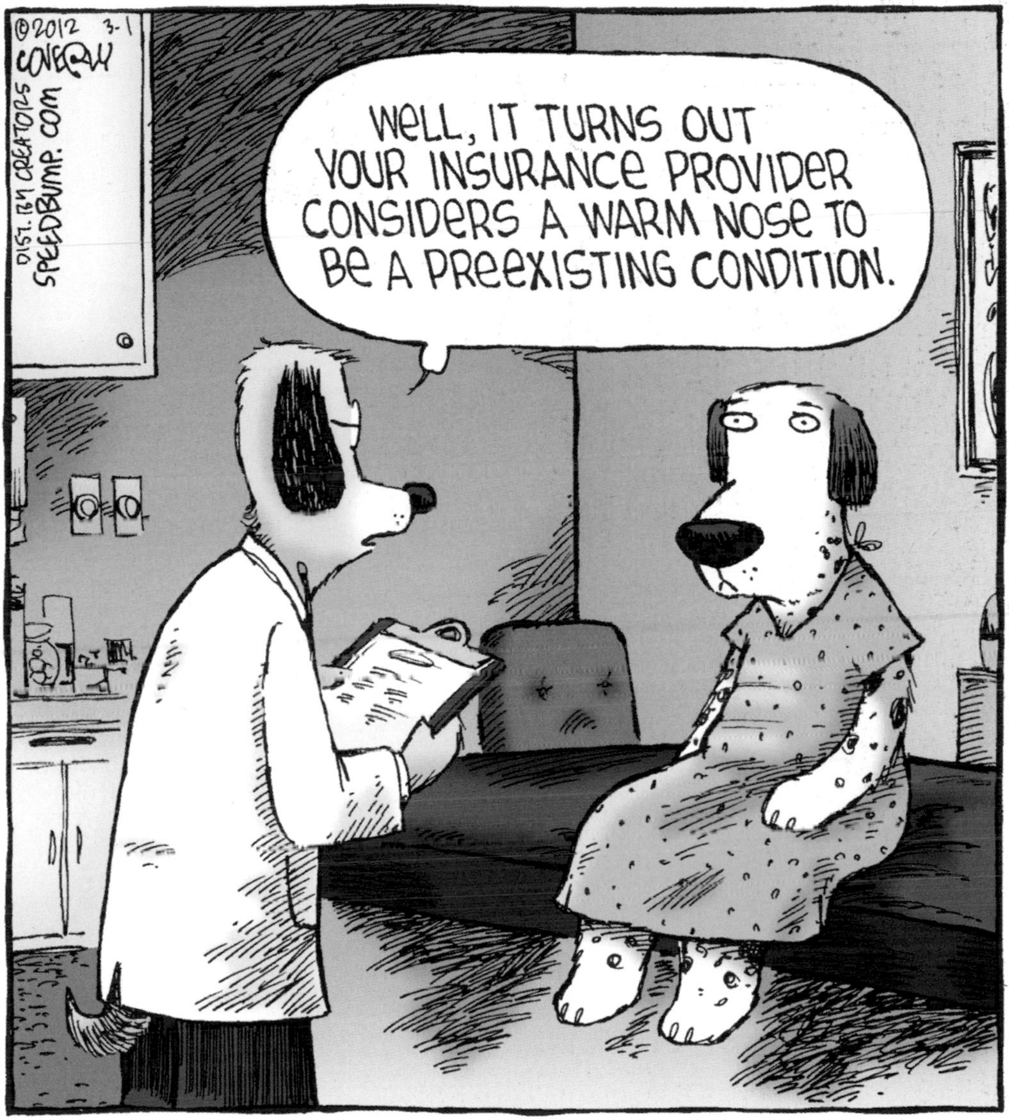
©2012 3-1
COVERLY
DIST. BY CREATORS
SPEEDBUMP. COM
WELL, IT TURNS OUT YOUR INSURANCE PROVIDER CONSIDERS A WARM NOSE TO BE A PREEXISTING CONDITION.

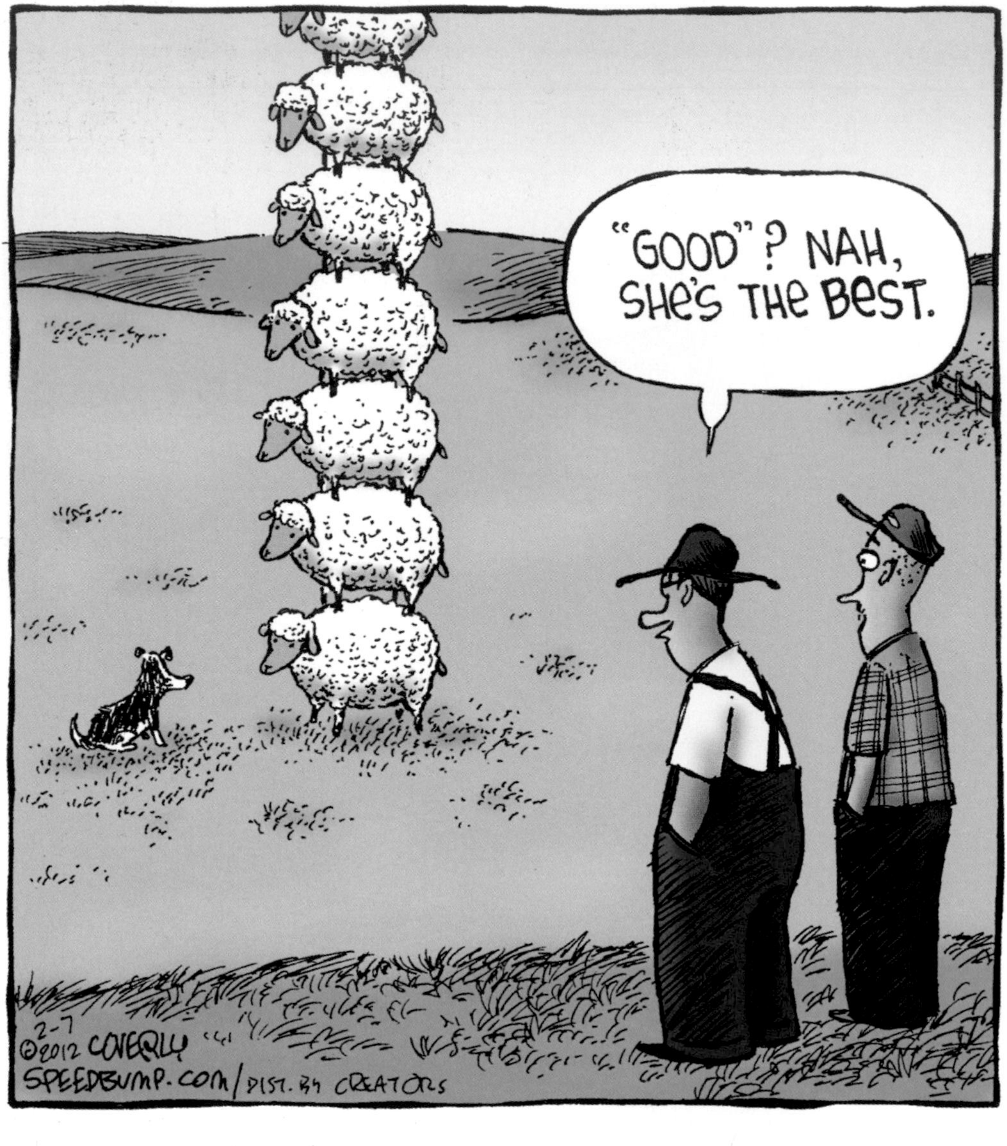
"GOOD"? NAH, SHE'S THE BEST.
2-7 ©2012 COVERLY SPEEDBUMP.COM/DIST. BY CREATORS

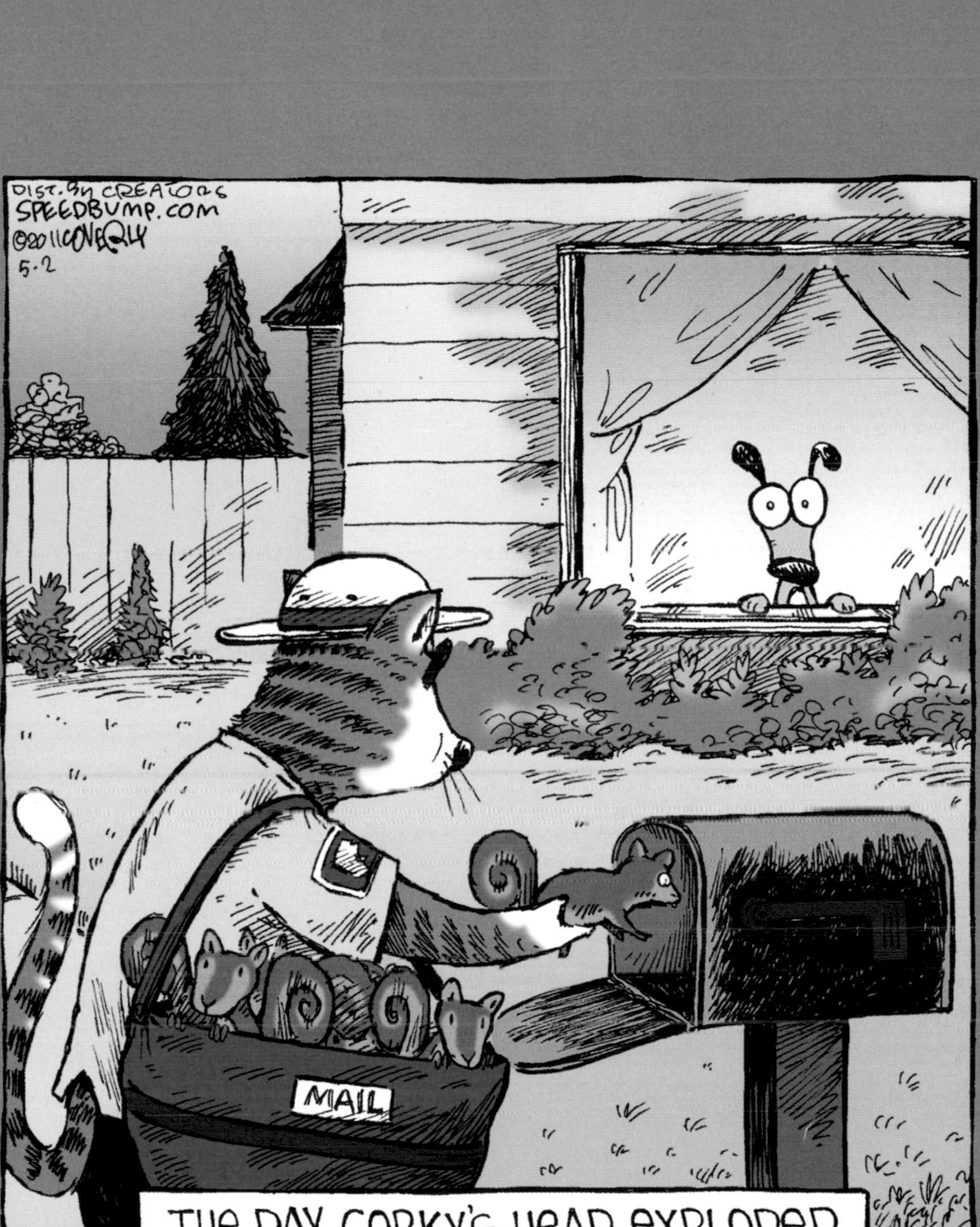
DIST. BY CREATORS
SPEEDBUMP.COM
©2011COVERLY
5-2
MAIL
THE DAY CORKY'S HEAD EXPLODED

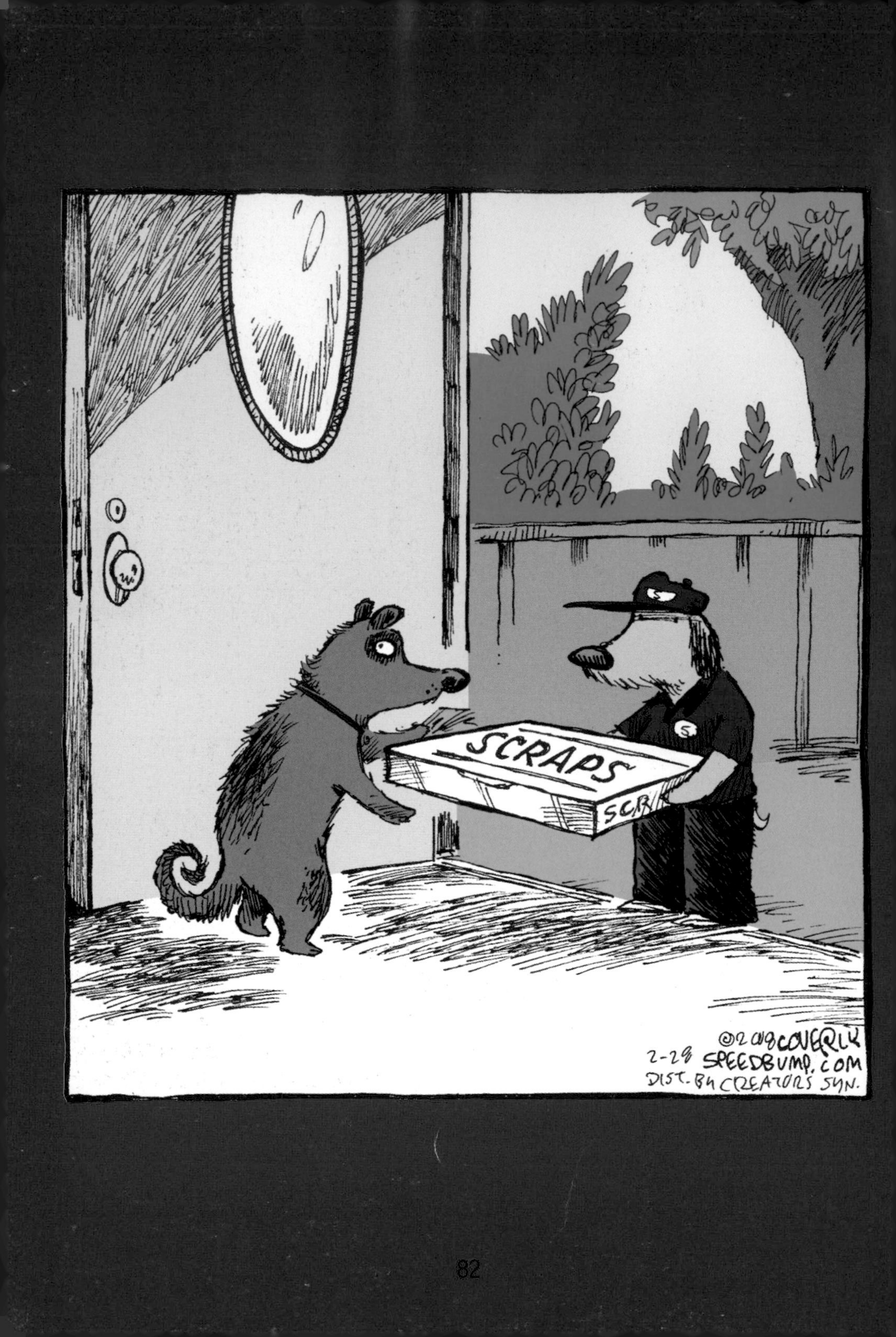
SCRAPS
SCR
©2018 COVERLY
2-28 SPEEDBUMP.COM
DIST. BY CREATORS SYN.

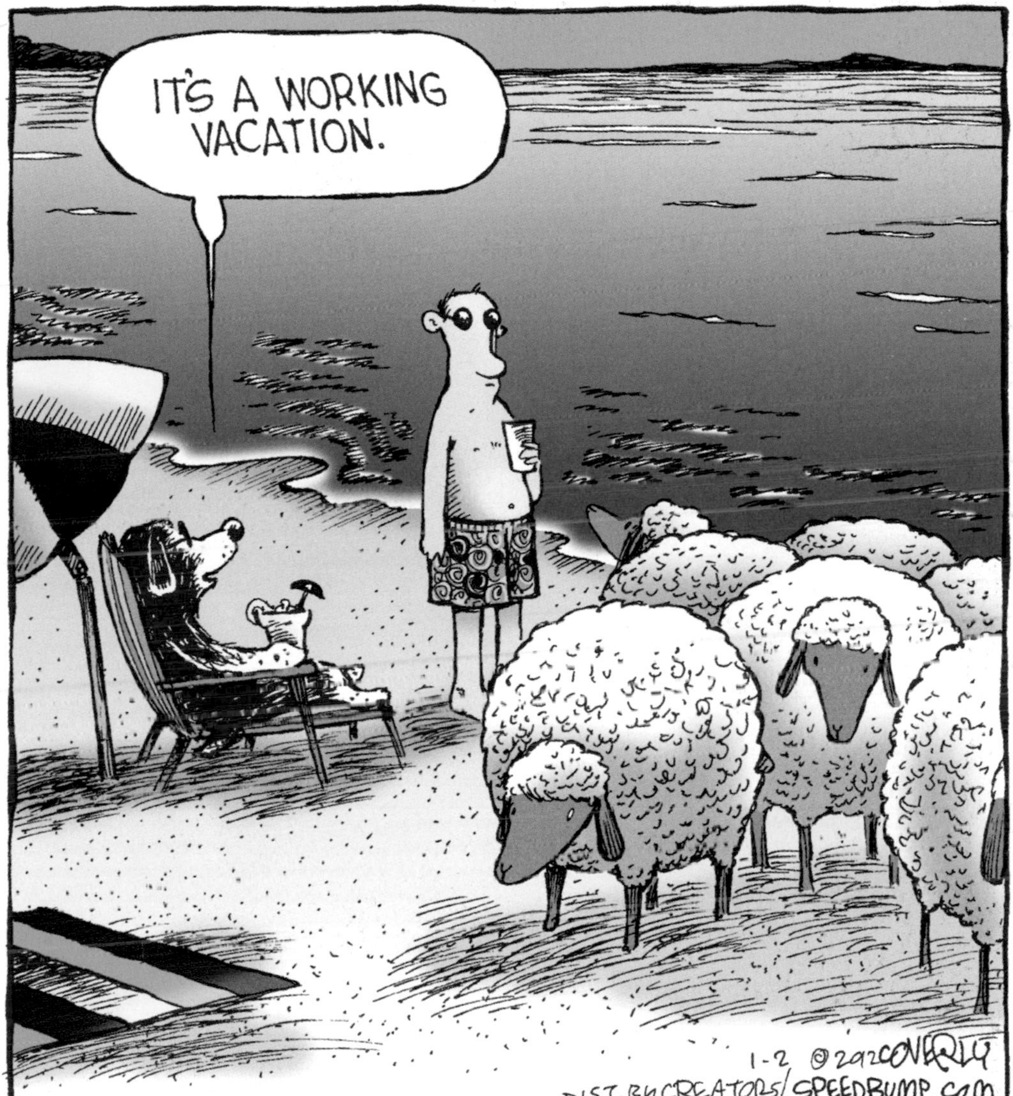
IT'S A WORKING VACATION.
1-2
DIST. BY CREATORS/ SPEEDBUMP.com

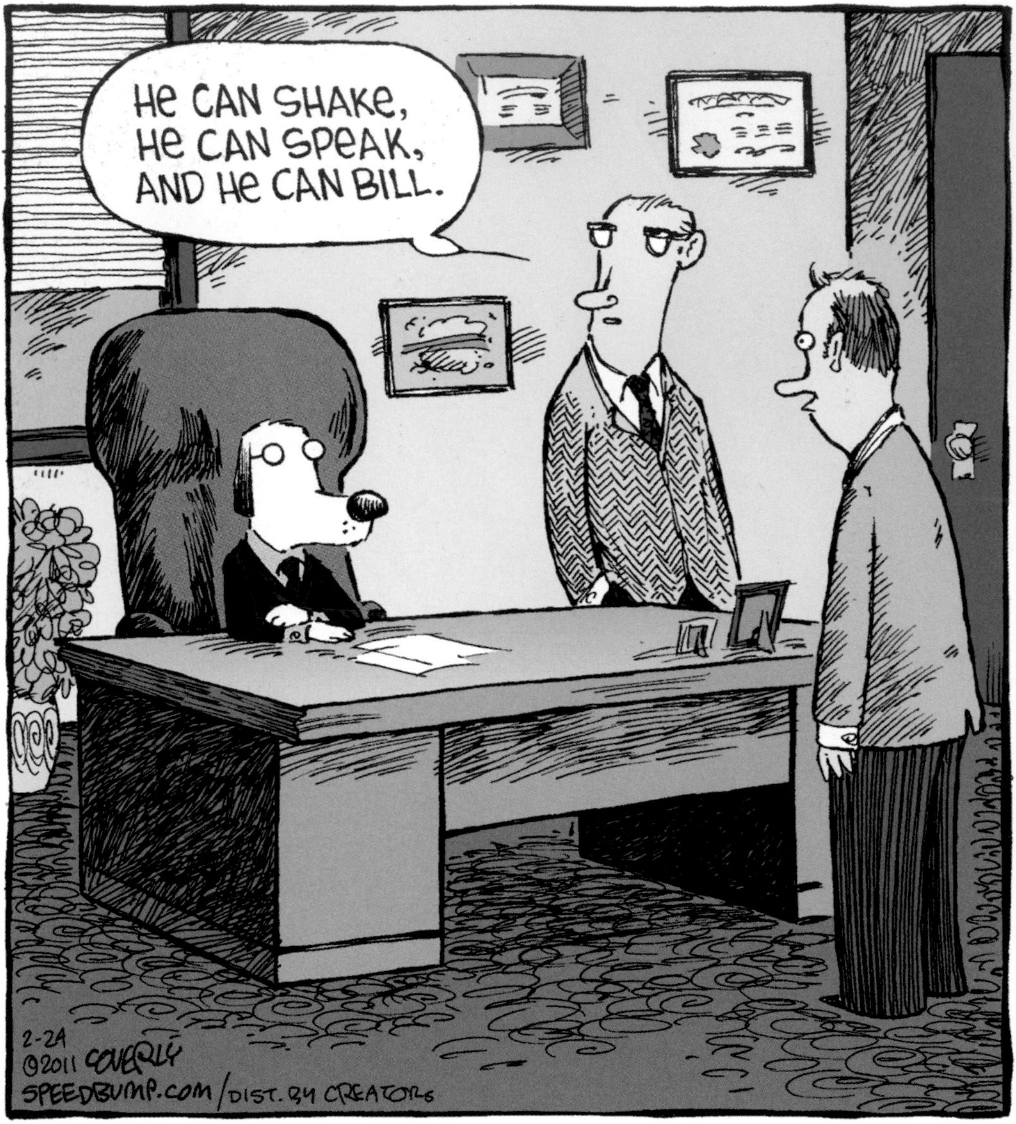
HE CAN SHAKE, HE CAN SPEAK, AND HE CAN BILL.
2-24
©2011 COVERLY
SPEEDBUMP.COM/DIST. BY CREATORS

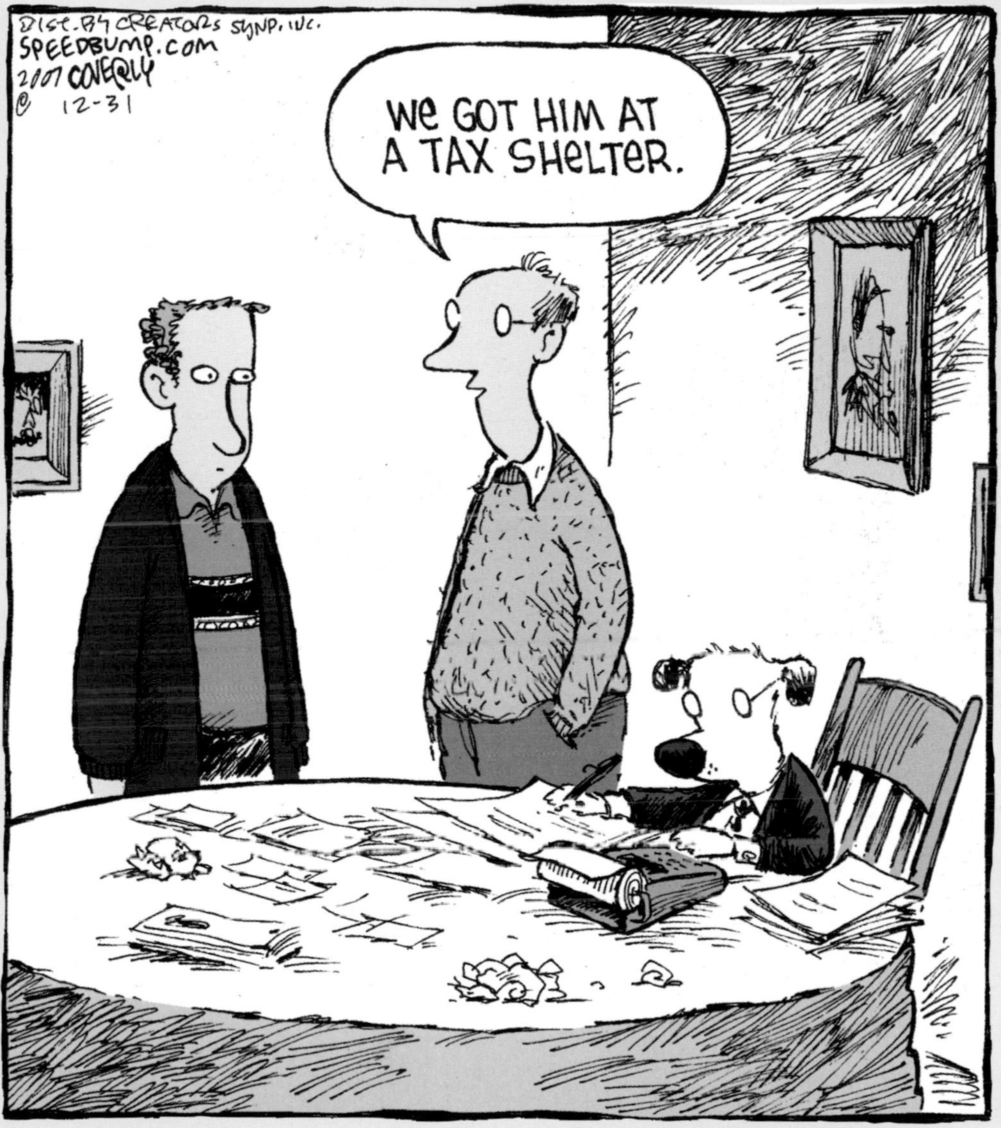
DIST. BY CREATORS SYND. INC.
SPEEDBUMP.COM
2007 COVERLY
© 12-31
WE GOT HIM AT A TAX SHELTER.

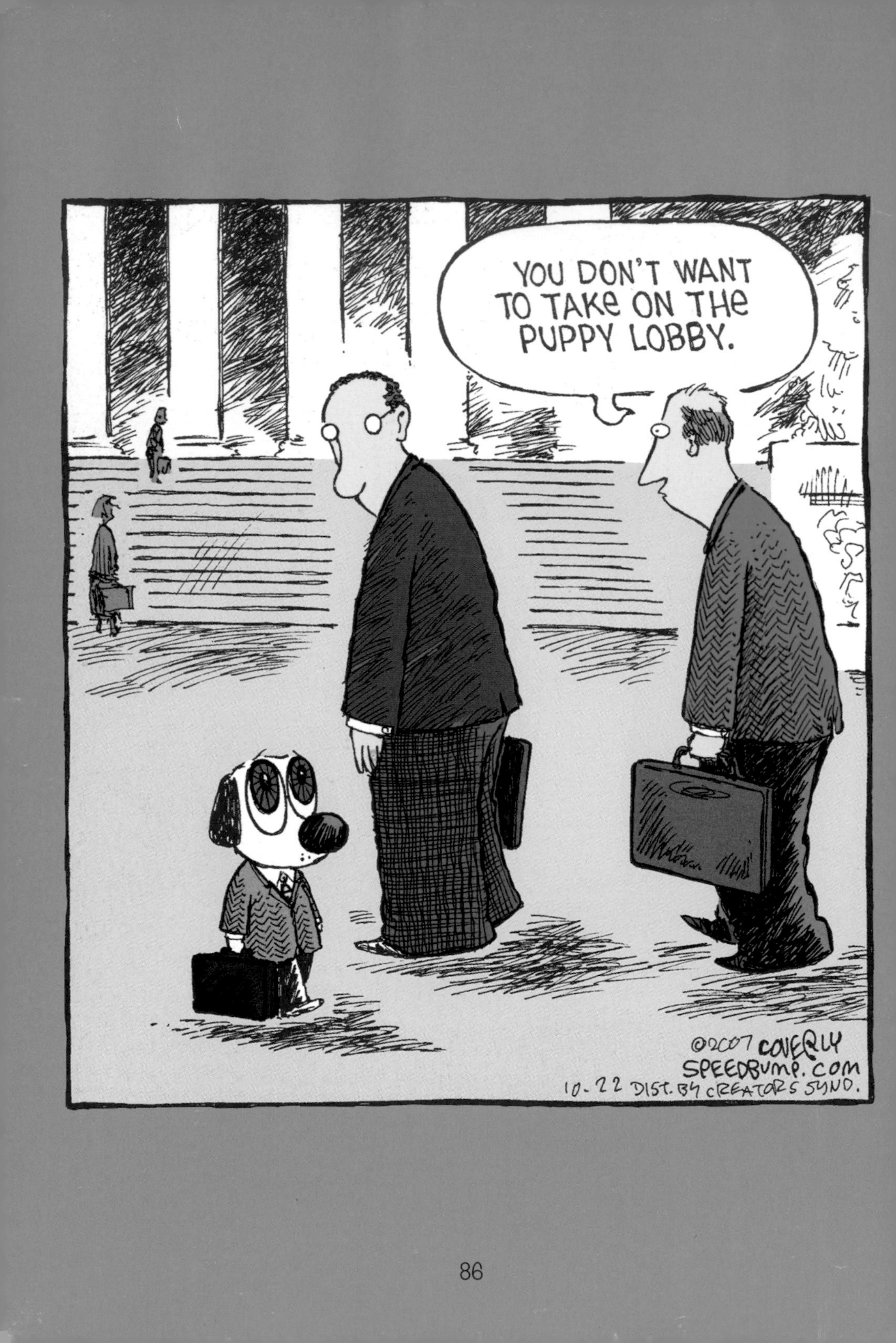
YOU DON'T WANT TO TAKE ON THE PUPPY LOBBY.
©2007 COVERLY
SPEEDBUMP.COM
10-22 DIST. BY CREATORS SYND.

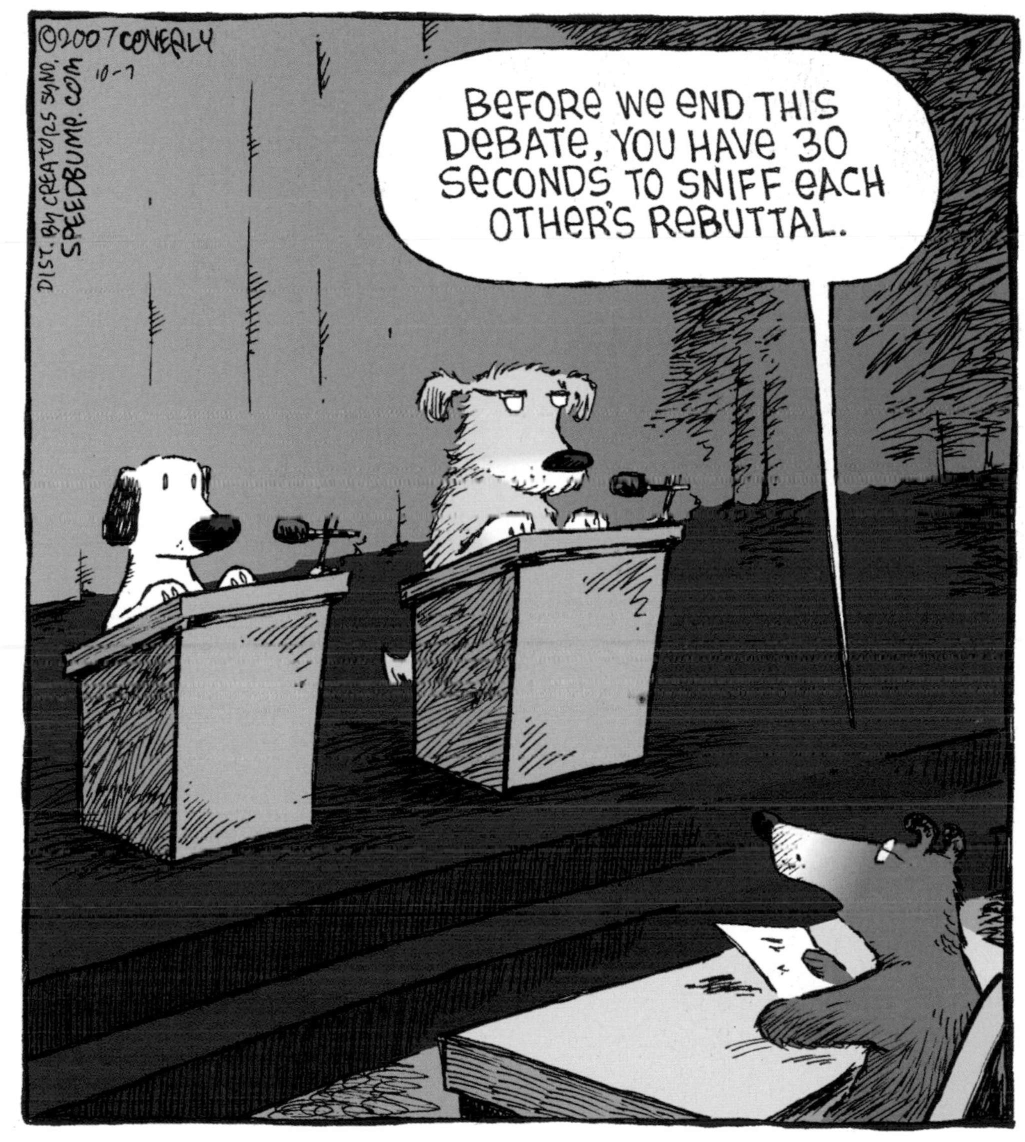

BEFORE WE END THIS DEBATE, YOU HAVE 30 SECONDS TO SNIFF EACH OTHER'S REBUTTAL.
©2007 COVERLY 10-7
DIST. BY CREATORS SYND. SPEEDBUMP.COM

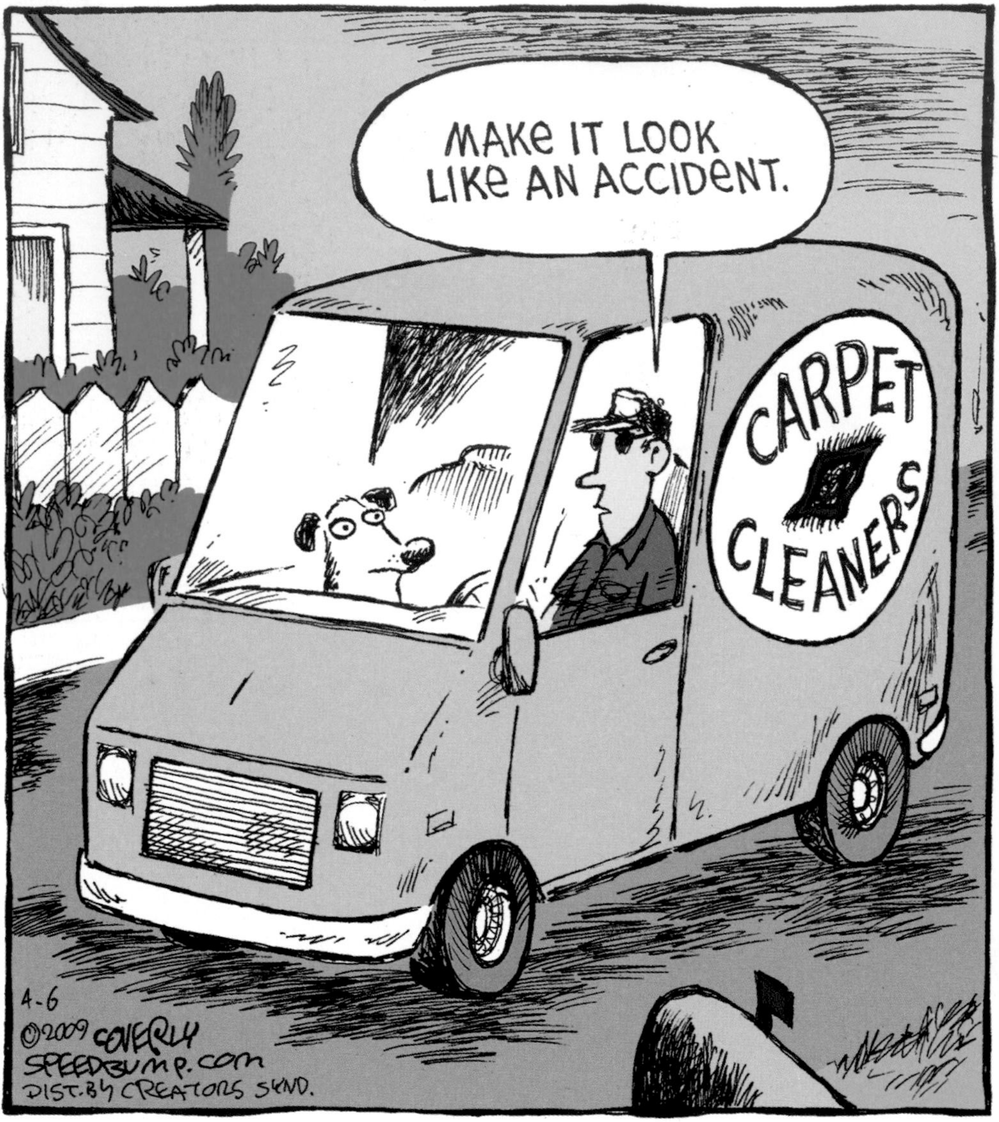
MAKE IT LOOK LIKE AN ACCIDENT.
CARPET CLEANERS
4-6
©2009 COVERLY
SPEEDBUMP.COM
DIST. BY CREATORS SYND.

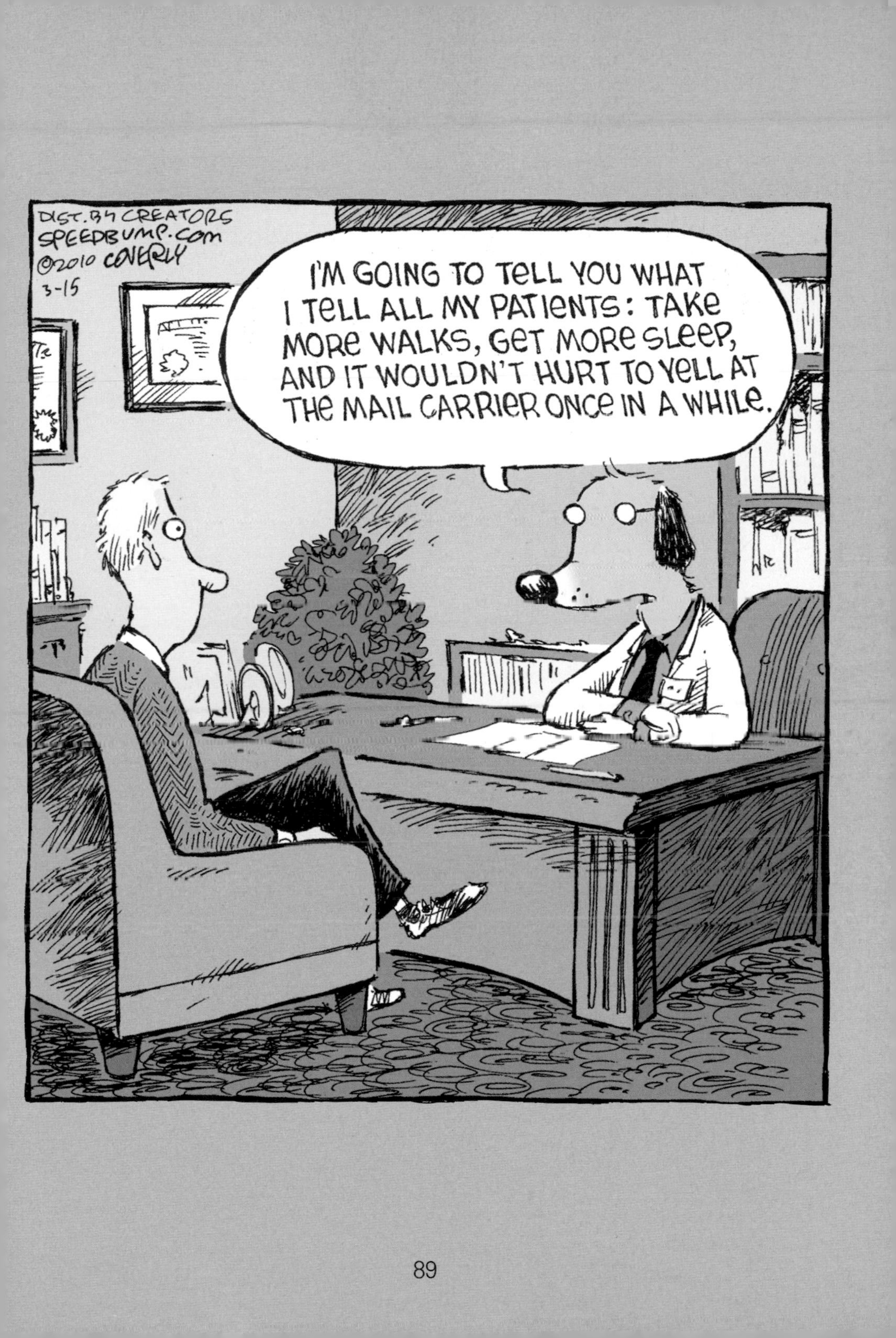
DIST. BY CREATORS
SPEEDBUMP.COM
©2010 COVERLY
3-15
I'M GOING TO TELL YOU WHAT I TELL ALL MY PATIENTS: TAKE MORE WALKS, GET MORE SLEEP, AND IT WOULDN'T HURT TO YELL AT THE MAIL CARRIER ONCE IN A WHILE.

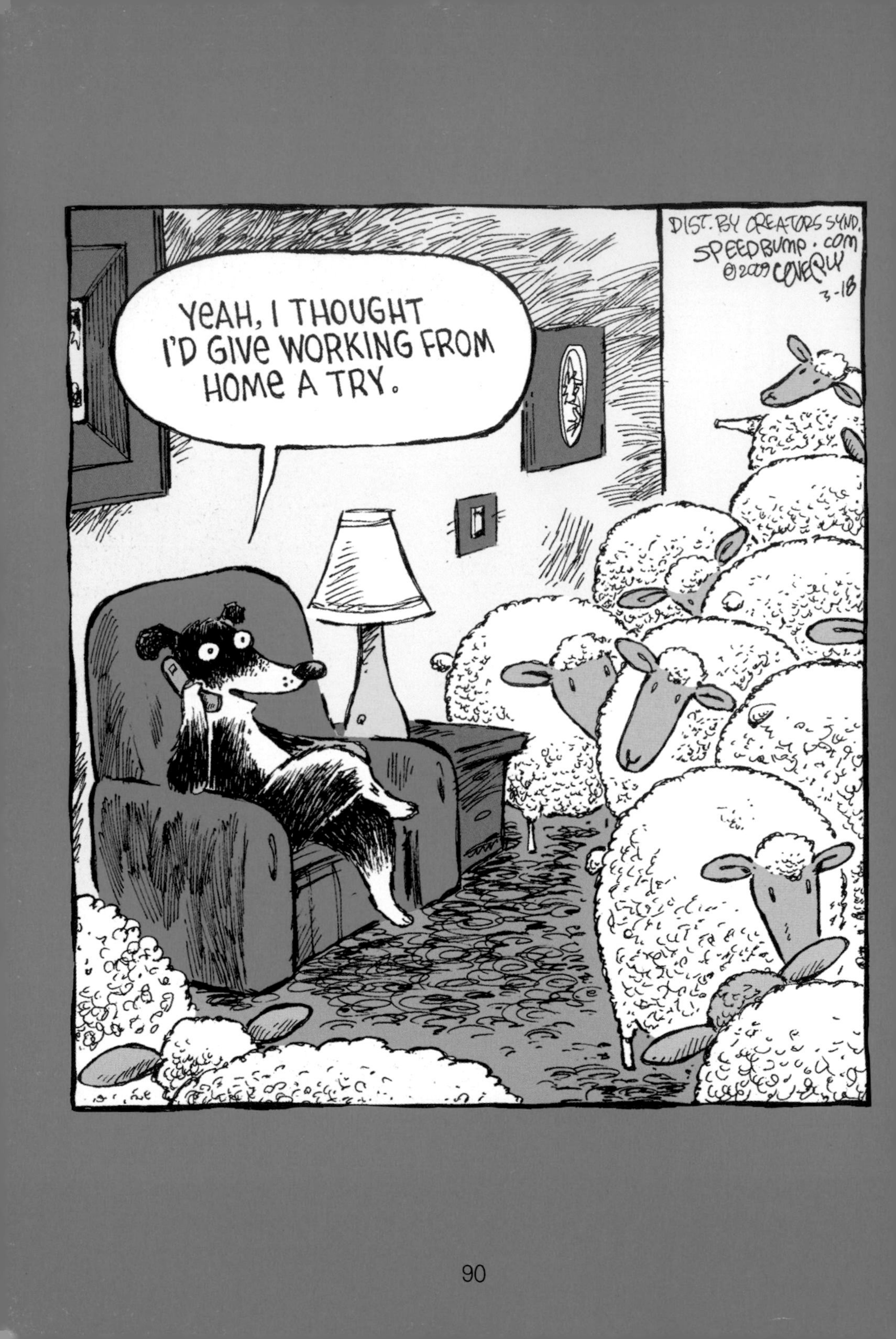
YEAH, I THOUGHT I'D GIVE WORKING FROM HOME A TRY.
DIST. BY CREATORS SYND.
SPEEDBUMP.COM
©2009 COVERLY
3-18

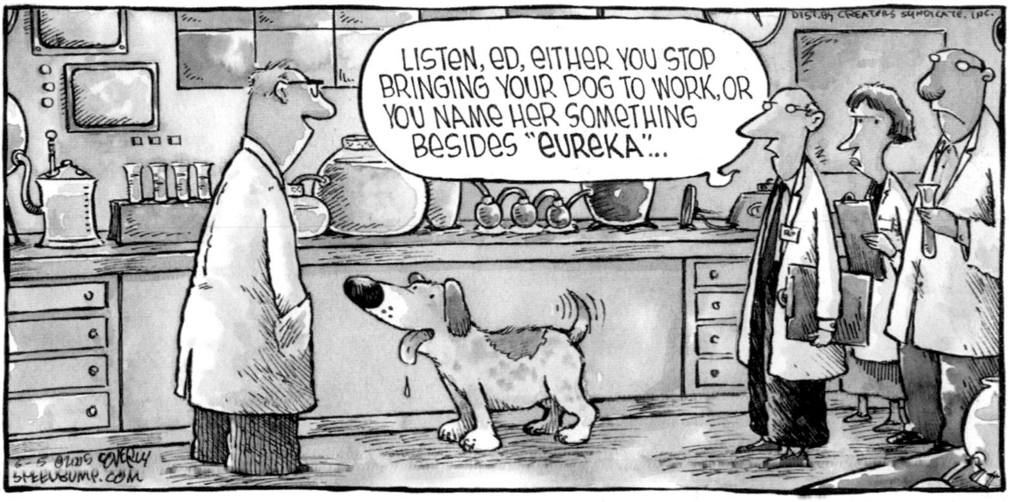
DIST. BY CREATORS SYNDICATE, INC.
LISTEN, ED, EITHER YOU STOP BRINGING YOUR DOG TO WORK, OR YOU NAME HER SOMETHING BESIDES "EUREKA"...
SPEEDBUMP.COM

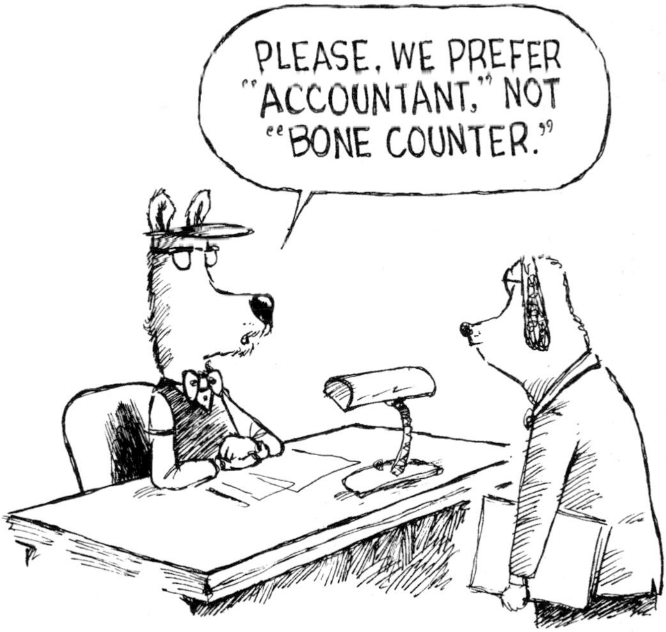
PLEASE, WE PREFER "ACCOUNTANT," NOT "BONE COUNTER."

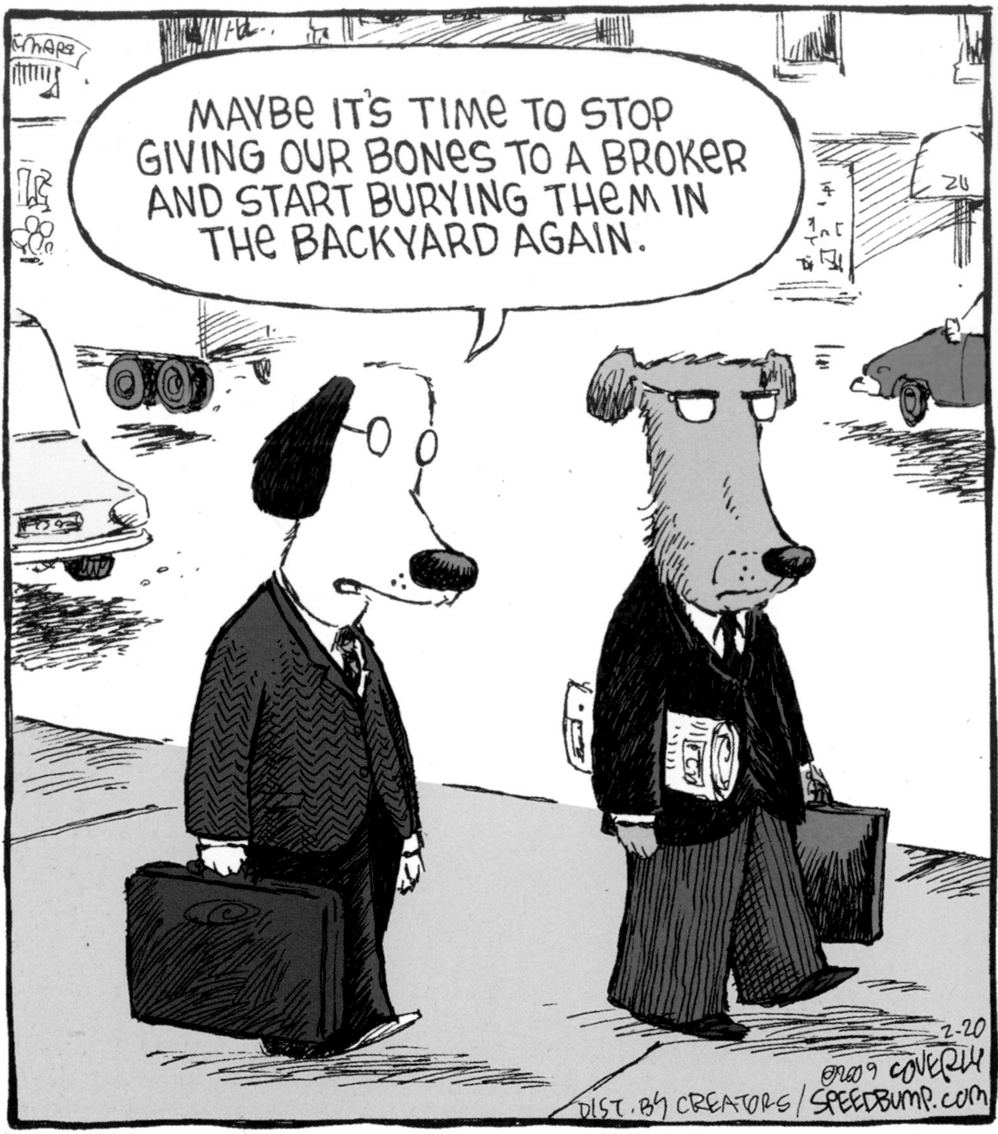
MAYBE IT'S TIME TO STOP GIVING OUR BONES TO A BROKER AND START BURYING THEM IN THE BACKYARD AGAIN.
2-20
©2009 COVERLY
DIST. BY CREATORS/ SPEEDBUMP.COM

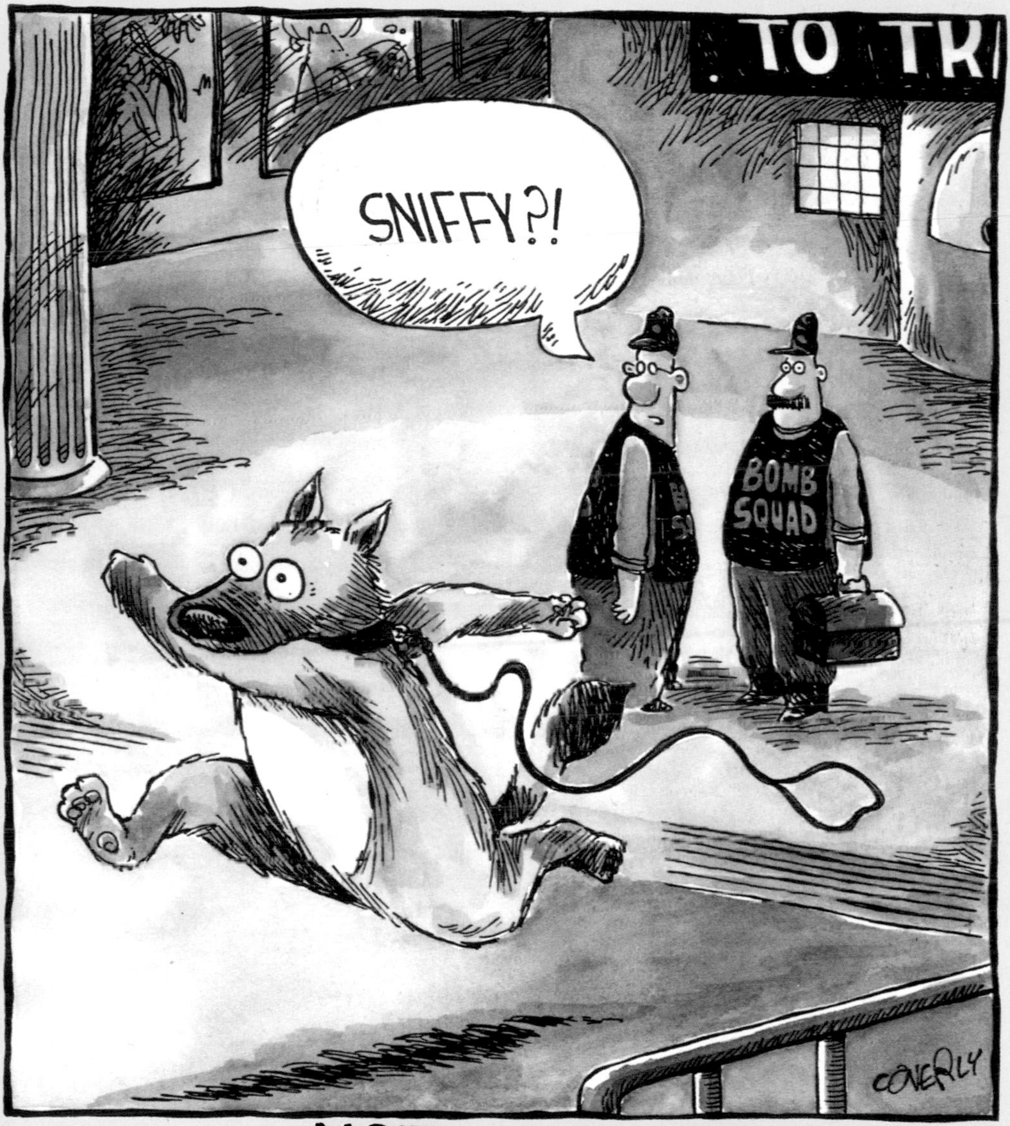
TO TR
SNIFFY?!
BOMB SQUAD
COVERLY

NOT A GOOD SIGN

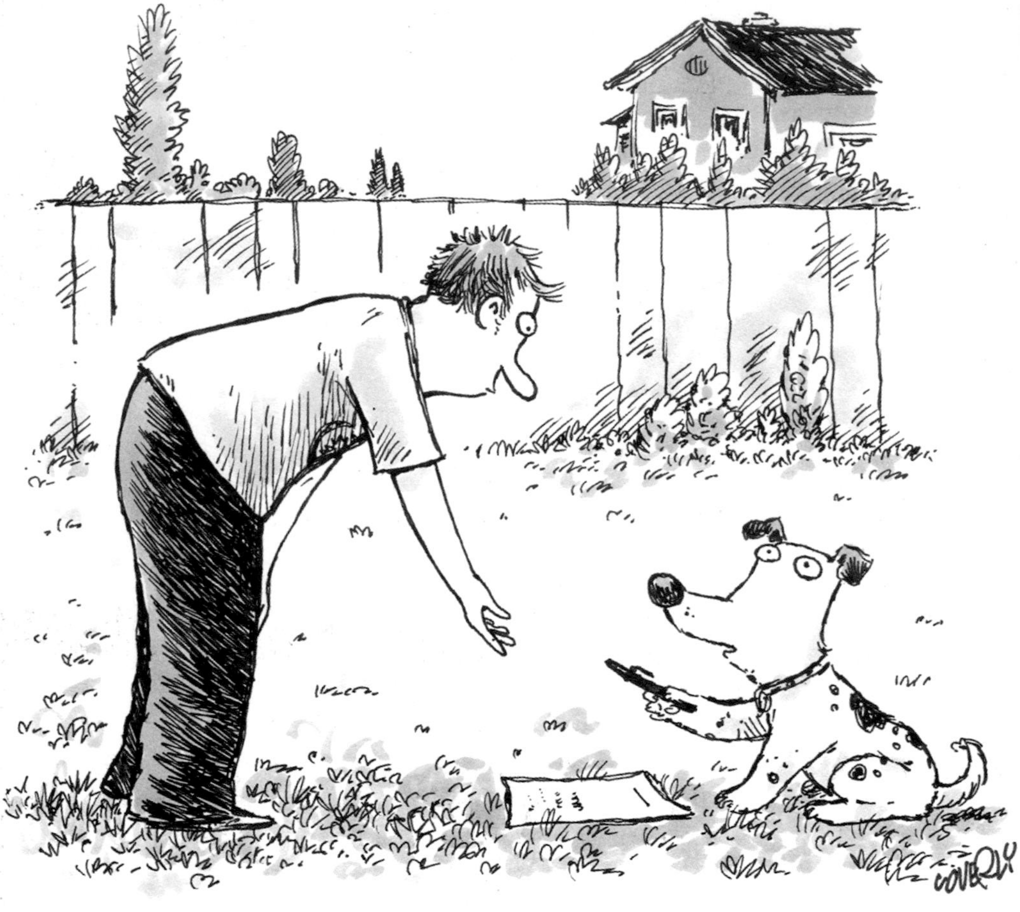

"Sorry, I don't shake. I only get things in writing."

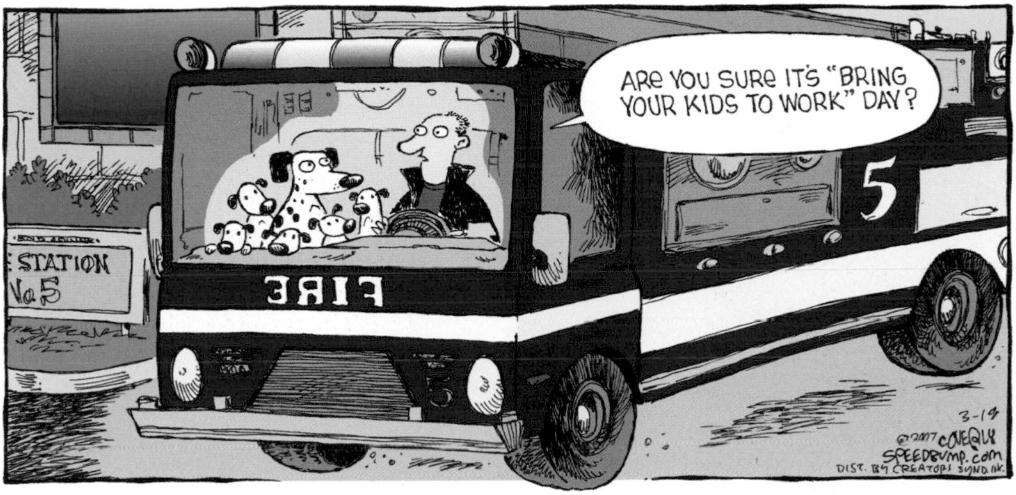
ARE YOU SURE IT'S "BRING YOUR KIDS TO WORK" DAY?
STATION No 5
FIRE
5
3-19
©2007 COVERLY
SPEEDBUMP.COM
DIST. BY CREATORS SYND. INC.

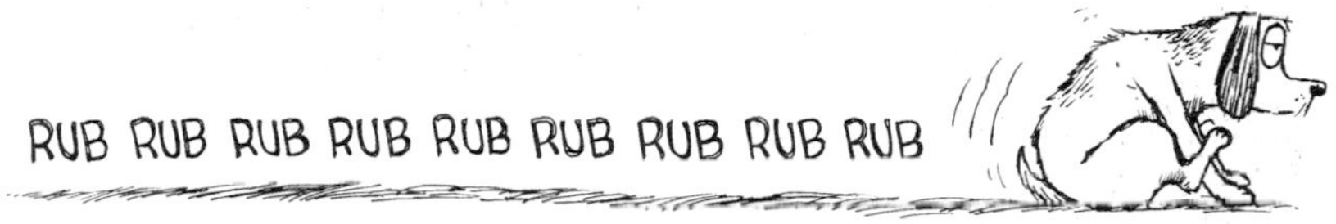
RUB RUB RUB RUB RUB RUB RUB RUB RUB

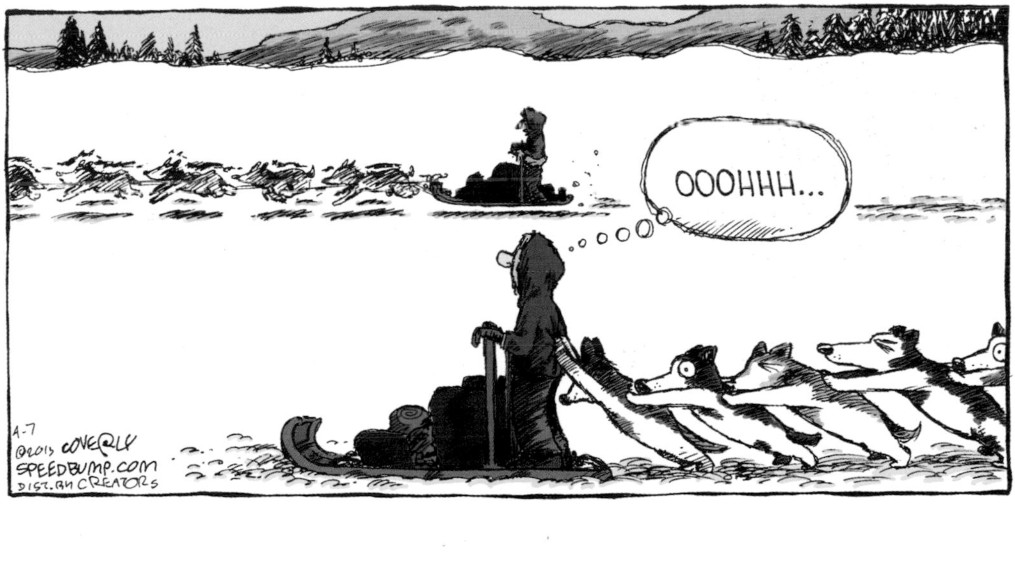
OOOHHH...
4-7
©2013 COVERLY
SPEEDBUMP.COM
DIST. BY CREATORS

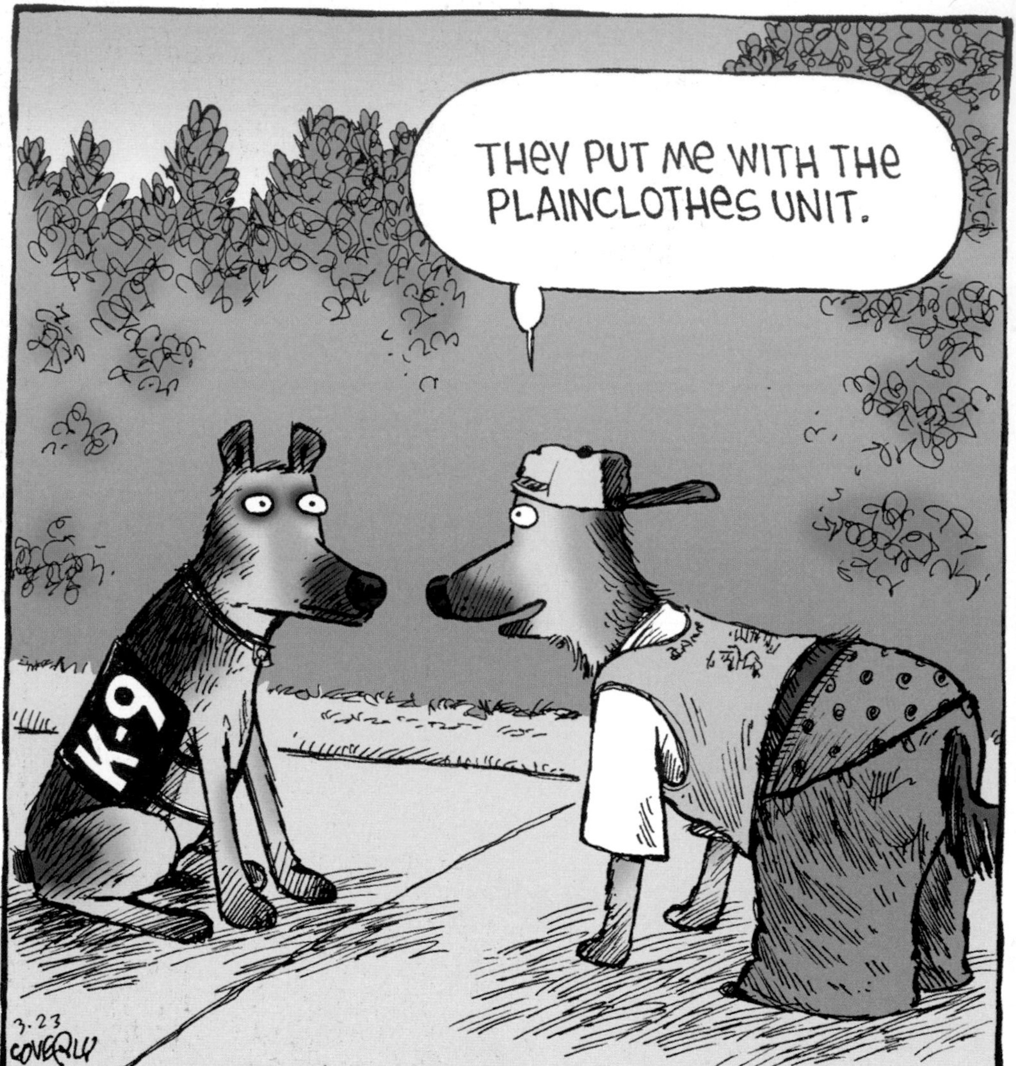
THEY PUT ME WITH THE PLAINCLOTHES UNIT.
K-9
3.23
COVERLY
©2011
SPEEDBUMP.COM/DIST.BY CREATORS

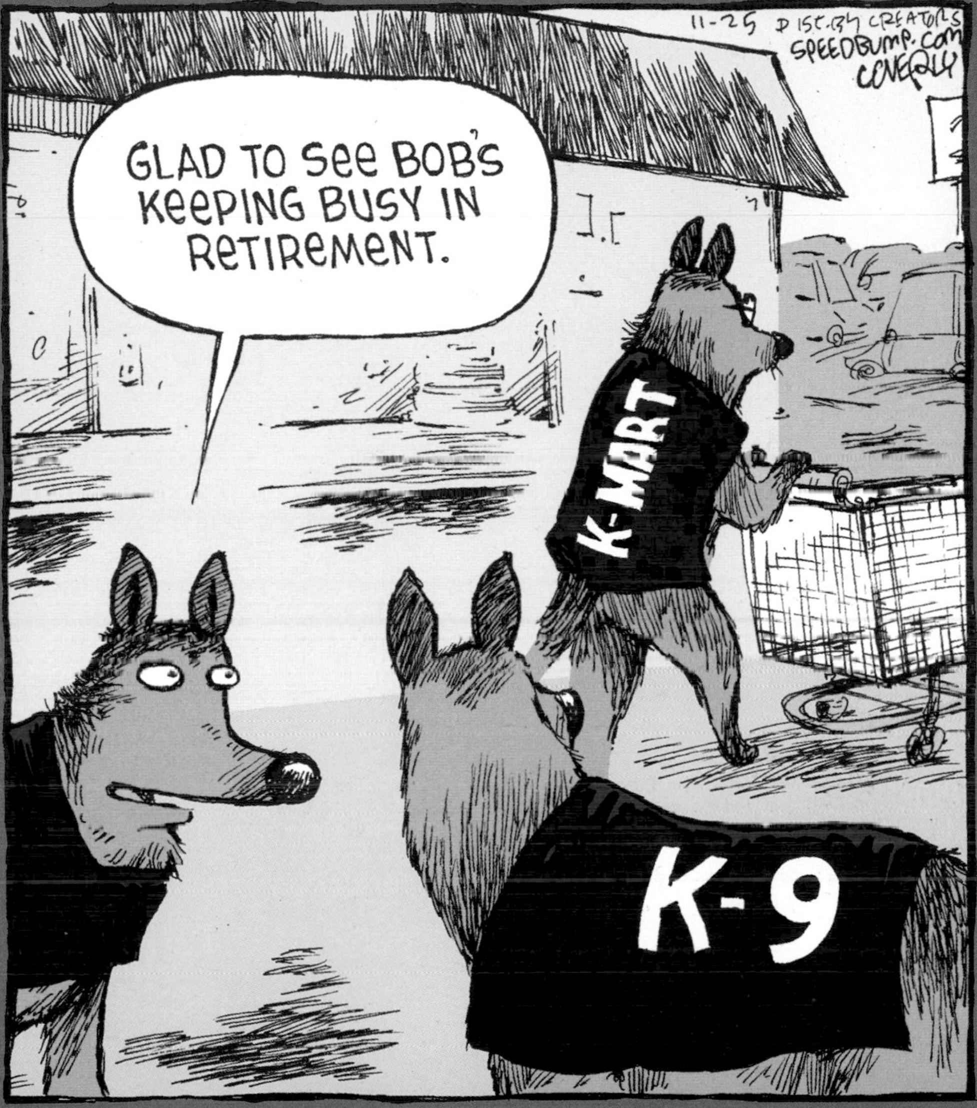
11-25 DIST. BY CREATORS
SPEEDBUMP.COM
COVERLY
GLAD TO SEE BOB'S KEEPING BUSY IN RETIREMENT.
K-MART
K-9

CHAPTER 4

TECHIE DOGS

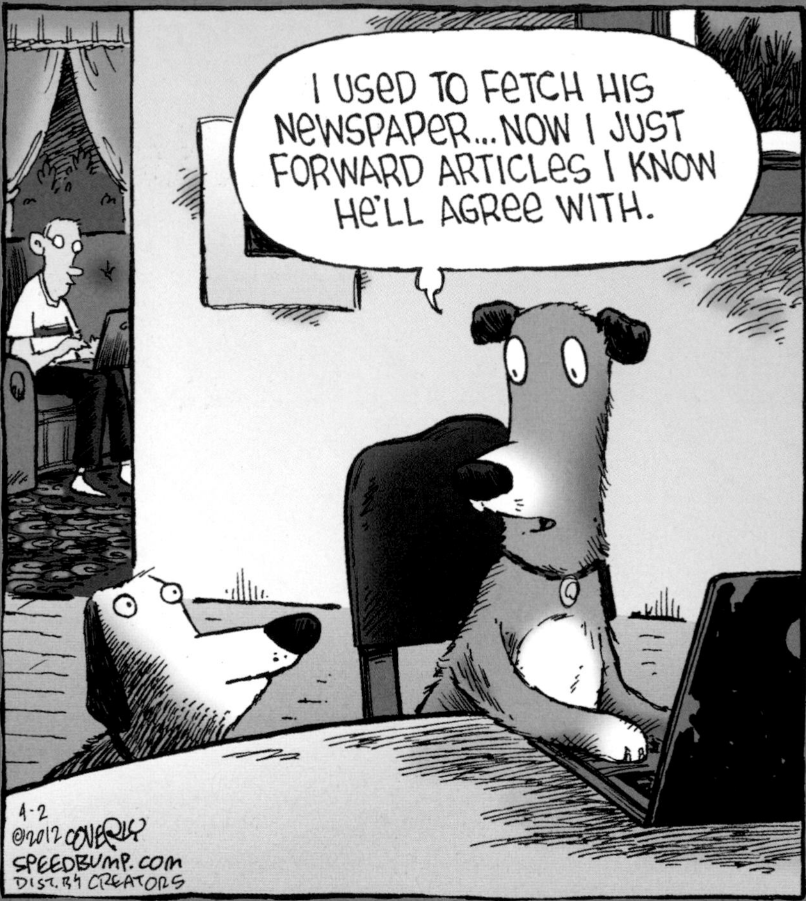
I USED TO FETCH HIS NEWSPAPER...NOW I JUST FORWARD ARTICLES I KNOW HE'LL AGREE WITH.
4-2
©2012 COVERLY
SPEEDBUMP.COM
DIST. BY CREATORS

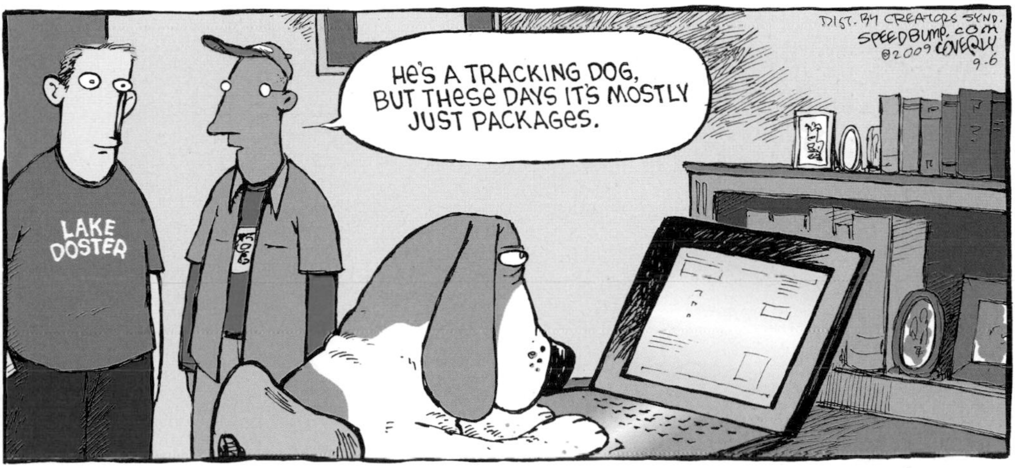
DIST. BY CREATORS SYND.
SPEEDBUMP.COM
©2009 COVERLY
9-6
HE'S A TRACKING DOG, BUT THESE DAYS IT'S MOSTLY JUST PACKAGES.
LAKE DOSTER

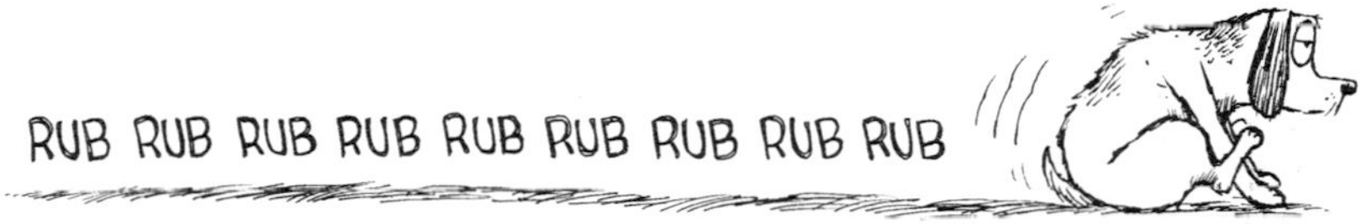
RUB RUB RUB RUB RUB RUB RUB RUB RUB

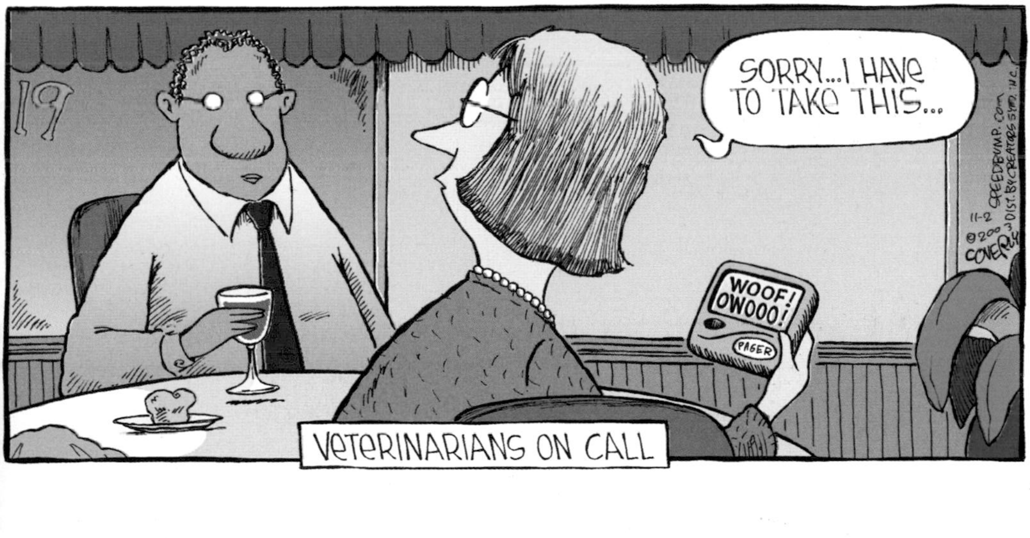
SORRY...I HAVE TO TAKE THIS...
SPEEDBUMP.COM
DIST. BY CREATORS SYND. INC.
11-2
COVERLY
WOOF! OWOOO!
PAGER
VETERINARIANS ON CALL

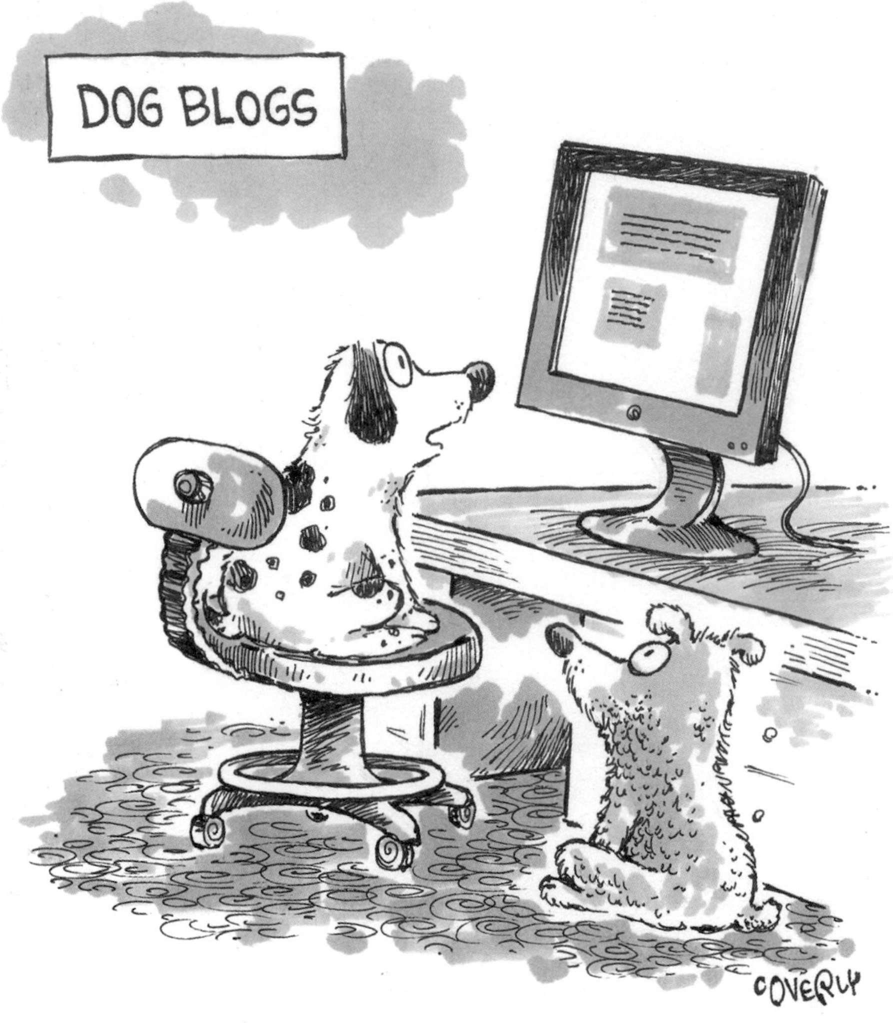
DOG BLOGS
COVERLY

"He slept, he ate, he barked at stuff, he went for a walk, he pooped...Geez, it's like he's living my life!"

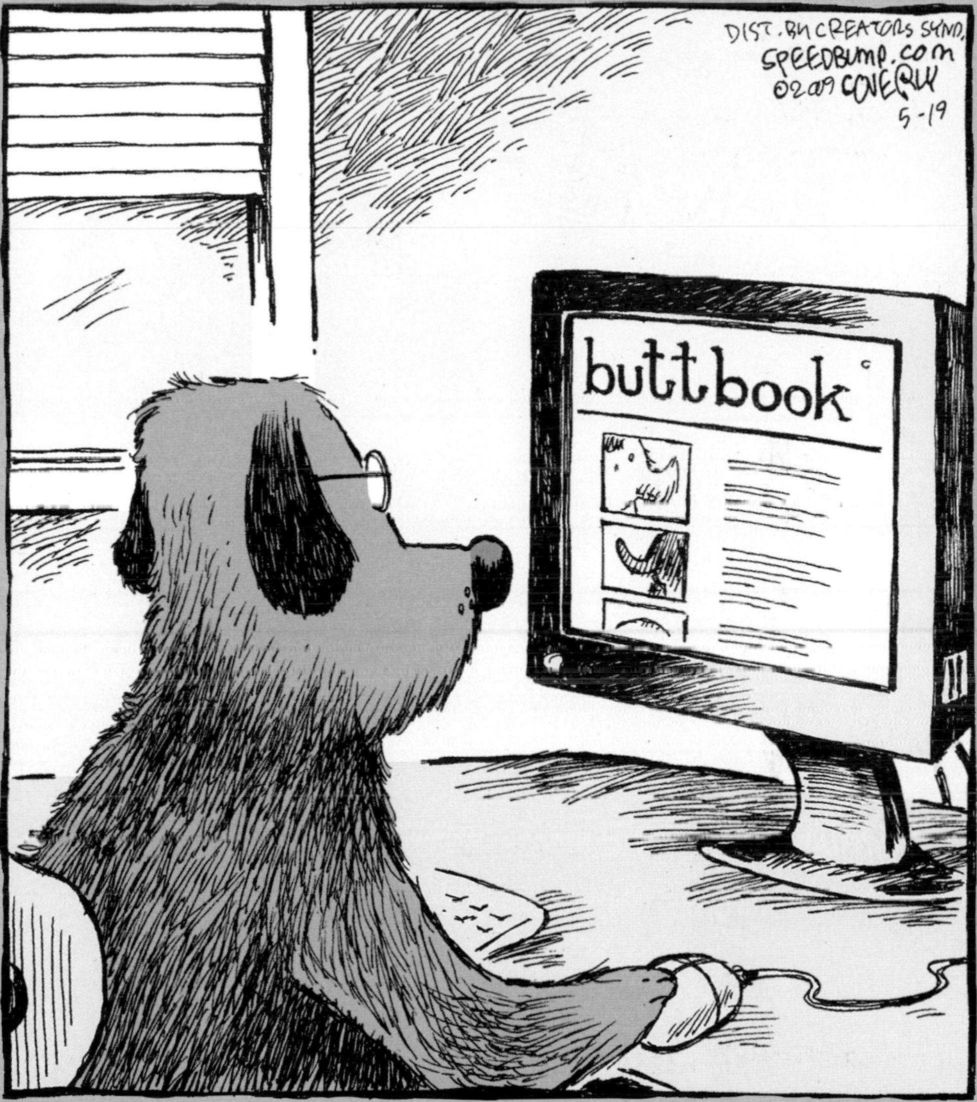
DIST. BY CREATORS SYND.
SPEEDBUMP.COM
©2009 COVERLY
5-19
buttbook

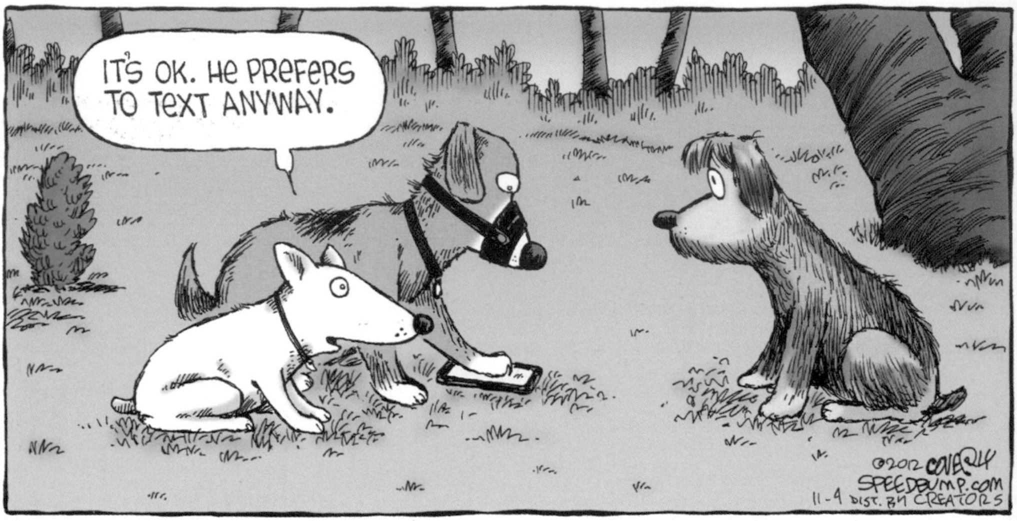
IT'S OK. HE PREFERS TO TEXT ANYWAY.
©2012 COVERLY
SPEEDBUMP.COM
11-4 DIST. BY CREATORS

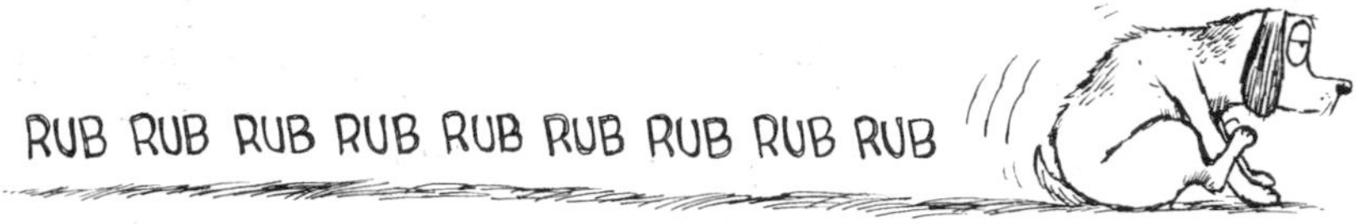
RUB RUB RUB RUB RUB RUB RUB RUB RUB

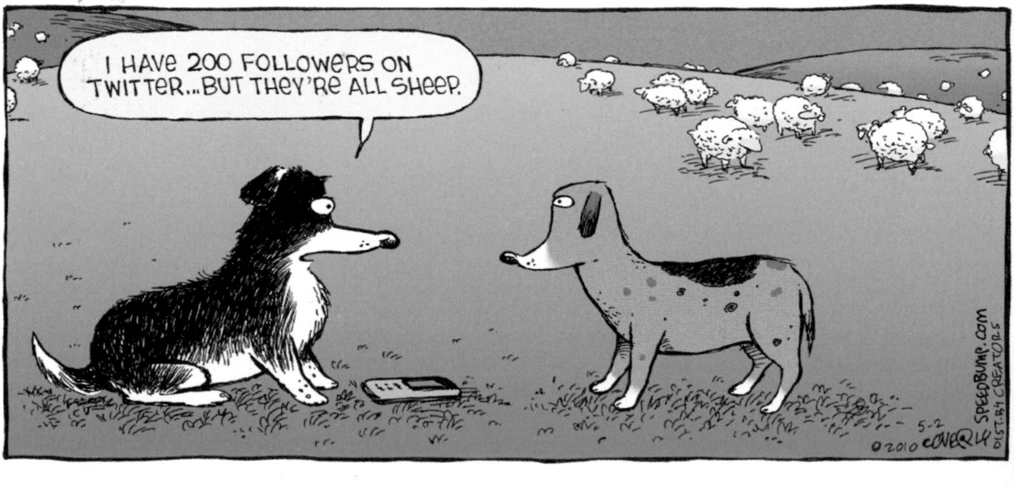
I HAVE 200 FOLLOWERS ON TWITTER...BUT THEY'RE ALL SHEEP.
SPEEDBUMP.COM
DIST. BY CREATORS
5-2
©2010 COVERLY

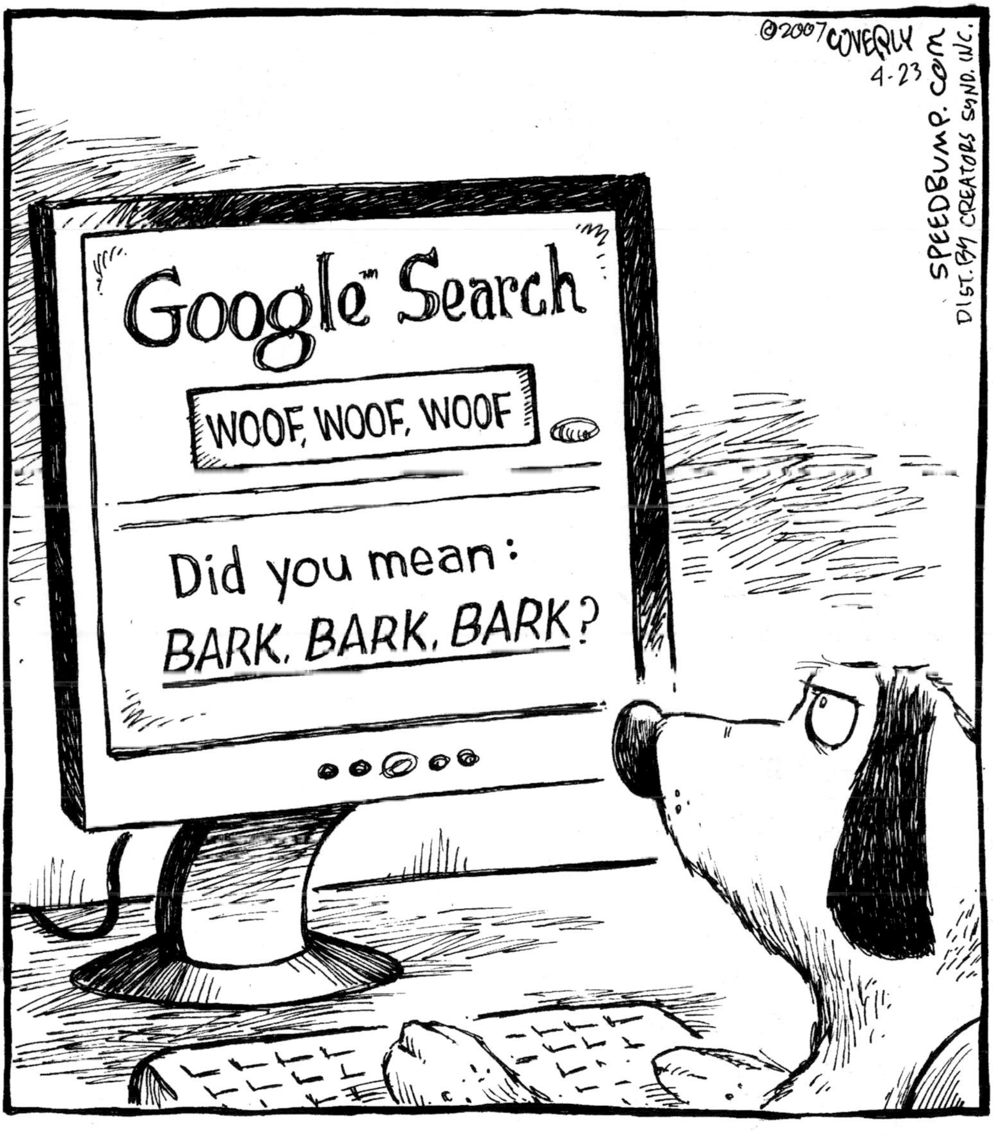
Google™ Search
WOOF, WOOF, WOOF
Did you mean:
BARK, BARK, BARK?
©2007 COVERLY 4-23
SPEEDBUMP.COM
DIST. BY CREATORS SYND. INC.

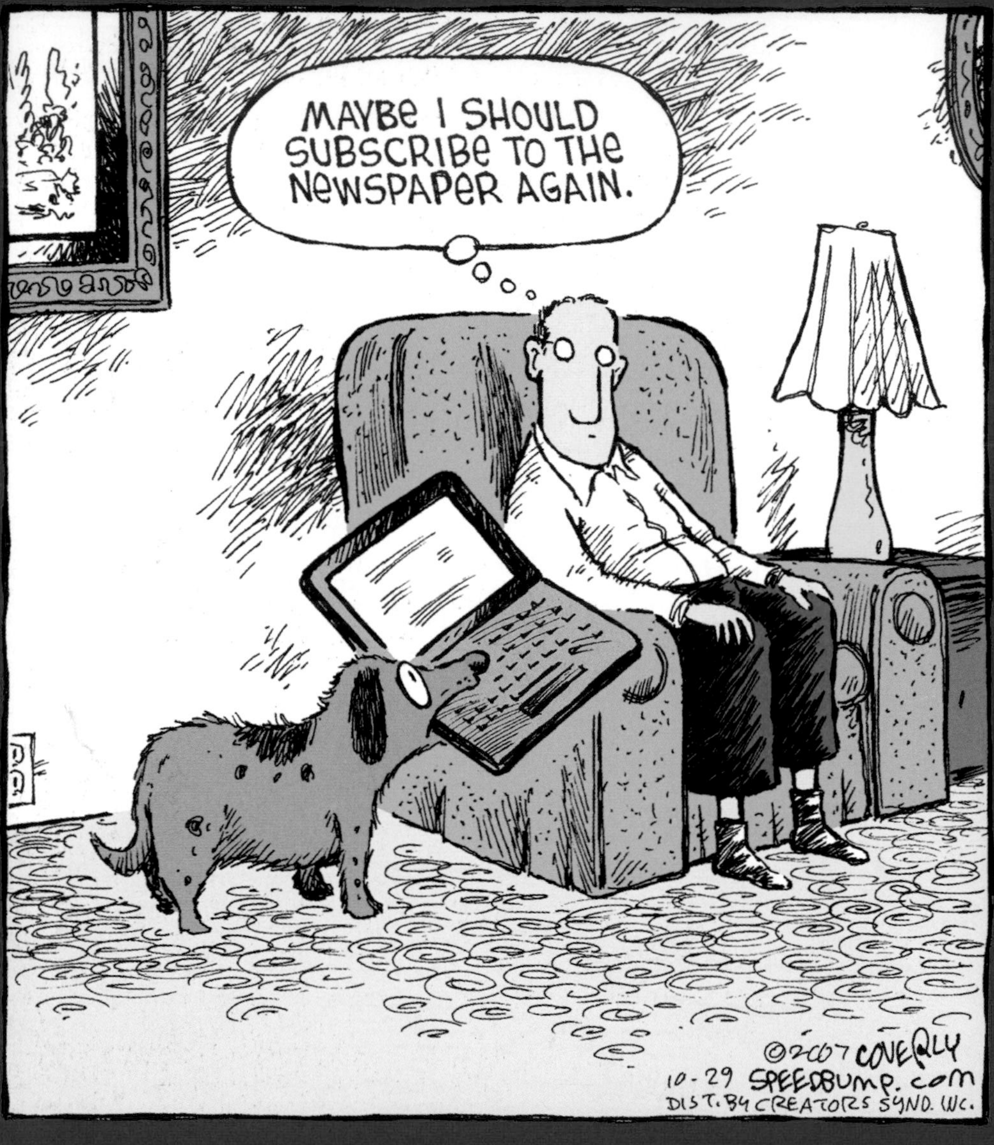
MAYBE I SHOULD SUBSCRIBE TO THE NEWSPAPER AGAIN.
©2007 COVERLY
10-29 SPEEDBUMP.com
DIST. BY CREATORS SYND. INC.

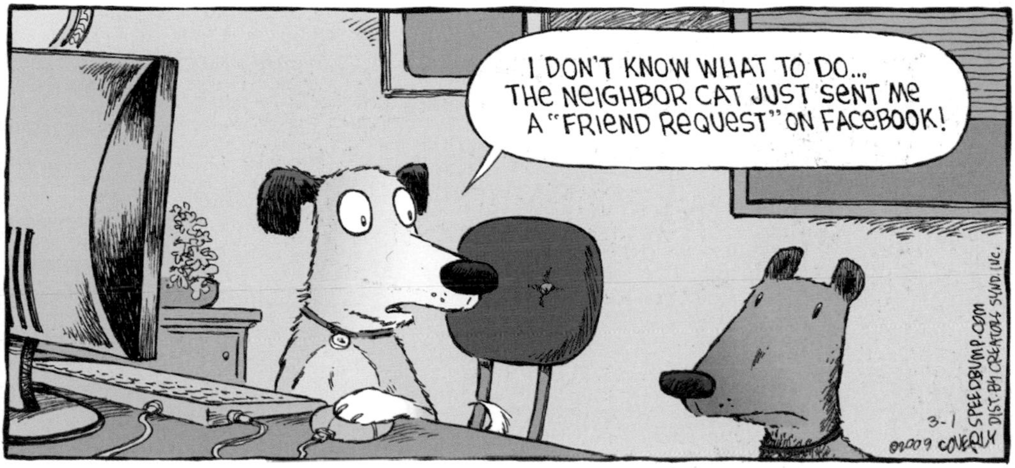
I DON'T KNOW WHAT TO DO...
THE NEIGHBOR CAT JUST SENT ME
A "FRIEND REQUEST" ON FACEBOOK!
3-1
SPEEDBUMP.COM
DIST. BY CREATORS SYND. INC.
©2009 COVERLY

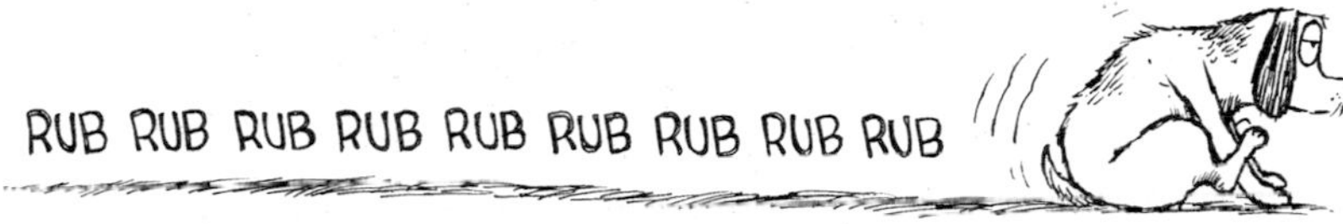
RUB RUB RUB RUB RUB RUB RUB RUB RUB

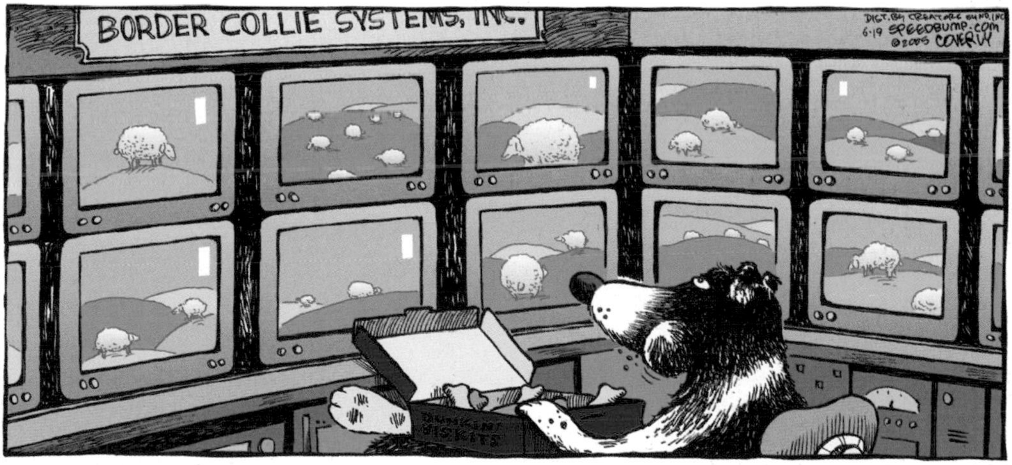
BORDER COLLIE SYSTEMS, INC.
6-19 SPEEDBUMP.COM
©2005 COVERLY

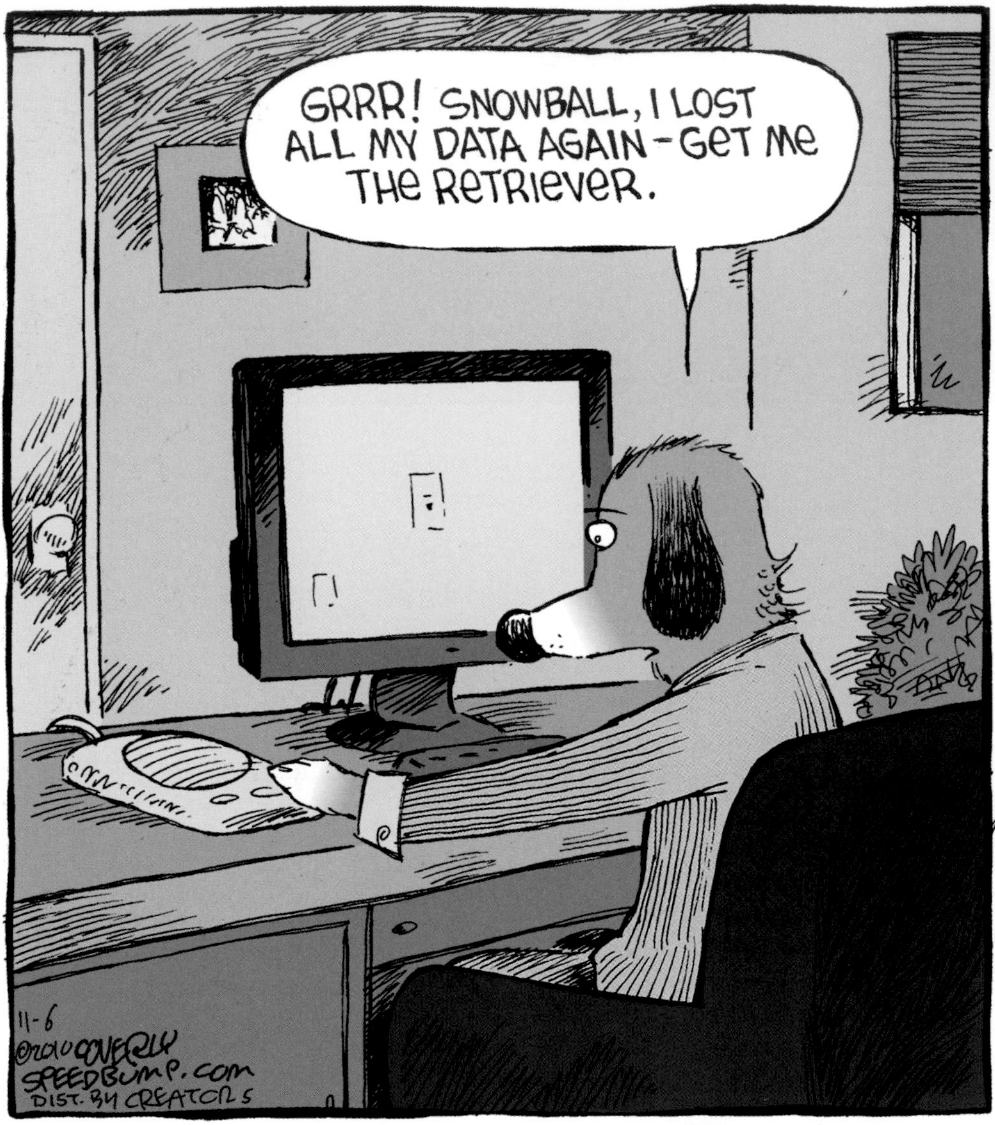
GRRR! SNOWBALL, I LOST ALL MY DATA AGAIN - GET ME THE RETRIEVER.
11-6
©2010 COVERLY
SPEEDBUMP.COM
DIST. BY CREATORS

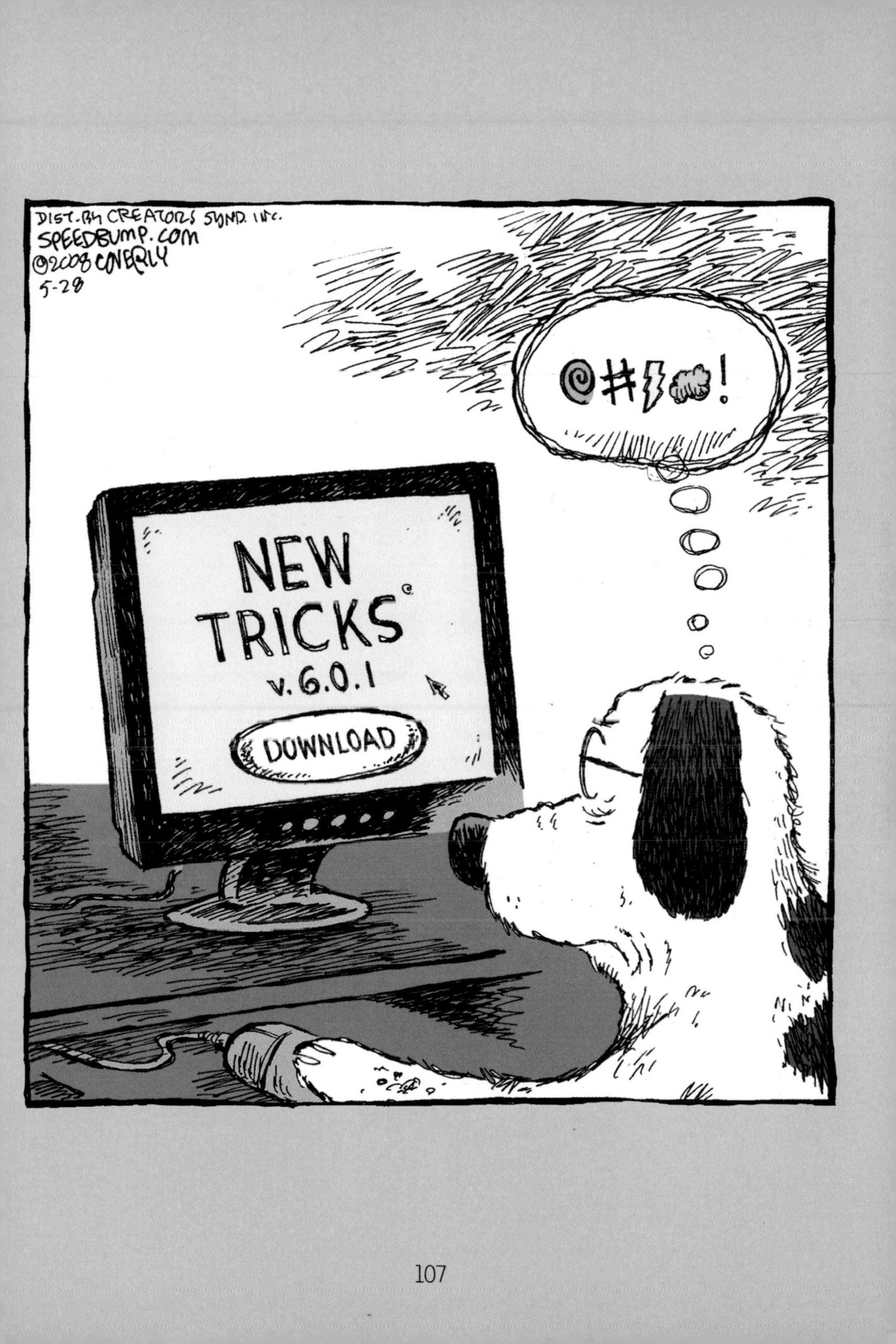
DIST. BY CREATORS SYND. INC.
SPEEDBUMP.COM
©2008 COVERLY
5-28
NEW TRICKS©
v.6.0.1
DOWNLOAD

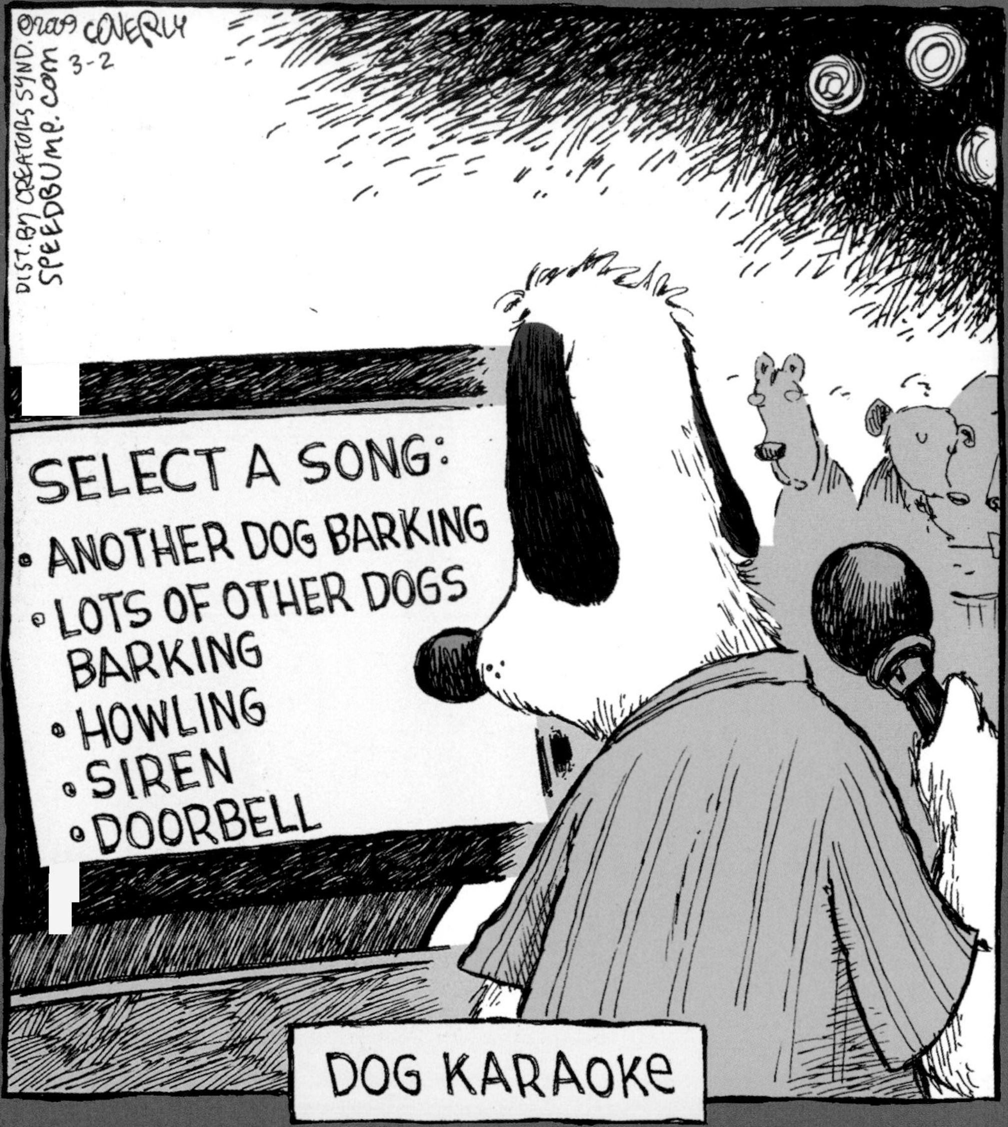
©2009 COVERLY
3-2
DIST. BY CREATORS SYND.
SPEEDBUMP.COM
SELECT A SONG:
• ANOTHER DOG BARKING
• LOTS OF OTHER DOGS BARKING
• HOWLING
• SIREN
• DOORBELL
DOG KARAOKE

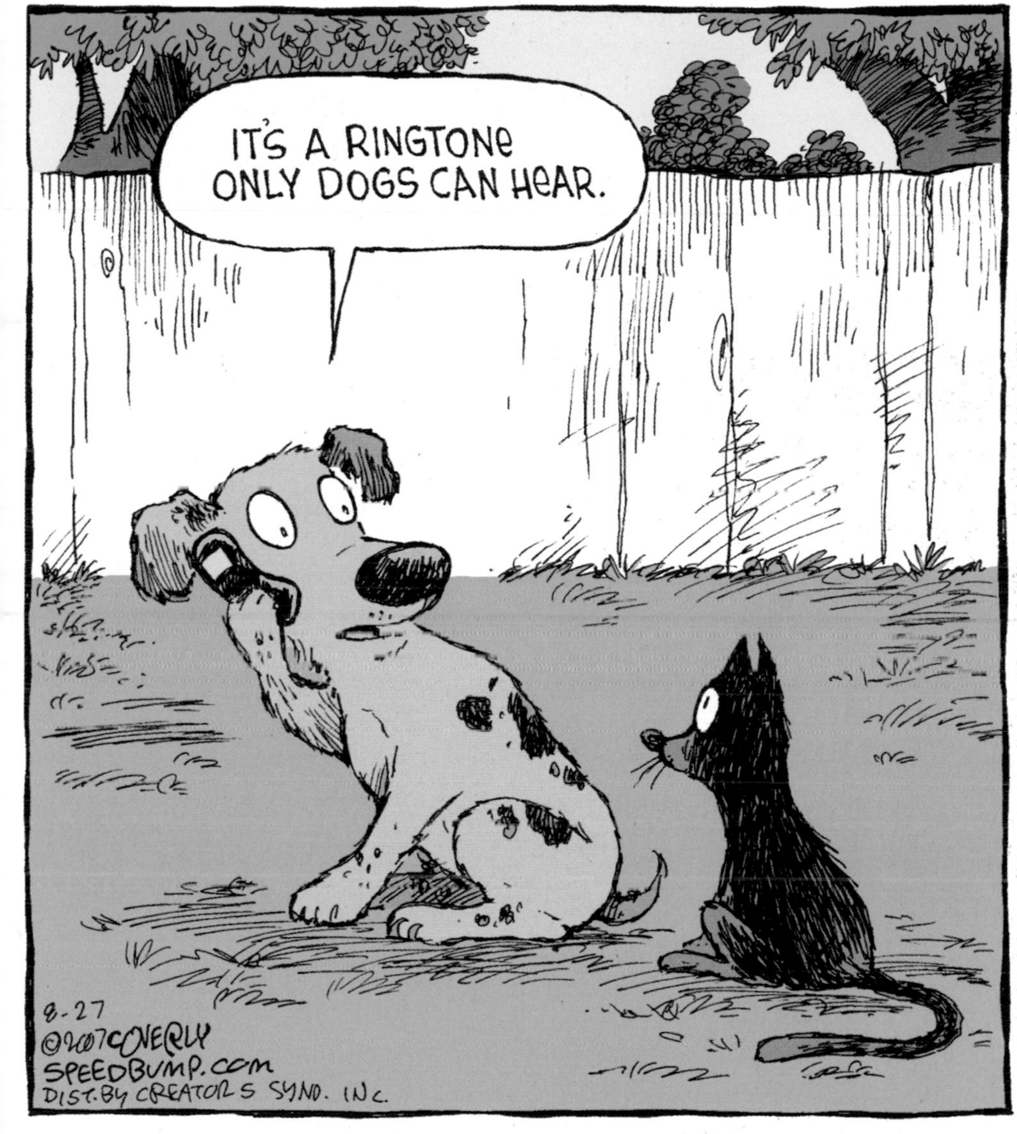
IT'S A RINGTONE ONLY DOGS CAN HEAR.
8-27
©2007 COVERLY
SPEEDBUMP.COM
DIST. BY CREATORS SYND. INC.

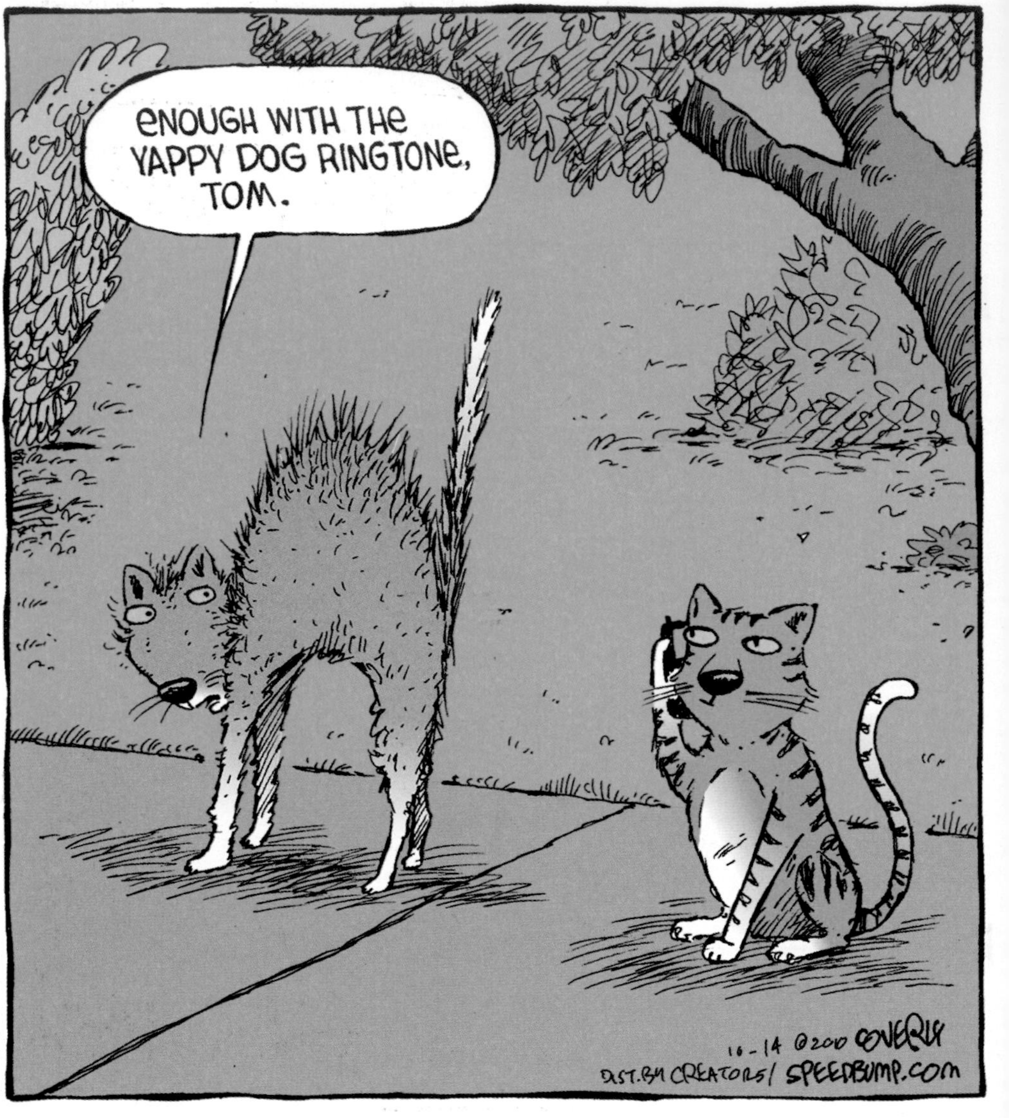
ENOUGH WITH THE YAPPY DOG RINGTONE, TOM.
10-14 ©2010 COVERLY
DIST. BY CREATORS/ SPEEDBUMP.COM

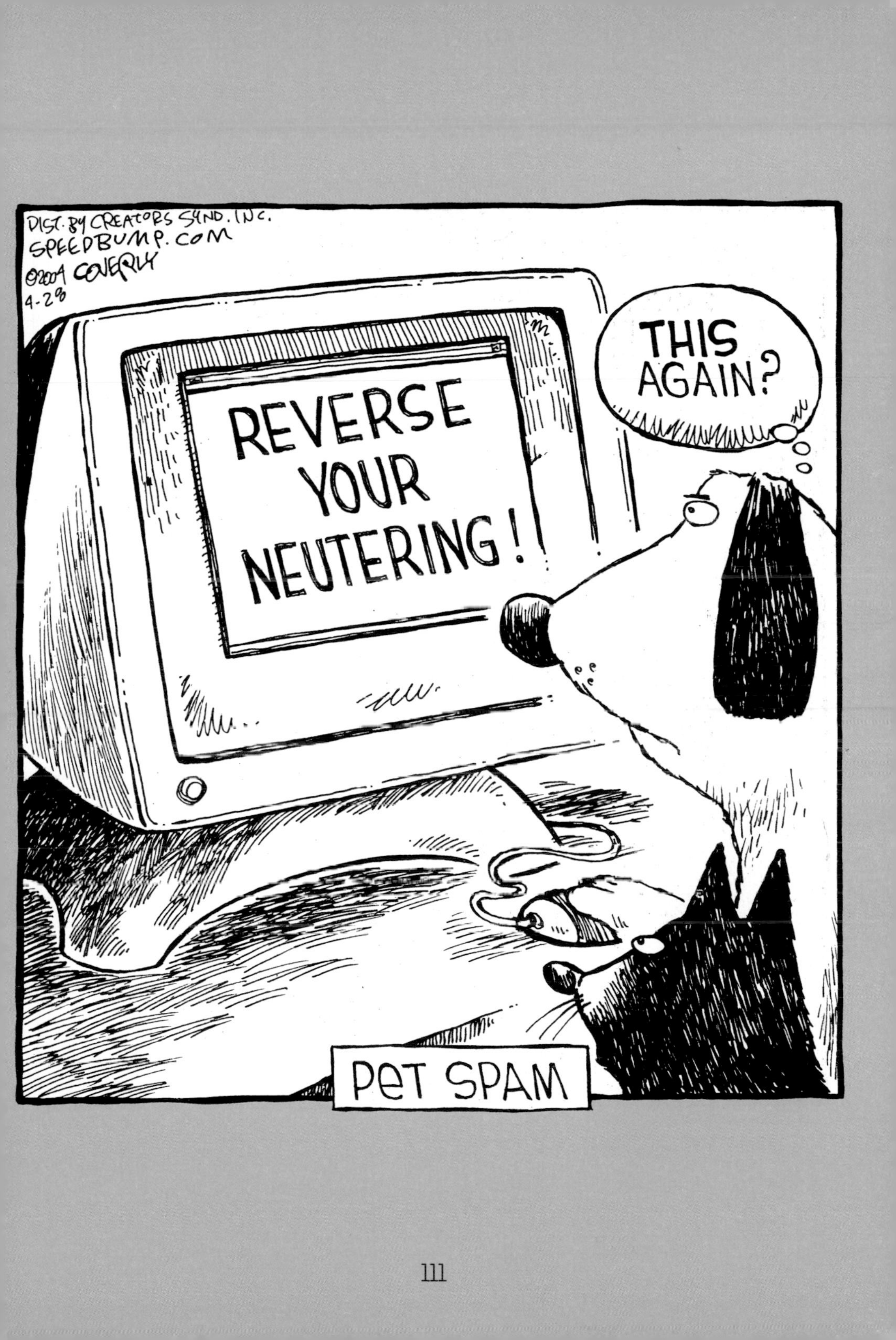
DIST. BY CREATORS SYND. INC.
SPEEDBUMP.COM
©2004 COVERLY
4-28
REVERSE YOUR NEUTERING!
THIS AGAIN?
PET SPAM

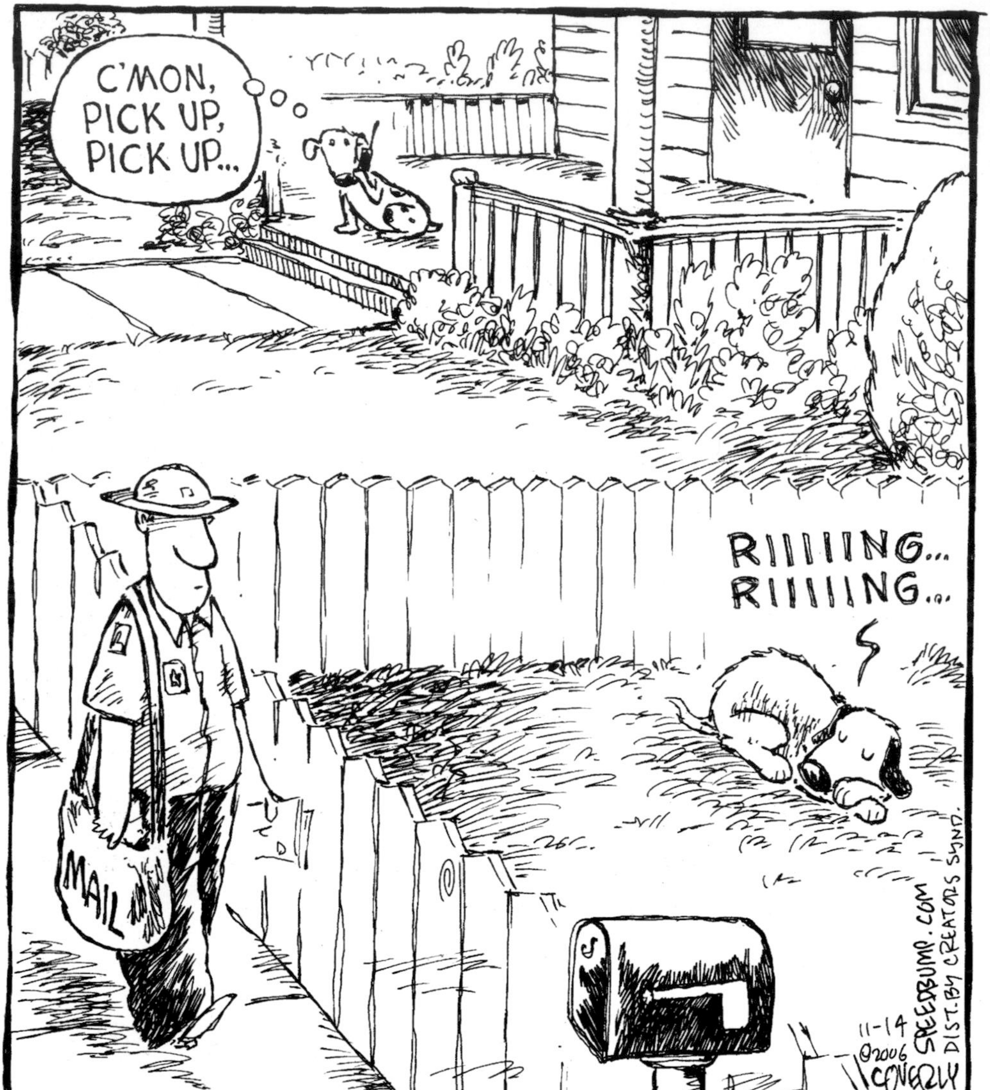
C'MON, PICK UP, PICK UP...
RIIIIING... RIIIIING...
MAIL
11-14
©2006
COVERLY
SPEEDBUMP.COM
DIST. BY CREATORS SYND.

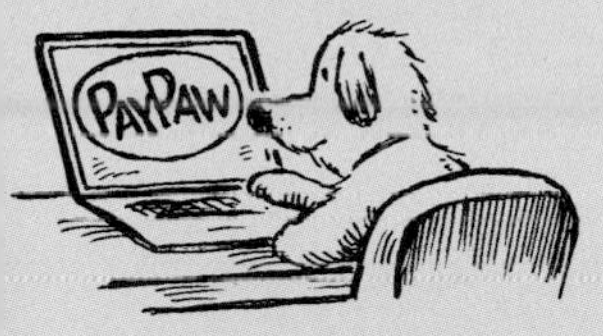
PAYPAW

STEVE

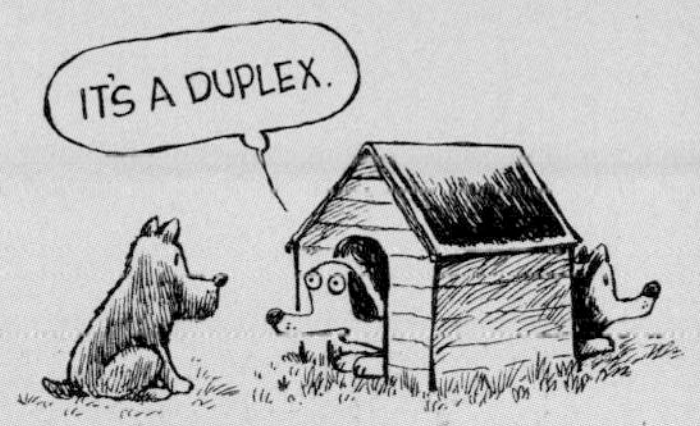
IT'S A DUPLEX.

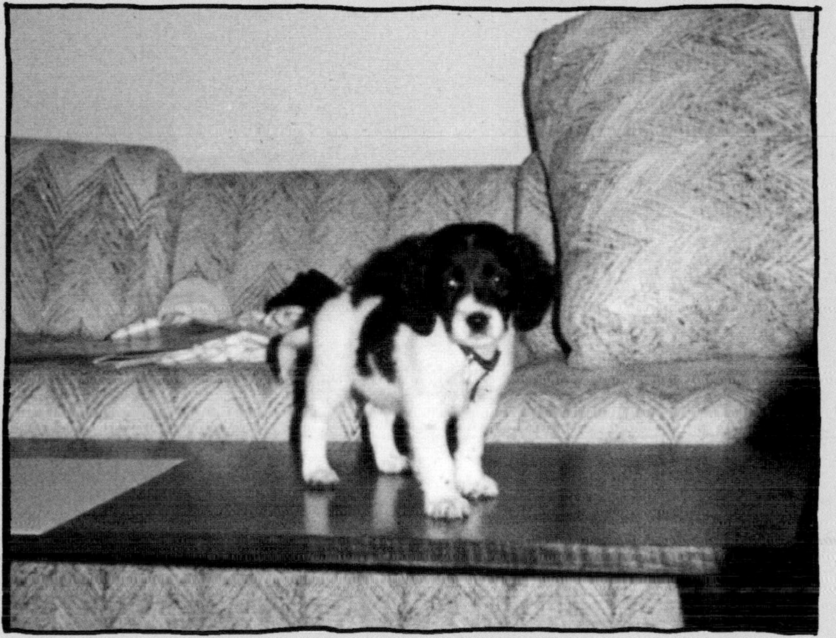

Steve dancing on the table, 1986.

The existence of Steve in my life is still a mystery. It was the spring of 1986, and I had just returned from a semester in England to an apartment just outside the campus of Eastern Michigan University. I had a full load of classes. I was on the tennis team. I was drawing cartoons for the school paper, the *Eastern Echo.* What random glitch in the universe compelled me to get a puppy . . . and to keep it in an apartment that didn't allow dogs? I can only guess it had something to do with Shag dying around that time.

Steve was a great little dog, friendly and beautiful. Friends and my girlfriend took him for tons of walks. And he must have had amazing karma, because when my landlord finally discovered him and enforced the No Pets policy, Steve landed with friends who not only had children, but lived on a fourteen-acre farm with lots of other animals. I'm certain he was never on a chain there. In fact, I heard Steve lived a long, busy life running that place.

I love happy endings.

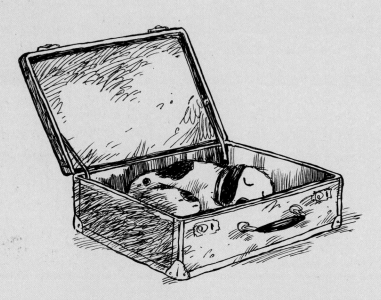

CHAPTER 5

DOGS BEHAVING BADLY

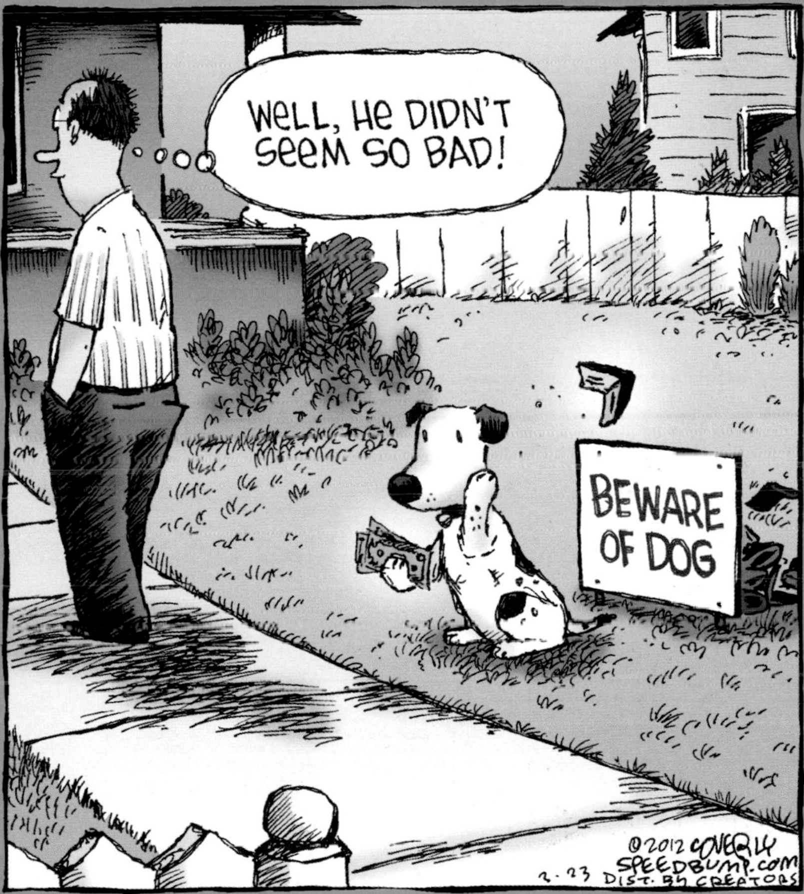
WELL, HE DIDN'T SEEM SO BAD!
BEWARE OF DOG
©2012 COVERLY
SPEEDBUMP.COM
2-23 DIST. BY CREATORS

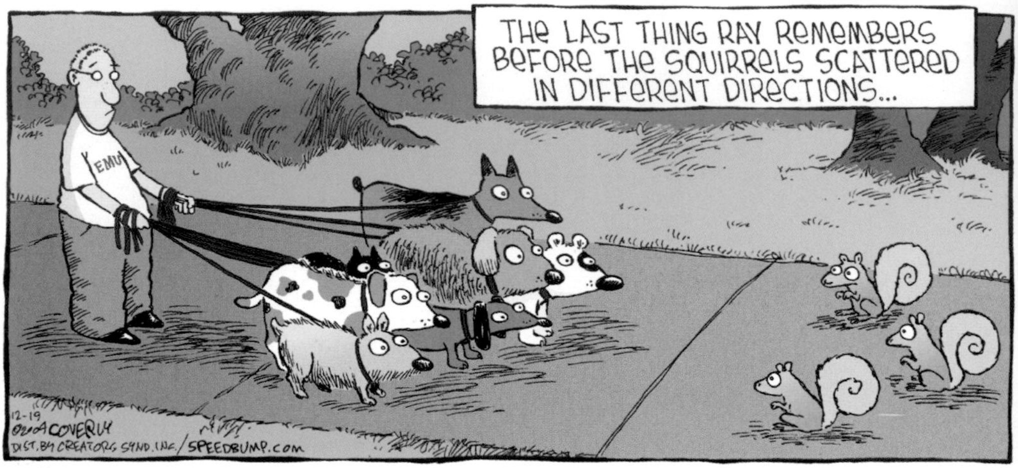
THE LAST THING RAY REMEMBERS BEFORE THE SQUIRRELS SCATTERED IN DIFFERENT DIRECTIONS...
EMU
12-19 ©2004 COVERLY
DIST. BY CREATORS SYND. INC./SPEEDBUMP.COM

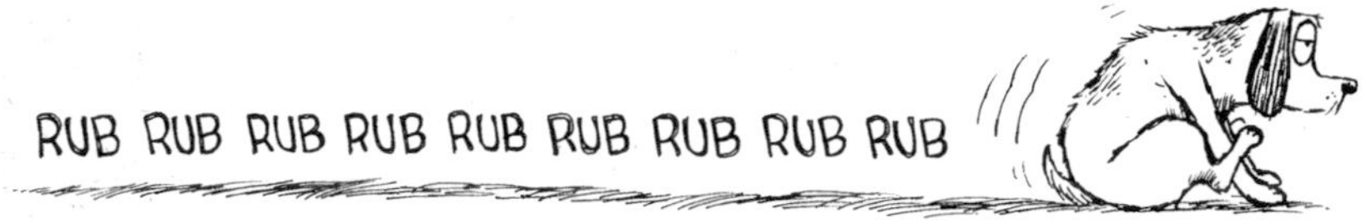
RUB RUB RUB RUB RUB RUB RUB RUB RUB

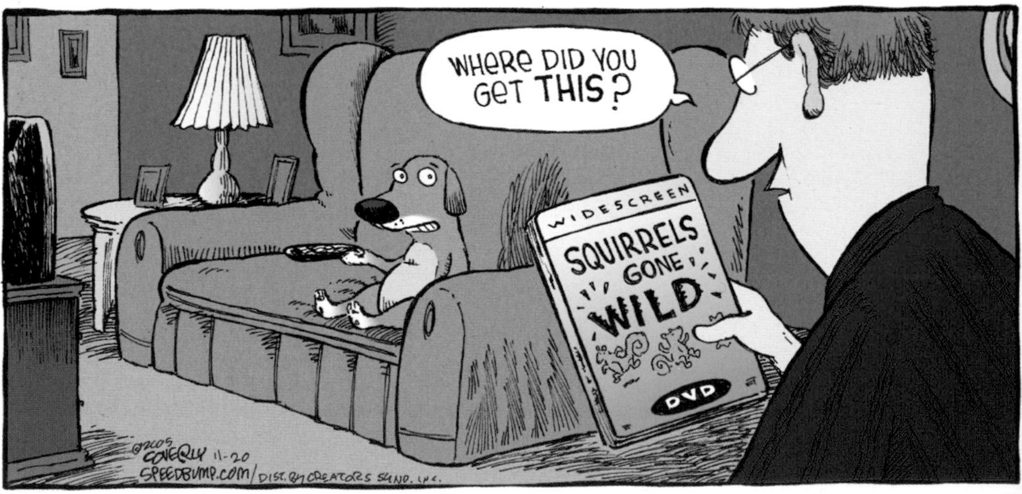
WHERE DID YOU GET THIS?
WIDESCREEN
SQUIRRELS GONE WILD
DVD
©2005 COVERLY 11-20
SPEEDBUMP.COM/DIST. BY CREATORS SYND. INC.

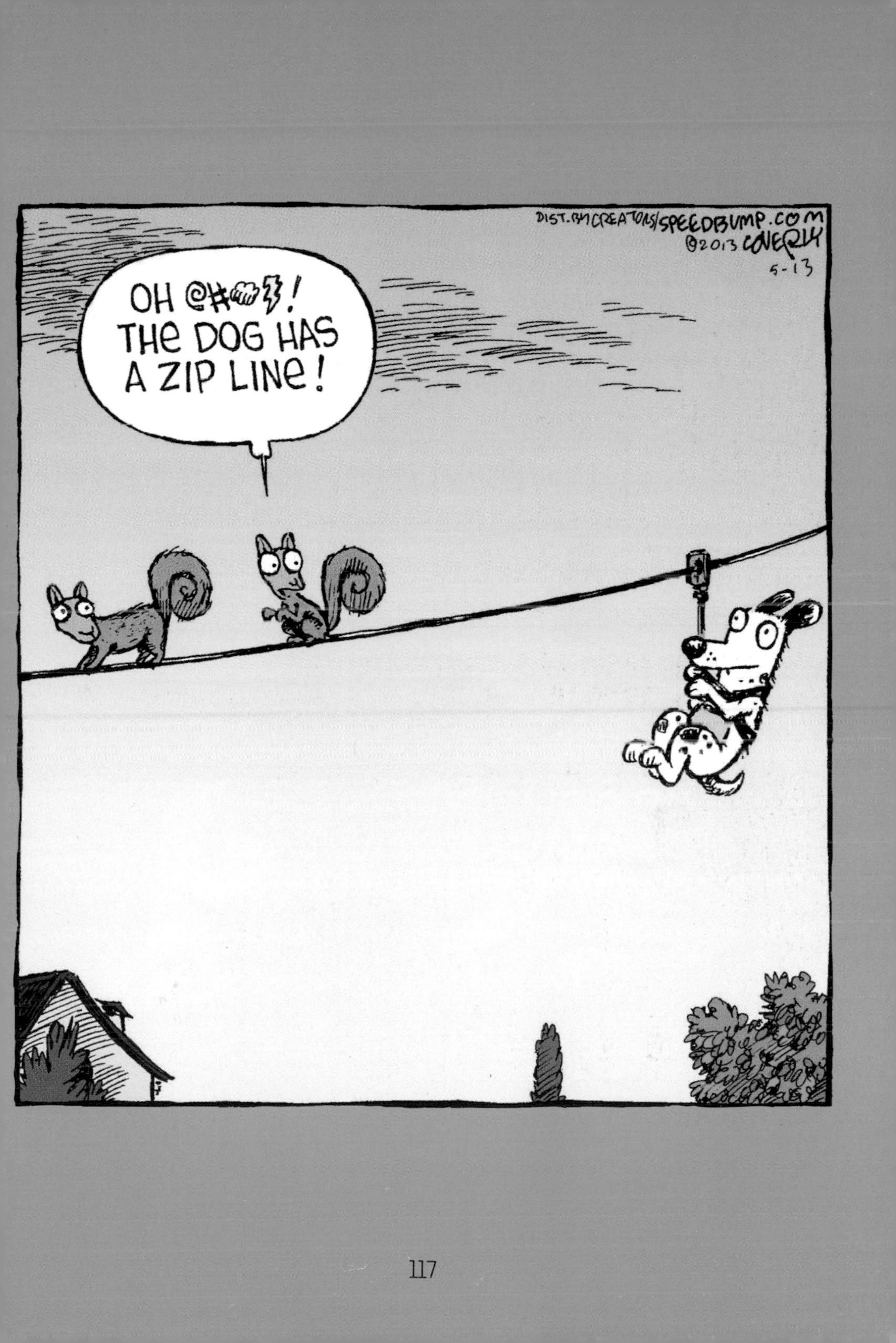
DIST. BY CREATORS/SPEEDBUMP.COM
©2013 COVERLY
5-13
OH @#☁⚡!
THE DOG HAS
A ZIP LINE!

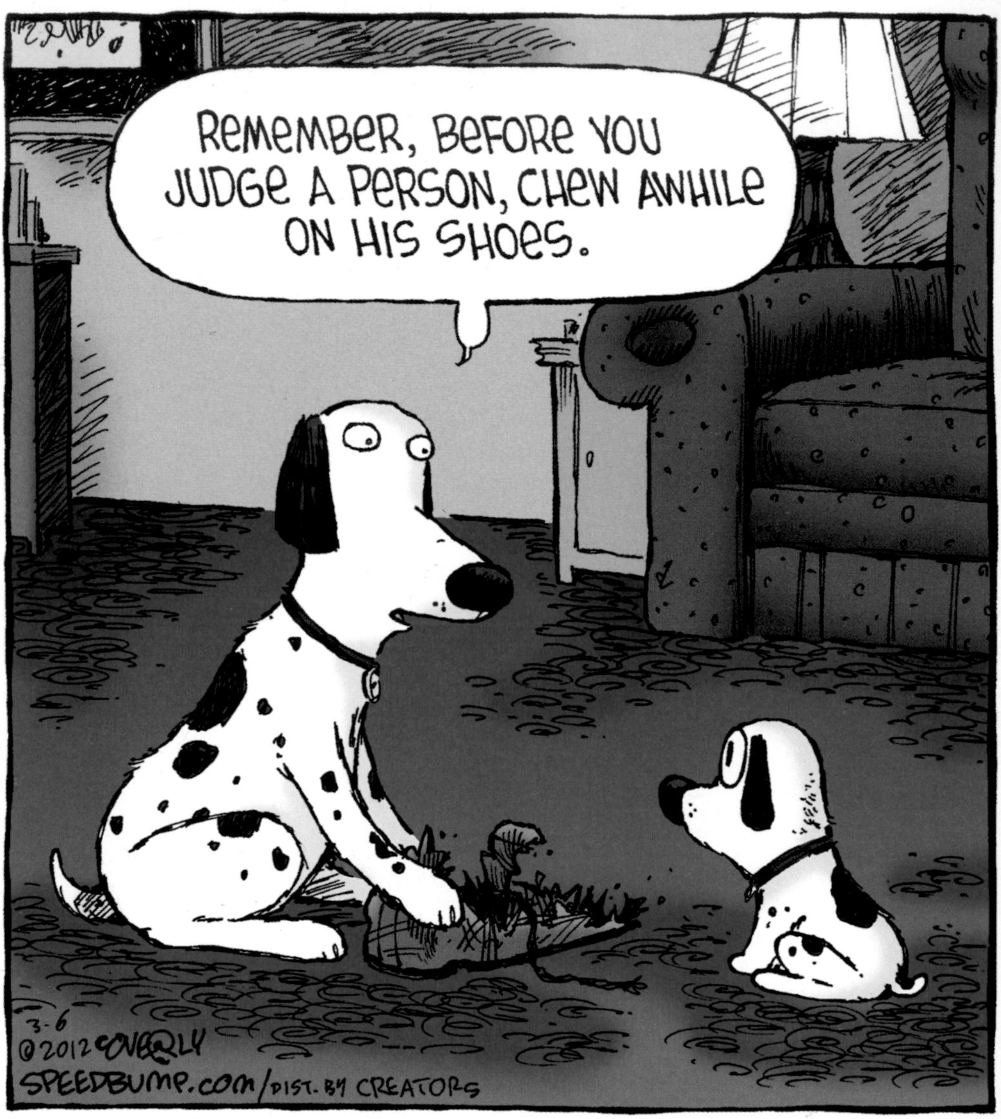
REMEMBER, BEFORE YOU JUDGE A PERSON, CHEW AWHILE ON HIS SHOES.
3-6
©2012 COVERLY
SPEEDBUMP.COM/DIST. BY CREATORS

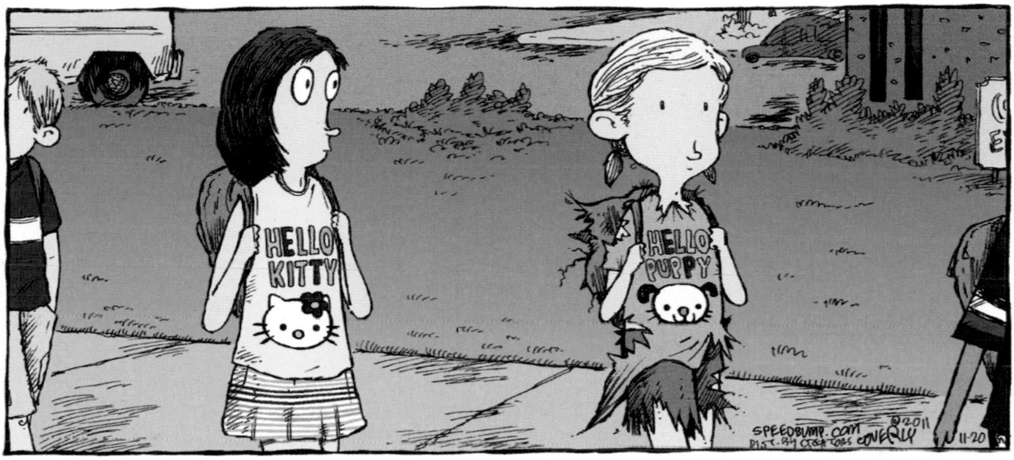
HELLO KITTY
HELLO PUPPY
SPEEDBUMP.com ©2011 DIST. BY CREATORS COVERLY 11-20

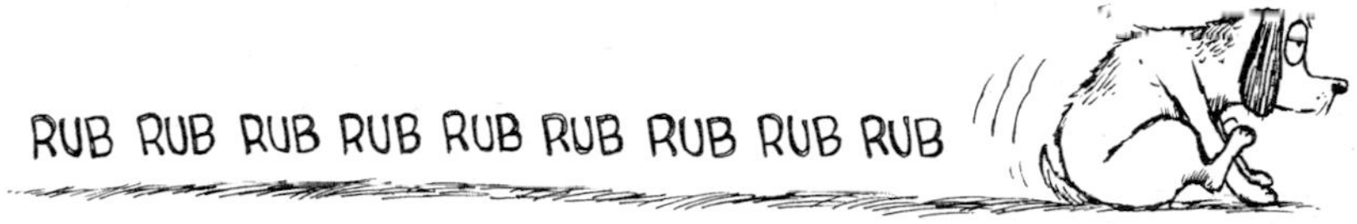
RUB RUB RUB RUB RUB RUB RUB RUB RUB

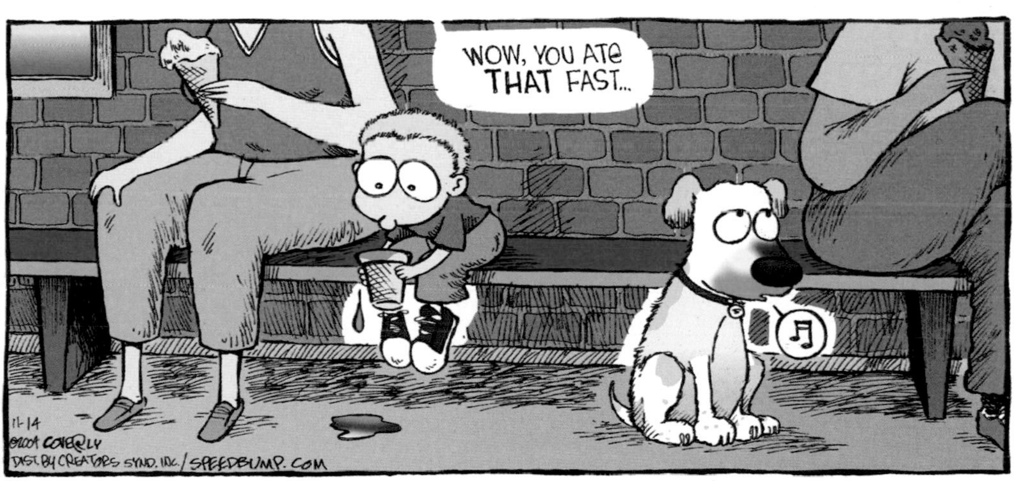
WOW, YOU ATE THAT FAST...
11-14 ©2004 COVERLY DIST. BY CREATORS SYND. INC./SPEEDBUMP.COM

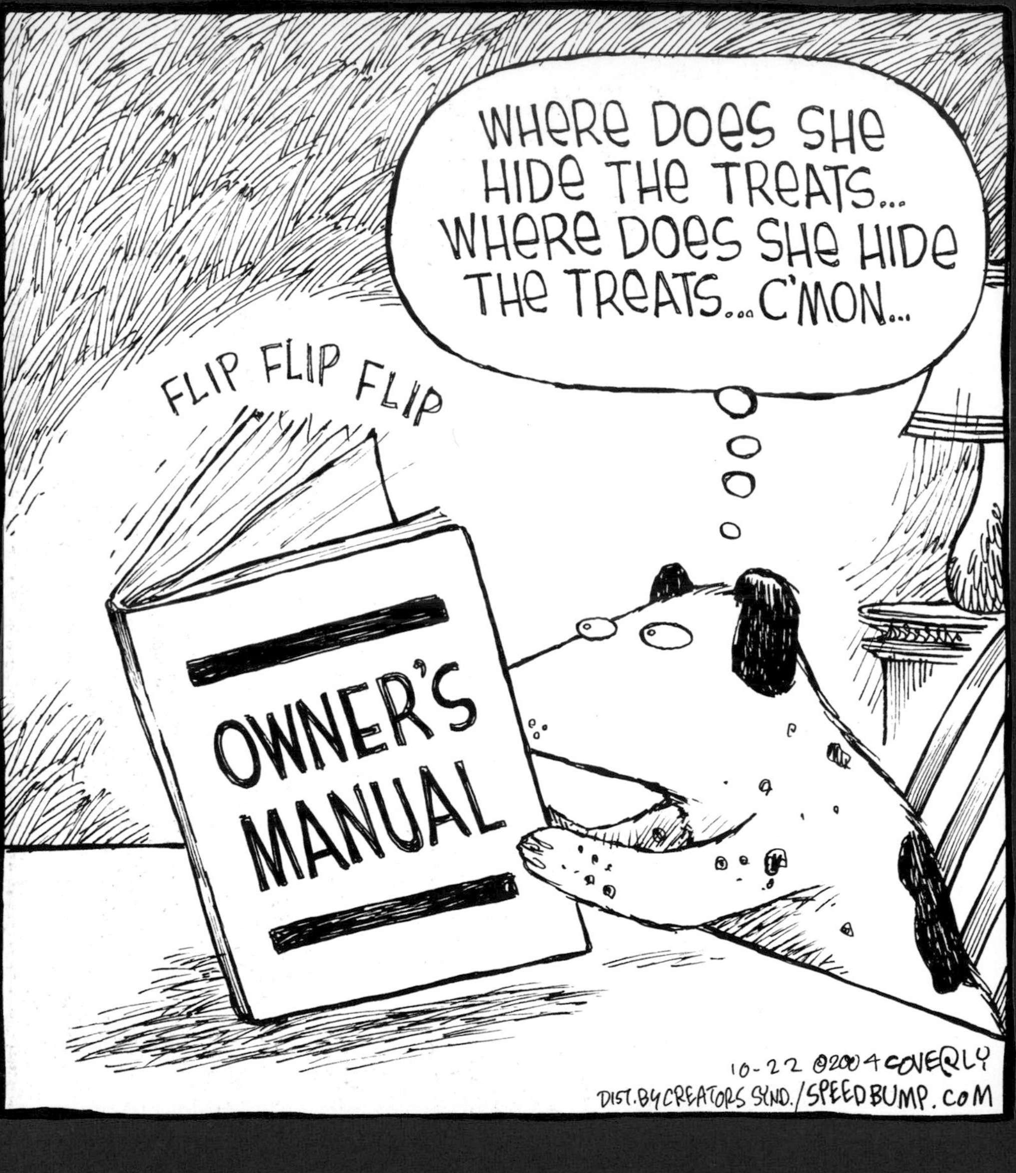
WHERE DOES SHE HIDE THE TREATS... WHERE DOES SHE HIDE THE TREATS... C'MON...
FLIP FLIP FLIP
OWNER'S MANUAL
10-22 ©2004 COVERLY
DIST. BY CREATORS SYND./SPEEDBUMP.COM

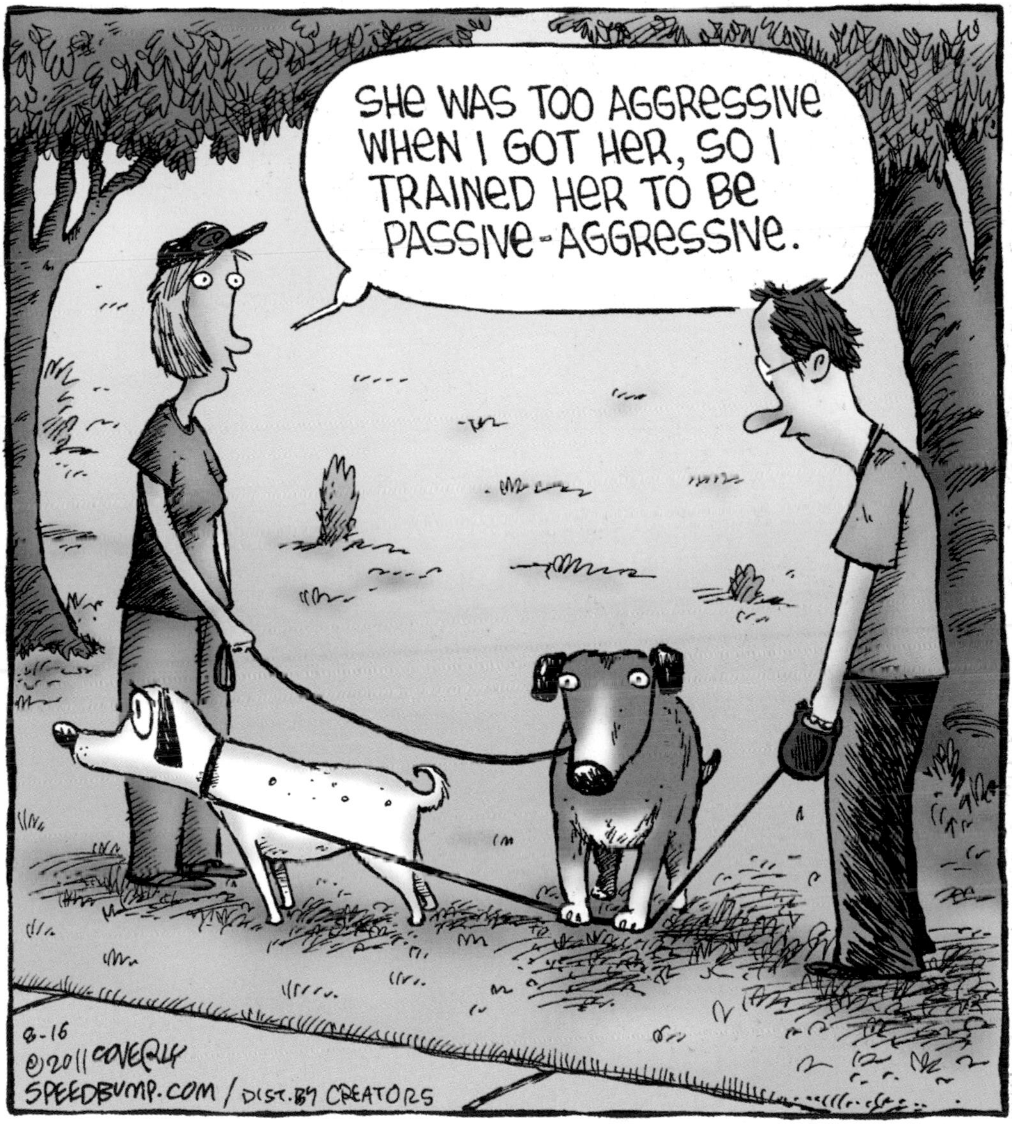
SHE WAS TOO AGGRESSIVE WHEN I GOT HER, SO I TRAINED HER TO BE PASSIVE-AGGRESSIVE.
8-16
©2011 COVERLY
SPEEDBUMP.COM / DIST. BY CREATORS

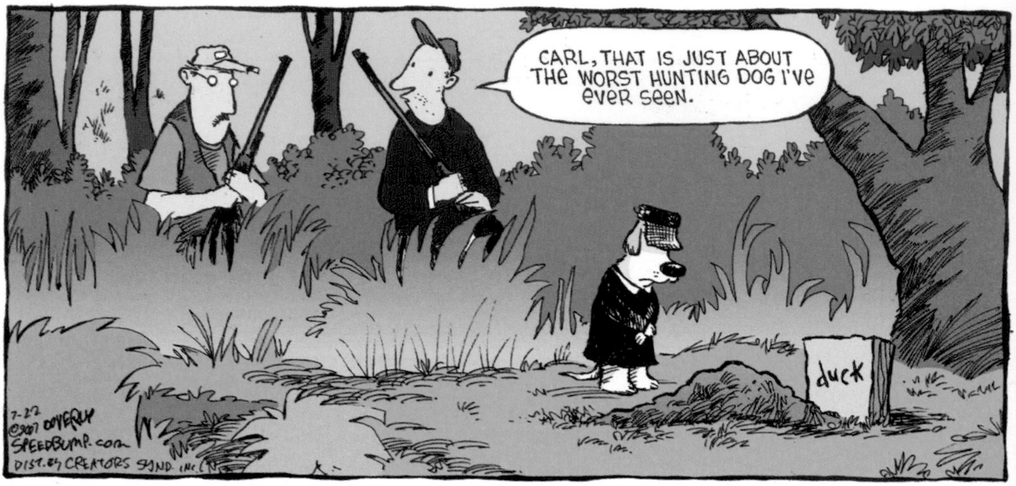
CARL, THAT IS JUST ABOUT THE WORST HUNTING DOG I'VE EVER SEEN.
duck
7-22 ©2007 COVERLY SPEEDBUMP.com DIST. BY CREATORS SYND. INC.

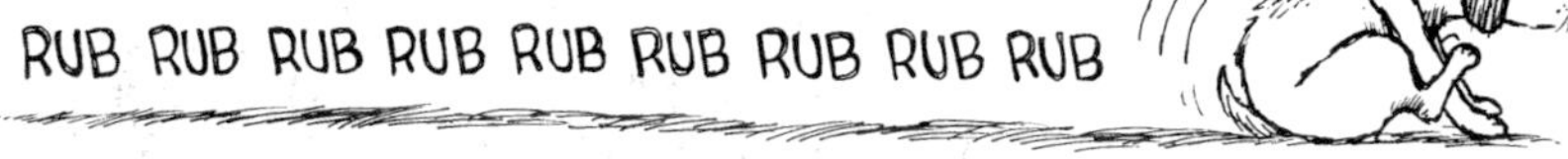
RUB RUB RUB RUB RUB RUB RUB RUB RUB

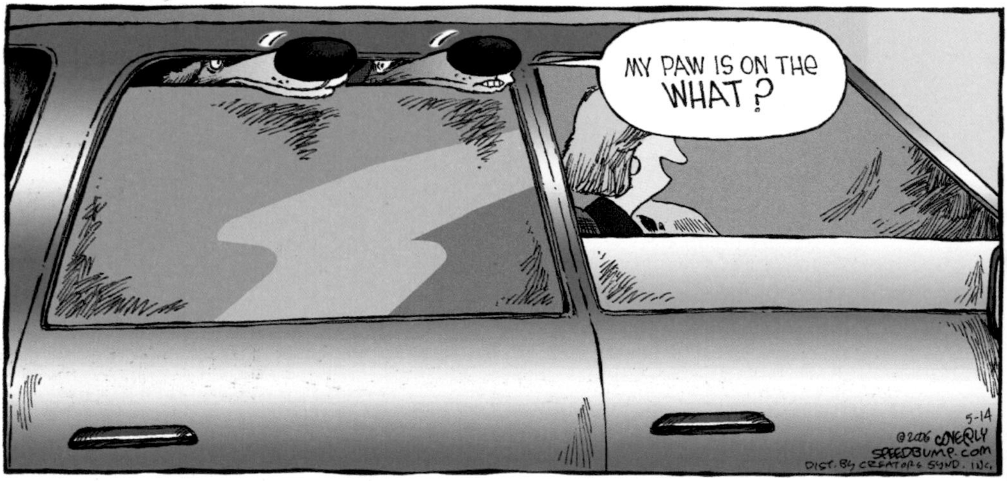
MY PAW IS ON THE WHAT?
5-14 ©2006 COVERLY SPEEDBUMP.com DIST. BY CREATORS SYND. INC.

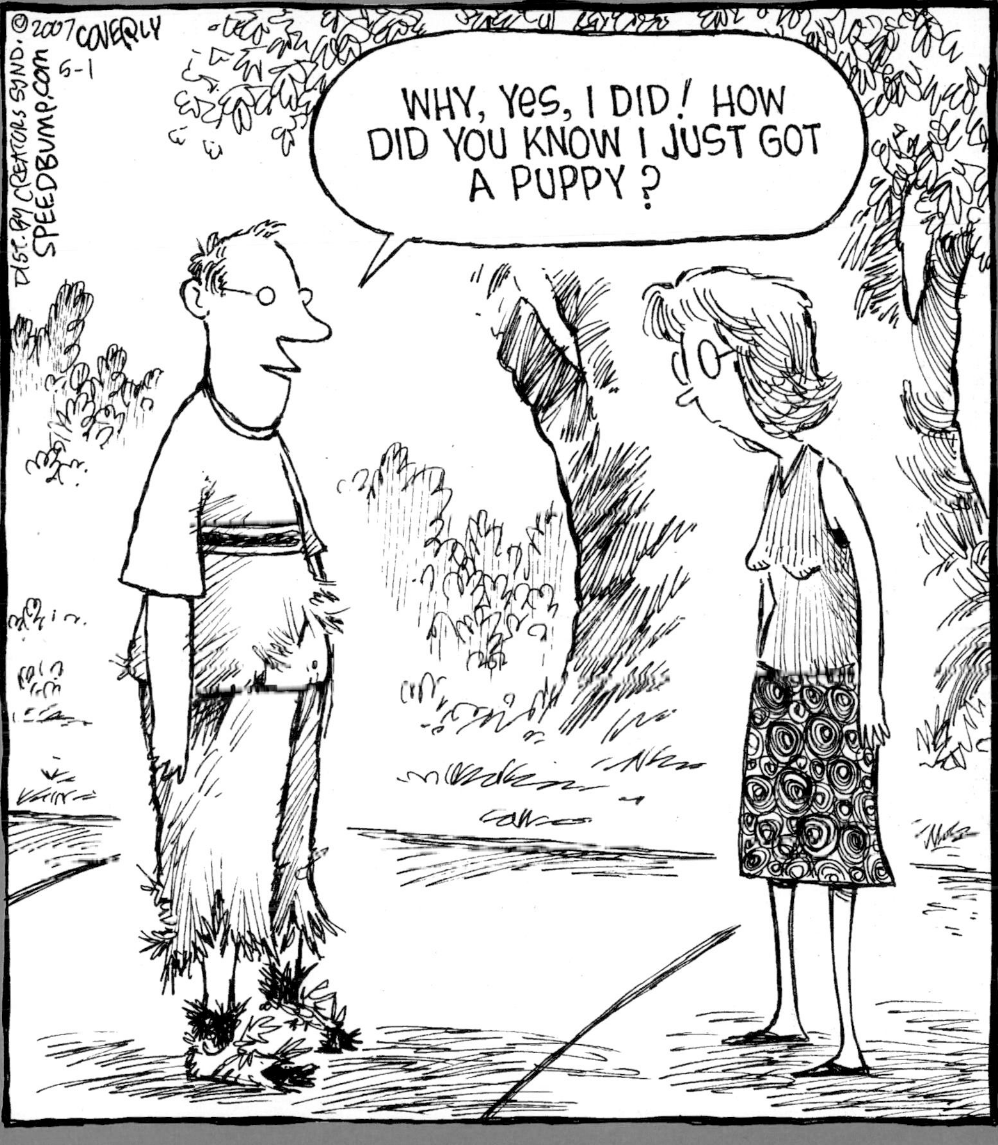
©2007 COVERLY
DIST. BY CREATORS SYND.
SPEEDBUMP.COM
5-1
WHY, YES, I DID! HOW DID YOU KNOW I JUST GOT A PUPPY?

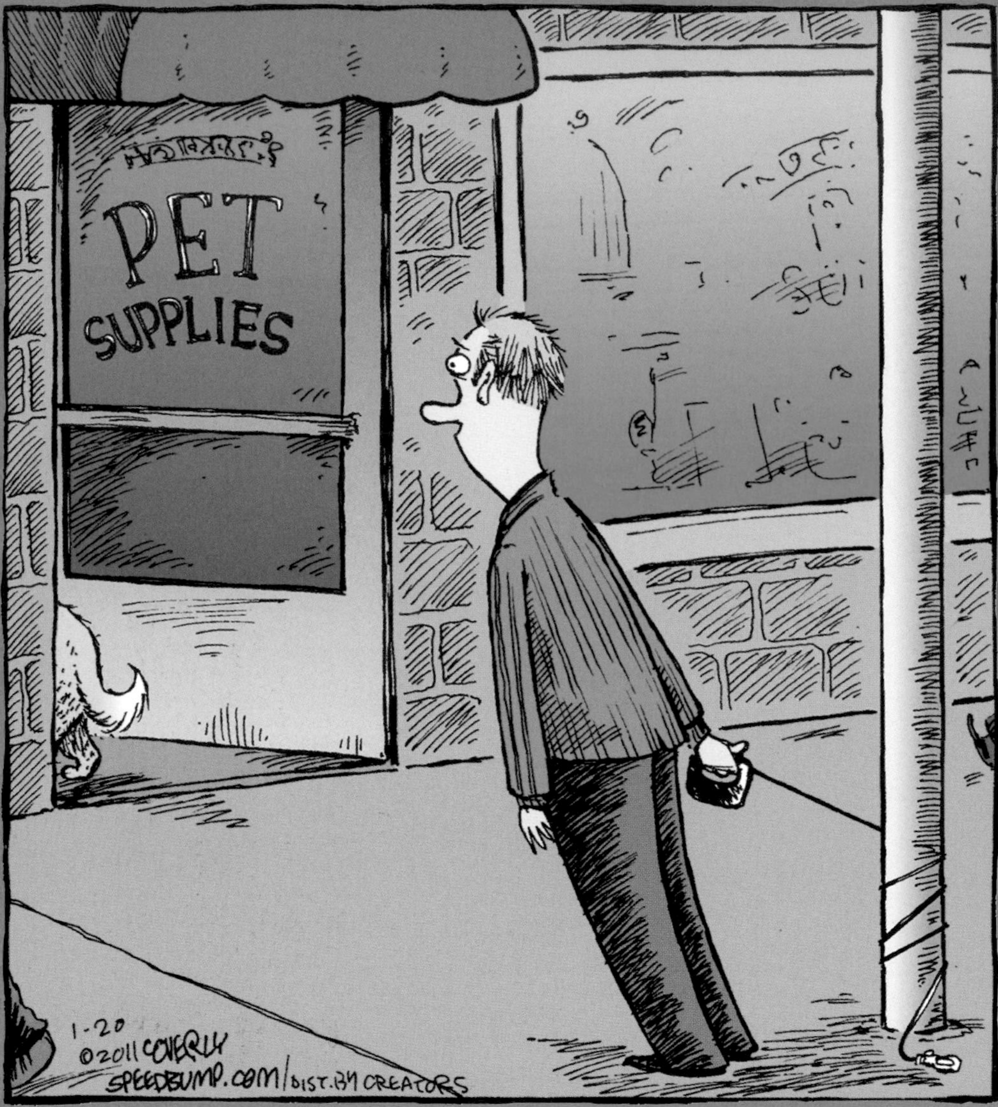
PET
SUPPLIES
1-20
©2011 COVERLY
SPEEDBUMP.COM/DIST. BY CREATORS

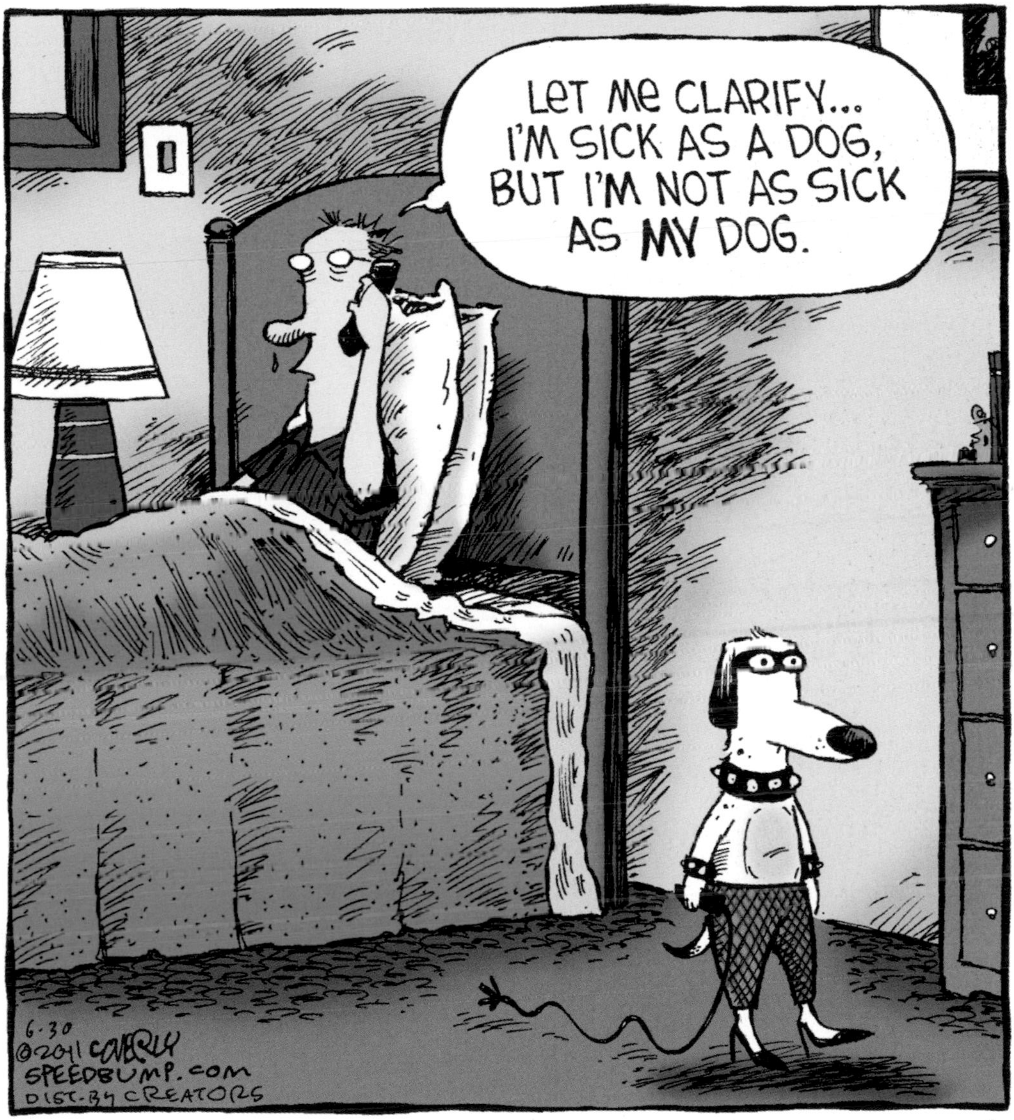
LET ME CLARIFY... I'M SICK AS A DOG, BUT I'M NOT AS SICK AS MY DOG.
6-30 ©2011 COVERLY SPEEDBUMP.COM DIST. BY CREATORS

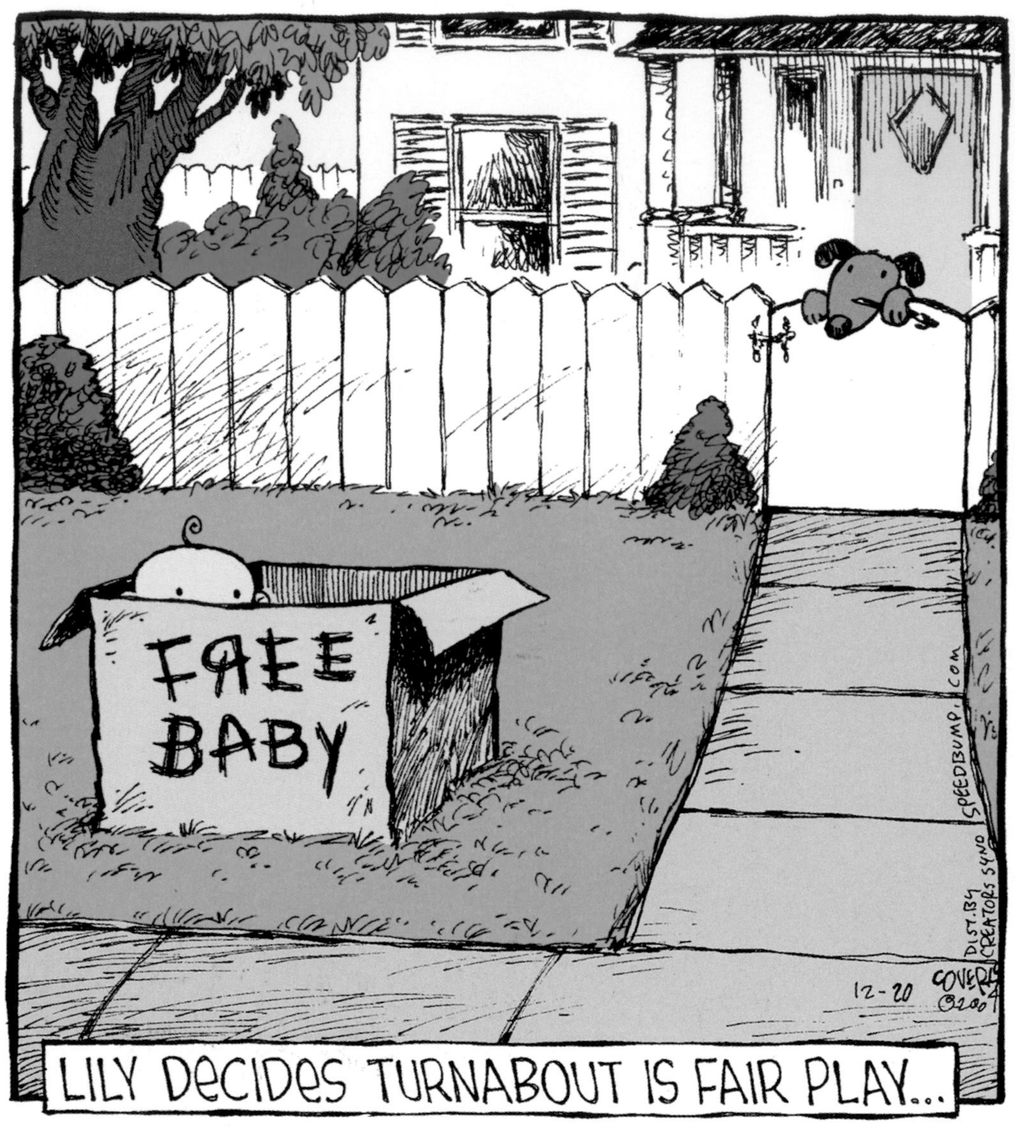
FREE
BABY
SPEEDBUMP.COM
DIST. BY CREATORS SYND
12-20

LILY DECIDES TURNABOUT IS FAIR PLAY...

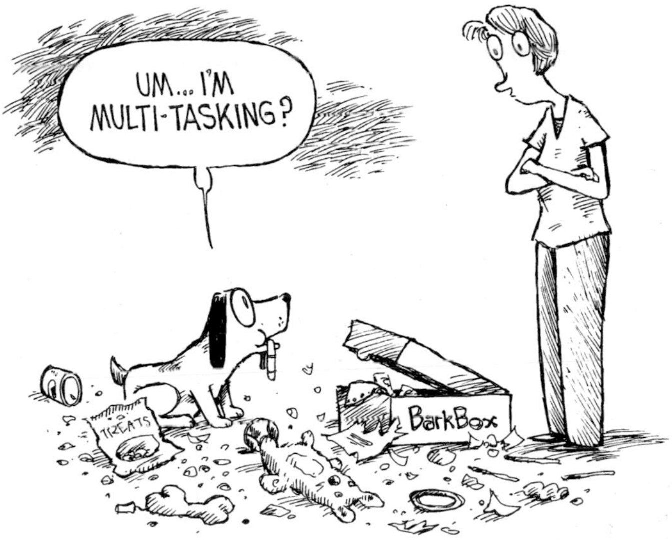
UM... I'M MULTI-TASKING?
TREATS
BarkBox

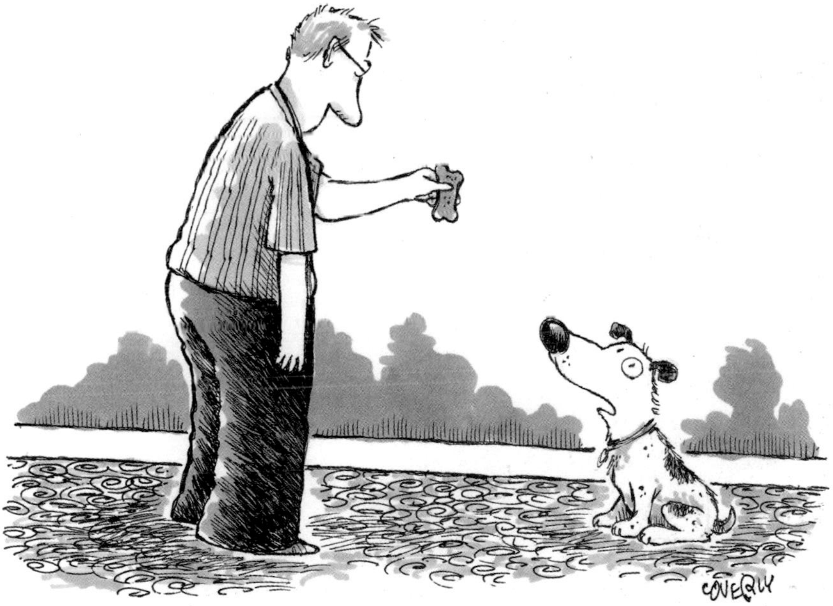

"Before I do the trick, I'd like half the treat up front."

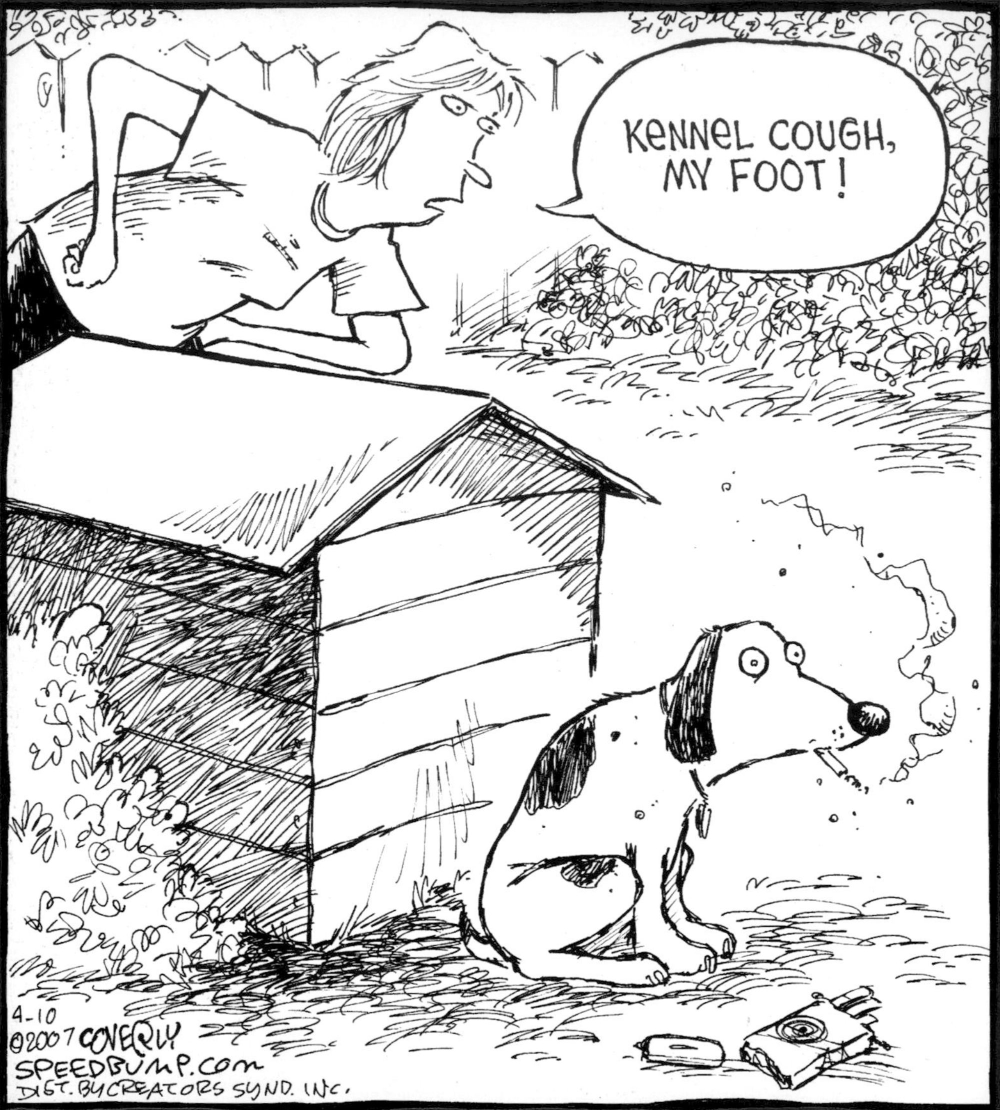
KENNEL COUGH, MY FOOT!
4-10
©2007 COVERLY
SPEEDBUMP.COM
DIST. BY CREATORS SYND. INC.

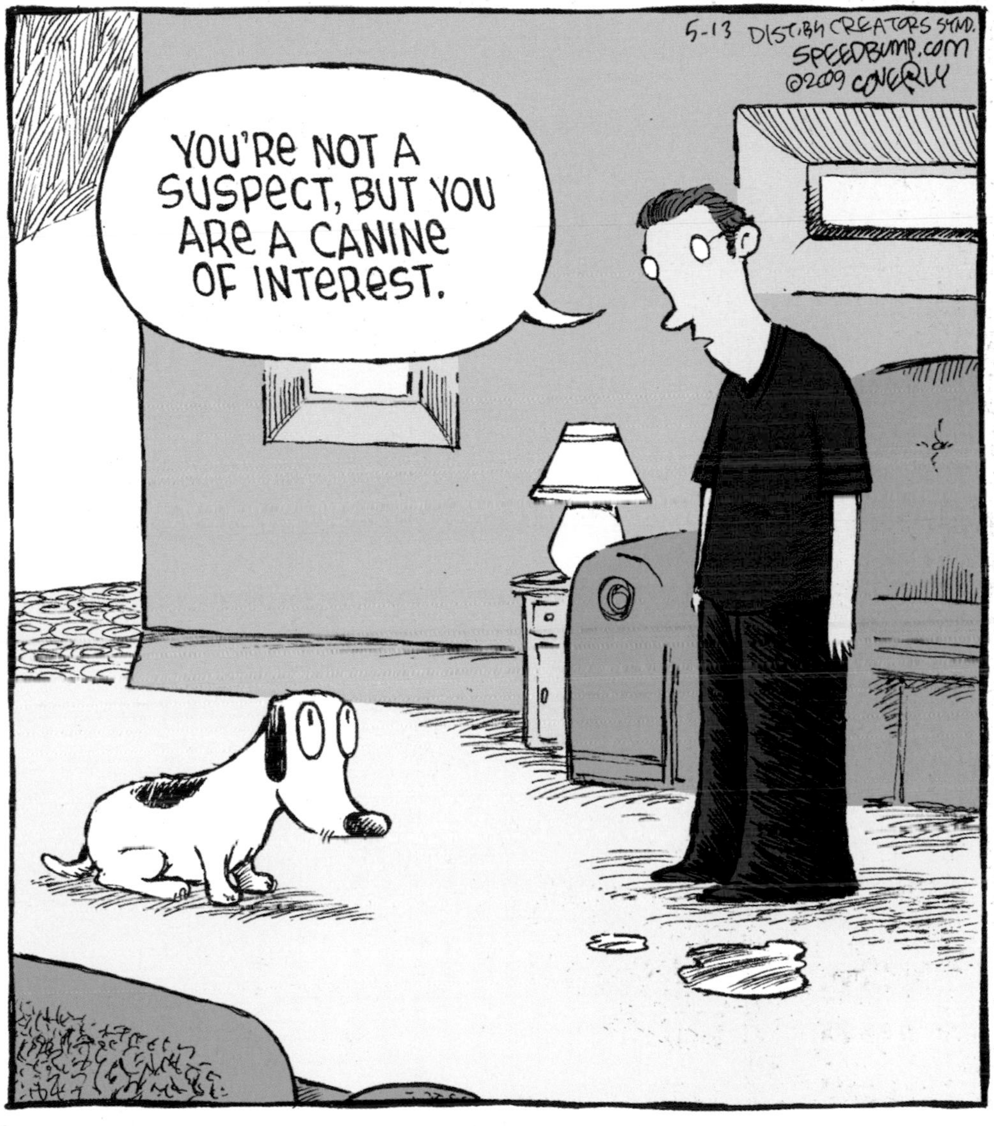
5-13 DISTIBY CREATORS SYND.
SPEEDBUMP.COM
©2009 COVERLY
YOU'RE NOT A SUSPECT, BUT YOU ARE A CANINE OF INTEREST.

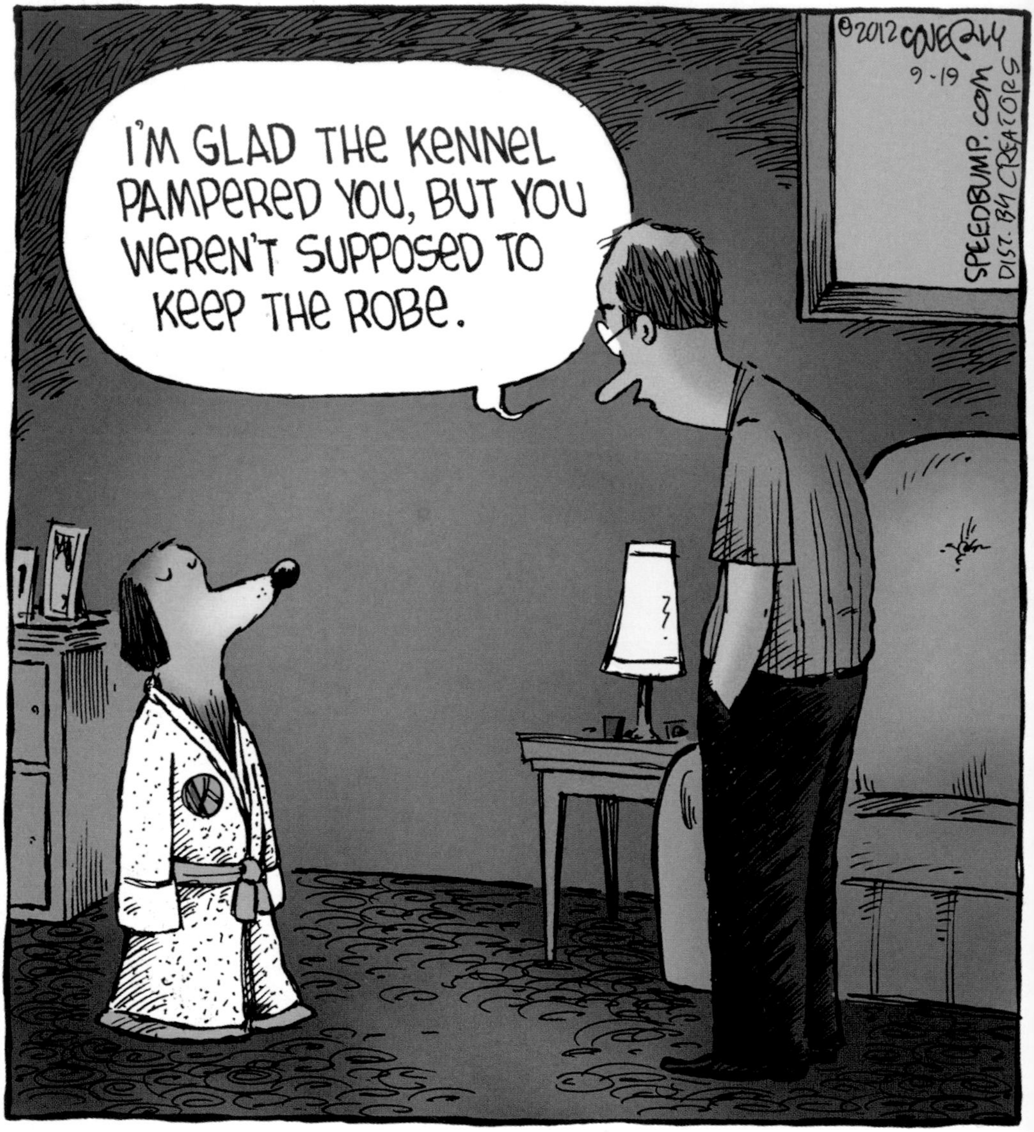
I'M GLAD THE KENNEL PAMPERED YOU, BUT YOU WEREN'T SUPPOSED TO KEEP THE ROBE.
©2012 COVERLY 9-19
SPEEDBUMP.COM
DIST. BY CREATORS

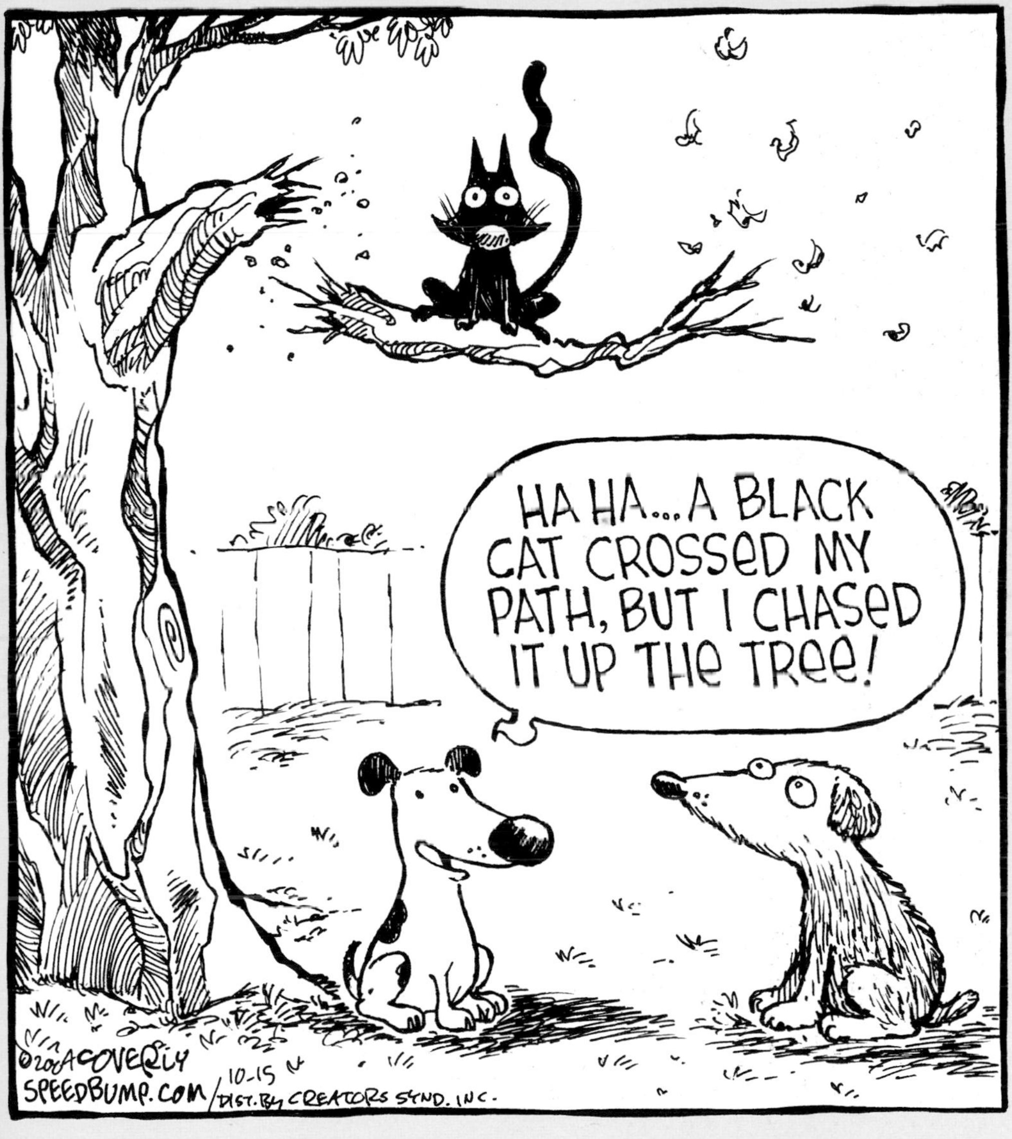
HA HA... A BLACK CAT CROSSED MY PATH, BUT I CHASED IT UP THE TREE!
©2008 COVERLY
SPEEDBUMP.COM
10-15
DIST. BY CREATORS SYND. INC.

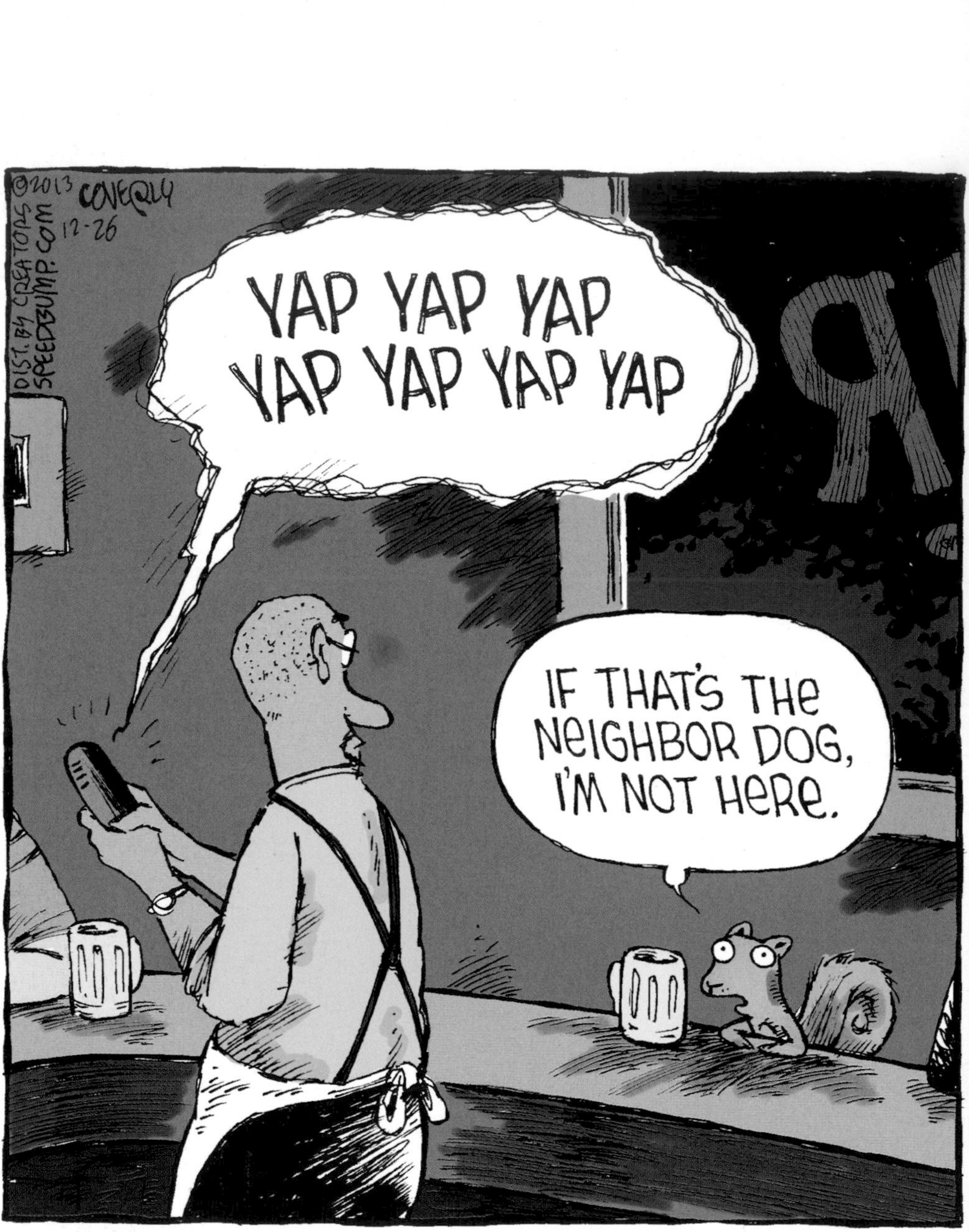
©2013 COVERLY
DIST. BY CREATORS
SPEEDBUMP.COM
12-26
YAP YAP YAP
YAP YAP YAP YAP
IF THAT'S THE
NEIGHBOR DOG,
I'M NOT HERE.

CHAPTER 6
ALL DOGS GO TO HEAVEN
(Even the Ones Who Behaved Badly)

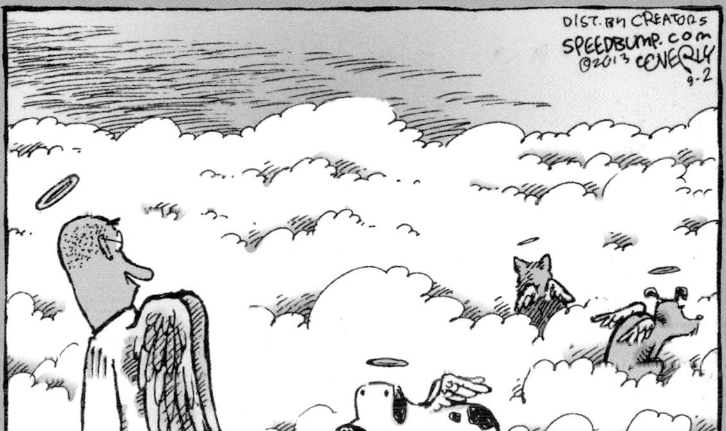
DIST. BY CREATORS
SPEEDBUMP.COM
©2013 COVERLY
9-2
DOG PARK
WHERE ANGELS FEAR TO TREAD

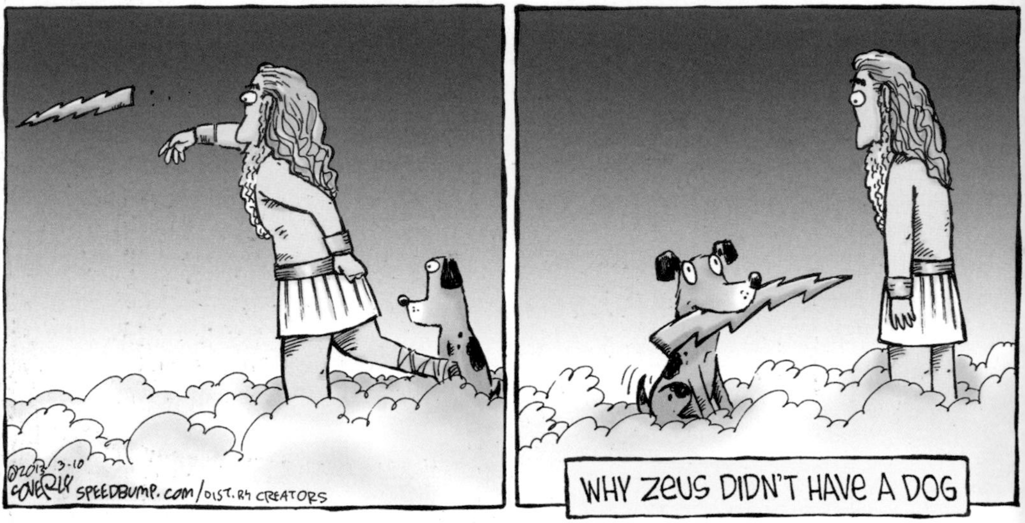
©2013 3-10
COVERLY SPEEDBUMP.COM/DIST. BY CREATORS
WHY ZEUS DIDN'T HAVE A DOG

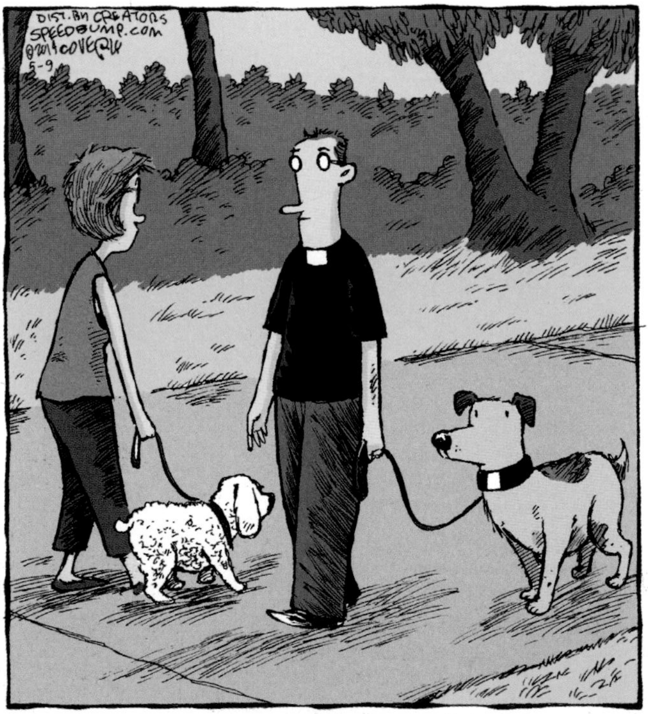
DIST. BY CREATORS
SPEEDBUMP.COM
5-9

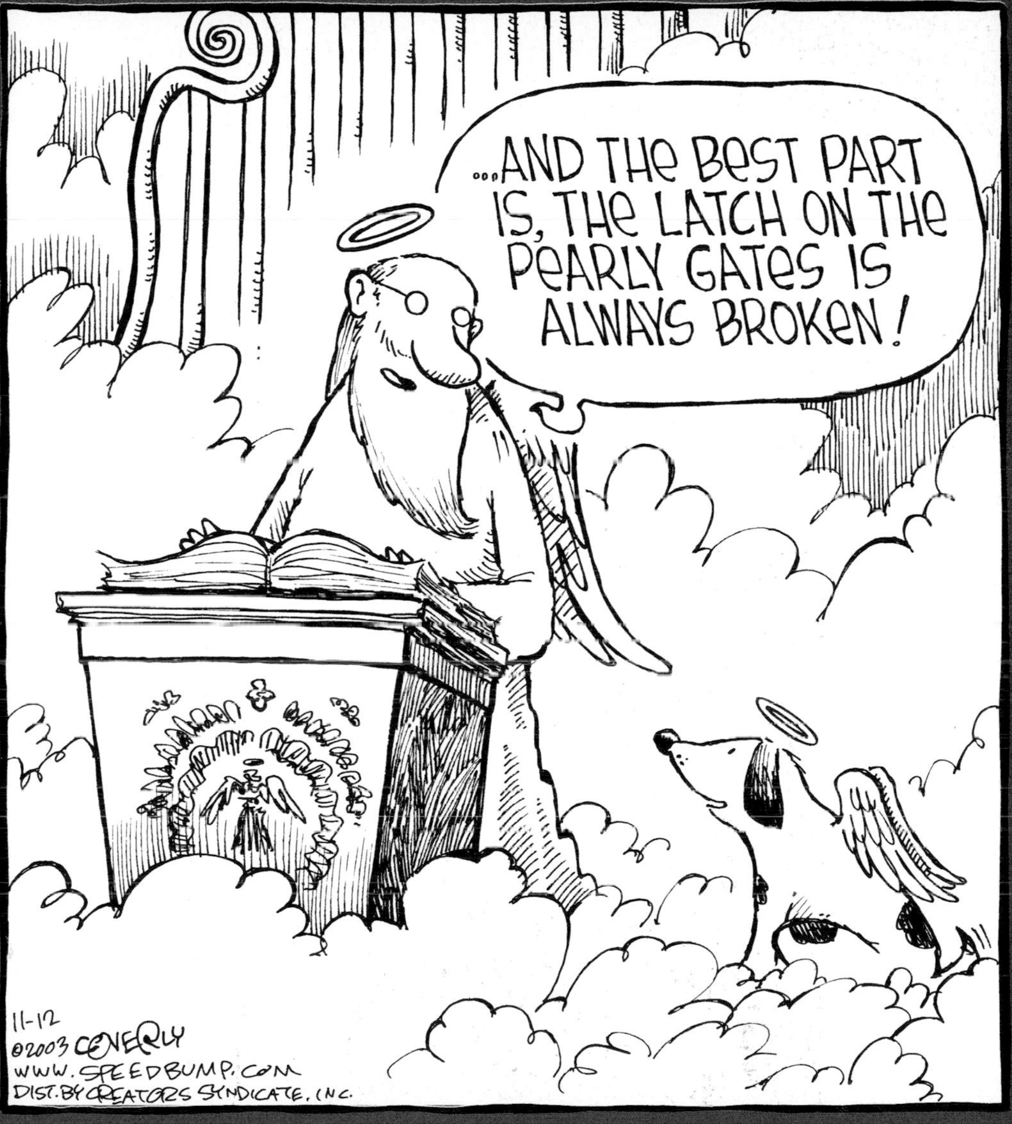
...AND THE BEST PART IS, THE LATCH ON THE PEARLY GATES IS ALWAYS BROKEN!
11-12
©2003 COVERLY
WWW.SPEEDBUMP.COM
DIST. BY CREATORS SYNDICATE, INC.

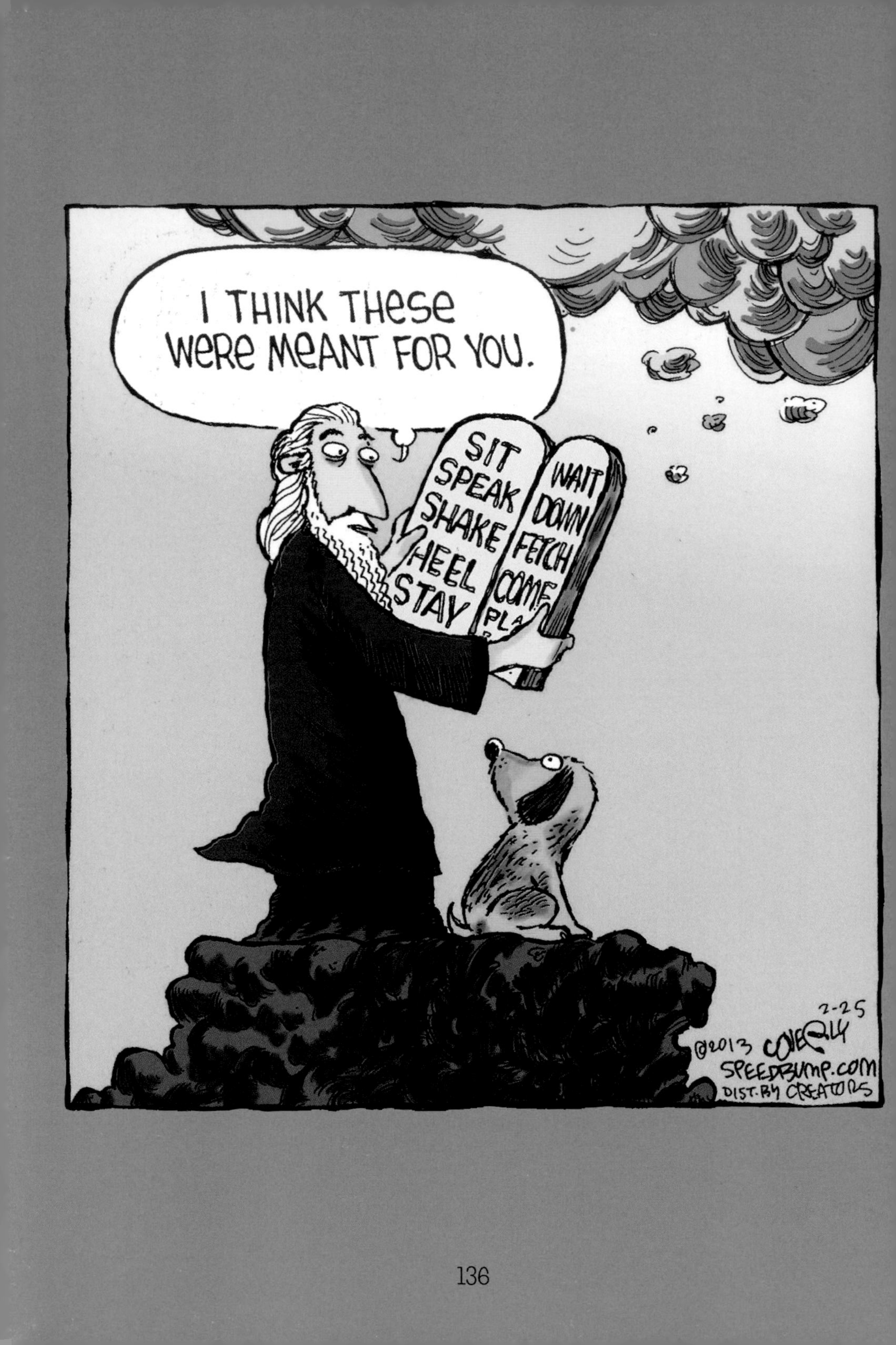
I THINK THESE WERE MEANT FOR YOU.
SIT
SPEAK
SHAKE
HEEL
STAY
WAIT
DOWN
FETCH
COME
2-25
©2013 COVERLY
SPEEDBUMP.COM
DIST. BY CREATORS

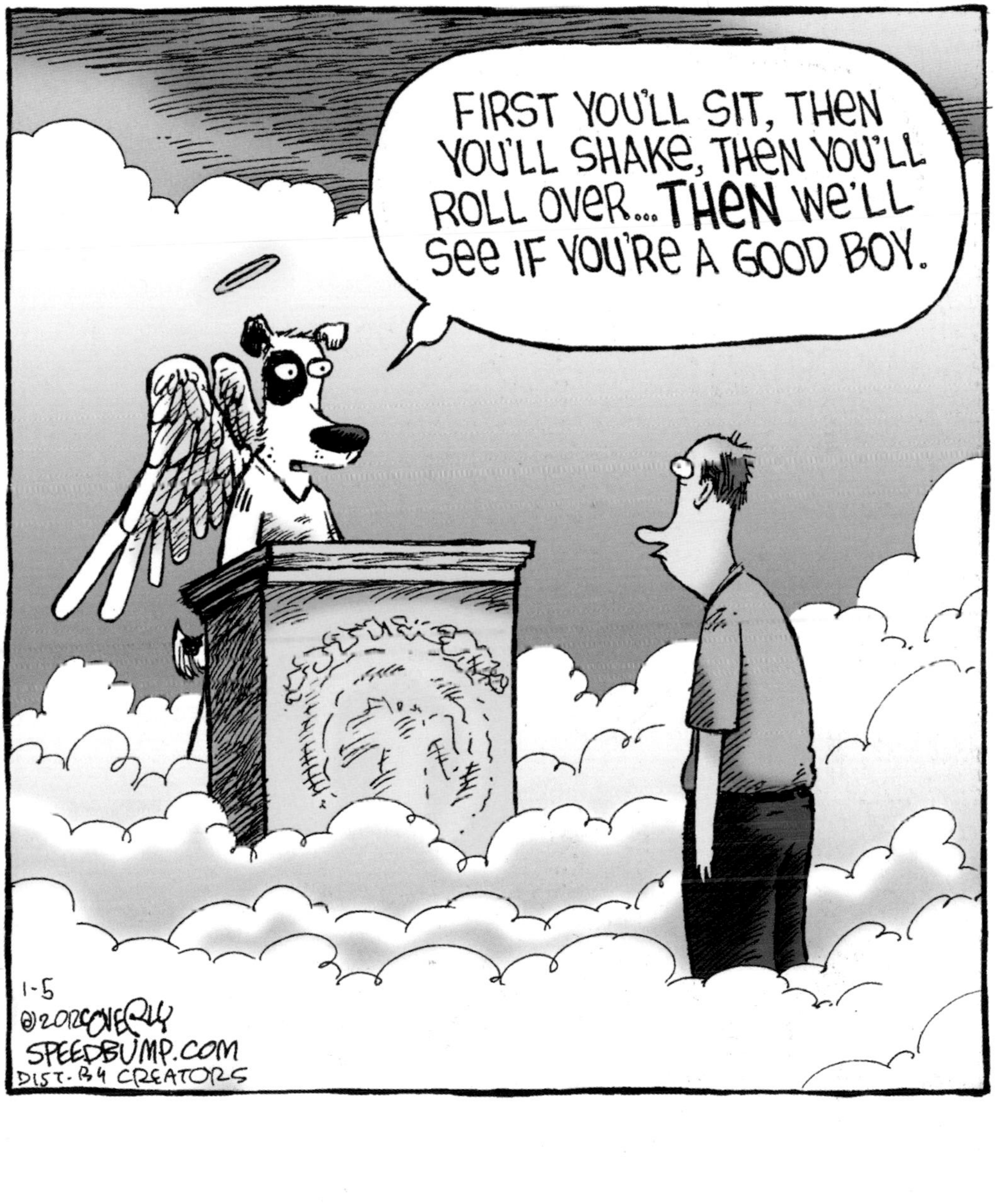
FIRST YOU'LL SIT, THEN YOU'LL SHAKE, THEN YOU'LL ROLL OVER...**THEN** WE'LL SEE IF YOU'RE A GOOD BOY.
1-5
©2012 COVERLY
SPEEDBUMP.COM
DIST. BY CREATORS

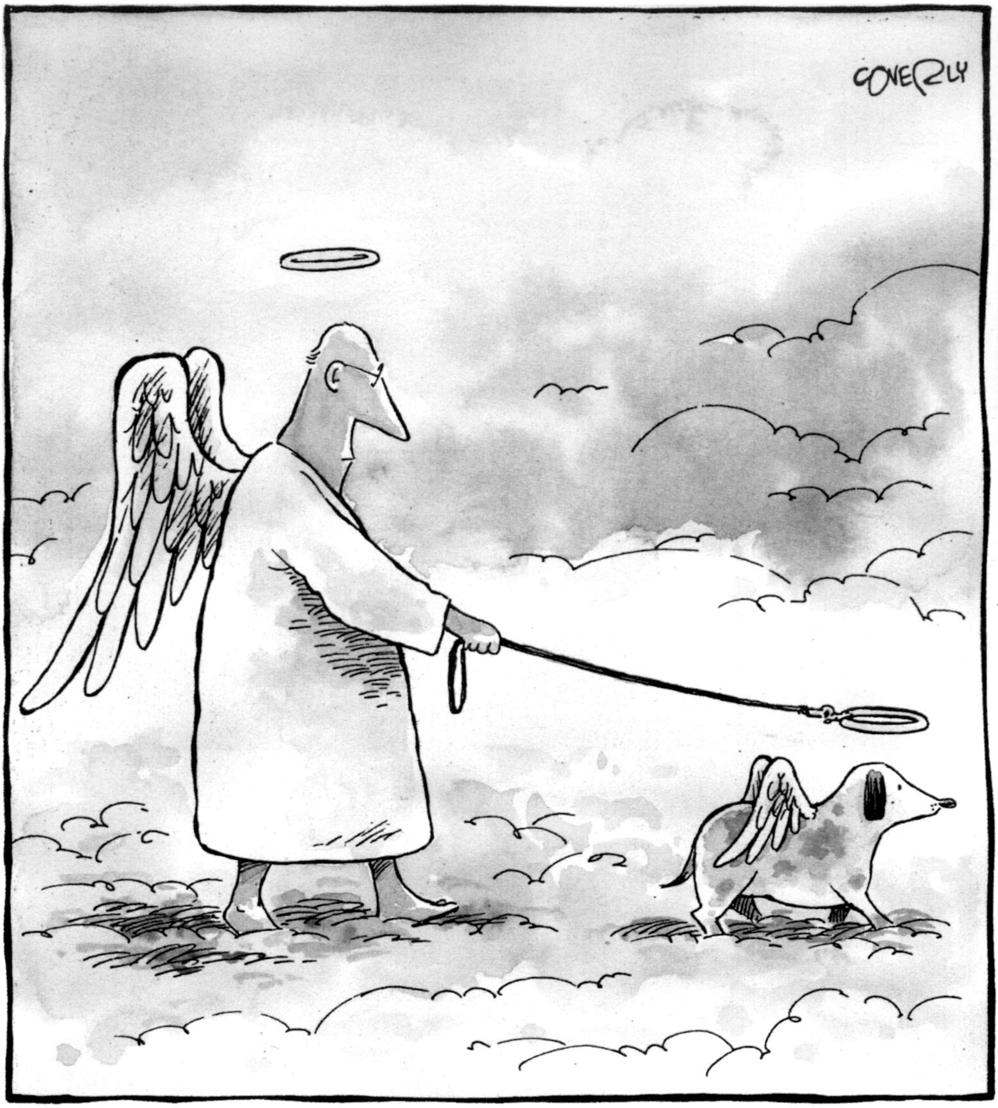
COVERLY

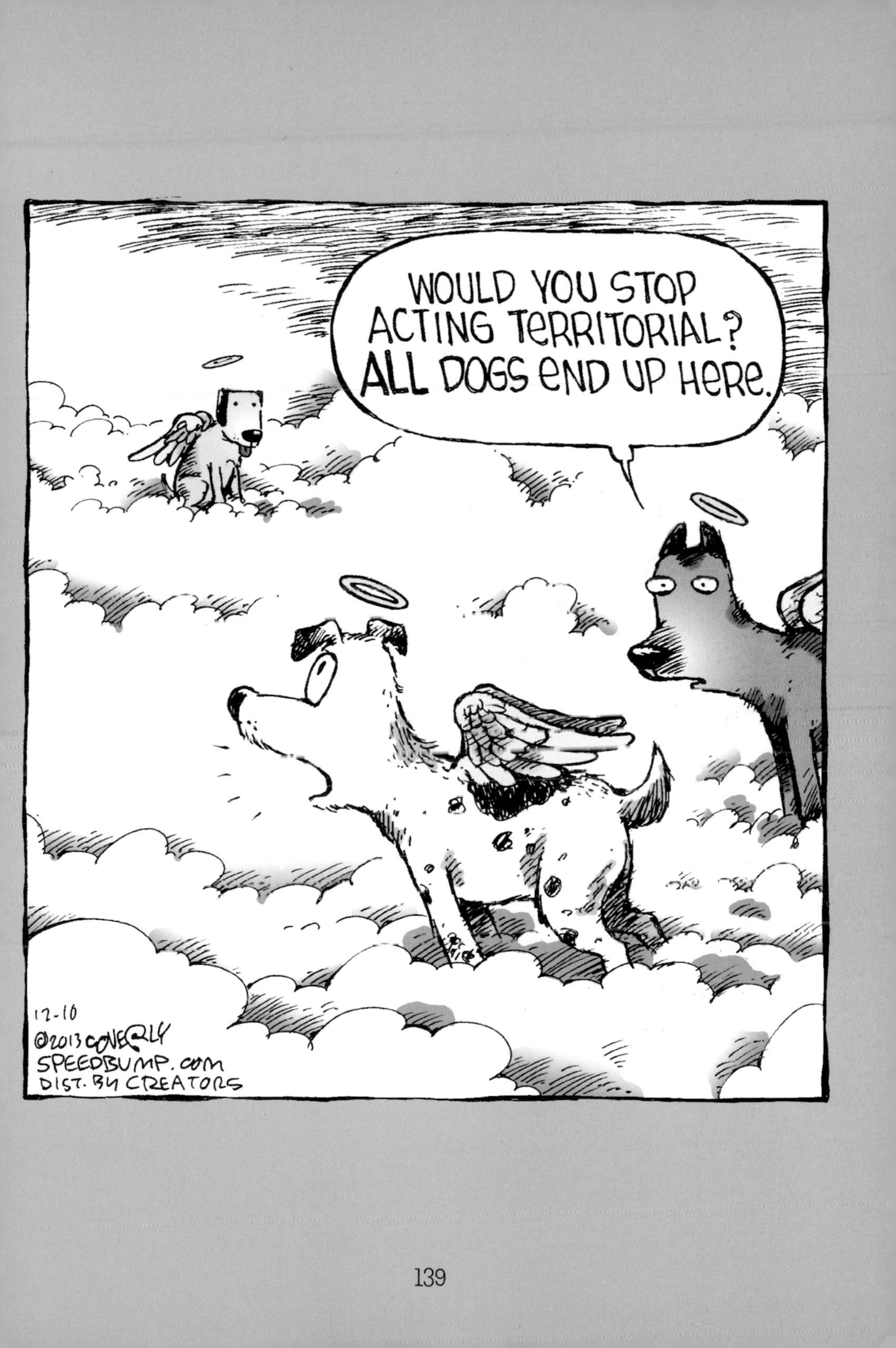
WOULD YOU STOP ACTING TERRITORIAL? ALL DOGS END UP HERE.
12-10
©2013 COVERLY
SPEEDBUMP.COM
DIST. BY CREATORS

YOU WON'T BELIEVE HOW THE DOCTOR TAKES YOUR TEMPERATURE!

KENZI

UGH, MORNINGS...
COFFEE

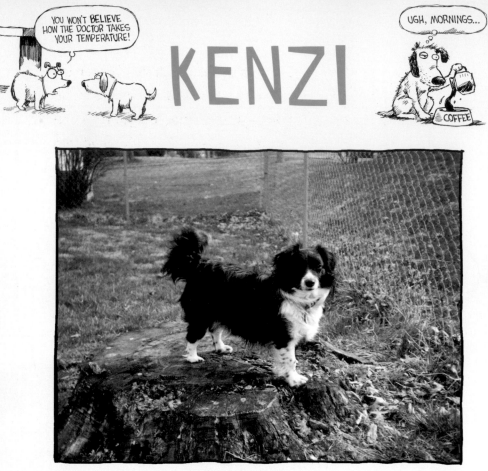

Kenzi, 1993.

In 1991, my wife, Chris, and I bought our first house in Bloomington, Indiana. Since we both grew up with dogs, we knew we were going to get one as soon as we got a house, so we picked a place with a large, fenced-in backyard. Within weeks, we were at the shelter, trying out dogs: some were too yappy, some weren't good with children, and some were just too distant. We were looking for a dog that, frankly, was looking for us. And, lucky for us, she found us.

A young dog had come into the shelter the day of our third

visit. She was small and black with white markings—she looked like a border collie cut off at the knees—and had been found in the woods with a collar but no tags. Since Bloomington is a university town, speculation was that she had been dropped into the woods by college students who had taken her as a puppy, realized puppies are a lot of work, and let her go (I mean, seriously, why would a STUDENT even WANT to get a . . . oh, wait, never mind).

When we arrived at the shelter, she ran to Chris first, then to me. She followed us around, and at one point, Chris even threw the dog up on her shoulder to see how easy-going she would be. The dog loved it (Full disclosure: Chris did the same thing to me when we first met.) We signed the adoption papers, but then we had to wait five days, by law, in case someone was actively looking for her. It was stupidly nerve-racking because, while we'd only just met her, she already felt like ours.

Five days later, we brought her home, and she slept on top of one of us for three days straight. And for the rest of her fourteen years, she never missed an opportunity to sleep on whoever happened to be available—Chris, me, our kids, other family, even unsuspecting visitors.

Eventually, she discovered that she could look out the front windows by resting on the back of the couch. It was at this point she got in touch with her Inner Yappy Dog, a trait we didn't know she had. But in fairness to her, she'd never had a family to protect before that.

She's lovingly remembered as the Best Dog Ever.

CHAPTER 7

FIVE AMAZING DOGS

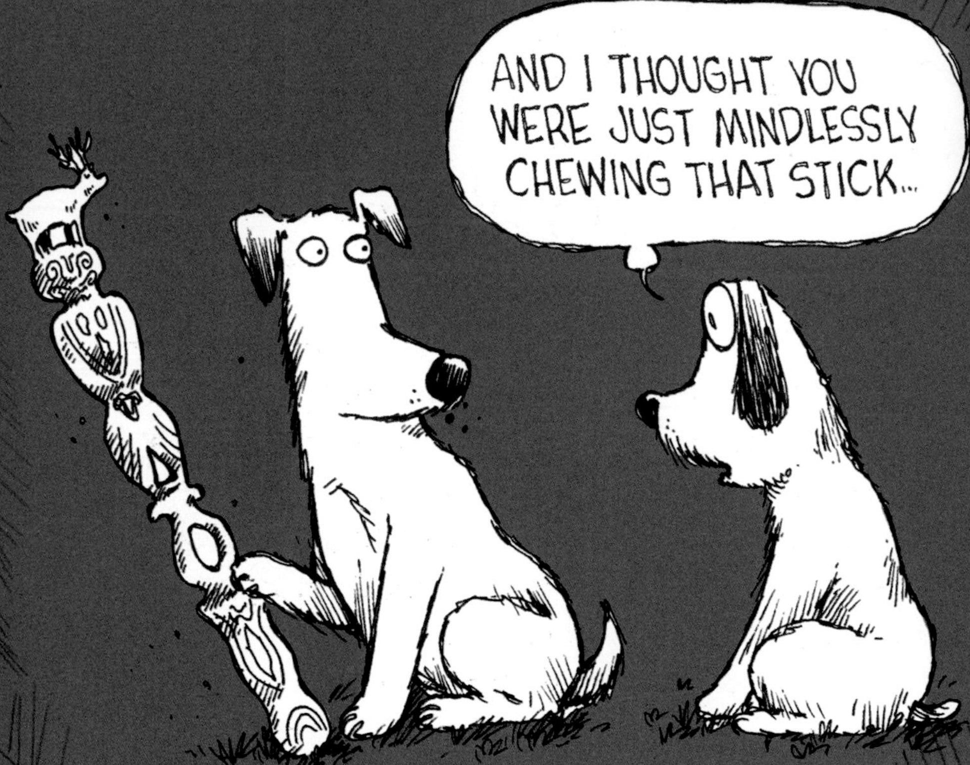

BARRY

I KNOW, BUT IT'S SO FUN TO DRAW ⇒

Maybe you've seen those cartoons of Saint Bernards that run around the Swiss Alps saving people stuck in the snow? You know, those big dogs with the little barrels full of first aid supplies attached to the front of their collars? Well, those cartoon dogs are based on a real dog named Barry. He was raised and trained by Swiss monks to help people lost in the Alps. Apparently, as the story goes (It's an old story), Barry was able to save about forty people during his career as a rescue dog, including one child whom he licked to keep warm and then, with the monks unable to reach them through the snow, carried on his back all the way to the monastery. In 1812, when Barry finally got too old to rescue people, he retired to live with the monks.

As for that barrel around the necks of Saint Bernards? Total fiction, made up by an English painter in the 1820s!

CHIPS

BEST DOG
COLLAR
EVER

Chips, a German shepherd/collie/husky mix, was the most decorated dog of the Second World War, given eight Battle Stars, a Theater Ribbon with an Arrowhead, a Silver Star, and a Purple Heart. (Sadly, he had to give back the Silver Star and the Purple Heart; apparently, those are meant only for people.) He was in the K9 unit in Sicily in 1943 when he and his handler became trapped on a beach by enemy fire. Chips dashed toward the gunmen, lucky not to be hit by flying bullets, and attacked them. His bravery inspired the soldiers—not to mention distracted the enemy—and led to the eventual surrender of the gunmen. Chips lived through the war and returned to his family when the war was over in 1945.

LAIKA

← SPACE SUIT: WAY COOLER THAN A DOGGIE SWEATER!

In 1957, during the cold war between the United States and the Soviet Union, the two countries were also engaged in a "race into space." The Soviets had developed a satellite called Sputnik 2, but they weren't sure a human could survive inside the capsule during a launch into space. So they decided to send a dog into space first as an experiment. Laika, a terrier–husky stray from the streets of Moscow, was trained and passed all the necessary tests, and on November 3 of that year, she was strapped into Sputnik 2 and shot into space. Sadly, she died during the flight, but her sacrifice taught the Soviet scientists a lot about the impact of these flights on a living being. And since *Laika* is Russian for "barker," you can be sure that heroic dog was making a lot of noise as she looked out that satellite window at a shrinking planet Earth.

ROBOT

NOT ACTUALLY DRAWN BY ROBOT...

Robot, a terrier, was responsible for one of the greatest historical discoveries of all time. He and four boys were exploring the woods in Dordogne, France, one day in 1940, looking for a tunnel that, legend had it, ran under the Vezere River and connected the Manor of Lascaux to the Castle of Montignac. Supposedly, there was treasure buried there. During their search, Robot ran ahead to a deep depression in the ground and began digging around the edge. The boys saw it led to a large, deep hole, so (being boys) they climbed down into it and discovered a cave. And not just any cave, but what is now known as the Cave of Lascaux, filled with brilliantly colored prehistoric paintings of large animals. Thanks to a curious little terrier with a futuristic name, we now have access to amazing historical works of art painted some 17,300 years ago.

SMOKY

← NOT EVEN AS BIG AS A HUMAN HEAD!

Smoky was a Yorkshire terrier found in an abandoned foxhole by a U.S. soldier in a New Guinea jungle during the Second World War. For the last two years of the war, she was cared for by Corporal William Wynne, who even took her on combat flights over the Pacific. Since there were no food rations given to dogs, she shared the food of the soldiers and slept in Wynne's tent. During the fighting, she stayed in a soldier's pack that also held his machine gun, and went on twelve combat missions, earning eight Battle Stars. Her ears and intuition allowed her to warn the soldiers of incoming shells; Wynne called her his "angel from a foxhole." After the war, she stayed in the service to visit injured soldiers in stateside hospitals, and she is now credited with being the country's first therapy dog.

CHAPTER 8

DOGS ARE A PERSON'S BEST FRIEND...

And Sometimes Even Another Dog's Best Friend

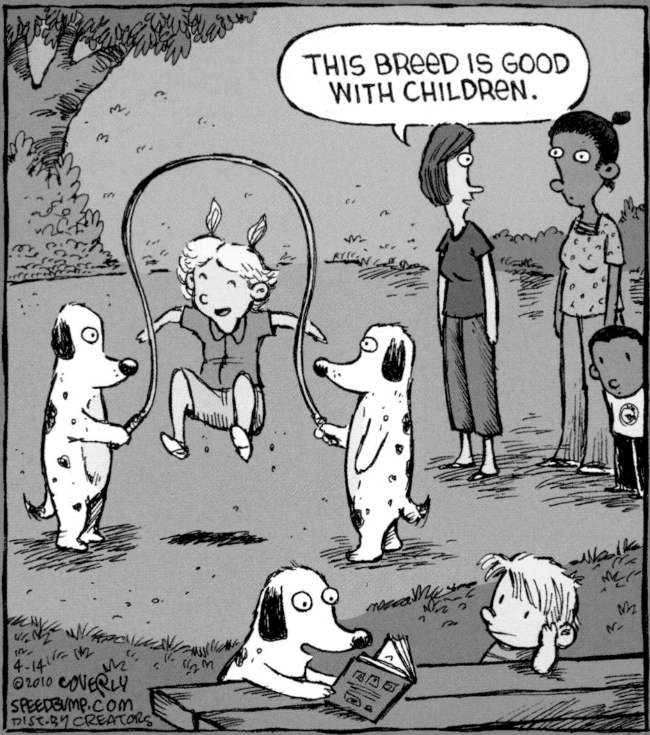
THIS BREED IS GOOD WITH CHILDREN.
4-14 ©2010 COVERLY
SPEEDBUMP.COM
DIST. BY CREATORS

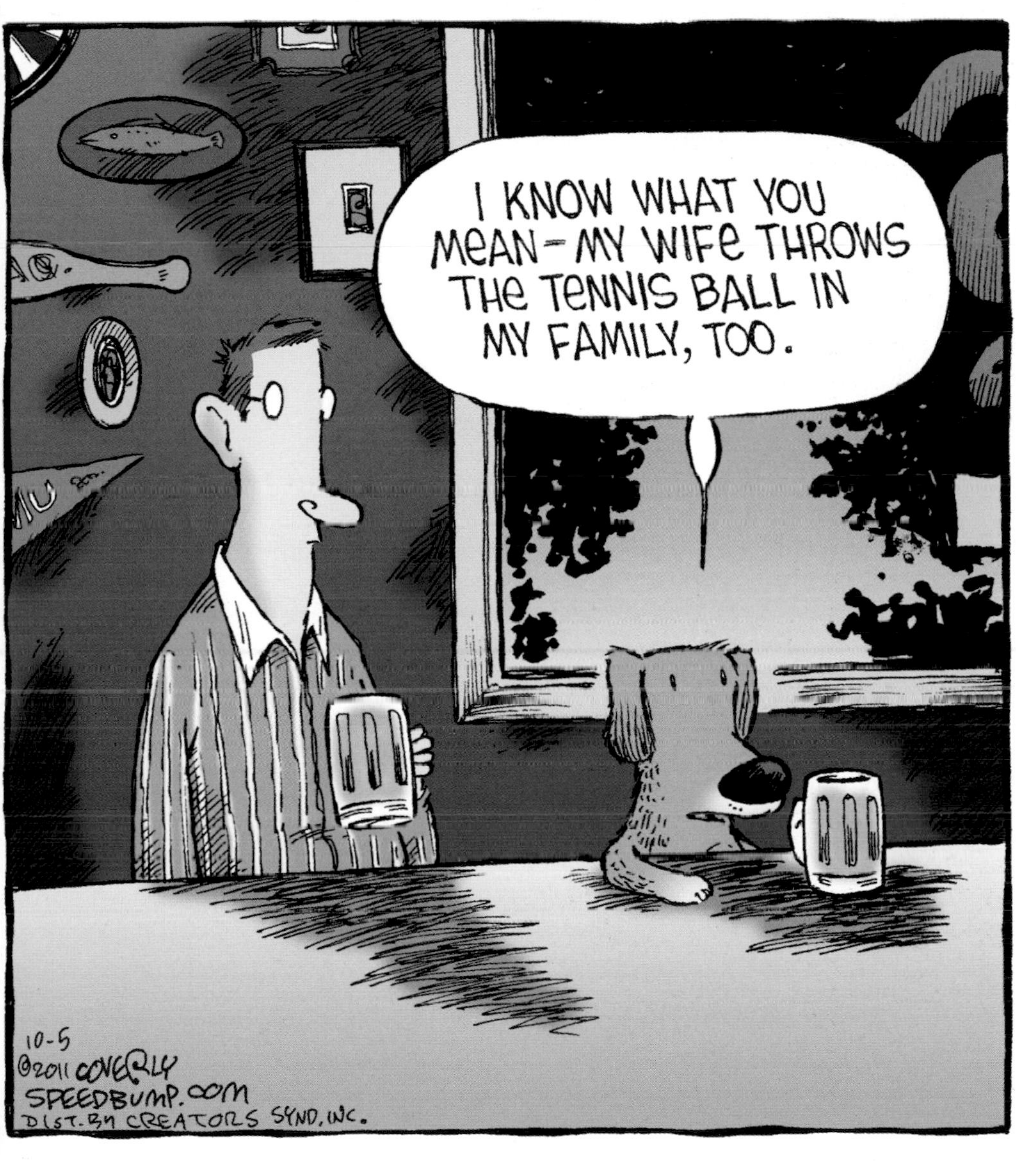
I KNOW WHAT YOU MEAN—MY WIFE THROWS THE TENNIS BALL IN MY FAMILY, TOO.
10-5
©2011 COVERLY
SPEEDBUMP.COM
DIST. BY CREATORS SYND, INC.

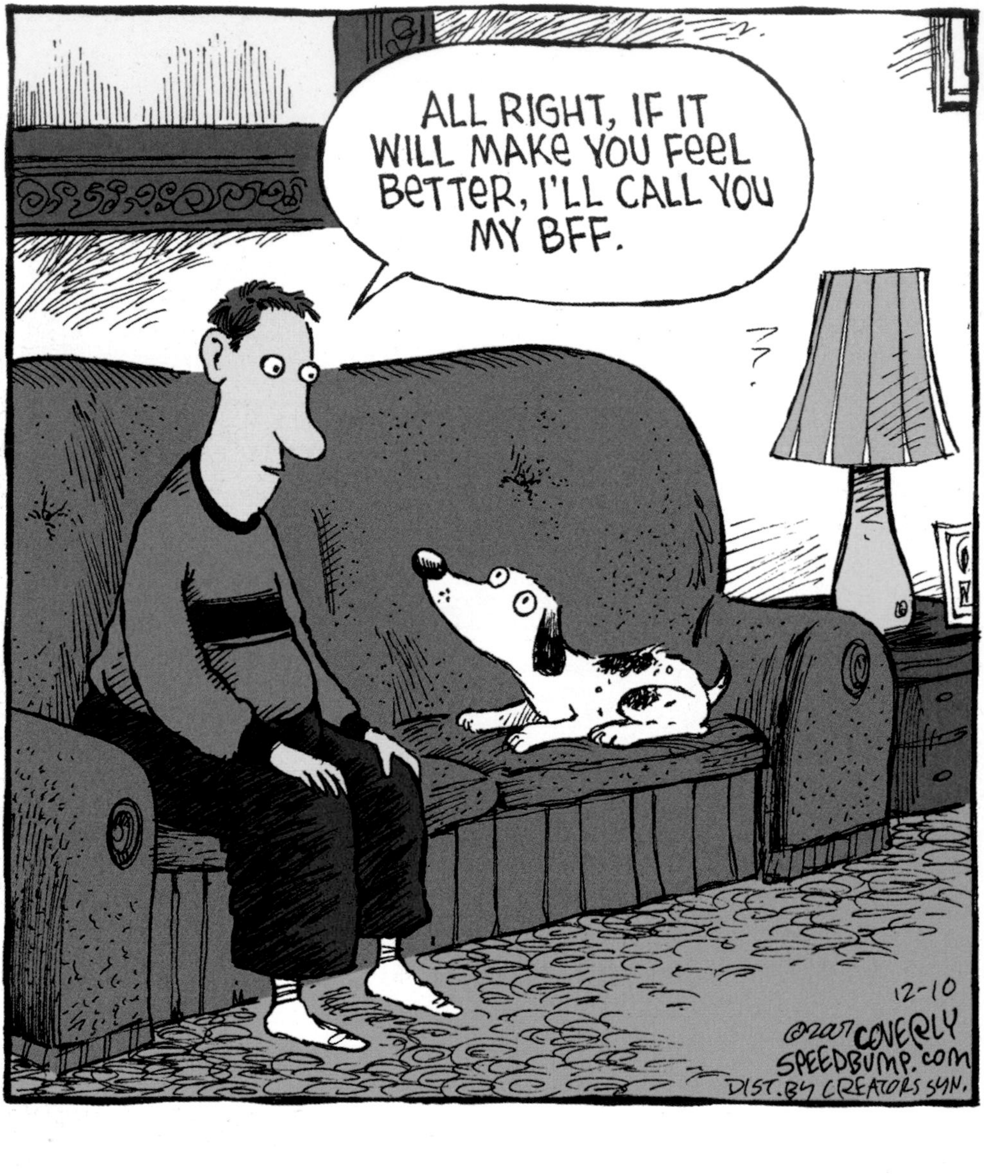
ALL RIGHT, IF IT WILL MAKE YOU FEEL BETTER, I'LL CALL YOU MY BFF.
12-10
©2007 COVERLY
SPEEDBUMP.COM
DIST. BY CREATORS SYN.

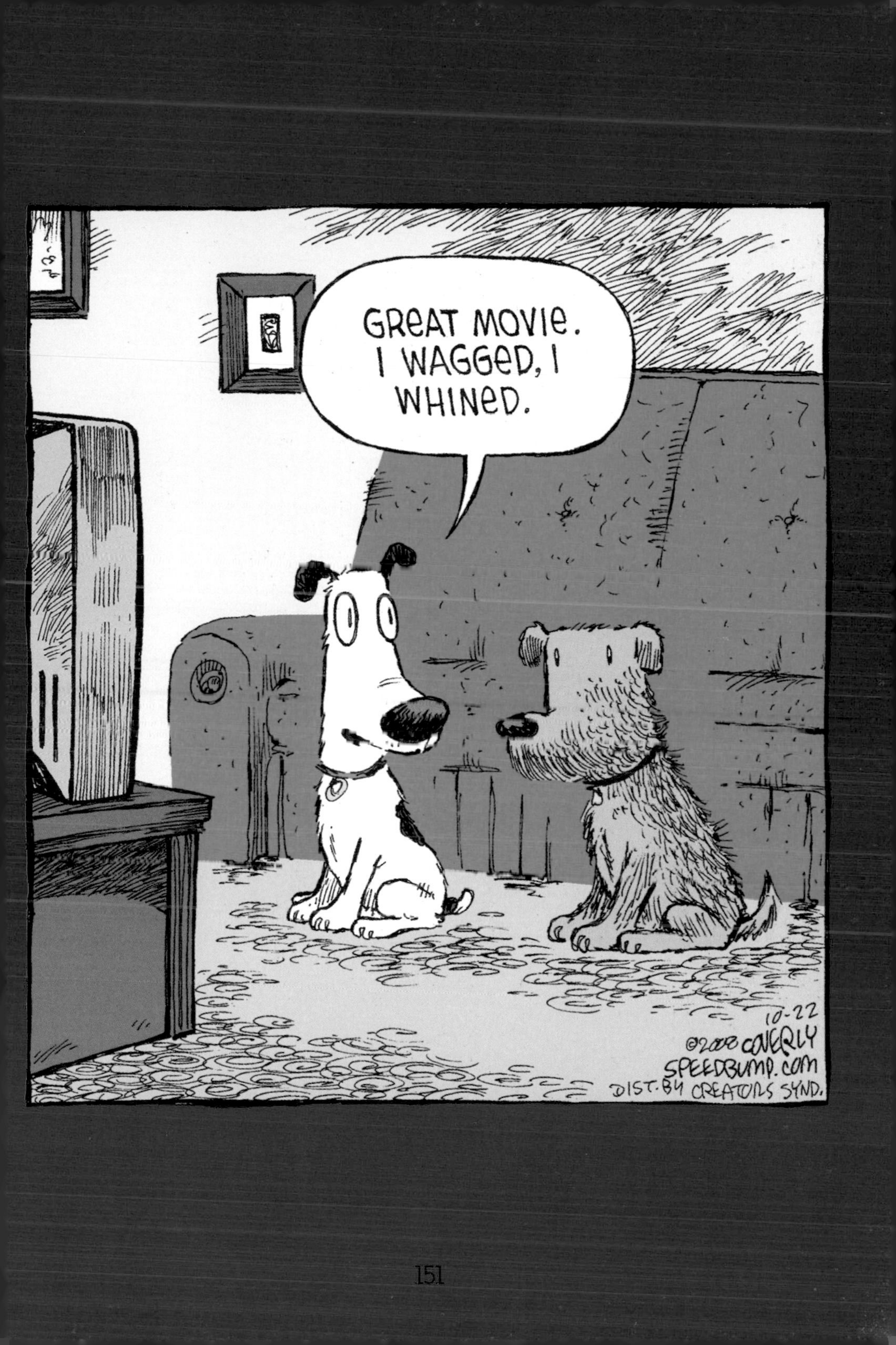
GREAT MOVIE. I WAGGED, I WHINED.
10-22
©2008 COVERLY
SPEEDBUMP.COM
DIST. BY CREATORS SYND.

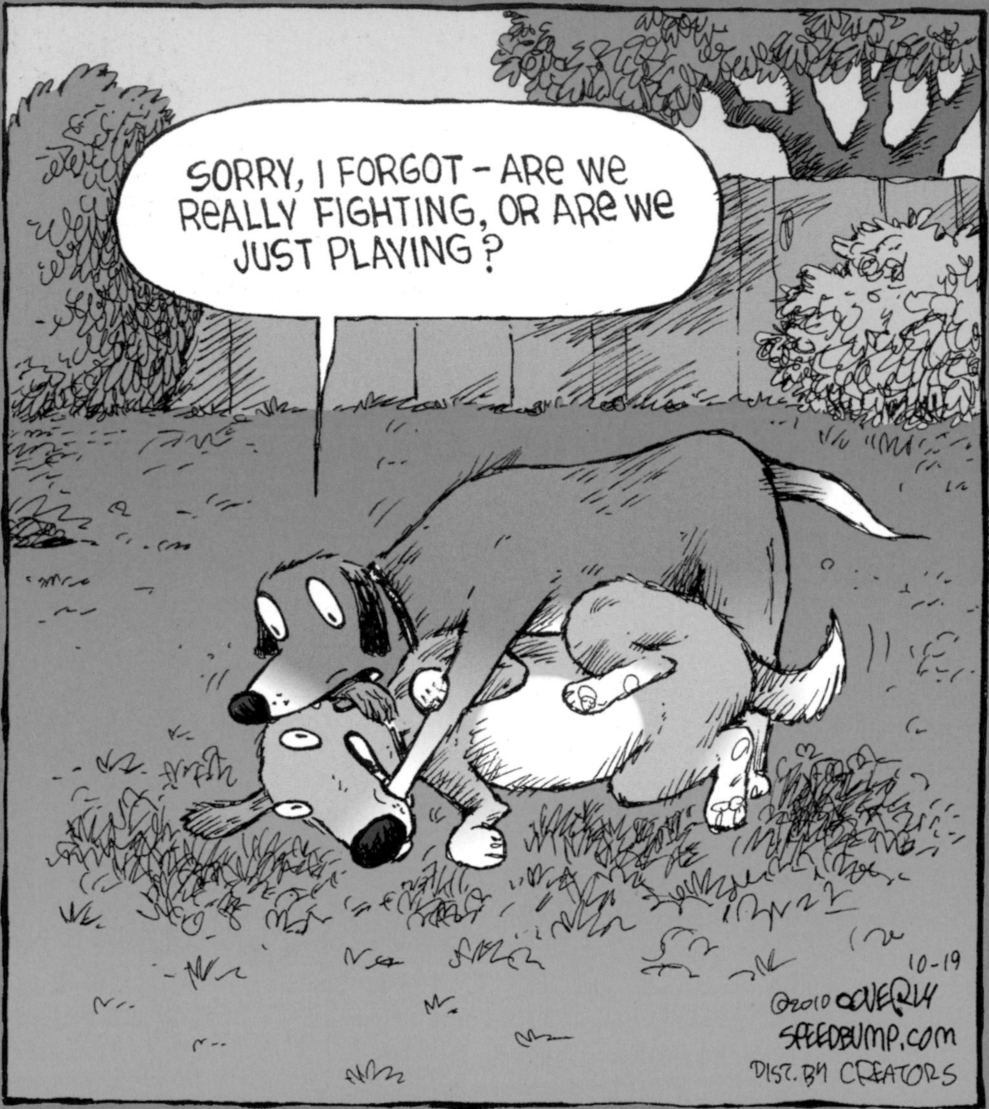
SORRY, I FORGOT - ARE WE REALLY FIGHTING, OR ARE WE JUST PLAYING?
10-19
©2010 COVERLY
SPEEDBUMP.COM
DIST. BY CREATORS

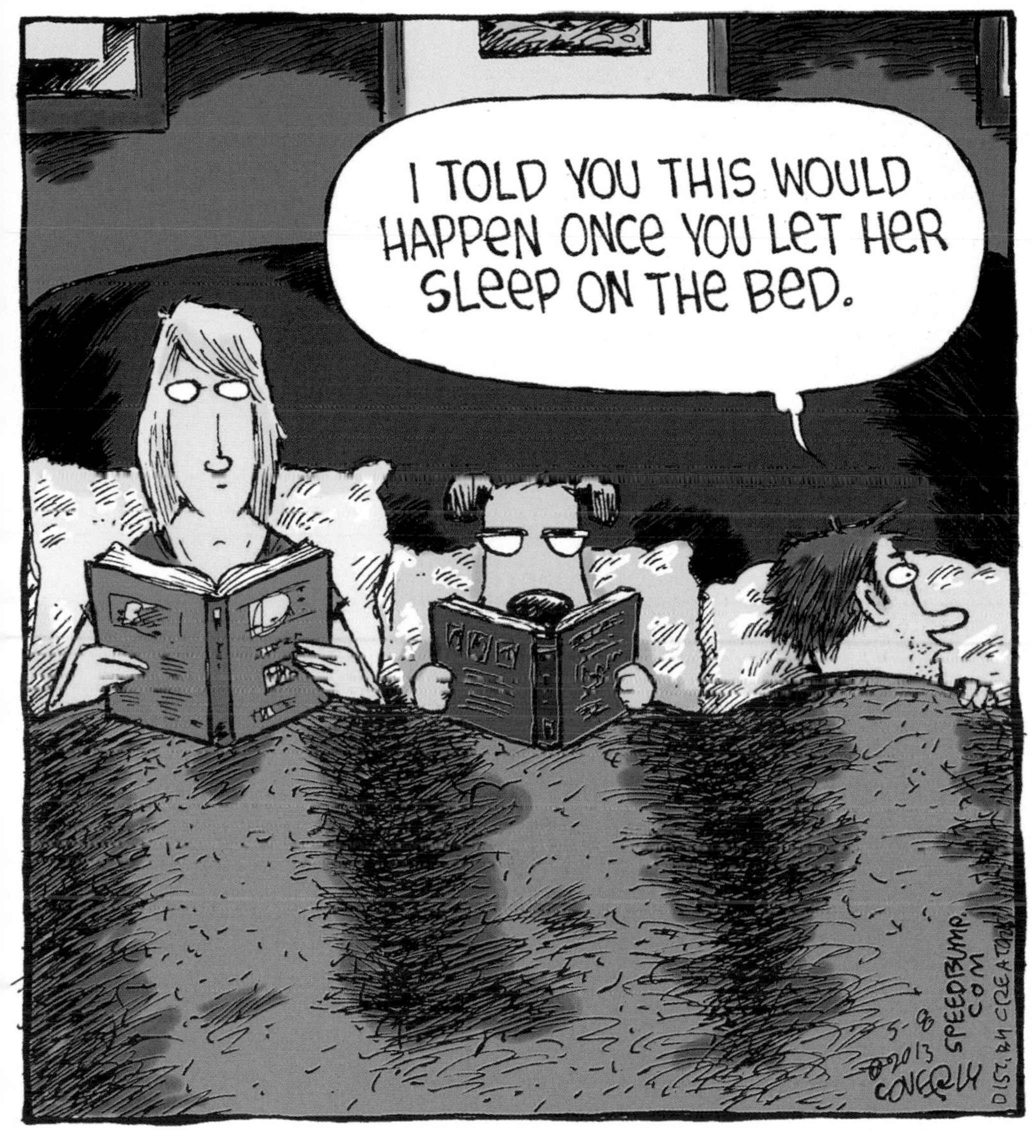
I TOLD YOU THIS WOULD HAPPEN ONCE YOU LET HER SLEEP ON THE BED.
©2013 COVERLY
SPEEDBUMP.COM
DIST. BY CREATORS

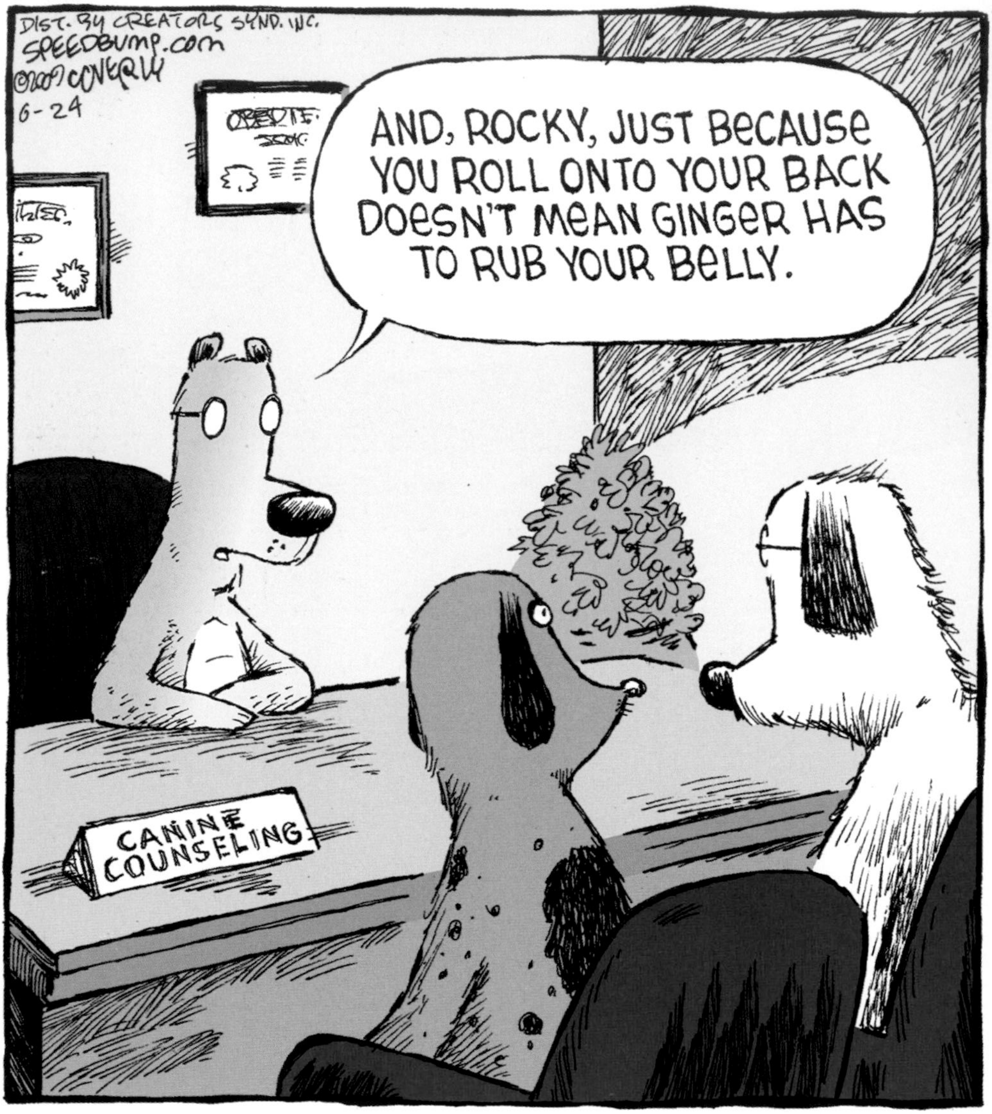
DIST. BY CREATORS SYND. INC.
SPEEDBUMP.COM
6-24
AND, ROCKY, JUST BECAUSE YOU ROLL ONTO YOUR BACK DOESN'T MEAN GINGER HAS TO RUB YOUR BELLY.
CANINE COUNSELING

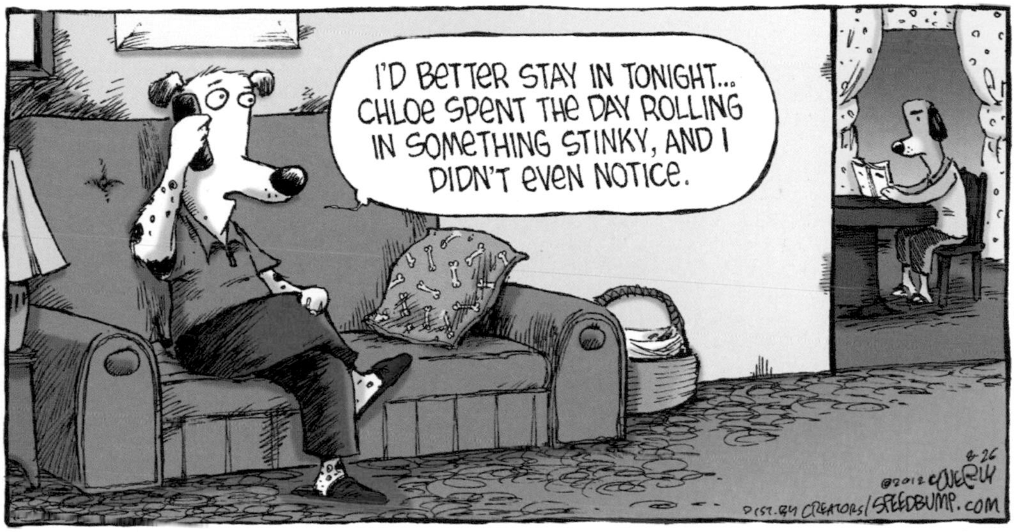
I'D BETTER STAY IN TONIGHT... CHLOE SPENT THE DAY ROLLING IN SOMETHING STINKY, AND I DIDN'T EVEN NOTICE.

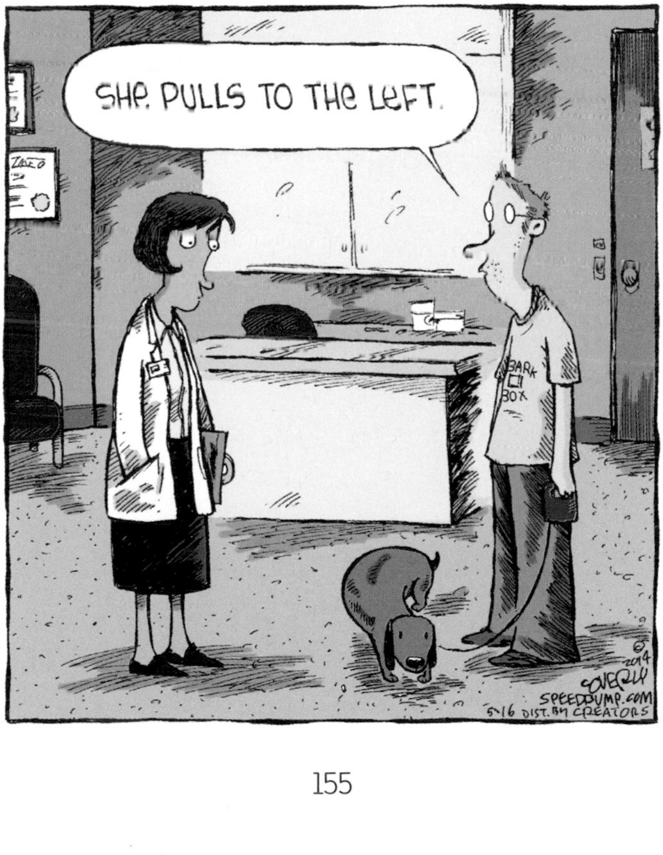
SHE PULLS TO THE LEFT.

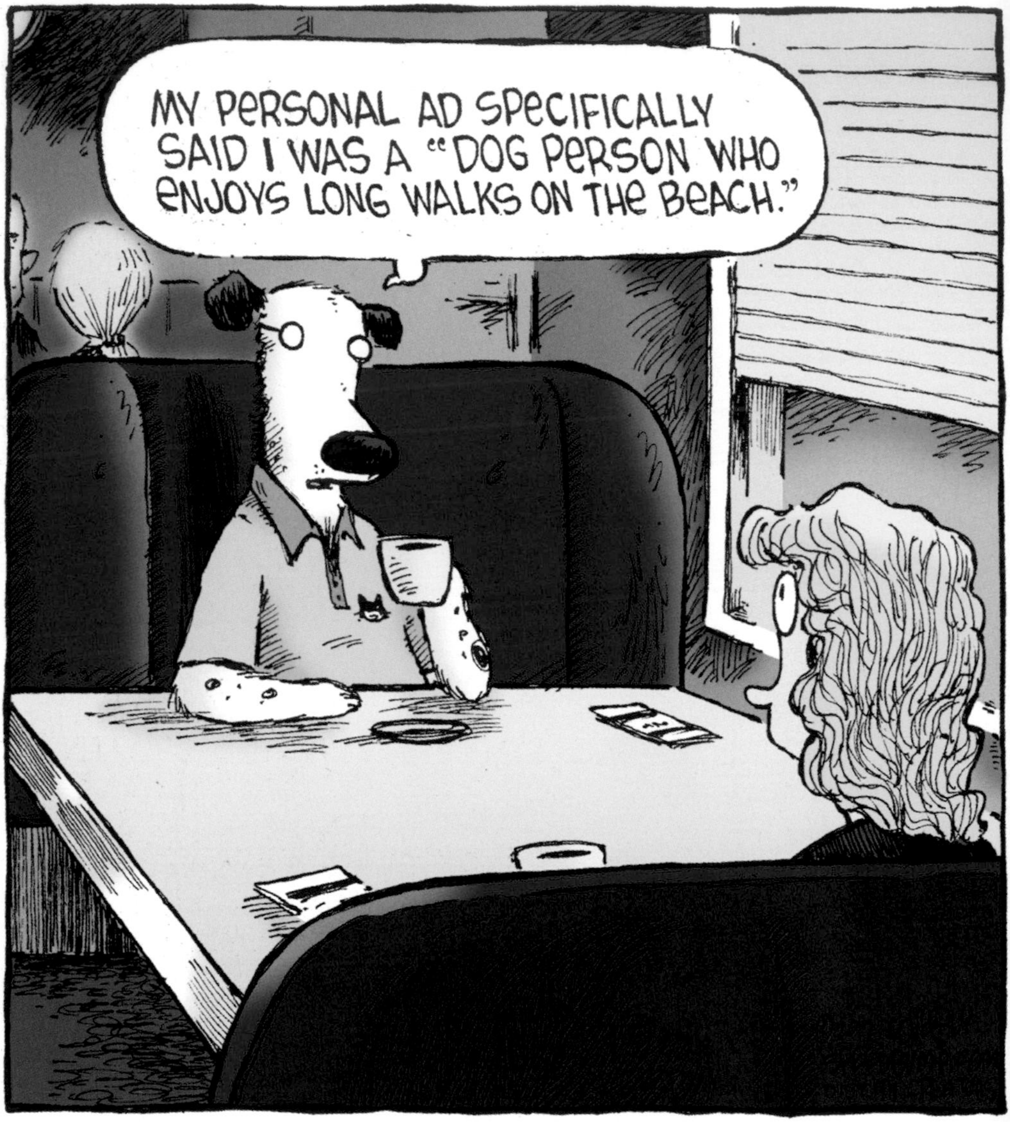
MY PERSONAL AD SPECIFICALLY SAID I WAS A "DOG PERSON WHO ENJOYS LONG WALKS ON THE BEACH."

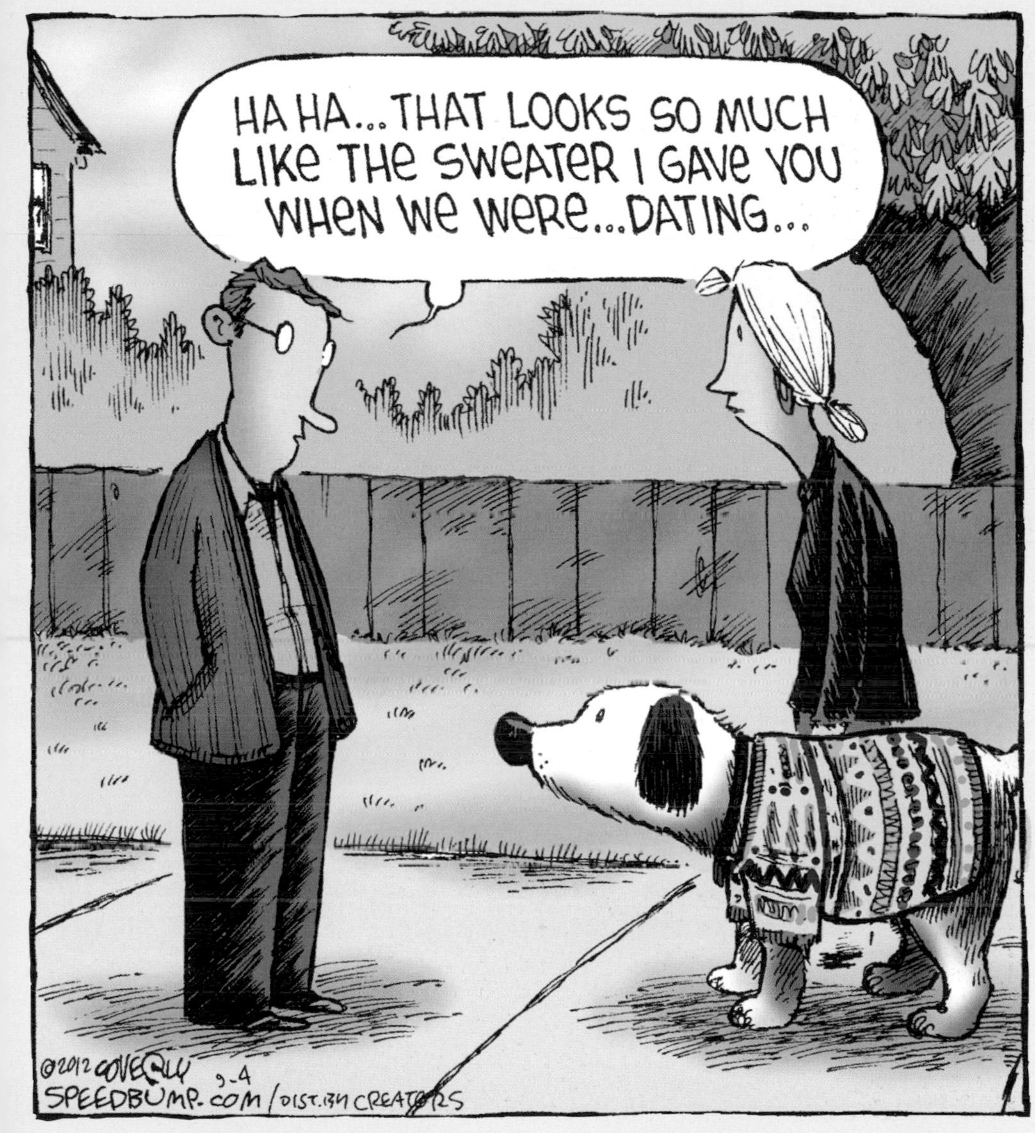
HA HA...THAT LOOKS SO MUCH LIKE THE SWEATER I GAVE YOU WHEN WE WERE...DATING...
©2012 COVERLY 9-4
SPEEDBUMP.COM / DIST. BY CREATORS

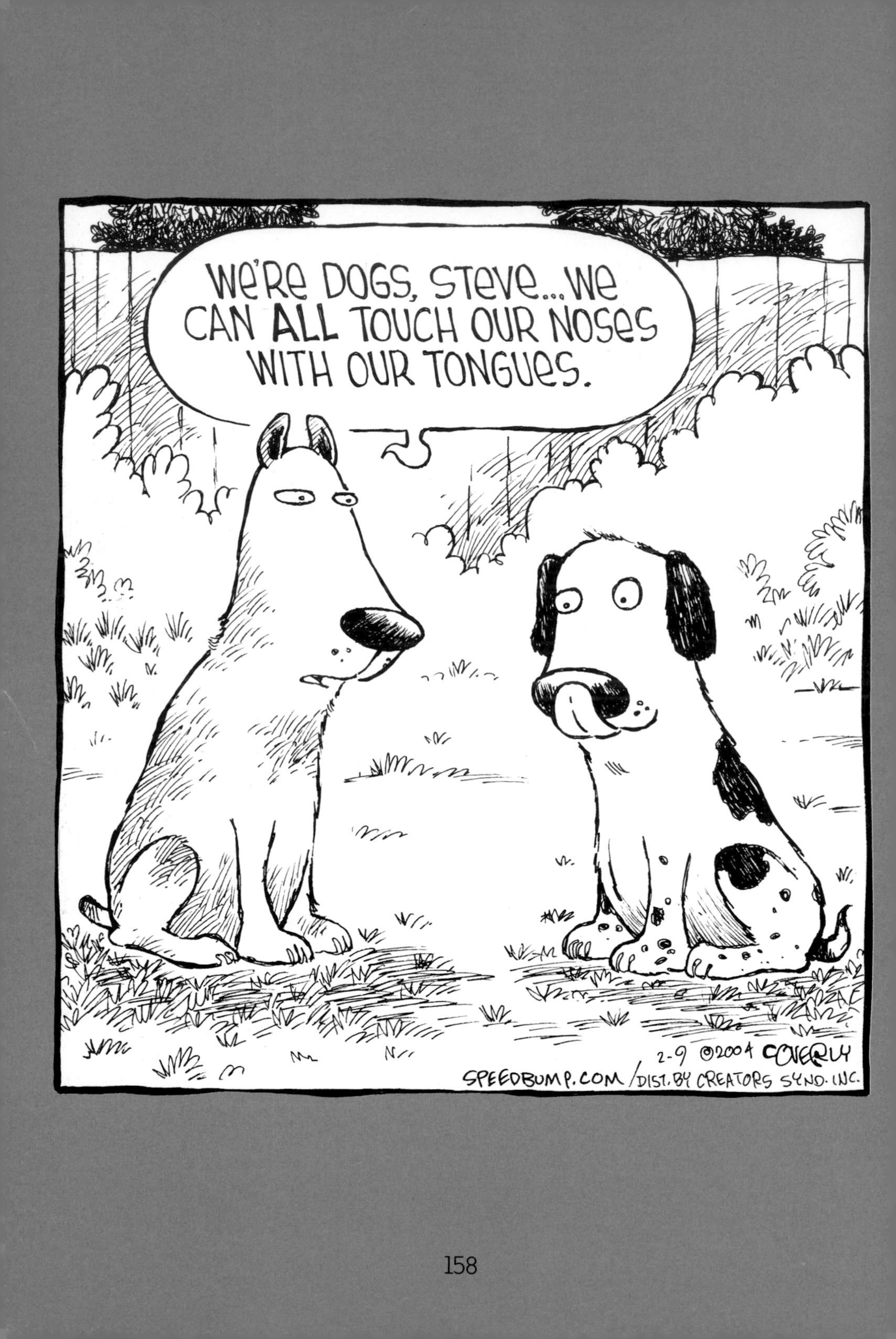
WE'RE DOGS, STEVE... WE CAN ALL TOUCH OUR NOSES WITH OUR TONGUES.
2-9 ©2004 COVERLY
SPEEDBUMP.COM / DIST. BY CREATORS SYND. INC.

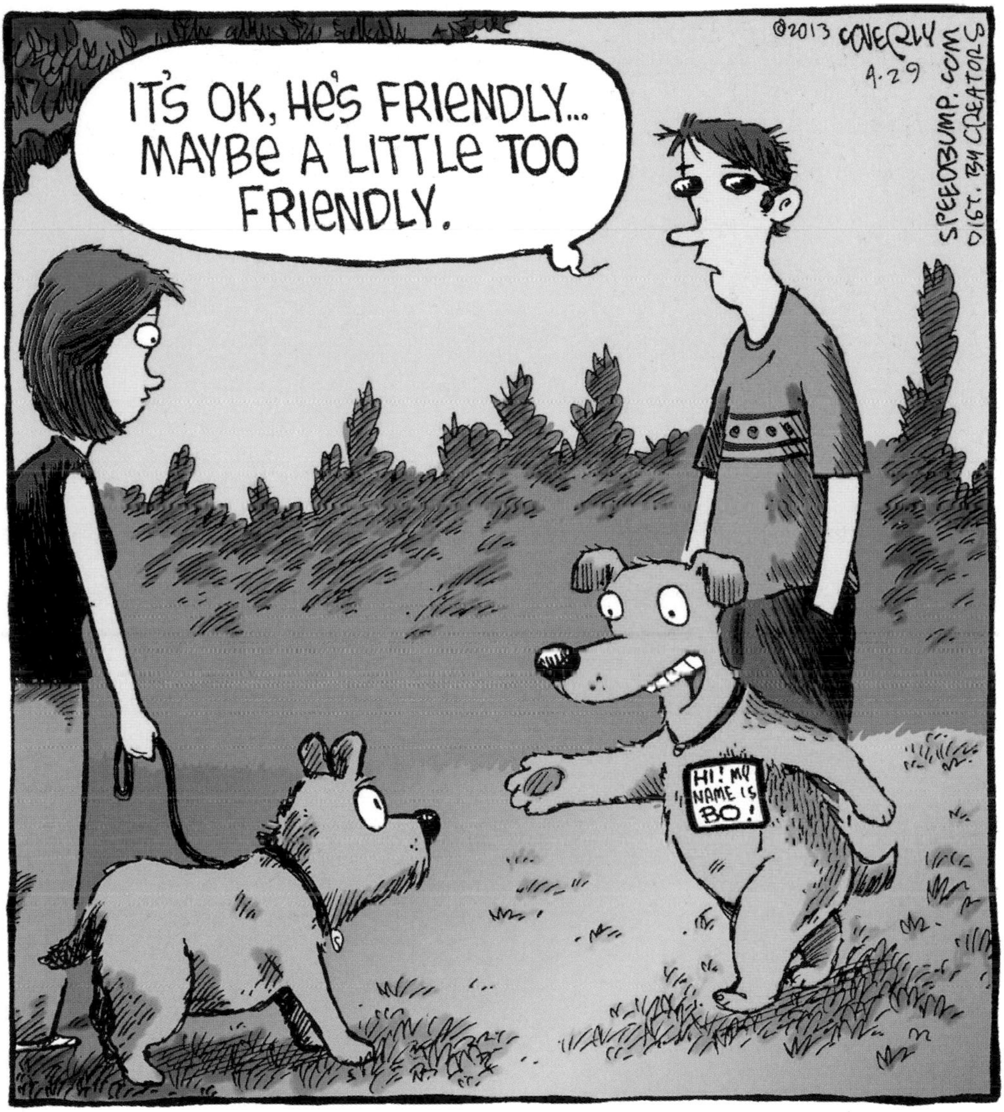
IT'S OK, HE'S FRIENDLY... MAYBE A LITTLE TOO FRIENDLY.
HI! MY NAME IS BO!
©2013 COVERLY 4.29
SPEEDBUMP.COM DIST. BY CREATORS

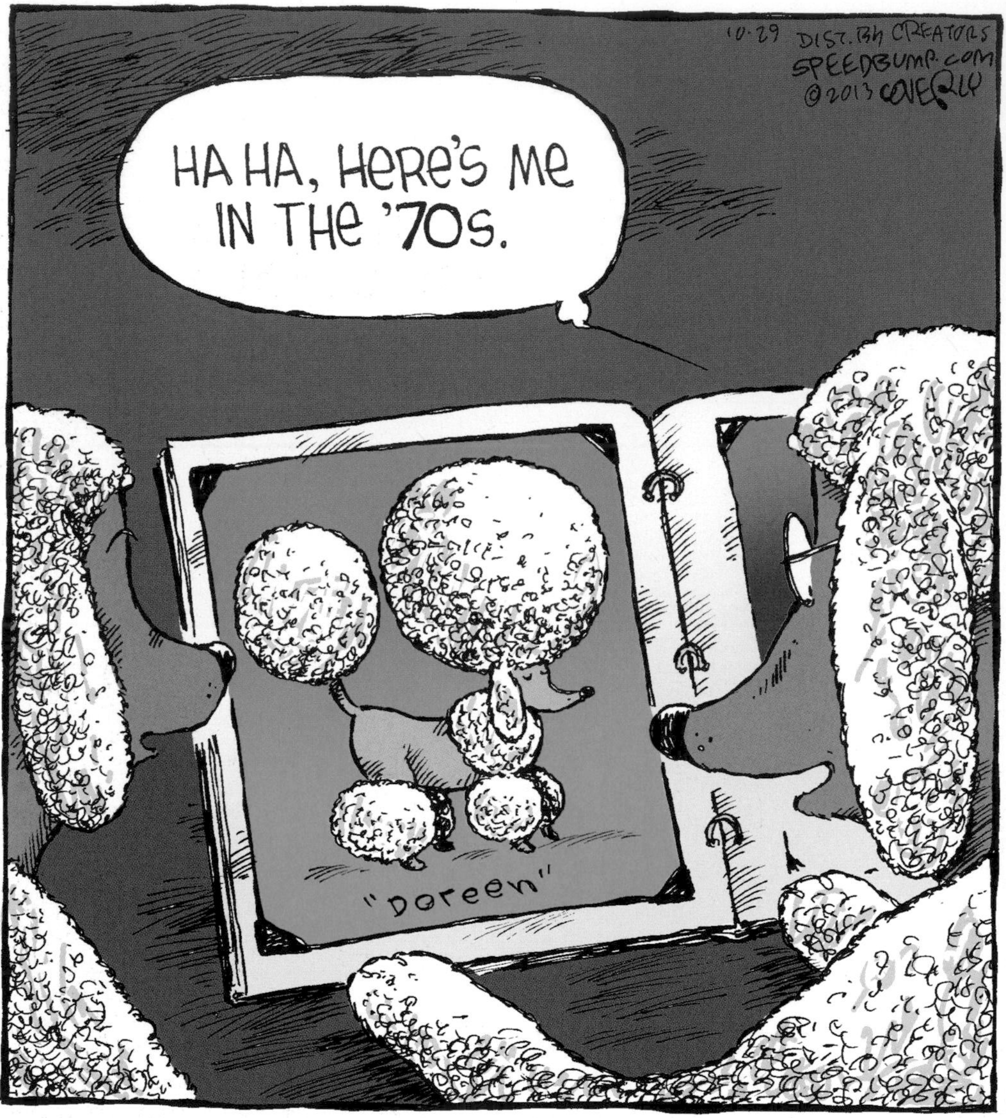
HA HA, HERE'S ME IN THE '70s.
"Doreen"
10·29 DIST. BY CREATORS
SPEEDBUMP.COM
©2013 COVERLY

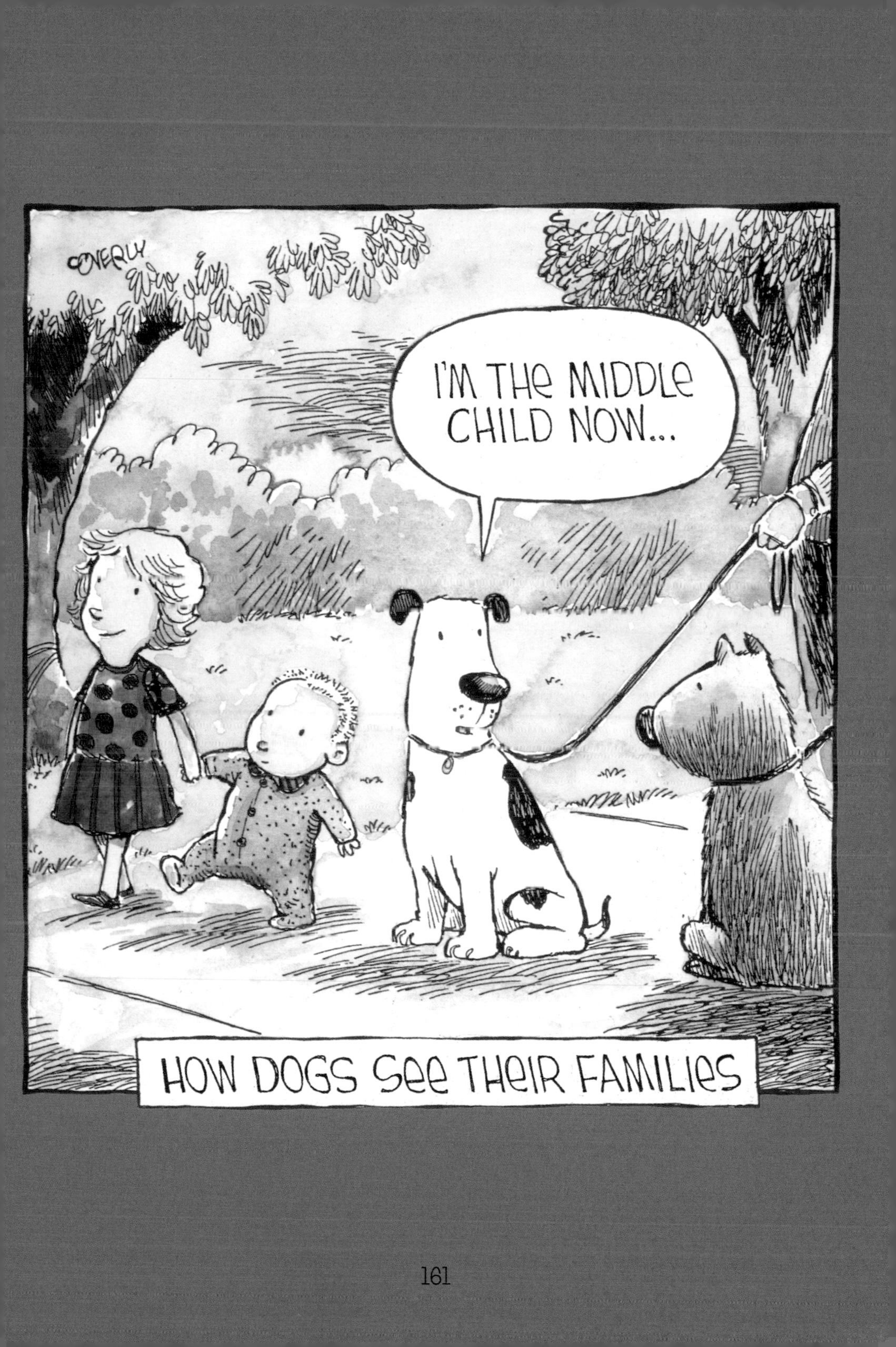
CONERLY
I'M THE MIDDLE CHILD NOW...
HOW DOGS SEE THEIR FAMILIES

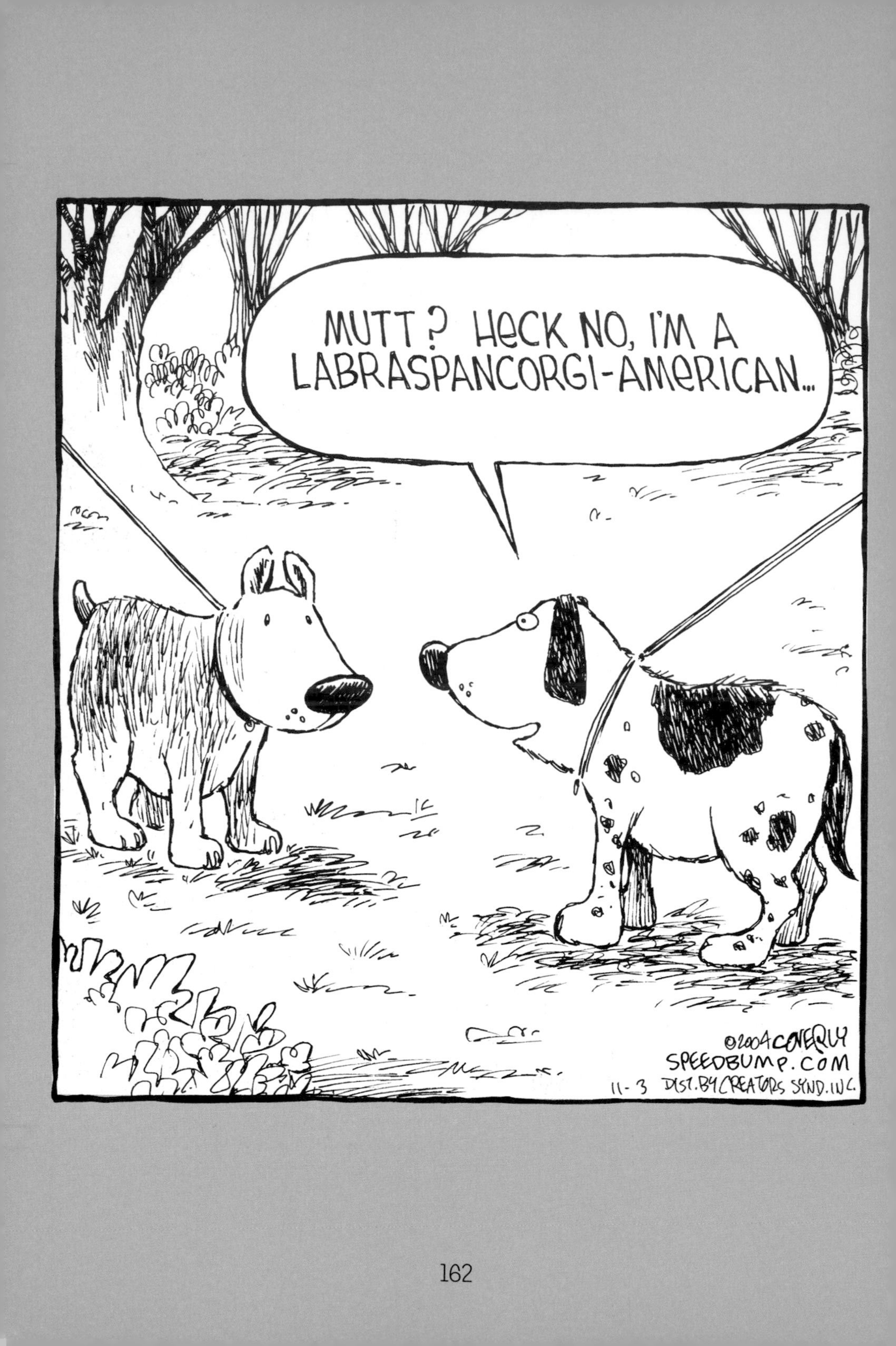
MUTT? HECK NO, I'M A LABRASPANCORGI-AMERICAN...
©2004 COVERLY
SPEEDBUMP.COM
11-3 DIST. BY CREATORS SYND. INC.

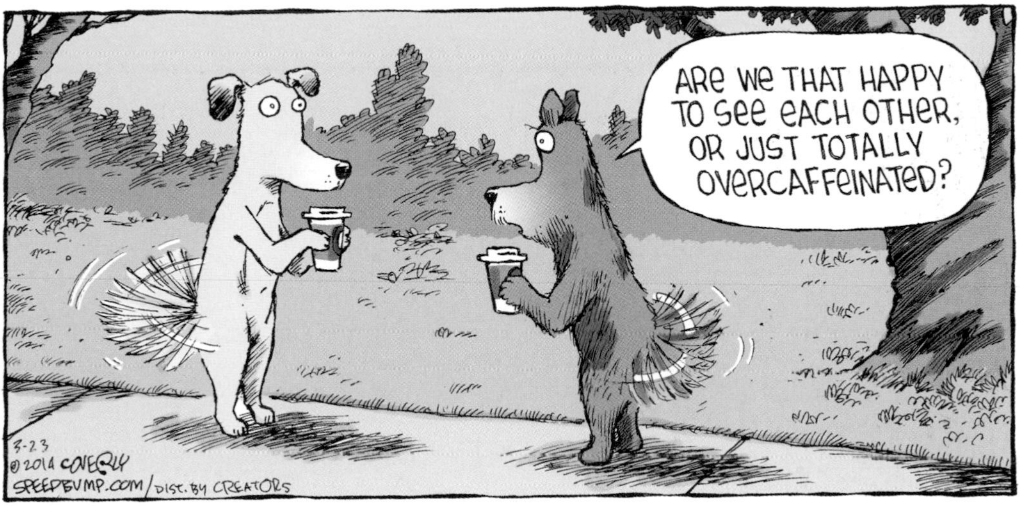
ARE WE THAT HAPPY TO SEE EACH OTHER, OR JUST TOTALLY OVERCAFFEINATED?
3-23
© 2014 COVERLY
SPEEDBUMP.COM / DIST. BY CREATORS

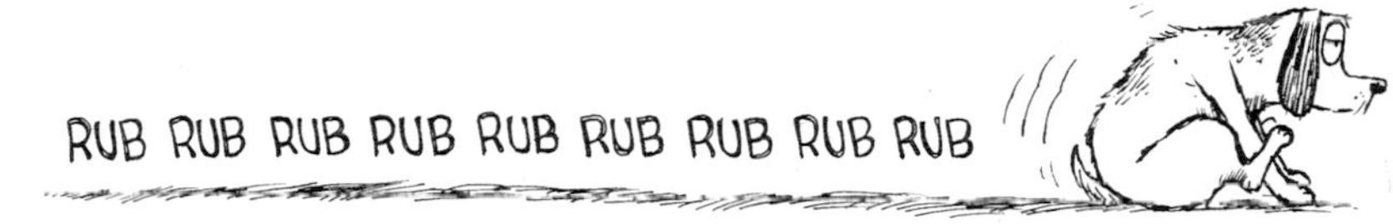
RUB RUB RUB RUB RUB RUB RUB RUB RUB

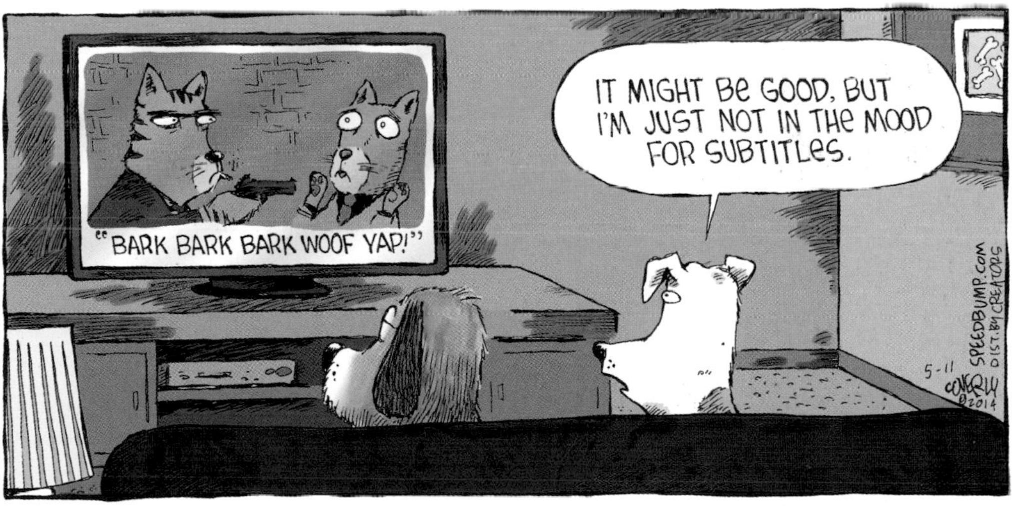
"BARK BARK BARK WOOF YAP!"
IT MIGHT BE GOOD, BUT I'M JUST NOT IN THE MOOD FOR SUBTITLES.
SPEEDBUMP.COM
DIST. BY CREATORS
5-11
COVERLY
©2014

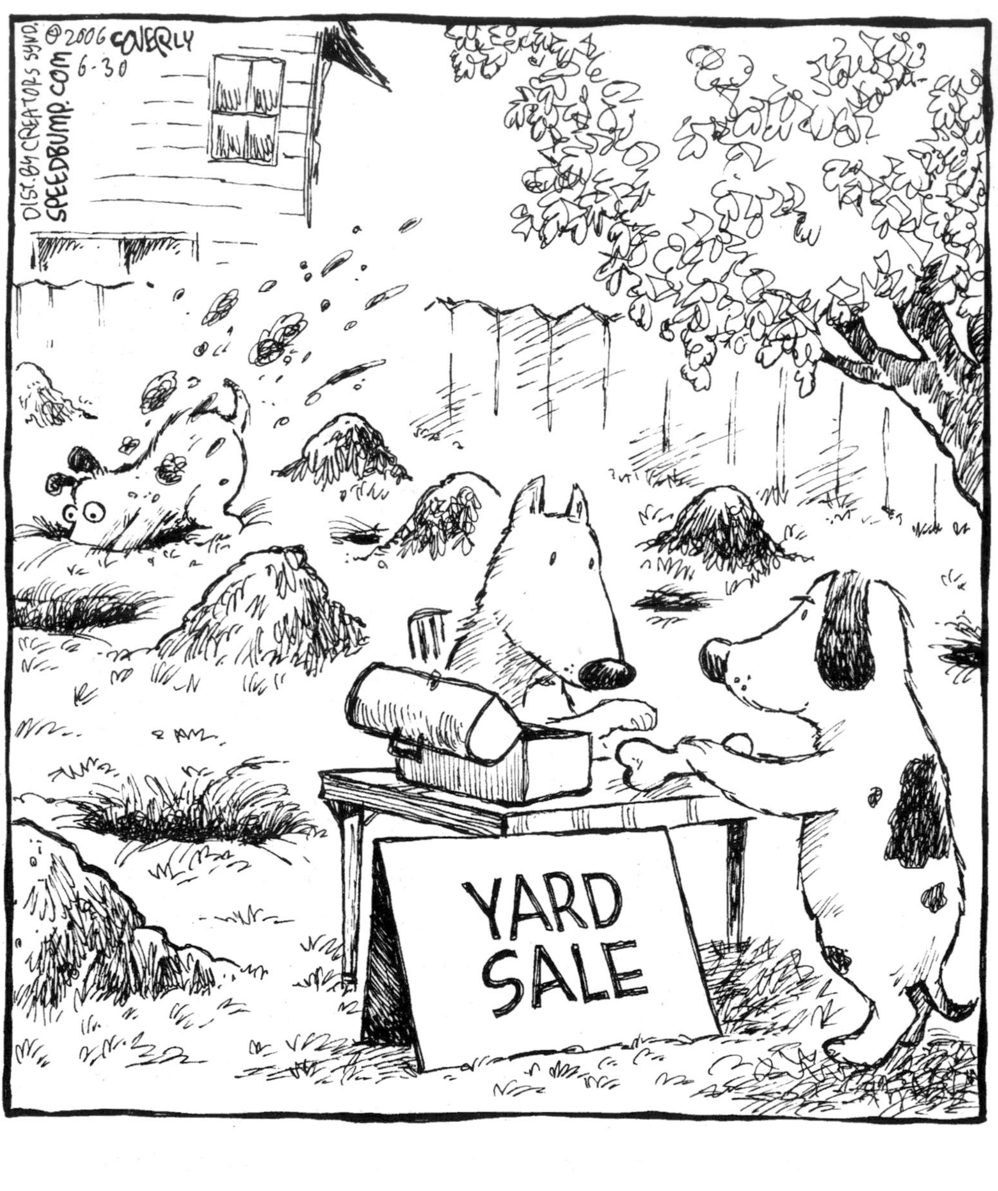
©2006 COVERLY
6-30
DIST. BY CREATORS SYND.
SPEEDBUMP.COM
YARD SALE

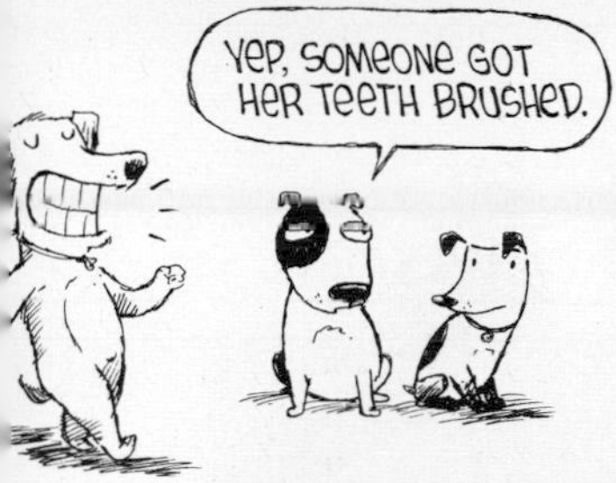
YEP, SOMEONE GOT HER TEETH BRUSHED.

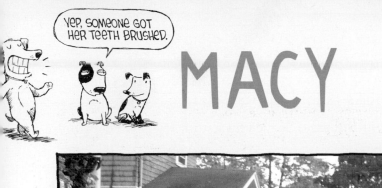

MACY

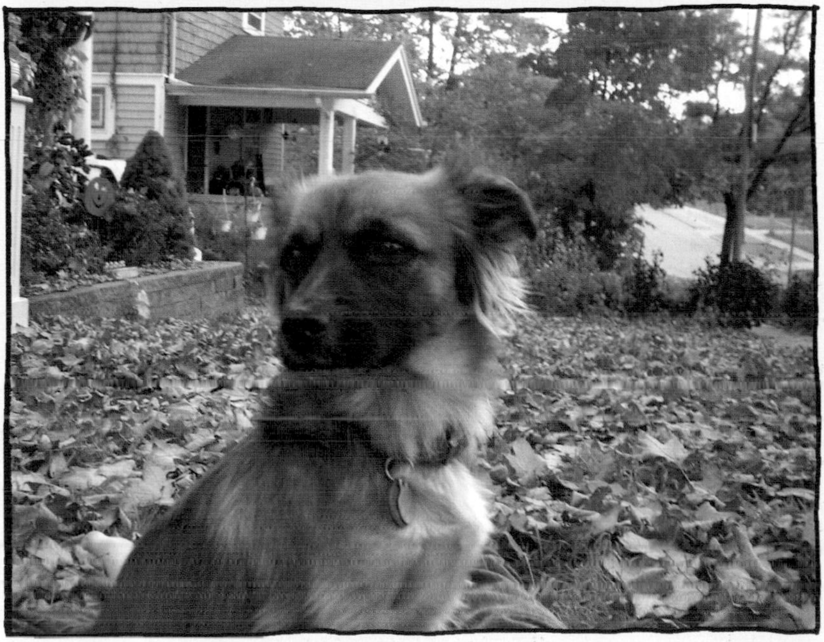

Macy, 2008.

When Kenzi passed away, it was obviously hard on our family, but particularly on our kids, Alayna, 11 at the time, and Simone, 7. Kenzi was a part of the family before they were born, so they'd never known a life without her. Chris and I agreed we wouldn't get another dog right away. It felt somehow disrespectful, and as anyone who's had a dog understands, each dog deserves to be mourned. We figured we'd wait maybe a year.

Ah, best-laid plans and all that . . . A couple months later, Alayna came home from school and began crying unexpectedly.

She missed being greeted at the door. The house felt empty. So Chris went online and secretly began researching rescue dogs and shelters in the area. She came across Homeward Bound, and on their site was a photo of an adorable puppy for adoption, along with three of its siblings. All of them were named after country music stars—Reba, Bonnie, Travis, and Cash. Chris made an appointment to visit the puppies despite this fact.

The backstory on these puppies is short but remarkable. Their mother, a sheltie, was pregnant, yet still scheduled to be euthanized. The owners of Homeward Bound heard about the euthanization through back channels (I imagine something similar to the midnight bark in *101 Dalmatians*), so a couple of volunteers hopped in their car to bring home the mother . . . a rescue that doesn't sound all that remarkable until you realize

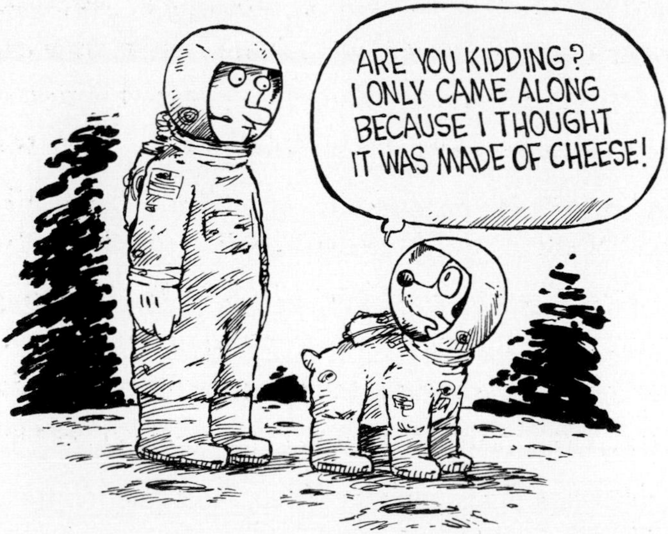
ARE YOU KIDDING? I ONLY CAME ALONG BECAUSE I THOUGHT IT WAS MADE OF CHEESE!

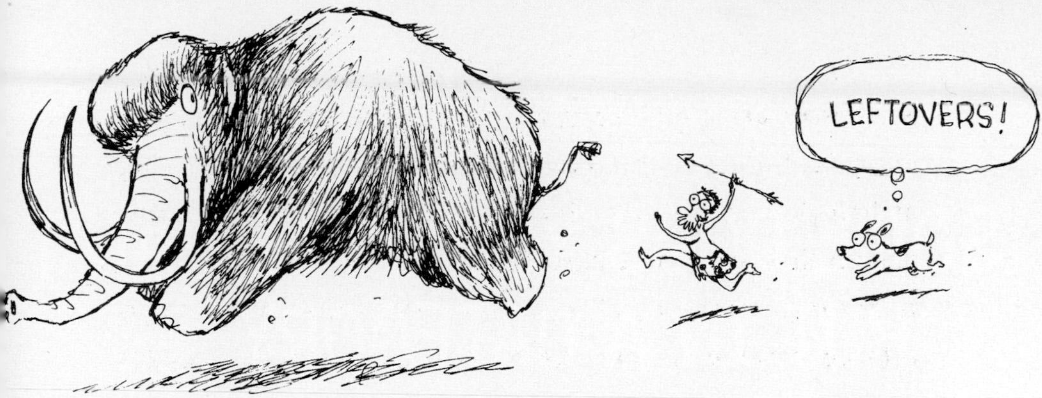
LEFTOVERS!

this Homeward Bound is in Michigan and the pregnant dog was in Georgia. Also, it was February. And they drove through a snowstorm to rescue the pregnant mother.

Our trip to pick out a puppy was a surprise to Alayna and Simone, so we covered the metal crate in the back of our car with a blanket and didn't tell them where we were going until we were nearly there. Both of them screamed, then Alayna began to cry with happiness, which caused her little sister to start crying. (Isn't it fascinating how crying, laughing, and yawning are contagious? Shared experiences are so powerful.) Our intent was to adopt Bonnie, the gorgeous sheltie–terrier mix in the website photo, but best-laid plans and all that . . . Bonnie and her two brothers were undeniably cute and were little balls of energy the day we visited. Reba, on the other hand, was the runt of the litter and must have been overtired, as she crawled up on Simone's lap and fell asleep. Then later she wandered over to Alayna and did the same. After having a dog like Kenzi, this sort of behavior won all of us over, and Reba became Macy, and Macy became a Coverly.

And her story is ongoing.

CHAPTER 9

SOME DOGS YOU JUST CAN'T PUT IN A CATEGORY . . . ER . . . DOG-ETORY

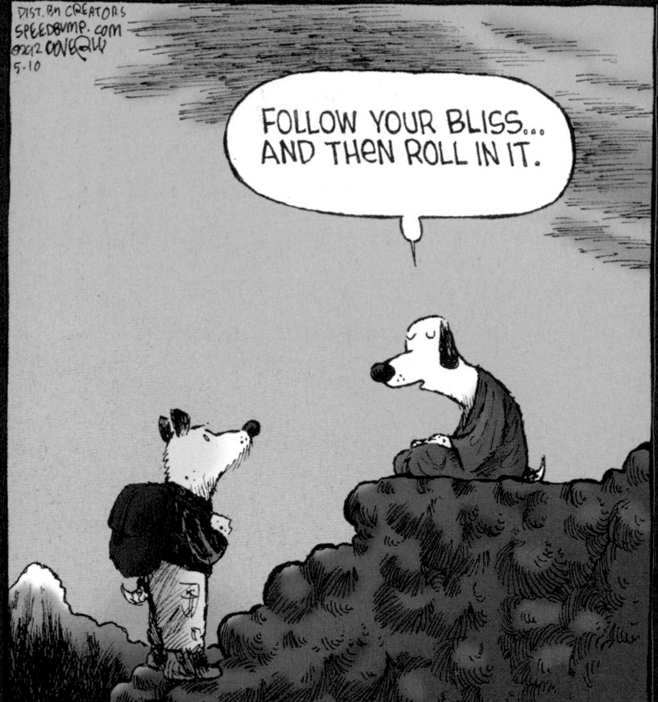
DIST. BY CREATORS
SPEEDBUMP.COM
FOLLOW YOUR BLISS...
AND THEN ROLL IN IT.

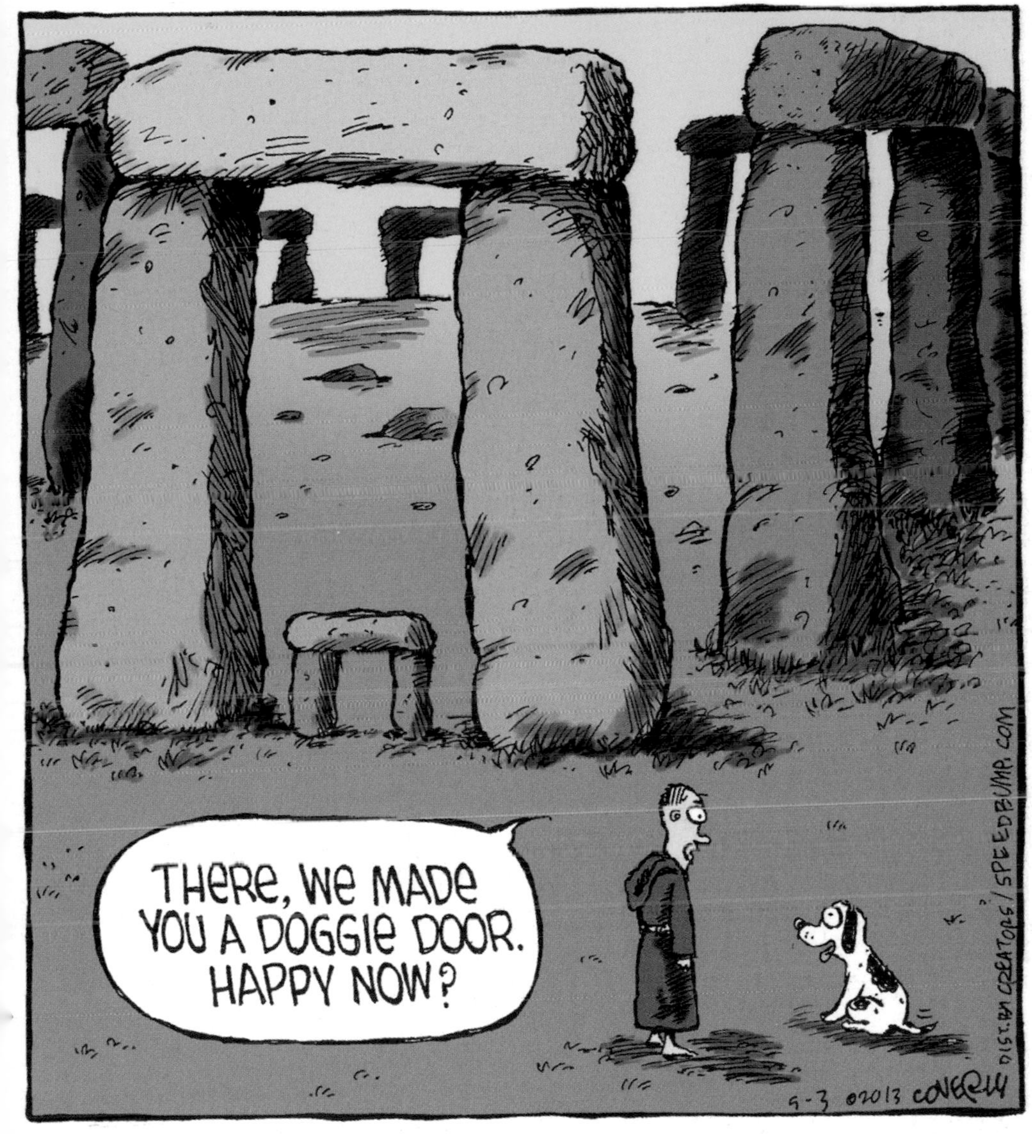
THERE, WE MADE YOU A DOGGIE DOOR. HAPPY NOW?
DIST. BY CREATORS / SPEEDBUMP.COM
5-3 ©2013 COVERLY

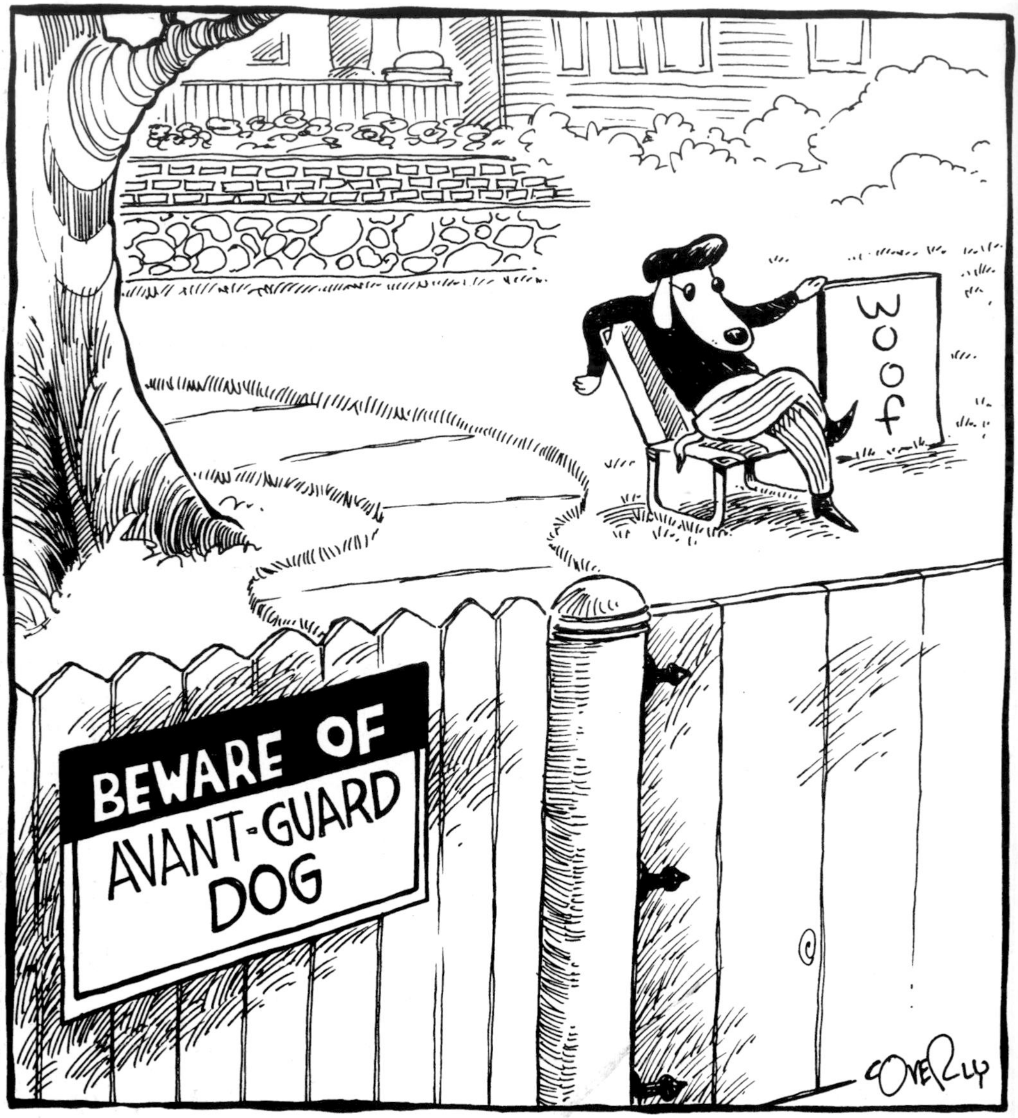
WOOF
BEWARE OF
AVANT-GUARD
DOG

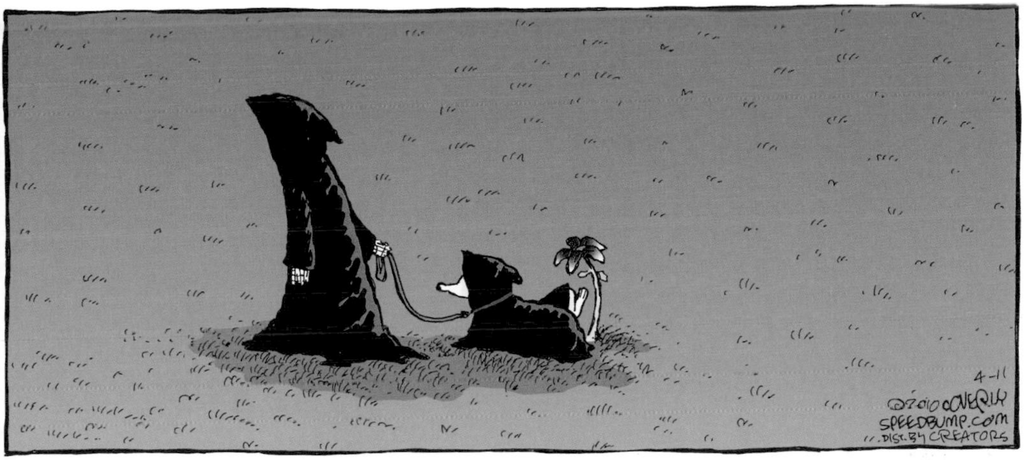
4-11
©2010 COVERLY
SPEEDBUMP.COM
DIST. BY CREATORS

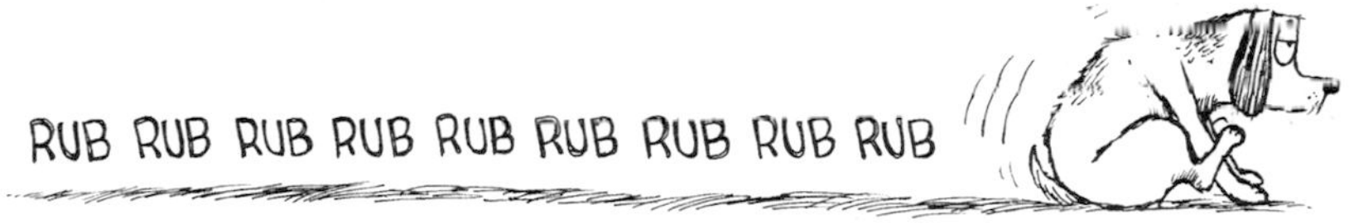
RUB RUB RUB RUB RUB RUB RUB RUB RUB

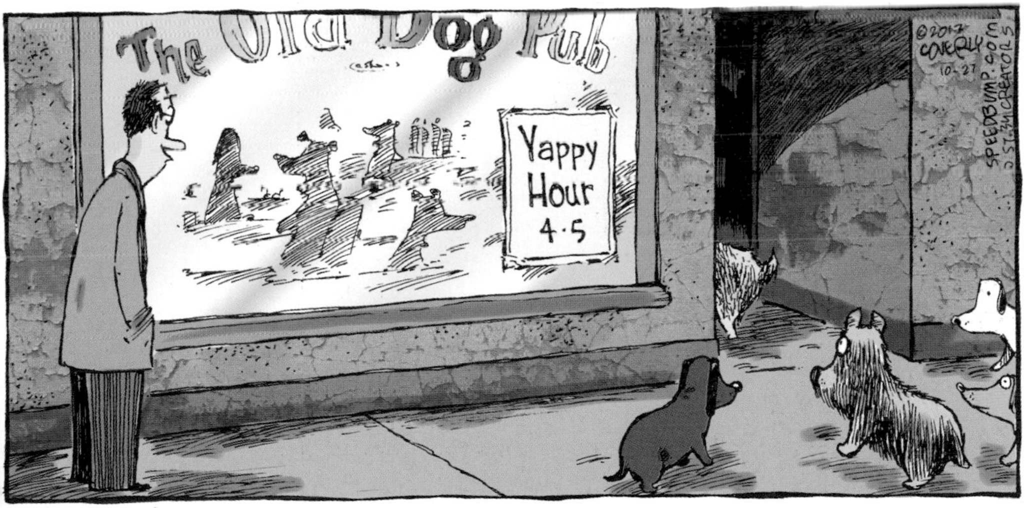
The Old Dog Pub
Yappy Hour 4-5
©2017 COVERLY 10-27
SPEEDBUMP.COM
DIST. BY CREATORS

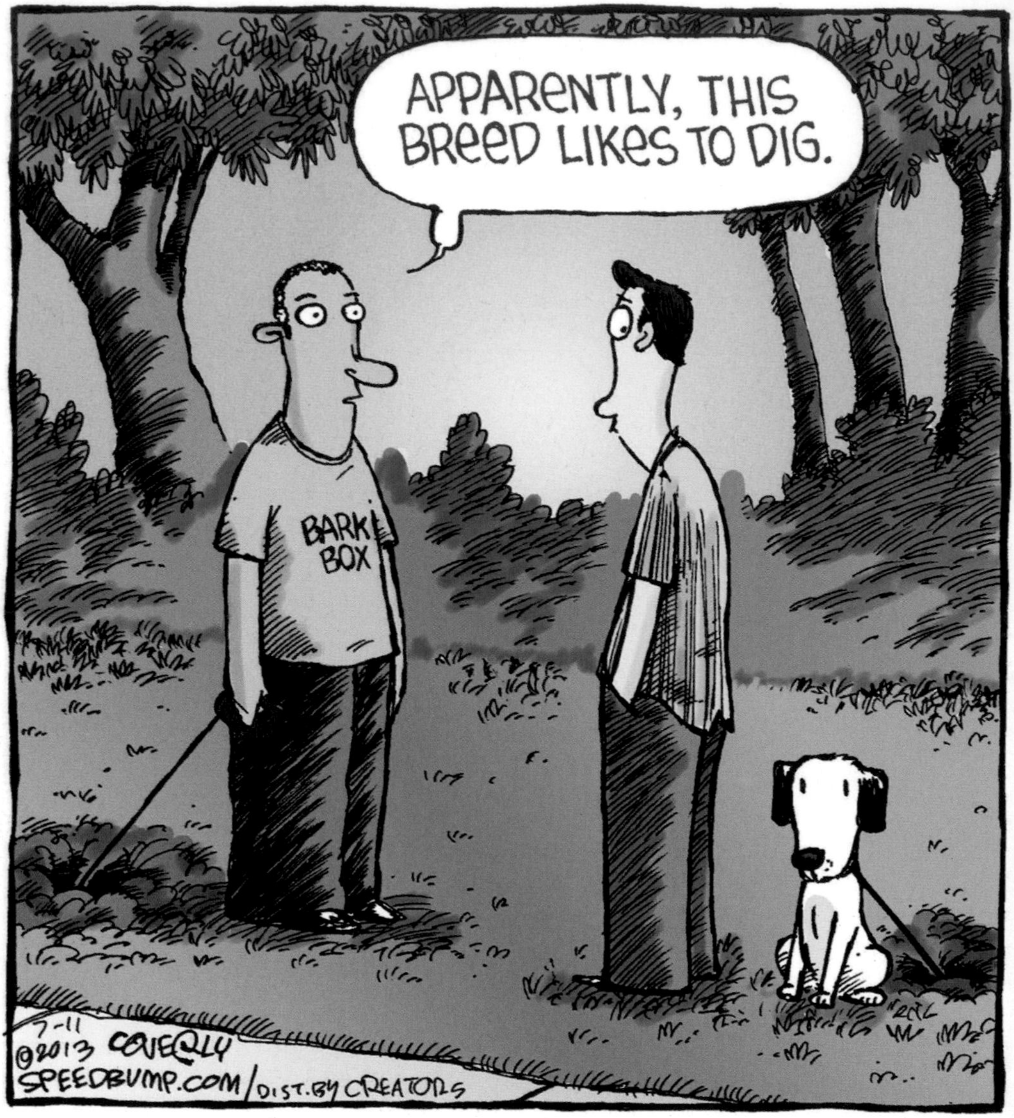
APPARENTLY, THIS BREED LIKES TO DIG.
BARK BOX
7-11 ©2013 COVERLY SPEEDBUMP.COM/DIST. BY CREATORS

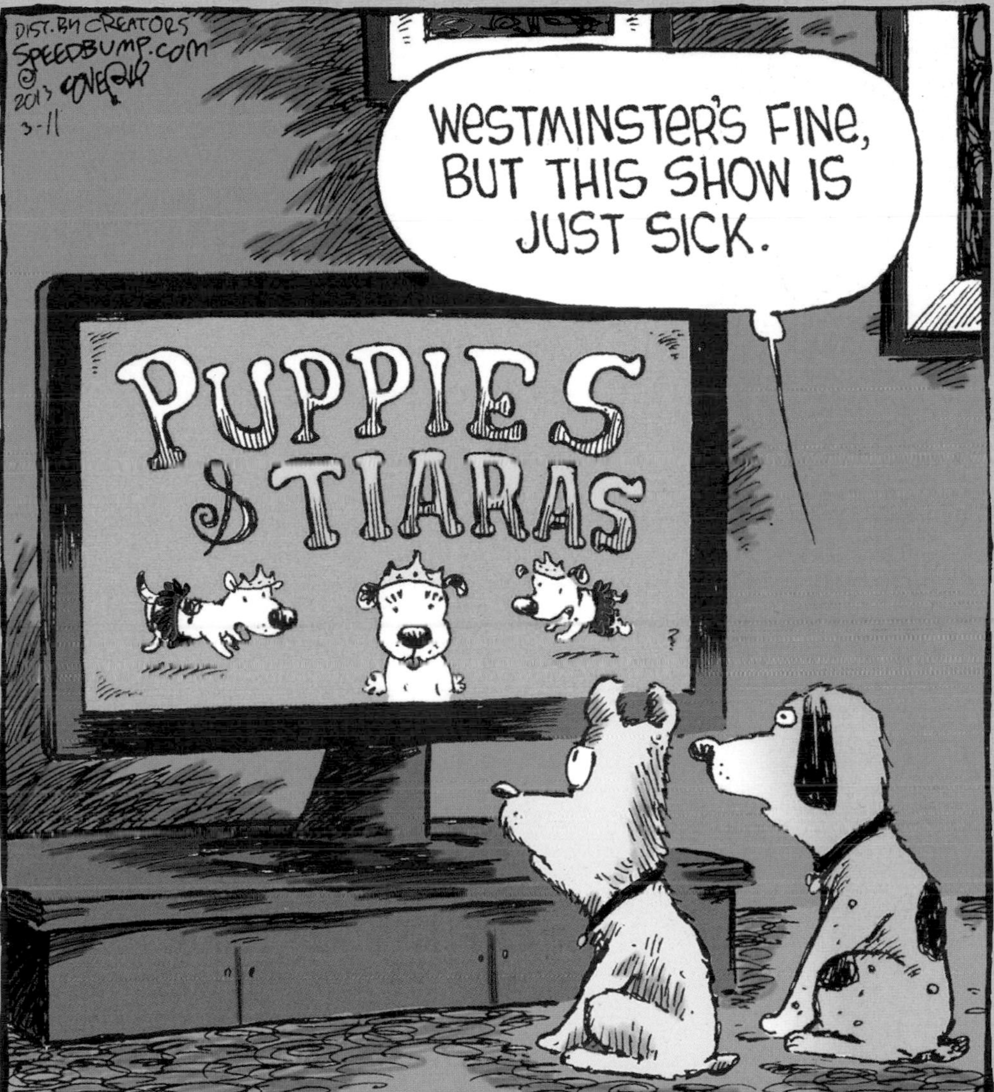
DIST. BY CREATORS
SPEEDBUMP.com
© 2013
3-11
WESTMINSTER'S FINE, BUT THIS SHOW IS JUST SICK.
PUPPIES & TIARAS

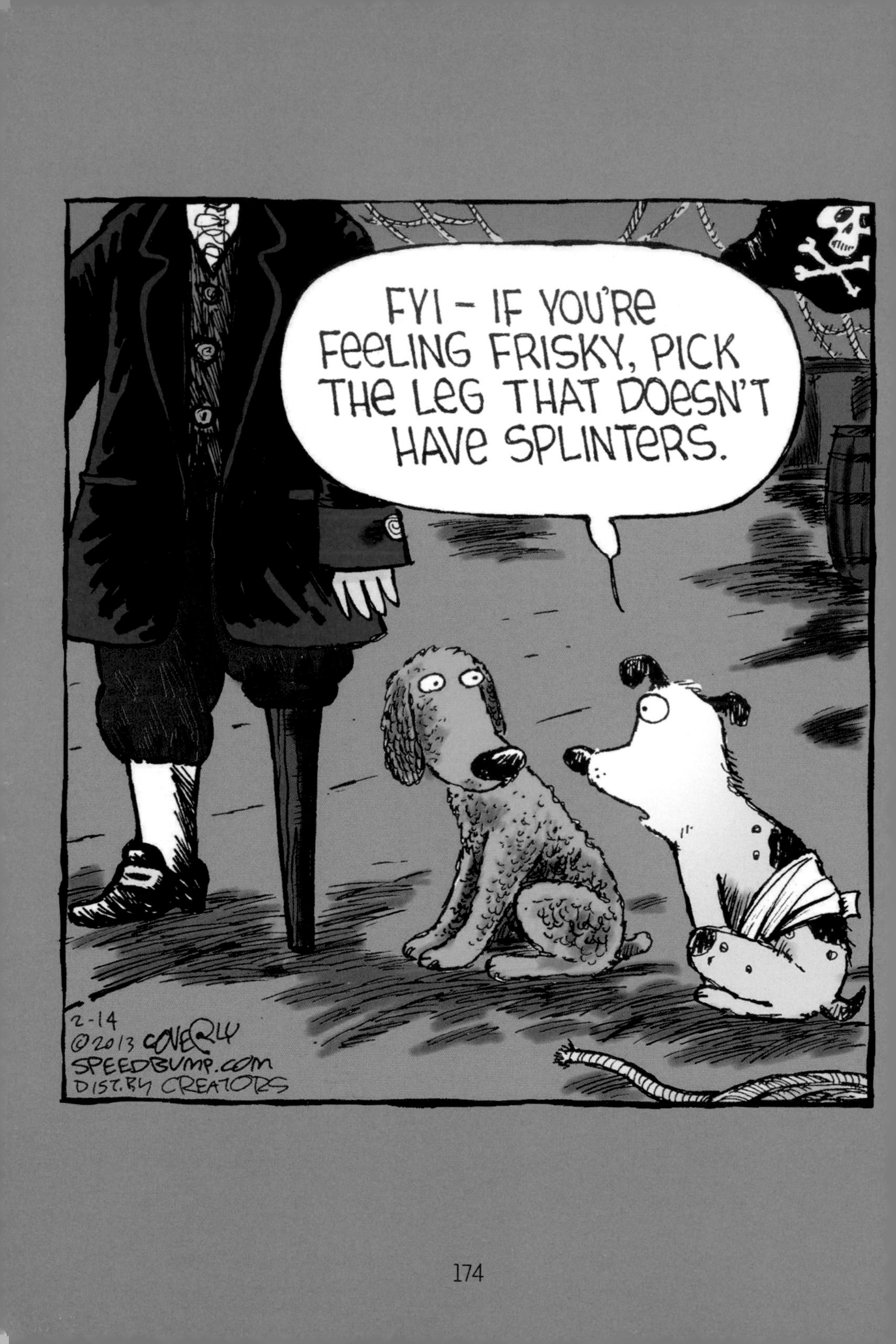
FYI - IF YOU'RE FEELING FRISKY, PICK THE LEG THAT DOESN'T HAVE SPLINTERS.
2-14 ©2013 COVERLY SPEEDBUMP.COM DIST. BY CREATORS

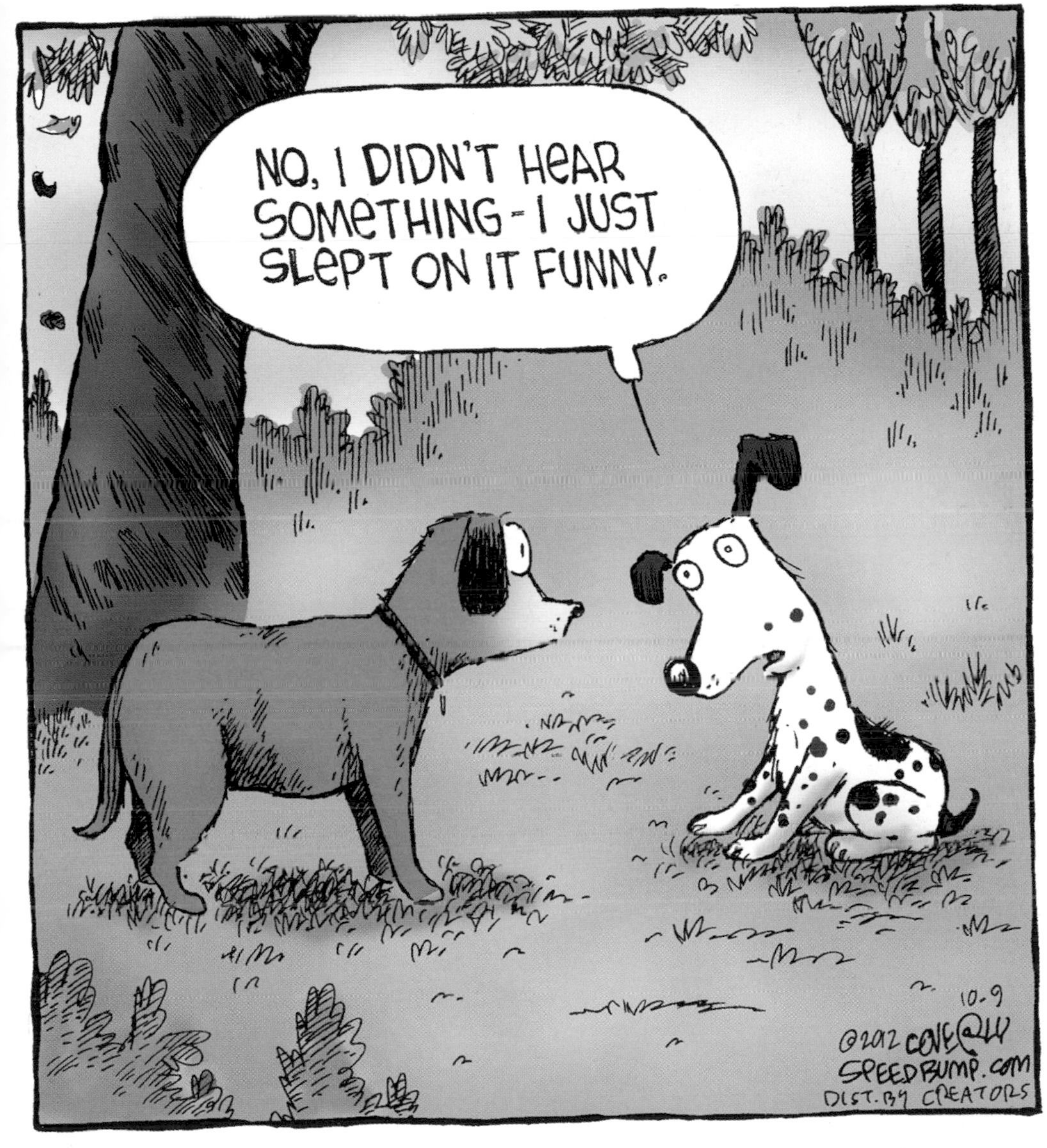
NO, I DIDN'T HEAR SOMETHING - I JUST SLEPT ON IT FUNNY.
10-9
©2012 COVERLY
SPEEDBUMP.COM
DIST. BY CREATORS

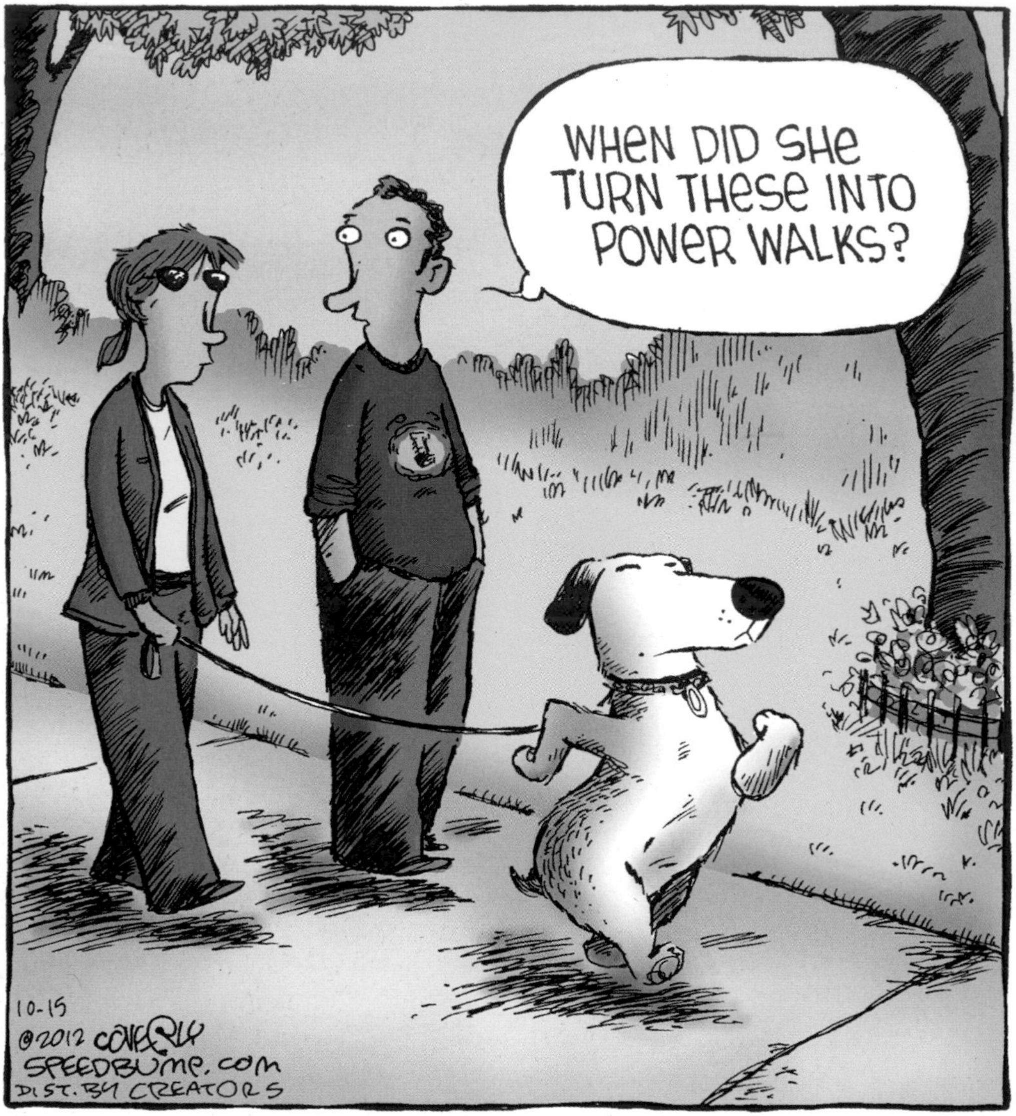
WHEN DID SHE TURN THESE INTO POWER WALKS?
10-15
©2012 COVERLY
SPEEDBUMP.COM
DIST. BY CREATORS

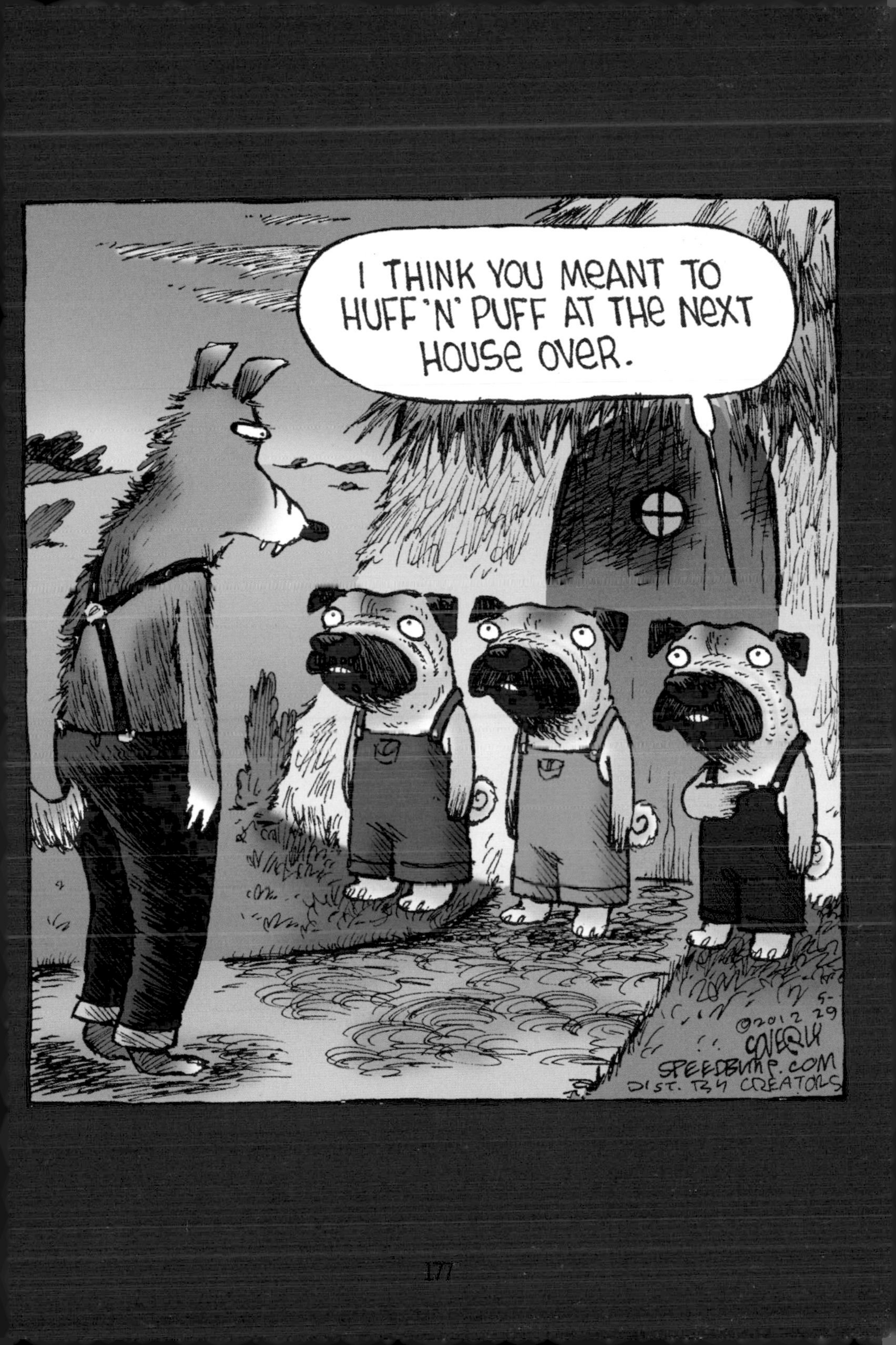
I THINK YOU MEANT TO HUFF 'N' PUFF AT THE NEXT HOUSE OVER.
©2012 5-29
COVERLY
SPEEDBUMP.COM
DIST. BY CREATORS

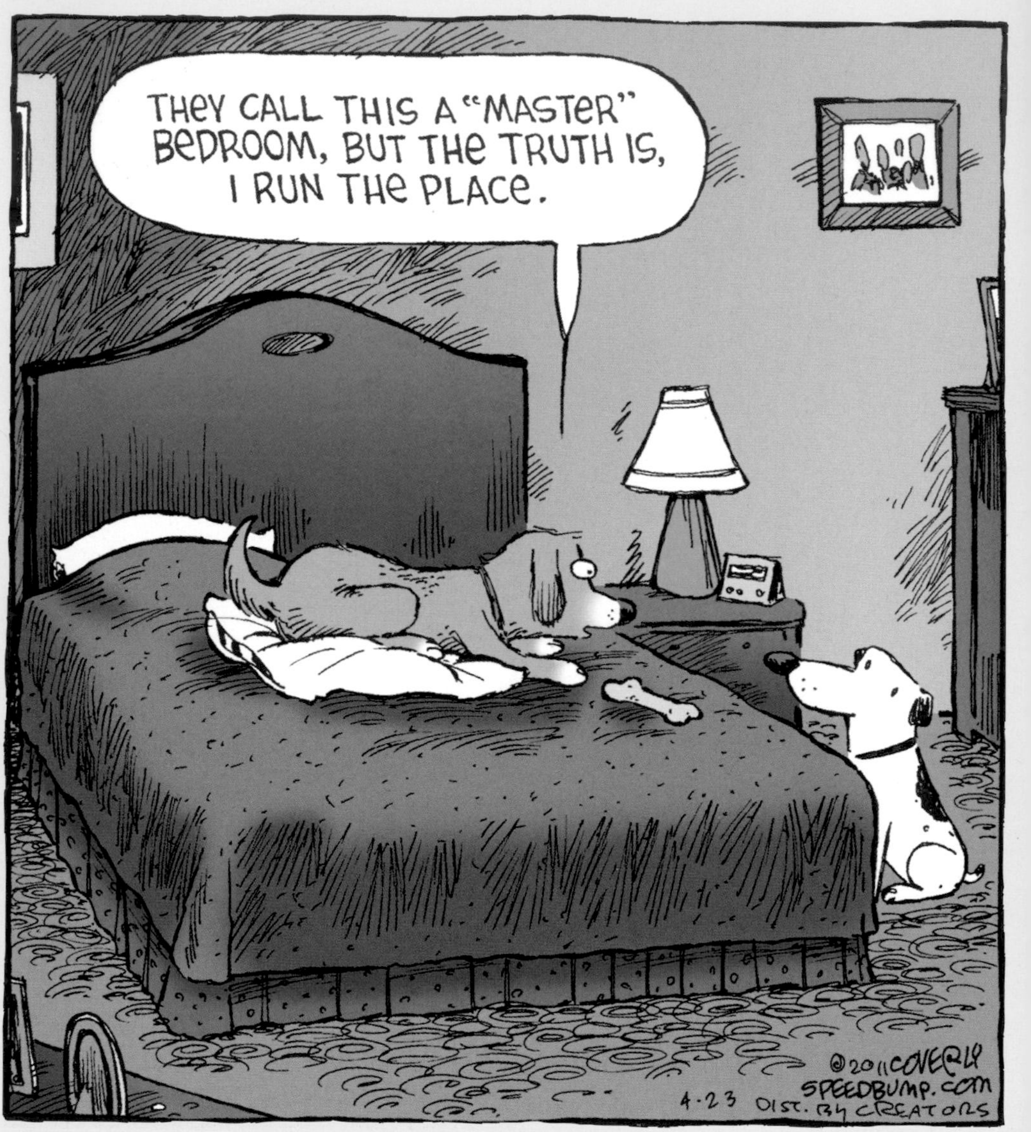
THEY CALL THIS A "MASTER" BEDROOM, BUT THE TRUTH IS, I RUN THE PLACE.
©2011 COVERLY
SPEEDBUMP.COM
4.23 DIST. BY CREATORS

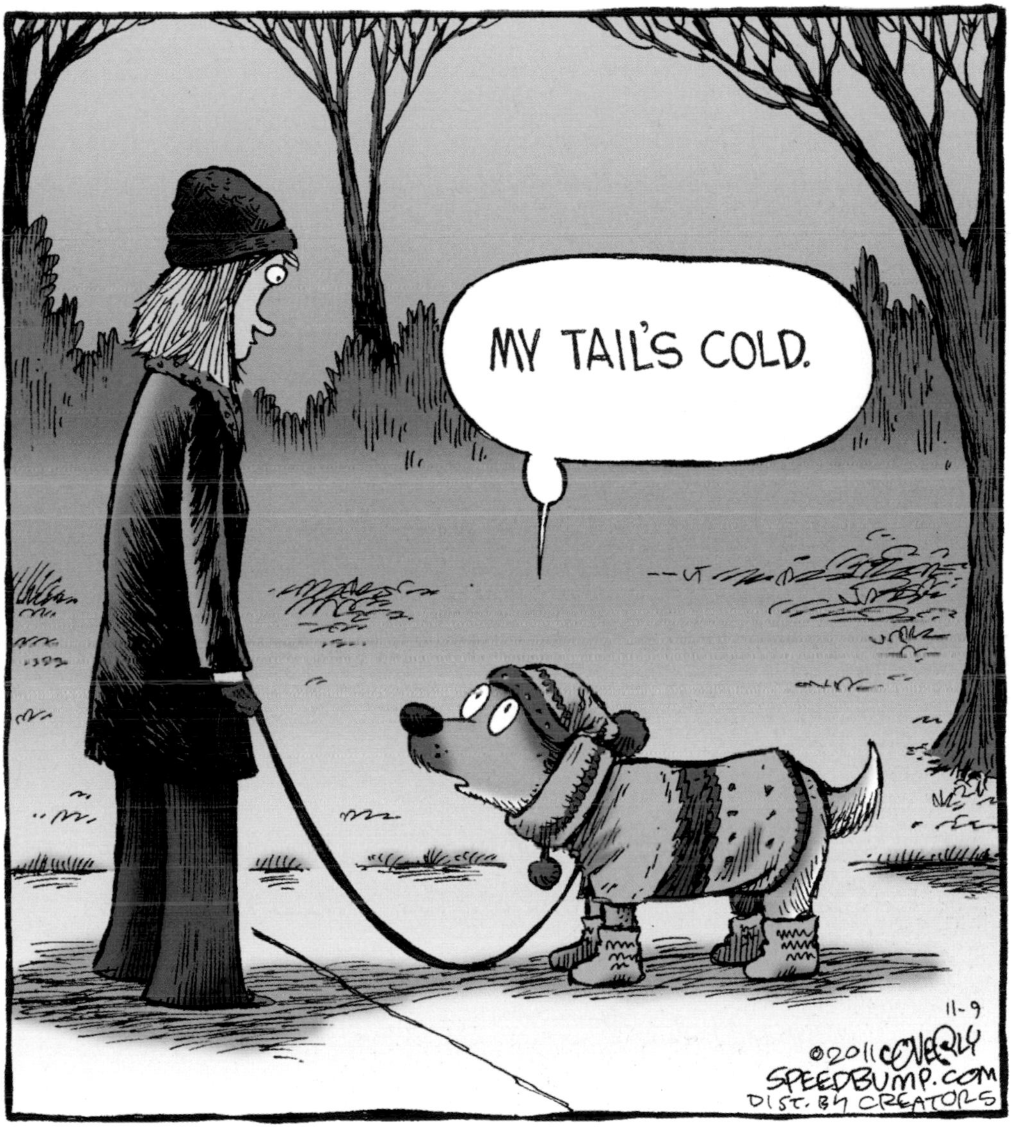
MY TAIL'S COLD.
11-9
©2011 COVERLY
SPEEDBUMP.COM
DIST. BY CREATORS

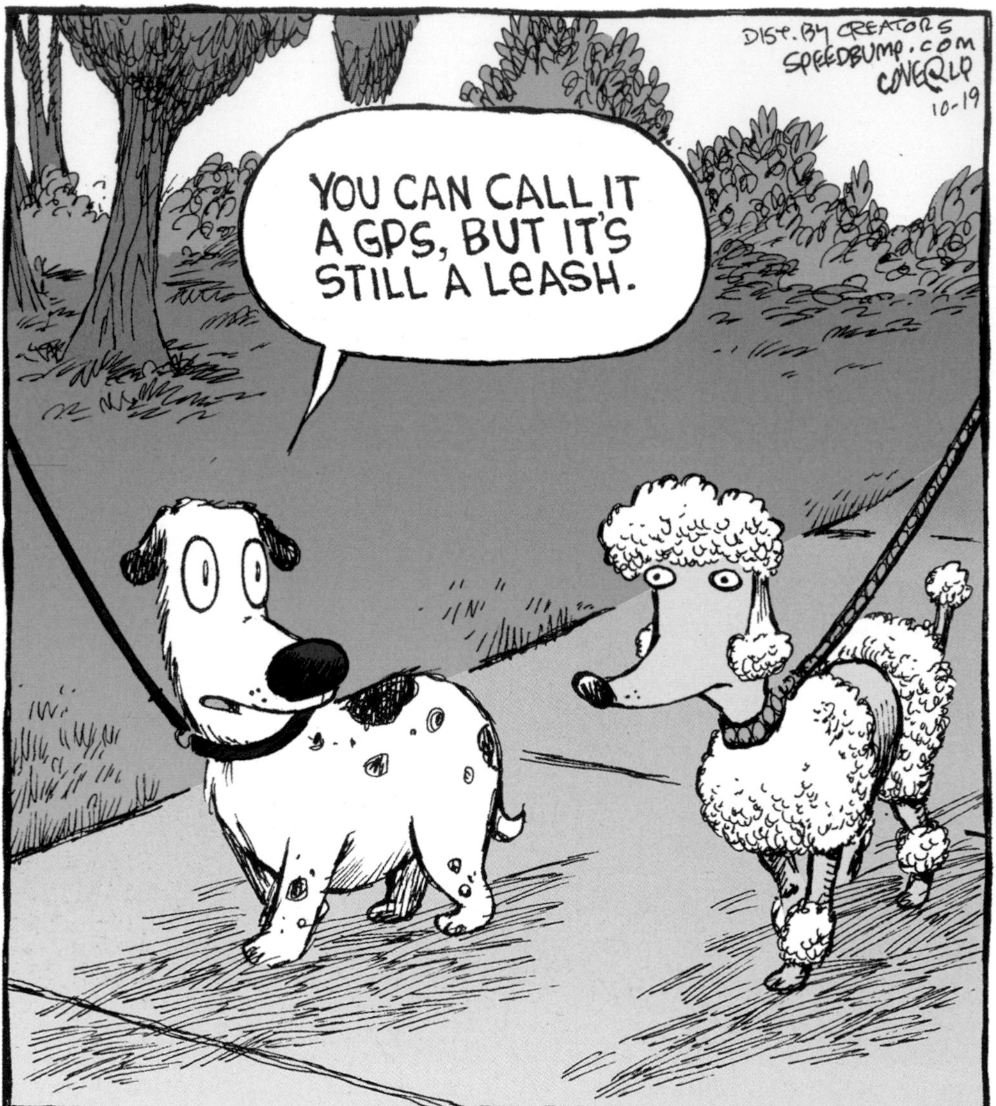
DIST. BY CREATORS
SPEEDBUMP.COM
COVERLY
10-19
YOU CAN CALL IT A GPS, BUT IT'S STILL A LEASH.

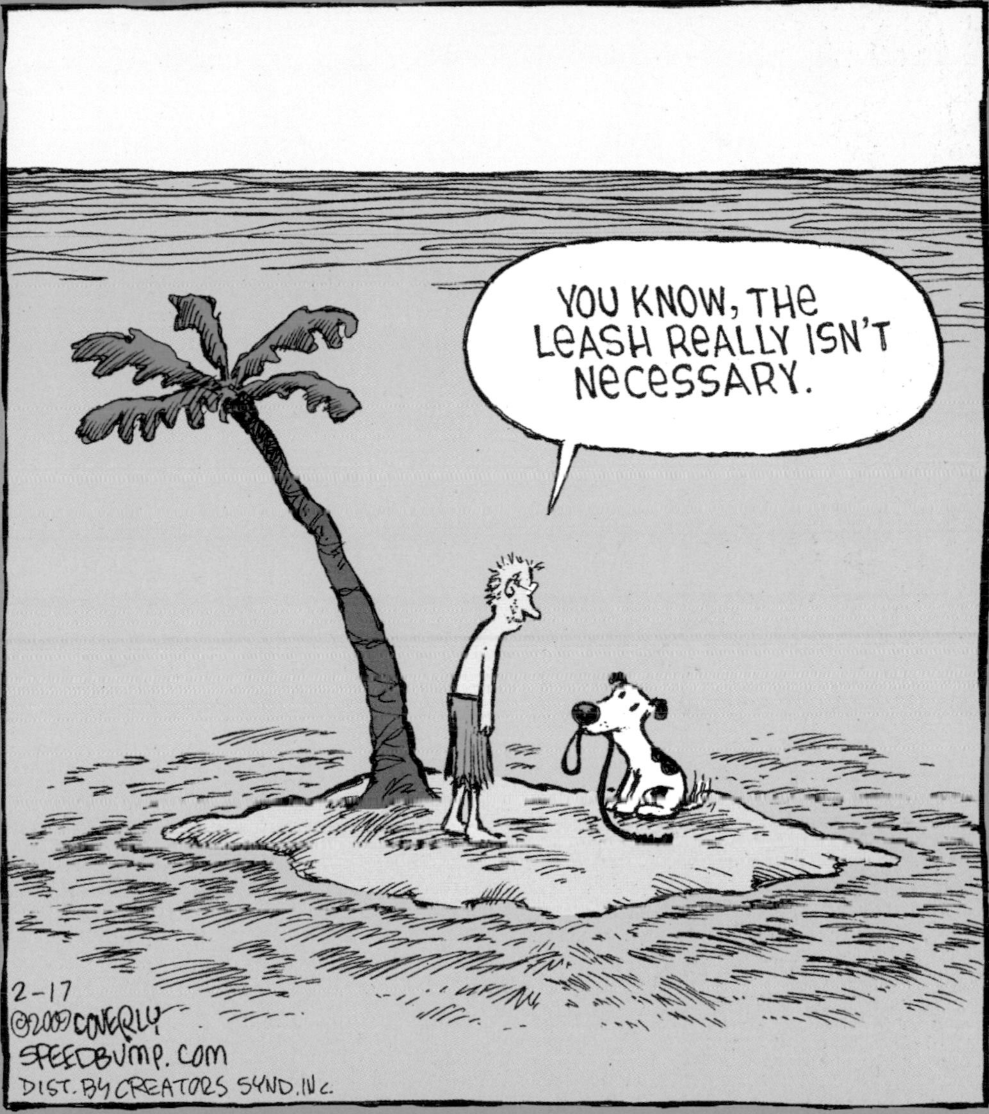
YOU KNOW, THE LEASH REALLY ISN'T NECESSARY.
2-17
©2009 COVERLY
SPEEDBUMP.COM
DIST. BY CREATORS SYND. INC.

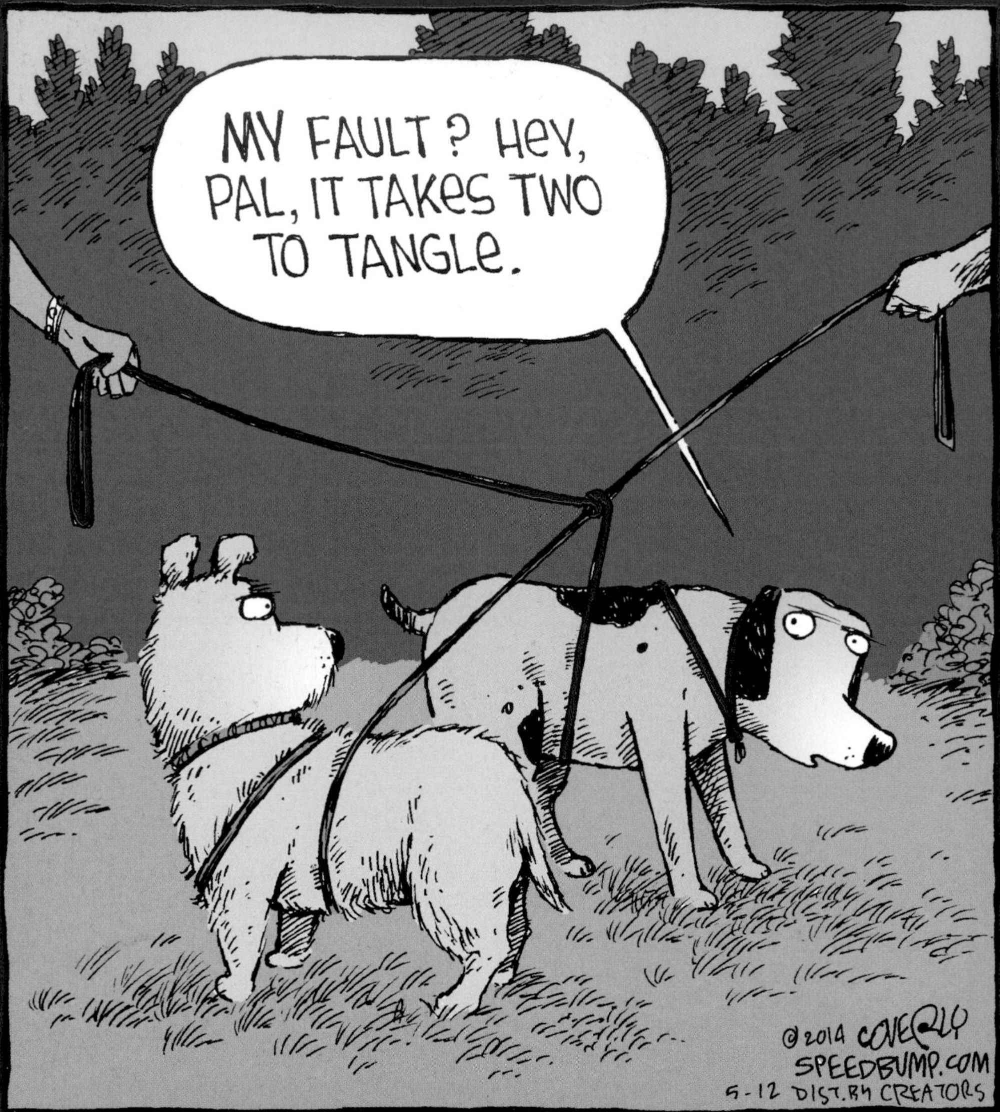
MY FAULT? HEY, PAL, IT TAKES TWO TO TANGLE.
©2014 COVERLY
SPEEDBUMP.COM
5-12 DIST. BY CREATORS

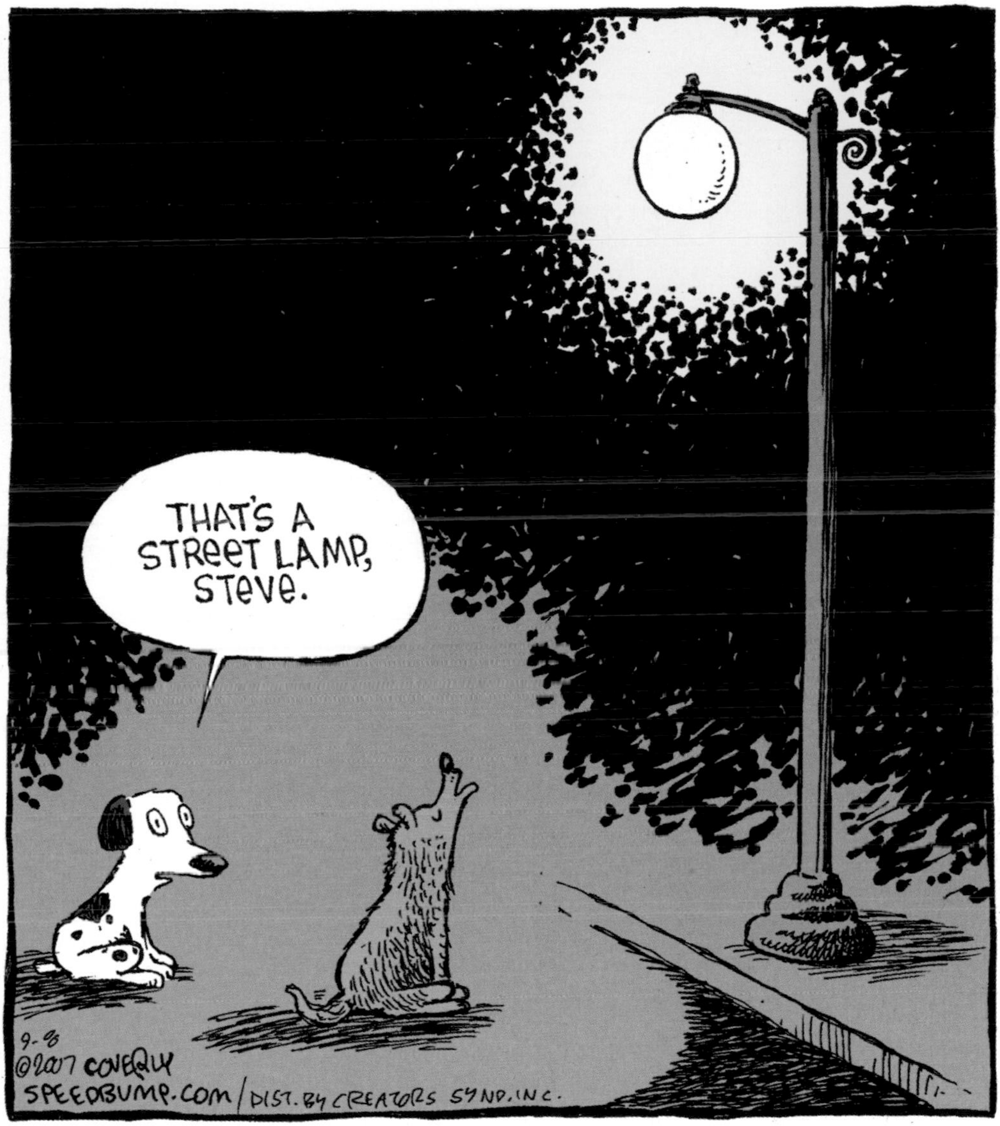
THAT'S A STREET LAMP, STEVE.
9-8
©2007 COVERLY
SPEEDBUMP.COM / DIST. BY CREATORS SYND. INC.

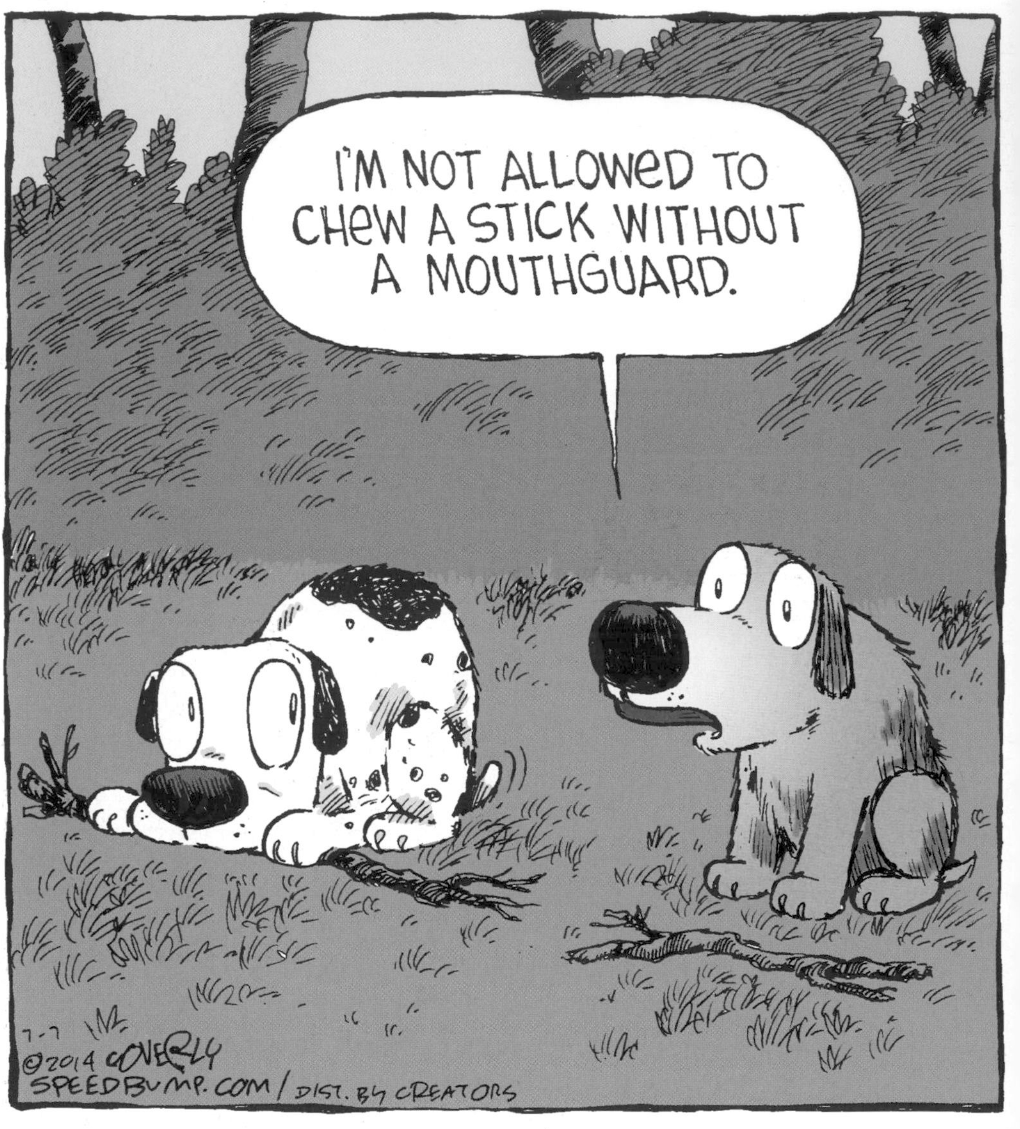
I'M NOT ALLOWED TO CHEW A STICK WITHOUT A MOUTHGUARD.
7-7
©2014 COVERLY
SPEEDBUMP.COM / DIST. BY CREATORS

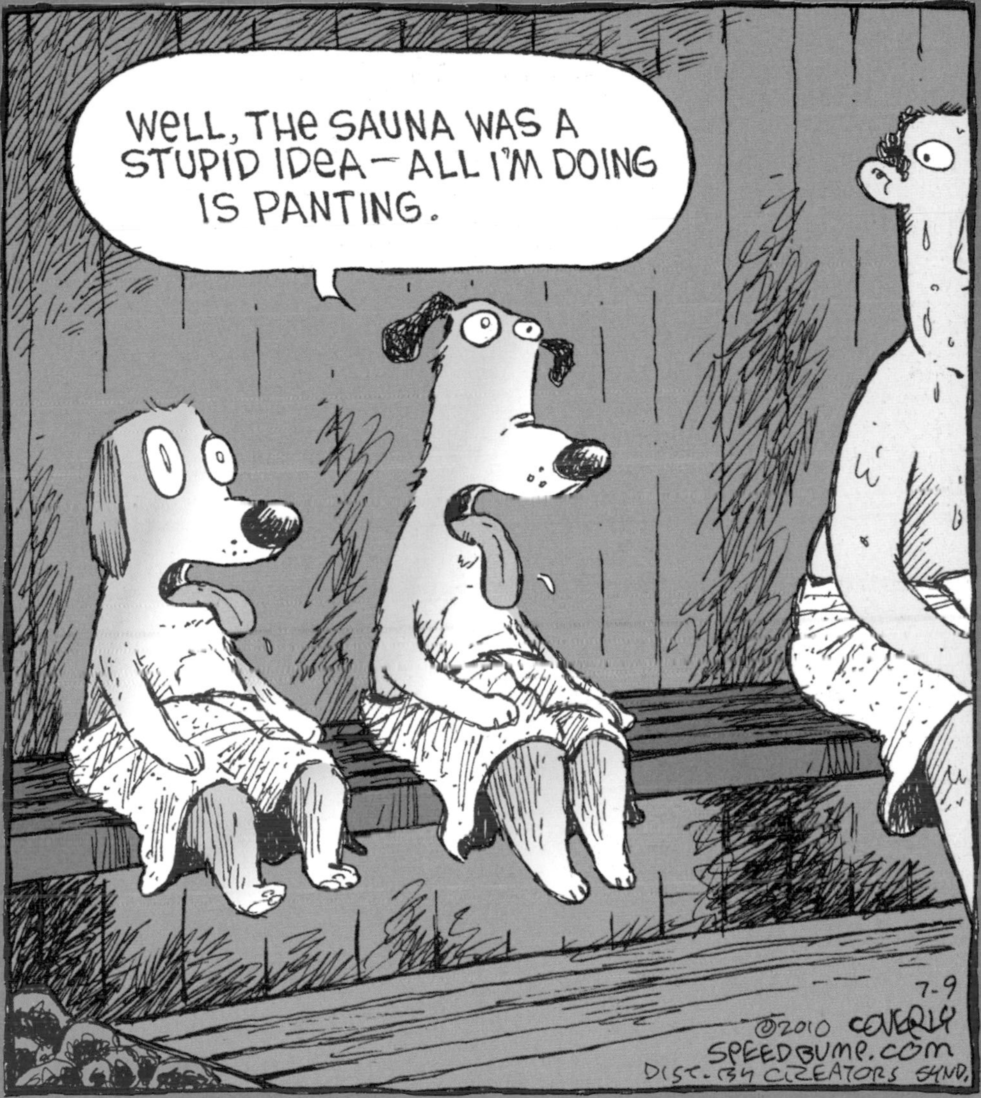
WELL, THE SAUNA WAS A STUPID IDEA—ALL I'M DOING IS PANTING.
7-9
©2010 COVERLY
SPEEDBUMP.COM
DIST. BY CREATORS SYND.

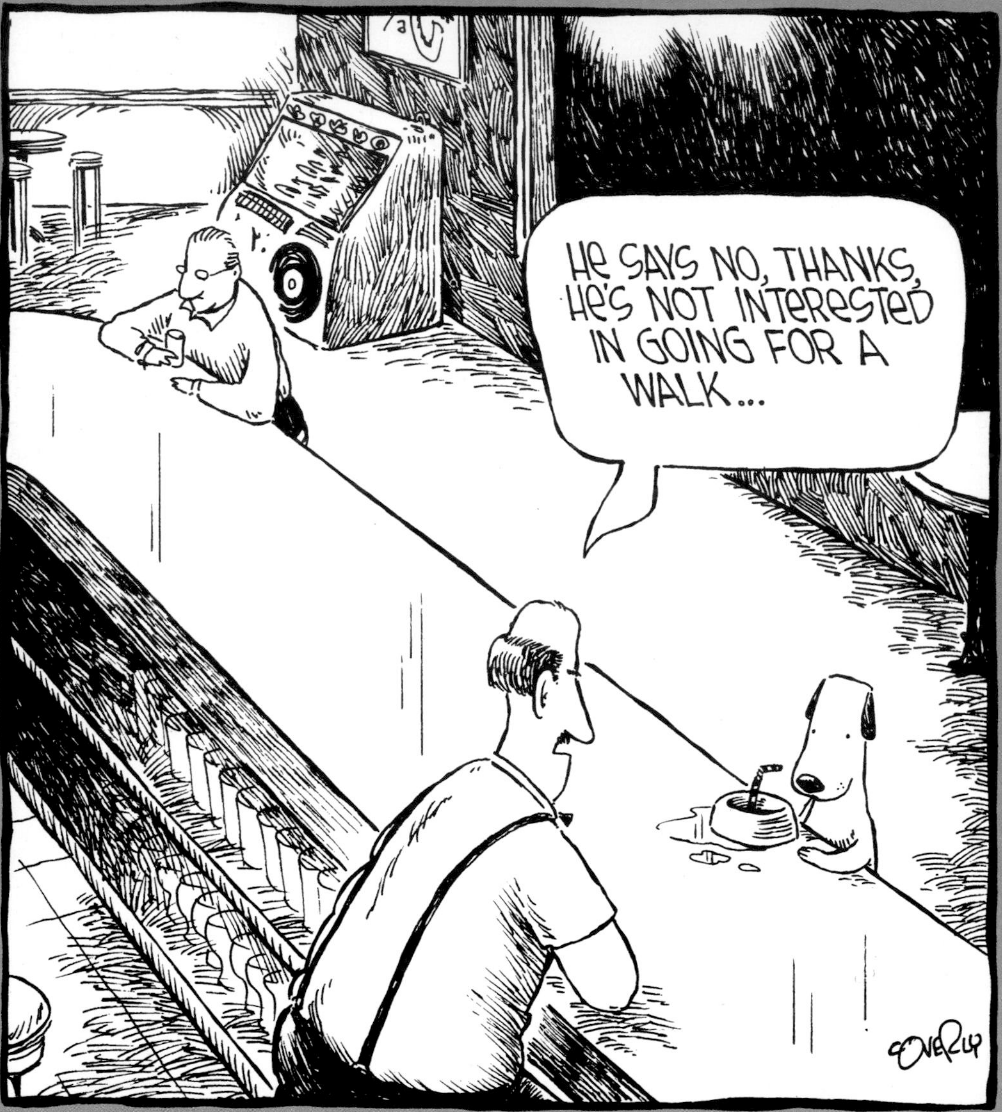
HE SAYS NO, THANKS, HE'S NOT INTERESTED IN GOING FOR A WALK...
COVERLY

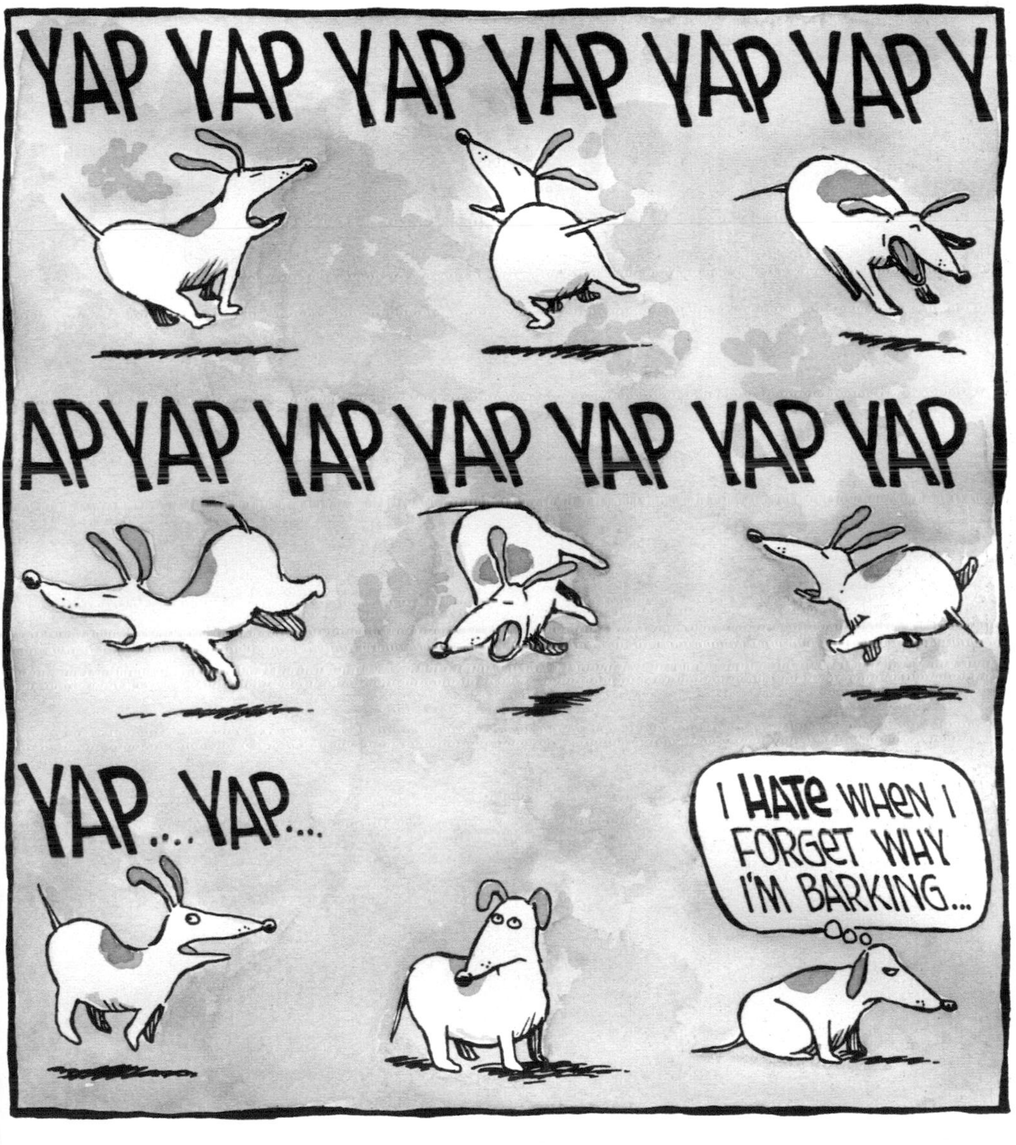
YAP YAP YAP YAP YAP YAP Y
APYAP YAP YAP YAP YAP YAP
YAP.... YAP....
I HATE WHEN I FORGET WHY I'M BARKING...

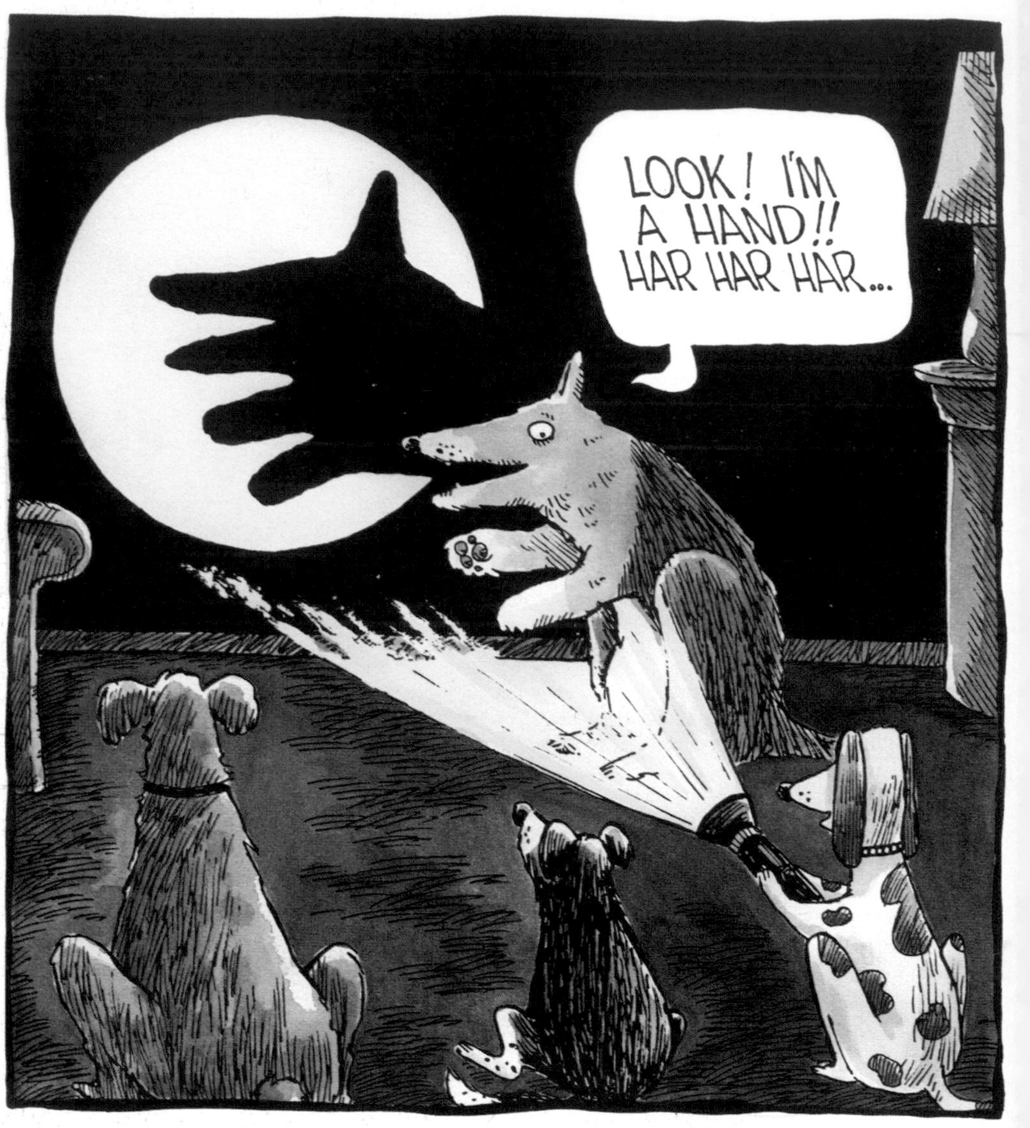
LOOK! I'M A HAND!! HAR HAR HAR...

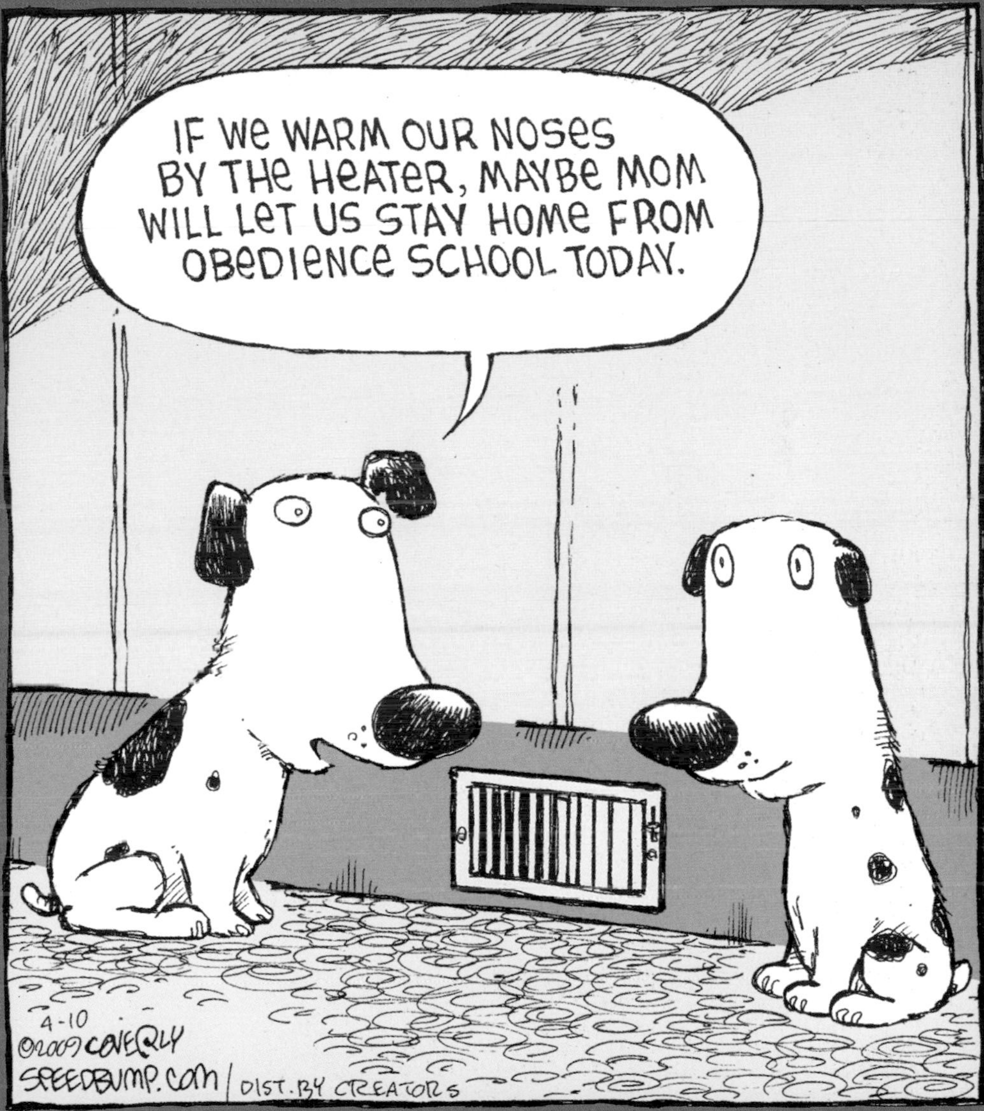
IF WE WARM OUR NOSES BY THE HEATER, MAYBE MOM WILL LET US STAY HOME FROM OBEDIENCE SCHOOL TODAY.
4-10
©2009 COVERLY
SPEEDBUMP.COM / DIST. BY CREATORS

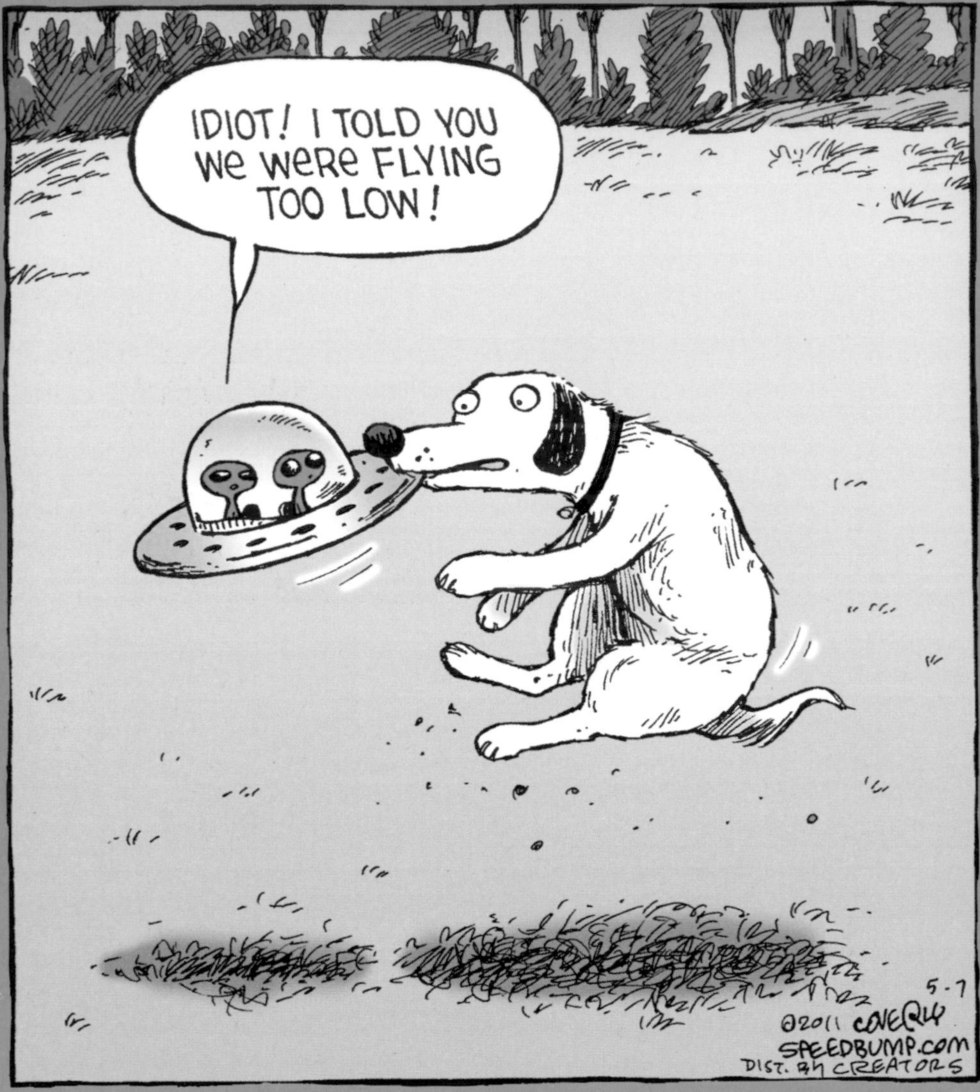
IDIOT! I TOLD YOU WE WERE FLYING TOO LOW!
5-7
©2011 COVERLY
SPEEDBUMP.COM
DIST. BY CREATORS

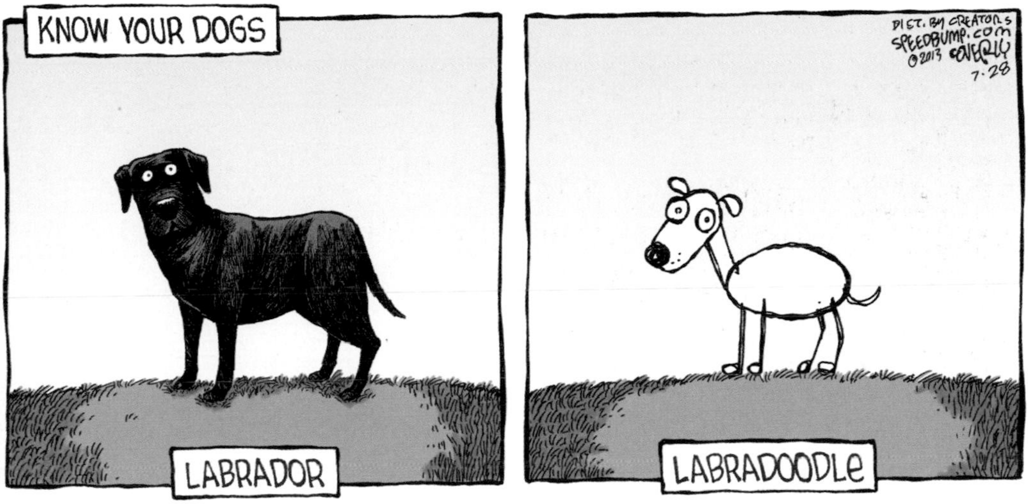
KNOW YOUR DOGS
LABRADOR
DIST. BY CREATORS
SPEEDBUMP.COM
©2013 COVERLY
7-28
LABRADOODLE

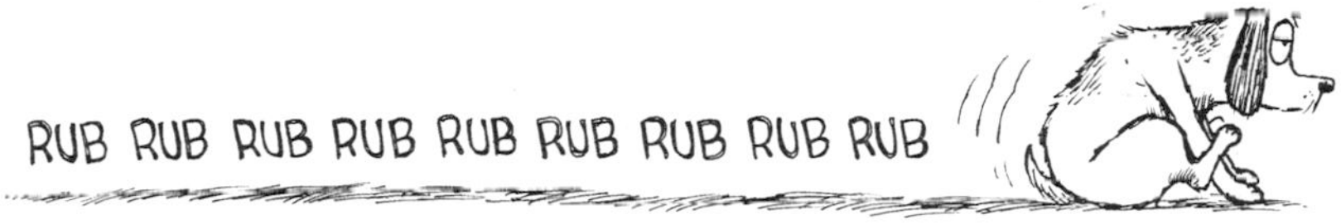
RUB RUB RUB RUB RUB RUB RUB RUB RUB

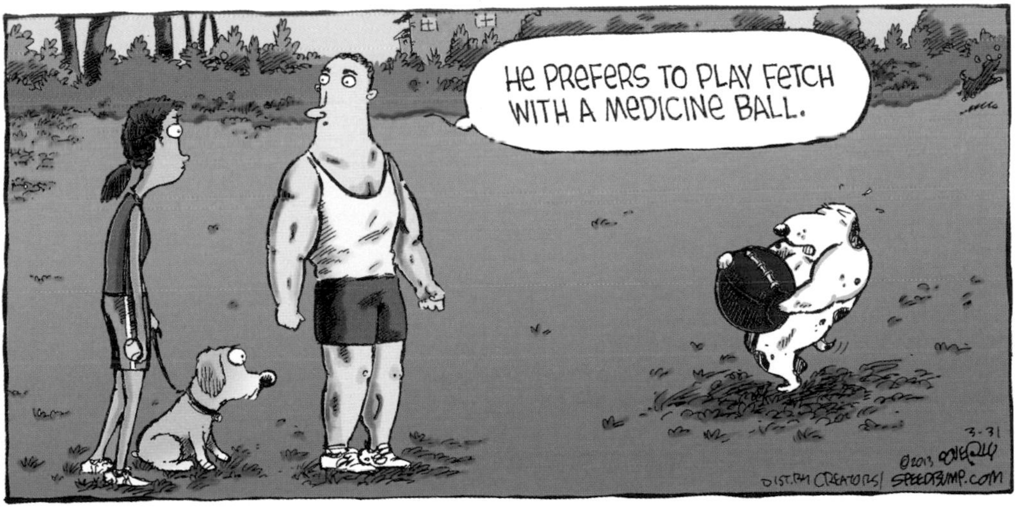
HE PREFERS TO PLAY FETCH WITH A MEDICINE BALL.
3-31
©2013 COVERLY
DIST. BY CREATORS/ SPEEDBUMP.COM

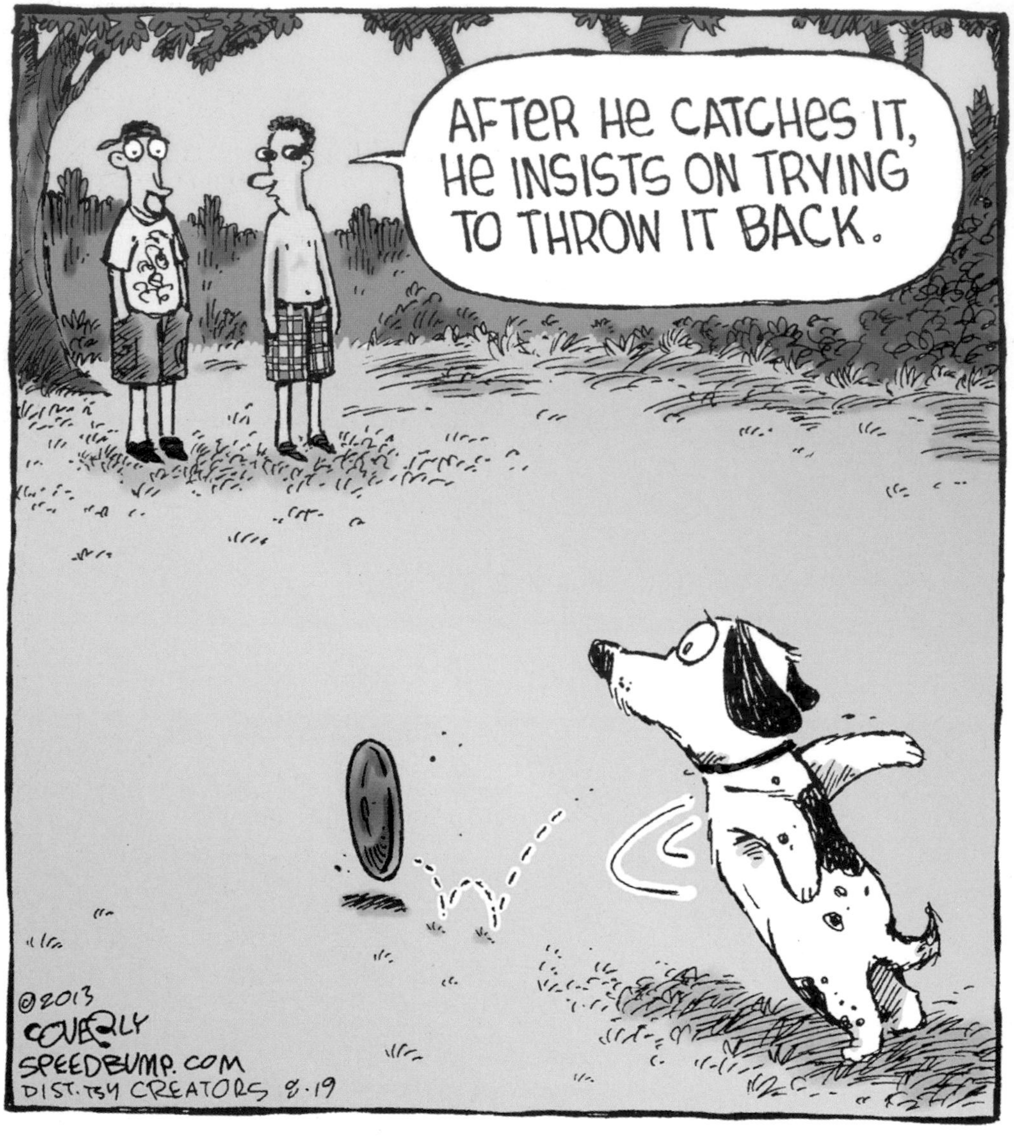
AFTER HE CATCHES IT, HE INSISTS ON TRYING TO THROW IT BACK.
©2013
COVERLY
SPEEDBUMP.COM
DIST. BY CREATORS 8·19

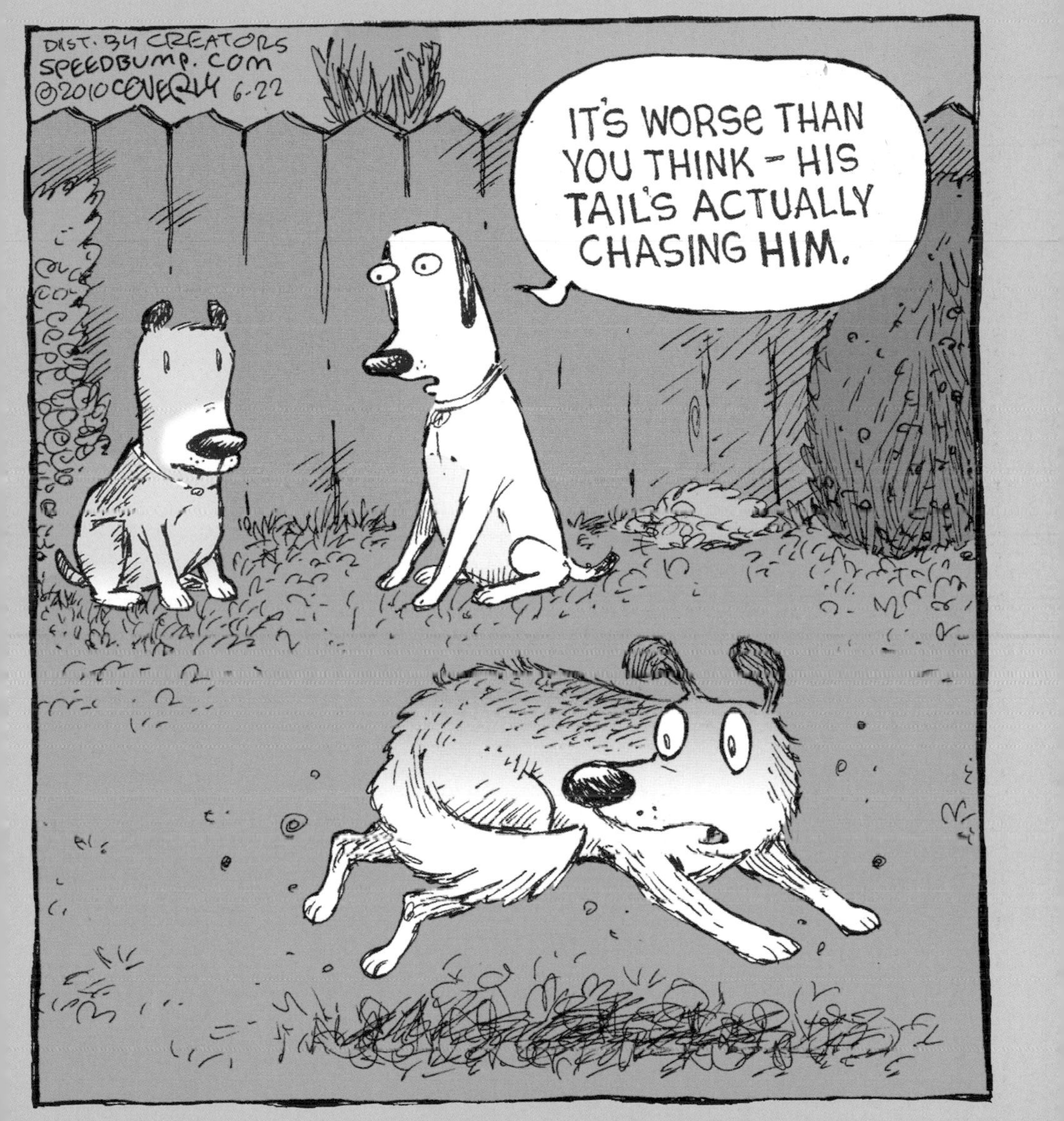
DIST. BY CREATORS
SPEEDBUMP.COM
©2010 COVERLY 6-22
IT'S WORSE THAN YOU THINK – HIS TAIL'S ACTUALLY CHASING **HIM**.

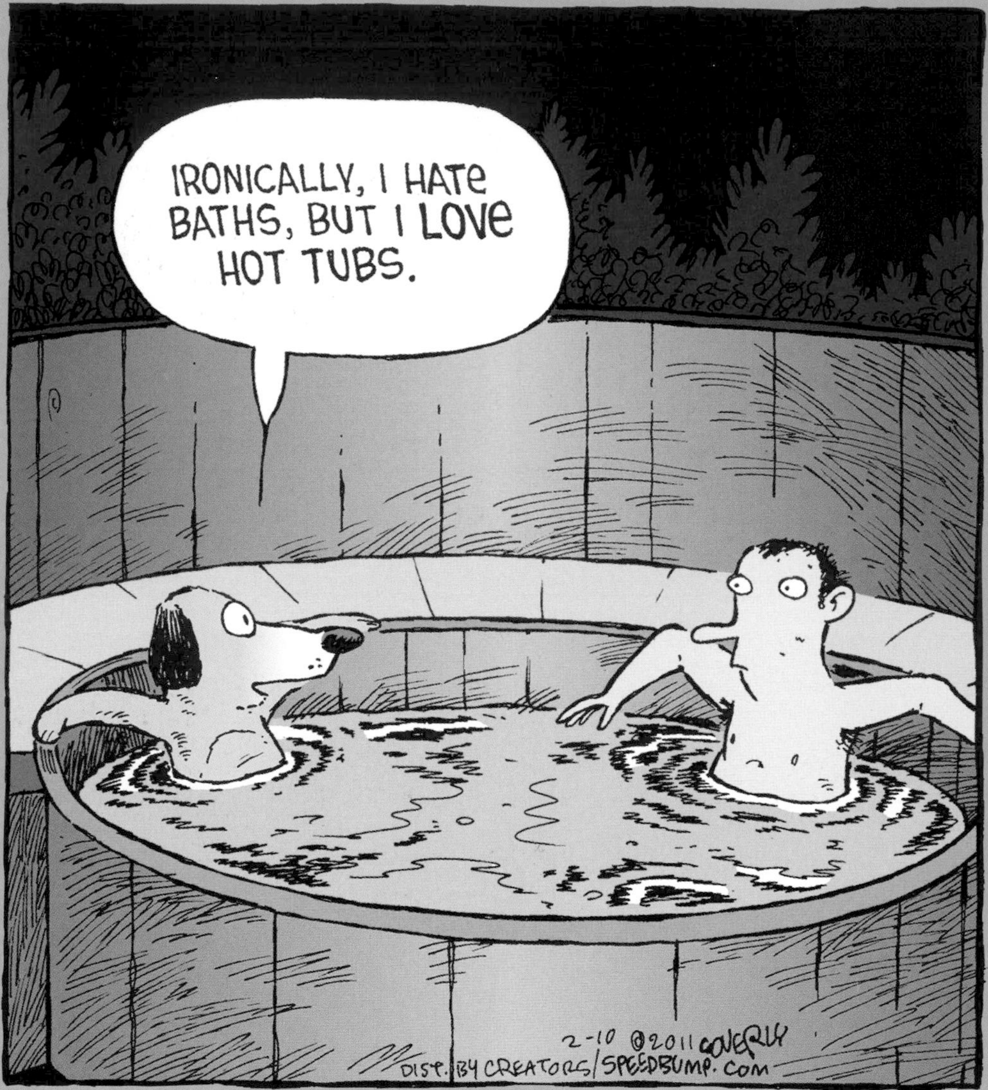
IRONICALLY, I HATE BATHS, BUT I LOVE HOT TUBS.
2-10 ©2011 COVERLY
DIST. BY CREATORS/SPEEDBUMP.COM

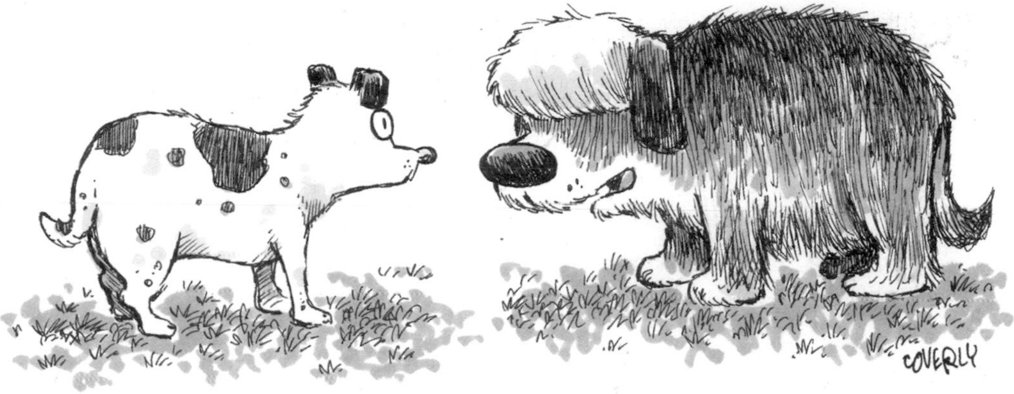
COVERLY

"Don't tell anyone, but they're just hair extensions."

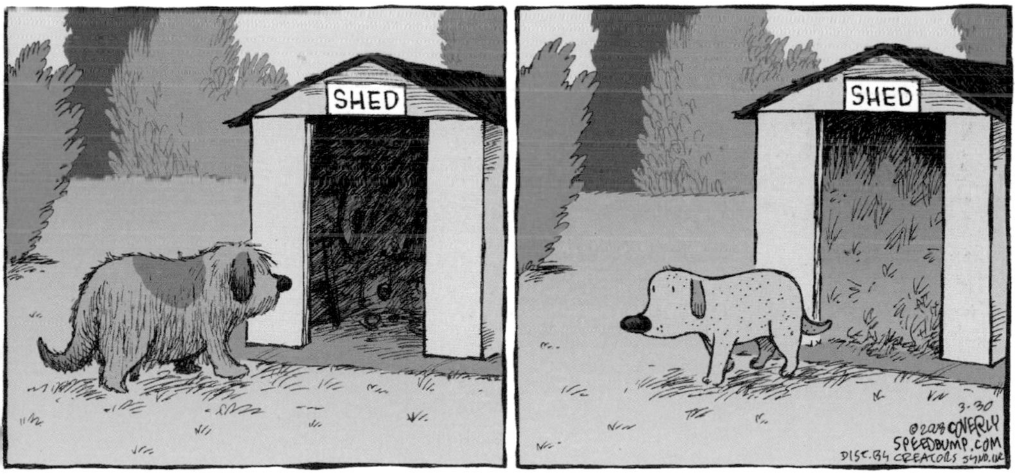
SHED
SHED
SPEEDBUMP.COM

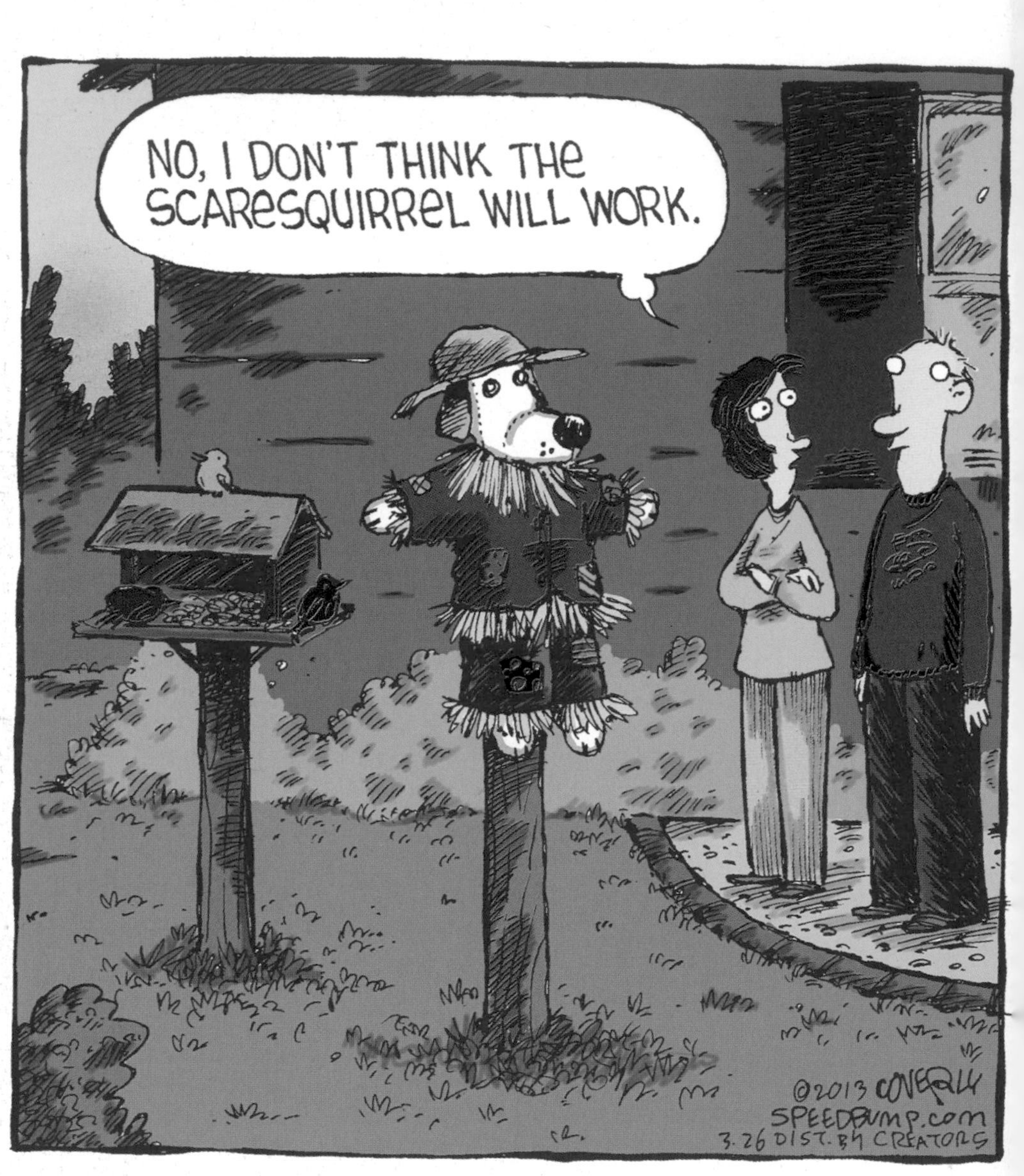
NO, I DON'T THINK THE SCARESQUIRREL WILL WORK.
©2013 COVERLY
SPEEDBUMP.com
3.26 DIST. BY CREATORS

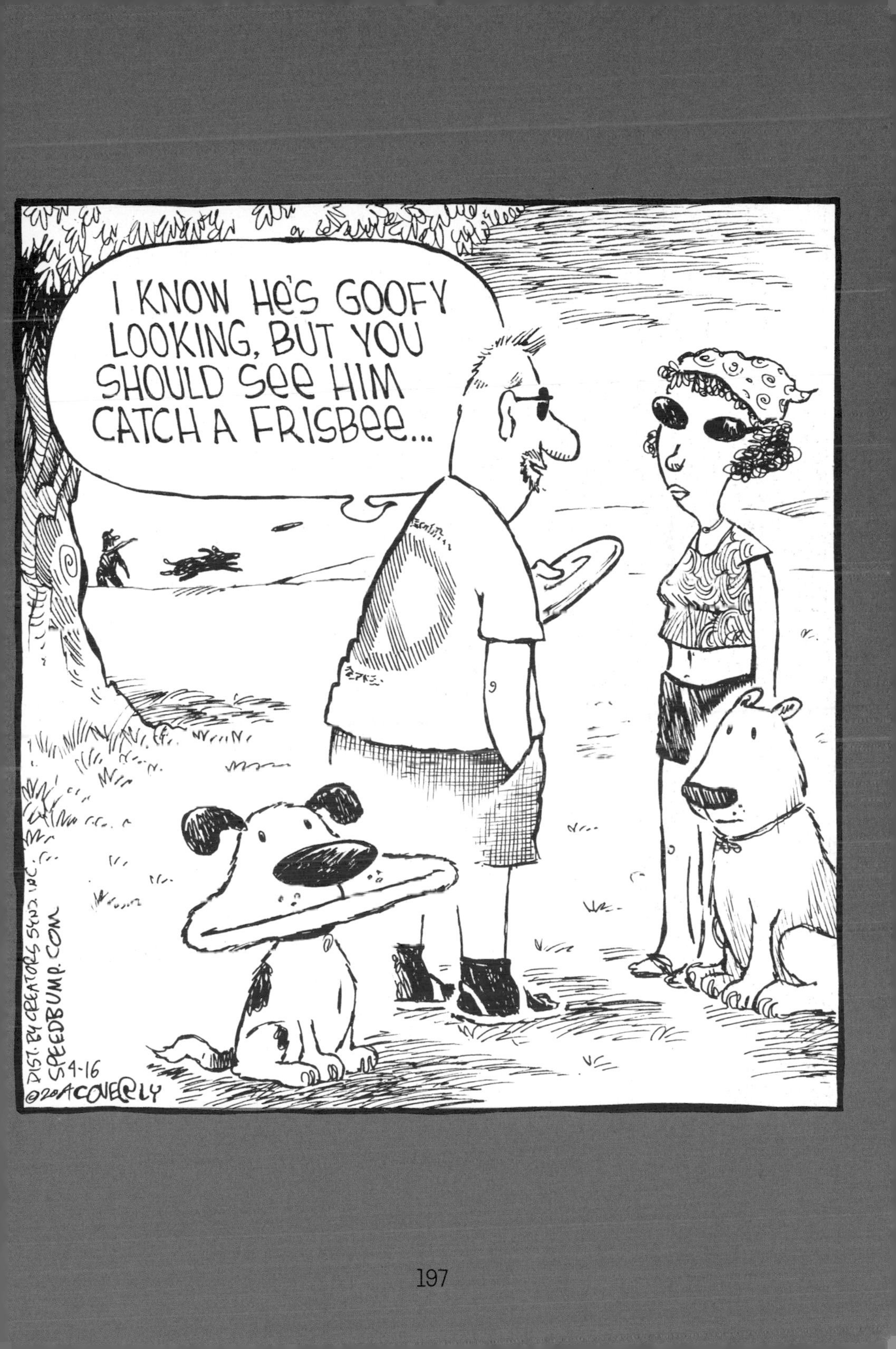
I KNOW HE'S GOOFY LOOKING, BUT YOU SHOULD SEE HIM CATCH A FRISBEE...
DIST. BY CREATORS SYND. INC.
SPEEDBUMP.COM
5-4-16
©2016 COVERLY

CHAPTER 10

FUN FACTS ABOUT OUR FURRY FRIENDS

When dogs drink water, they form a cup
with the back of their tongue.

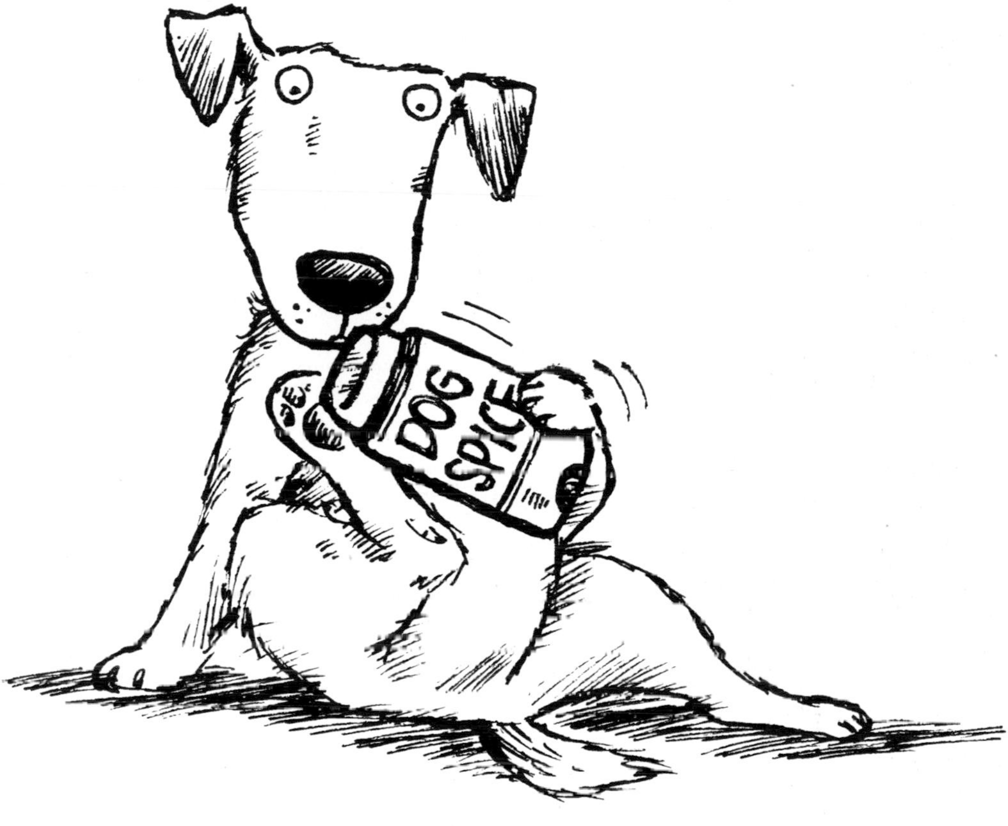
DOG SPICE

Dogs sweat through the pads of their feet, which are covered in bacteria from touching the ground, so when you smell a dog's feet, that's doggie B.O.!

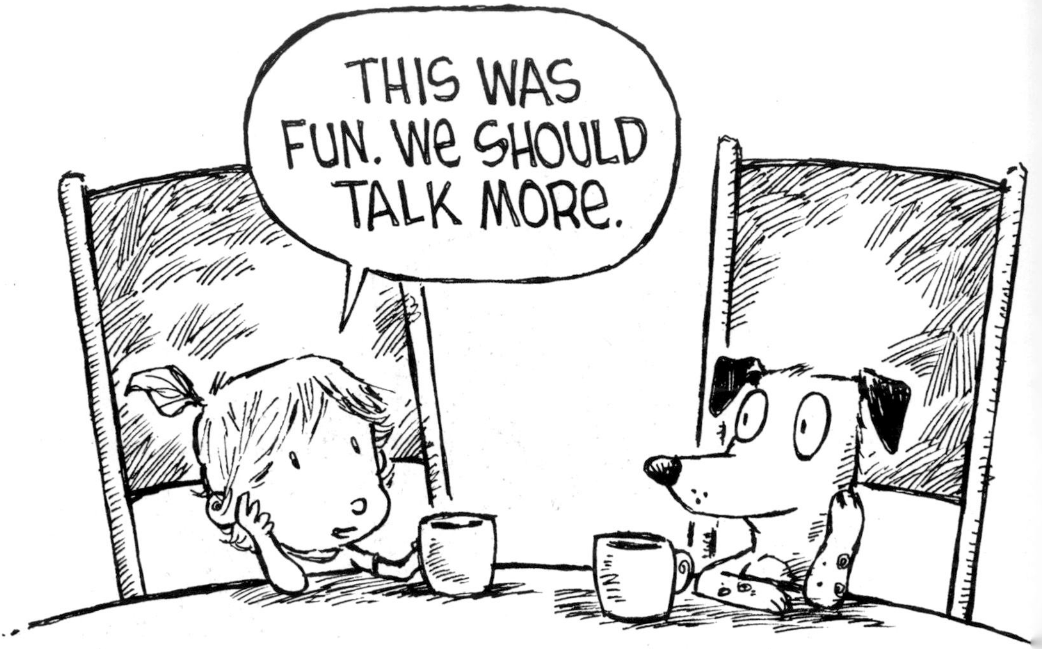
THIS WAS FUN. WE SHOULD TALK MORE.

Dogs basically have the same intelligence as a two-year-old and can understand up to 250 words. They can also count up to five.

Paul McCartney recorded a high-pitched
whistle that only dogs can hear and put it
in the Beatles' song "A Day in the Life"
so that his own dog would enjoy it.

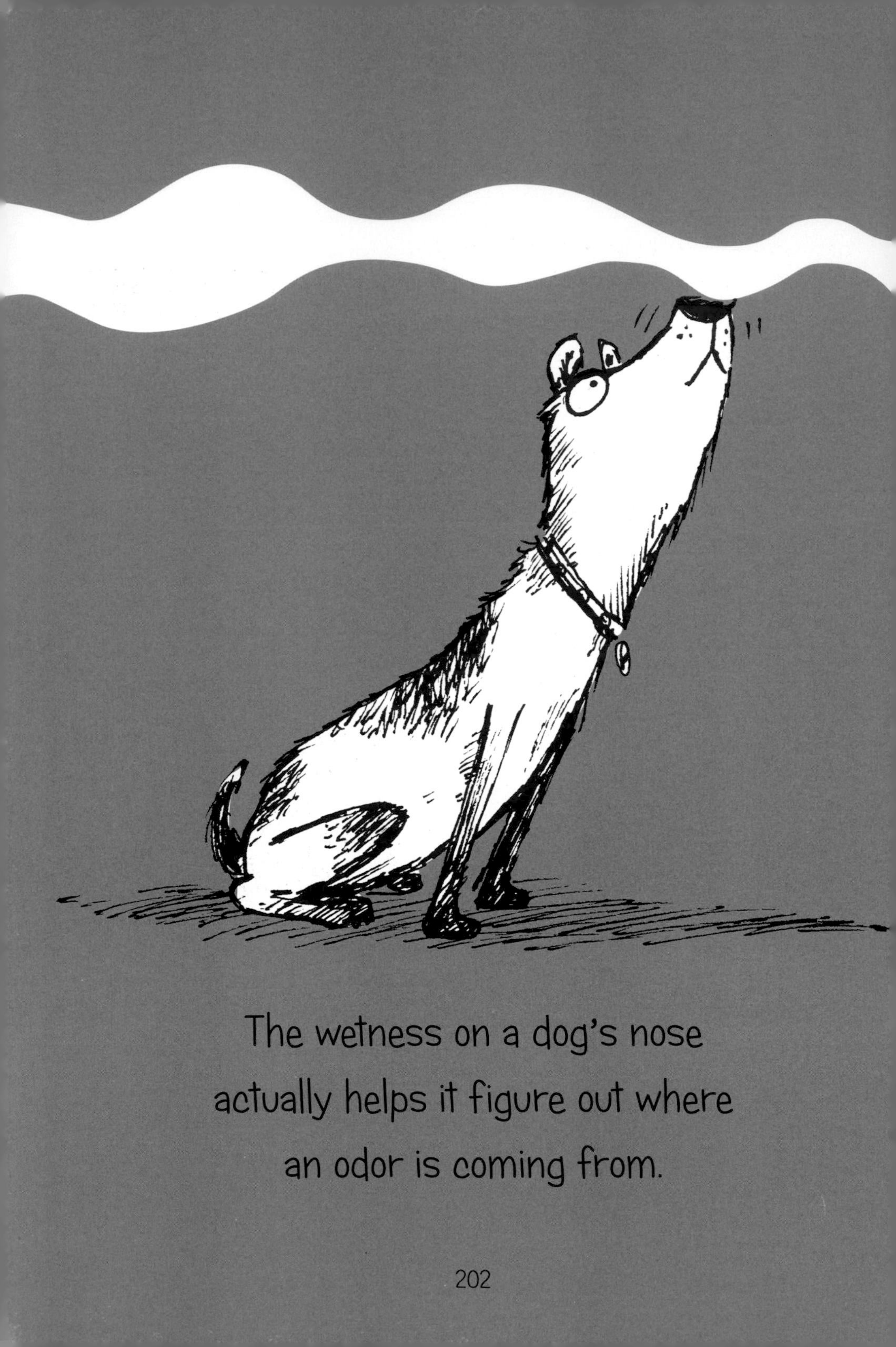

The wetness on a dog's nose actually helps it figure out where an odor is coming from.

DOG DOODLES

LIVING WITH AN EMOTIONALLY NEEDY DOG...

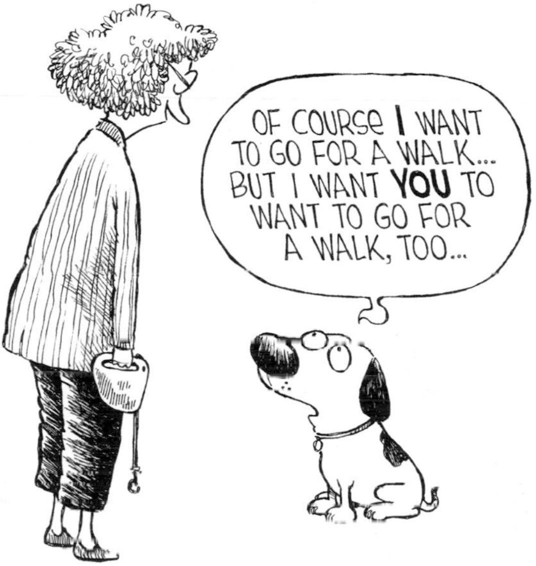
OF COURSE I WANT TO GO FOR A WALK... BUT I WANT **YOU** TO WANT TO GO FOR A WALK, TOO...

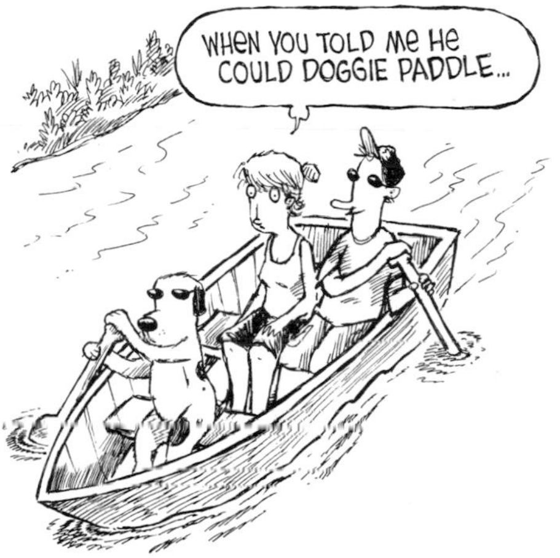
WHEN YOU TOLD ME HE COULD DOGGIE PADDLE...

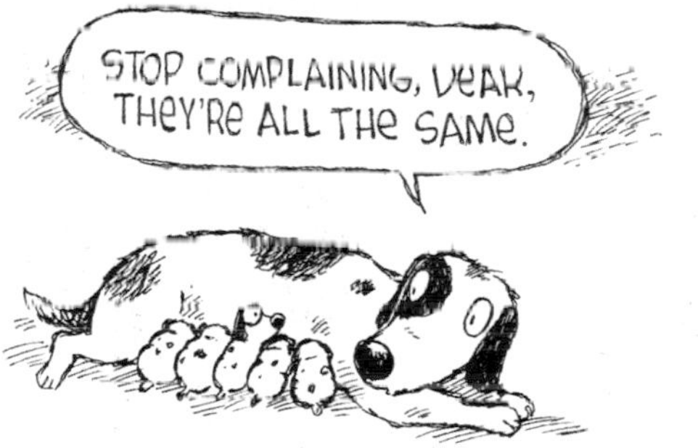
STOP COMPLAINING, DEAR, THEY'RE ALL THE SAME.

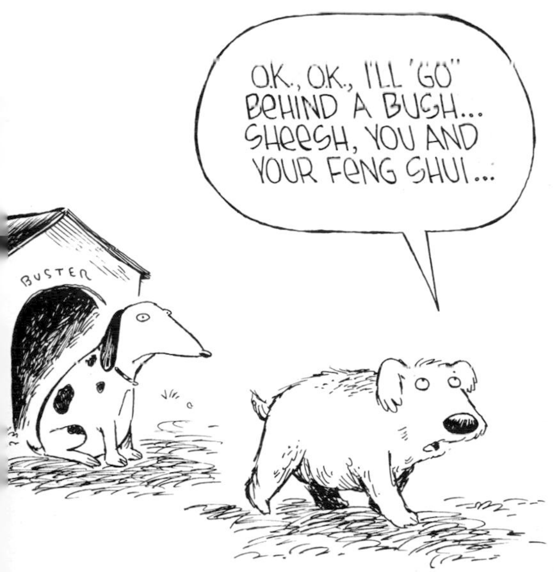
O.K., O.K., I'LL "GO" BEHIND A BUSH... SHEESH, YOU AND YOUR FENG SHUI...
BUSTER

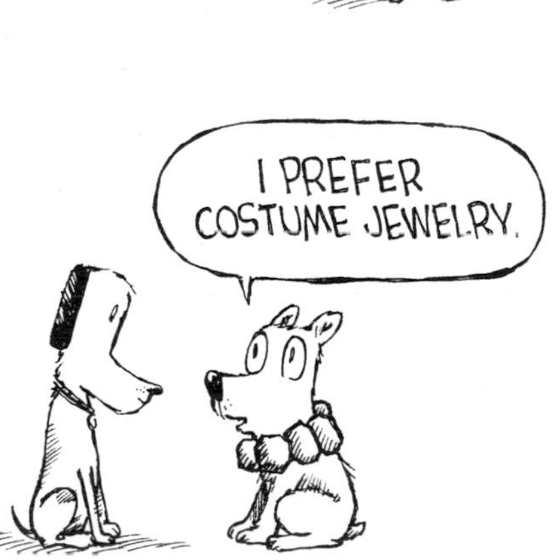
I PREFER COSTUME JEWELRY.

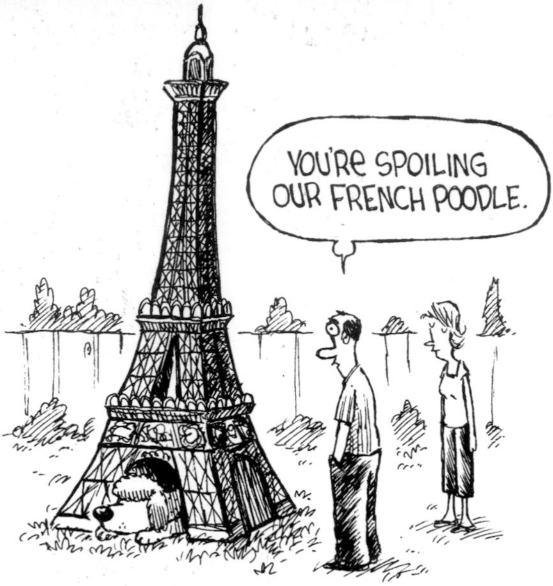
YOU'RE SPOILING OUR FRENCH POODLE.

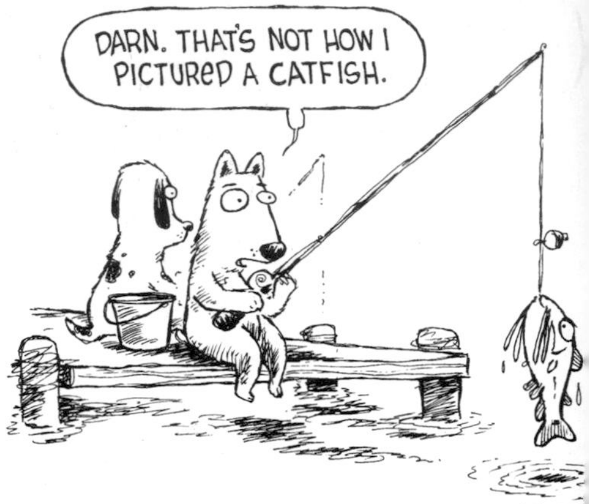
DARN. THAT'S NOT HOW I PICTURED A CATFISH.

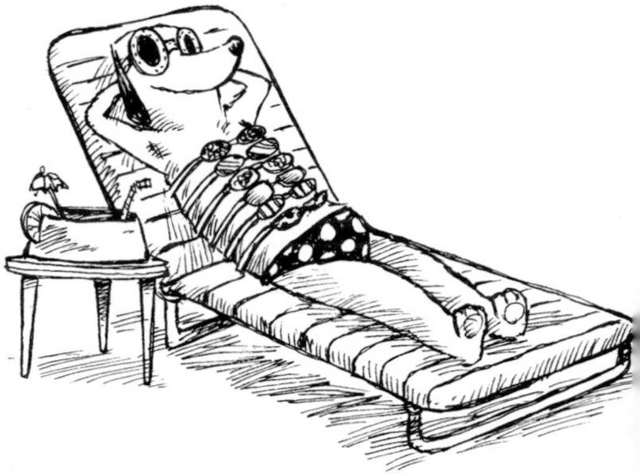

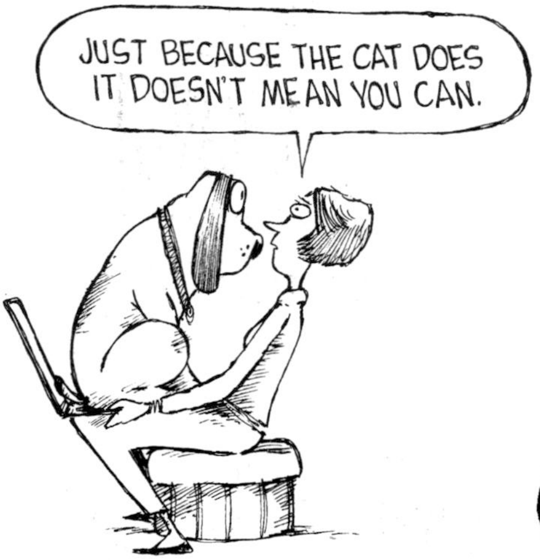
JUST BECAUSE THE CAT DOES IT DOESN'T MEAN YOU CAN.

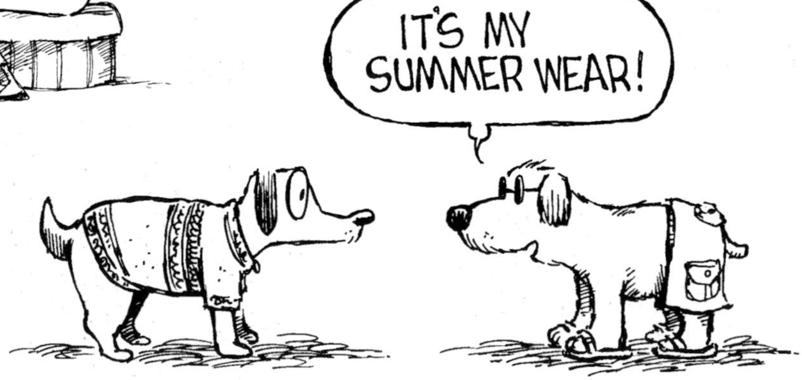
IT'S MY SUMMER WEAR!

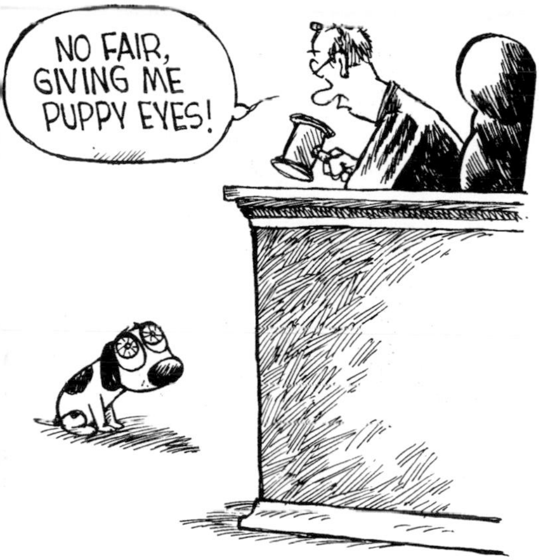
NO FAIR, GIVING ME PUPPY EYES!

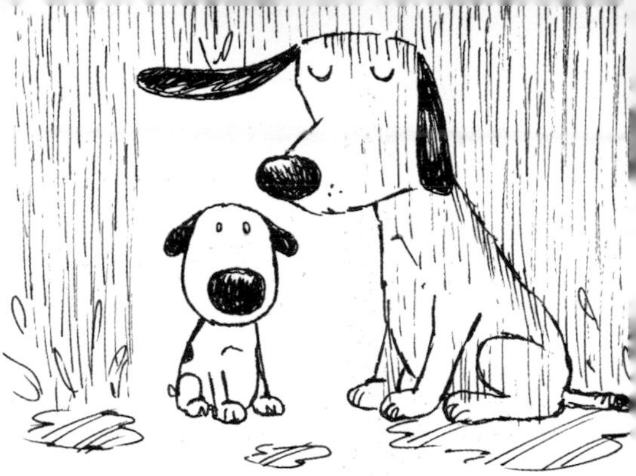

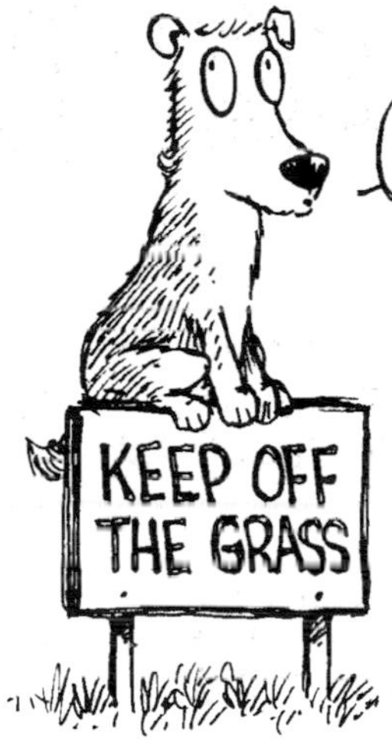
KEEP OFF THE GRASS

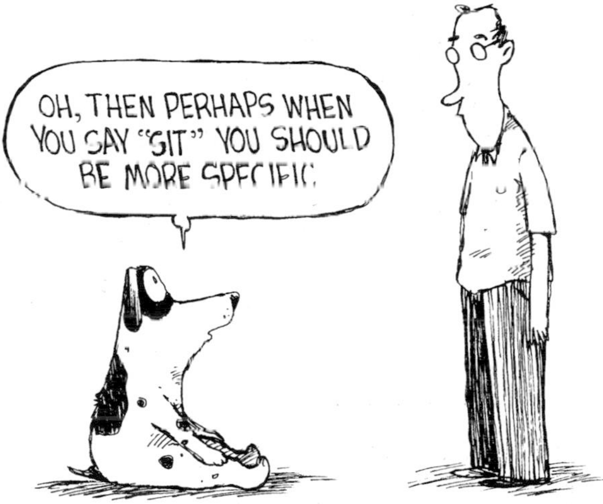
OH, THEN PERHAPS WHEN YOU SAY "GIT" YOU SHOULD BE MORE SPECIFIC

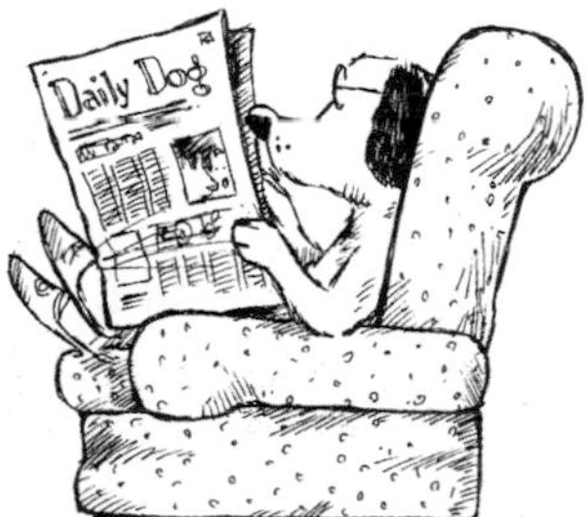
Daily Dog

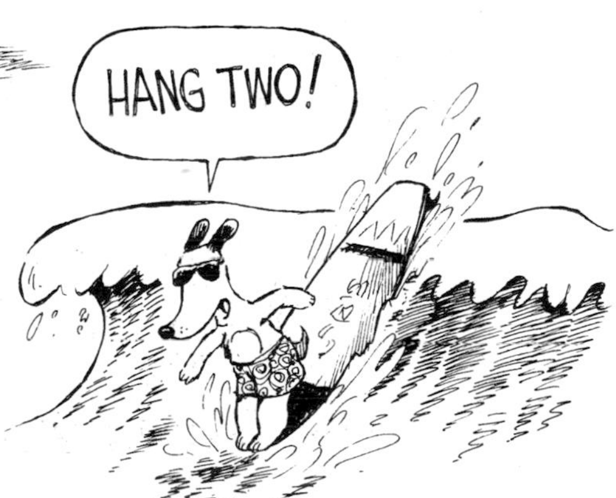
HANG TWO!

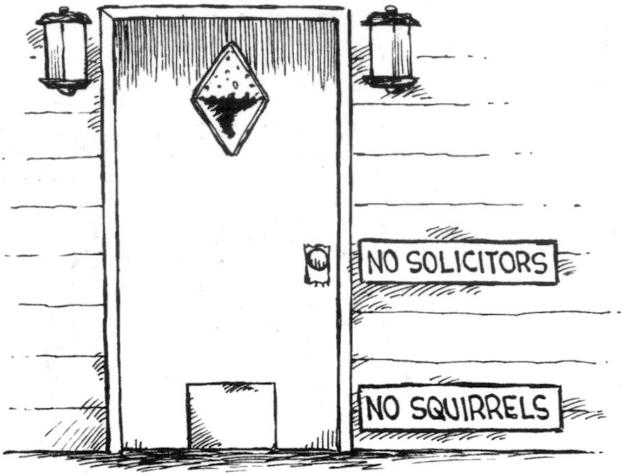
NO SOLICITORS
NO SQUIRRELS

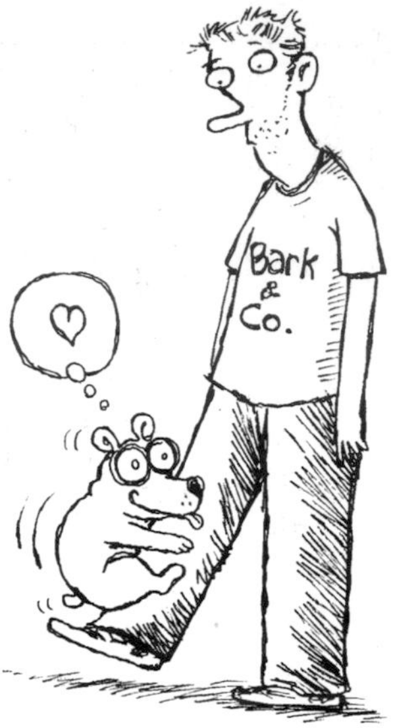
Bark & Co.

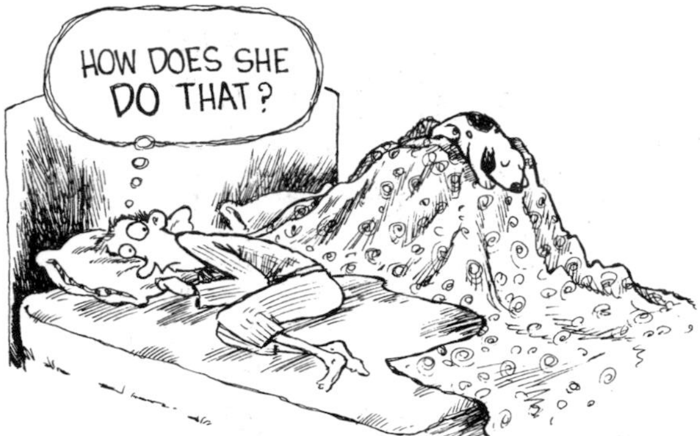
HOW DOES SHE DO THAT?

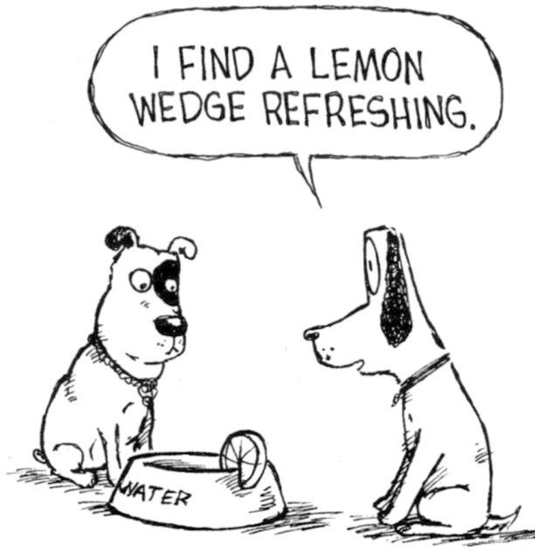
I FIND A LEMON WEDGE REFRESHING.
WATER

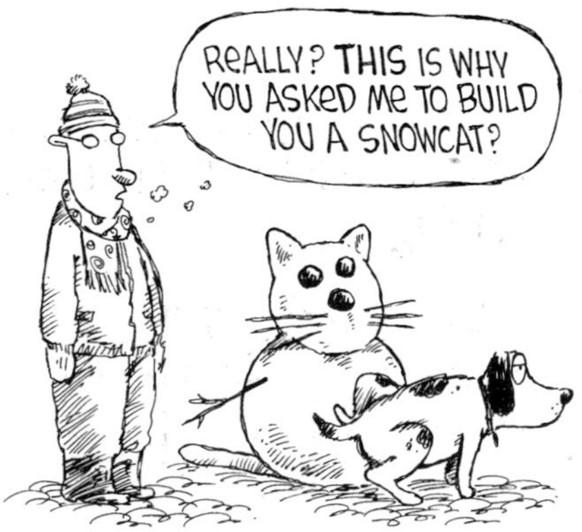
REALLY? THIS IS WHY YOU ASKED ME TO BUILD YOU A SNOWCAT?

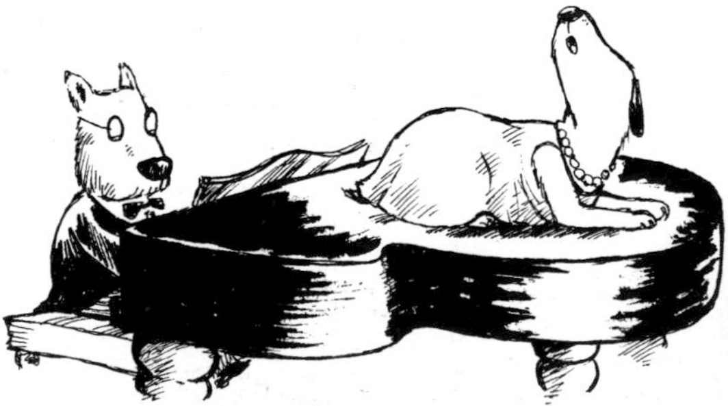

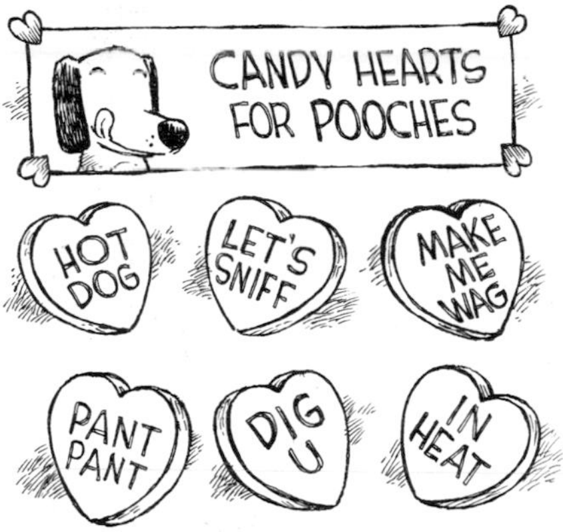
CANDY HEARTS FOR POOCHES
HOT DOG
LET'S SNIFF
MAKE ME WAG
PANT PANT
DIG U
IN HEAT

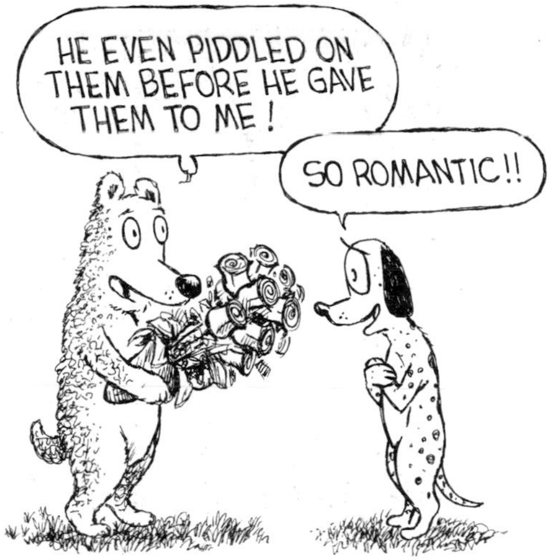
HE EVEN PIDDLED ON THEM BEFORE HE GAVE THEM TO ME!
SO ROMANTIC!!

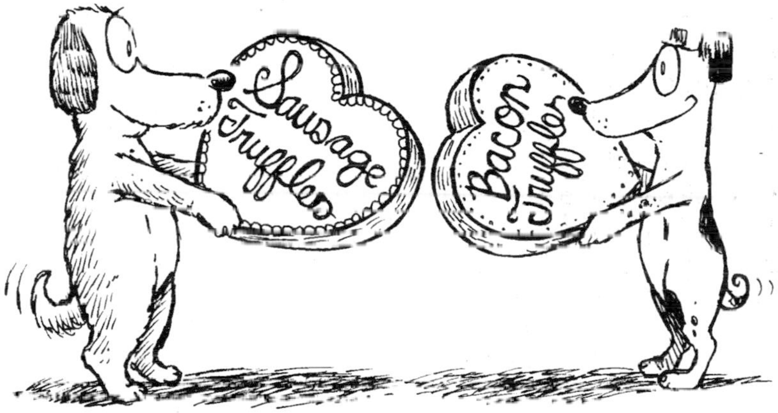
Sausage Truffles
Bacon Truffles

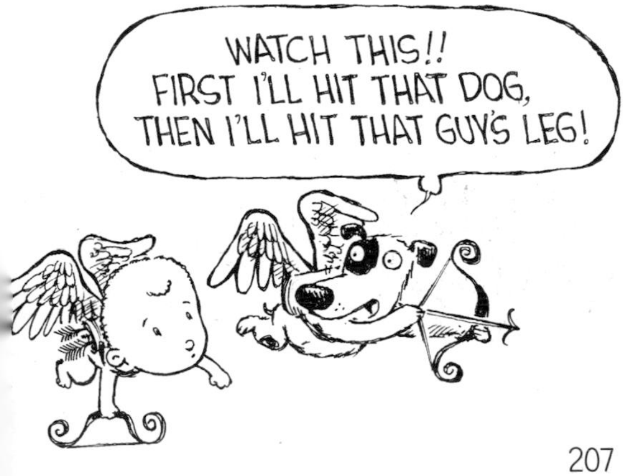
WATCH THIS!! FIRST I'LL HIT THAT DOG, THEN I'LL HIT THAT GUY'S LEG!

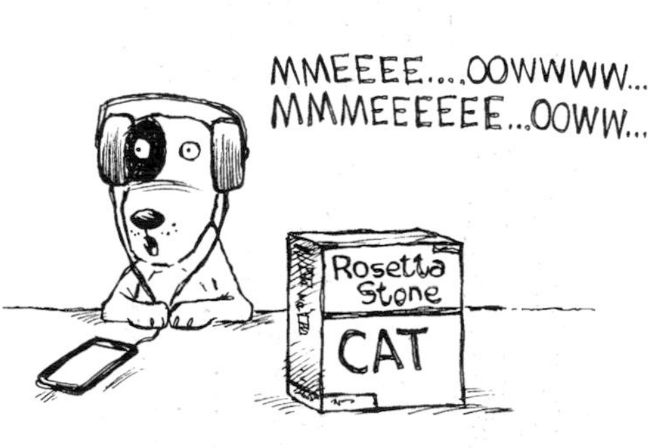
MMEEEE....OOWWWW...
MMMEEEEEE...OOWW...
Rosetta Stone
CAT

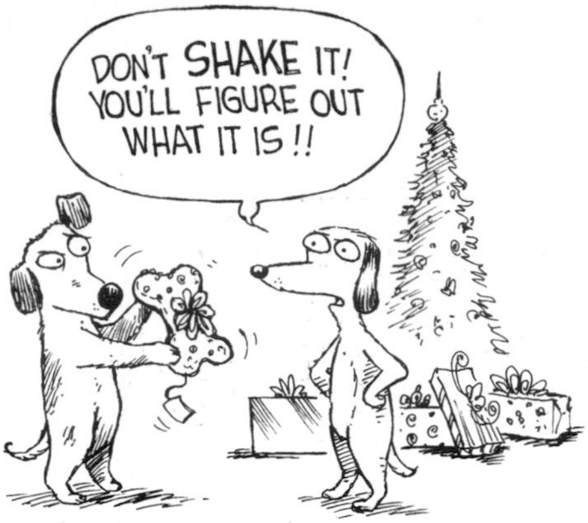
DON'T SHAKE IT! YOU'LL FIGURE OUT WHAT IT IS!!

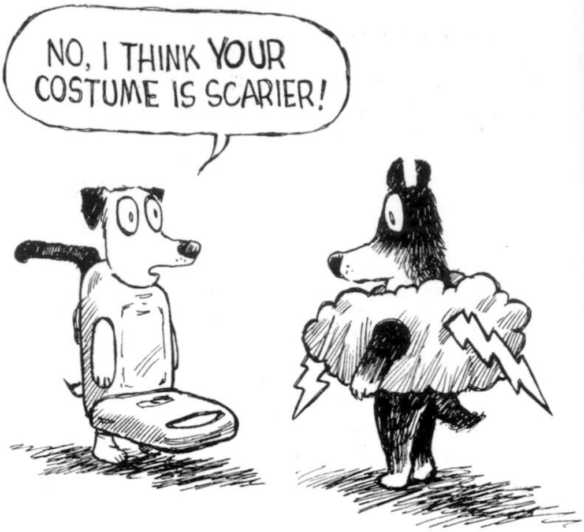
NO, I THINK YOUR COSTUME IS SCARIER!

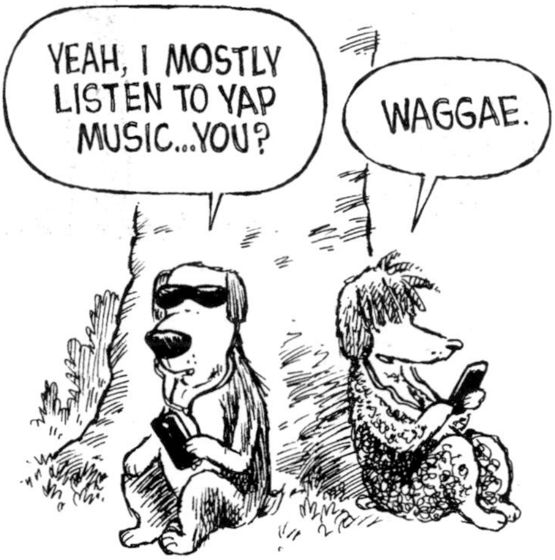
YEAH, I MOSTLY LISTEN TO YAP MUSIC...YOU?
WAGGAE.
People
Dogs

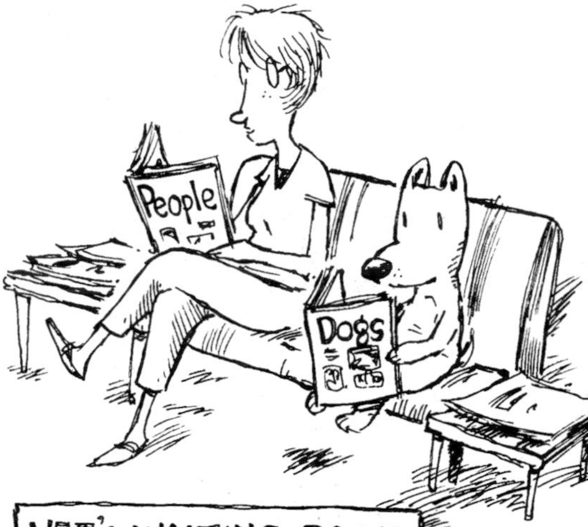
People
Dogs

VET'S WAITING ROOM

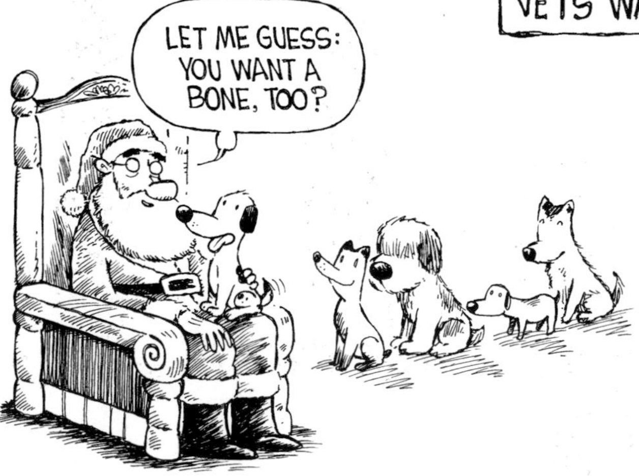
LET ME GUESS: YOU WANT A BONE, TOO?

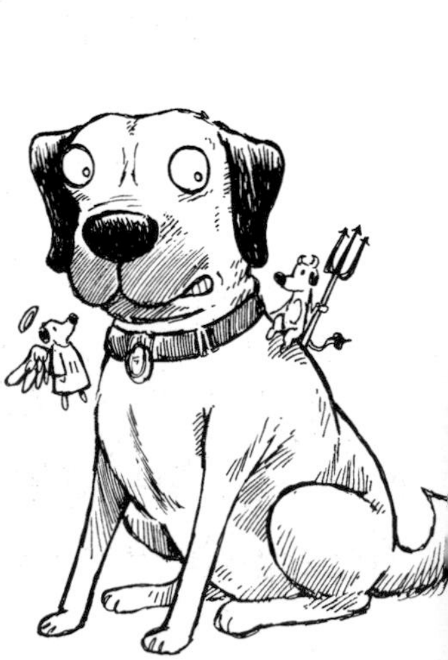

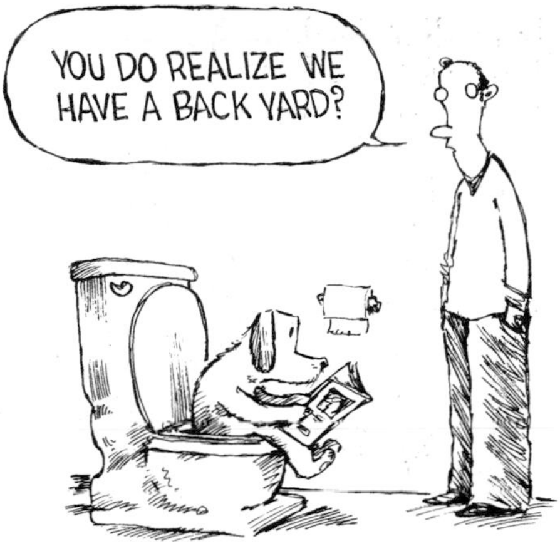
YOU DO REALIZE WE HAVE A BACK YARD?

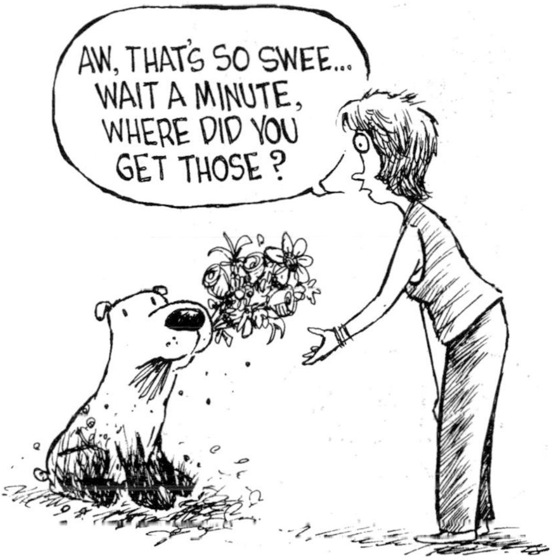
AW, THAT'S SO SWEE... WAIT A MINUTE, WHERE DID YOU GET THOSE ?

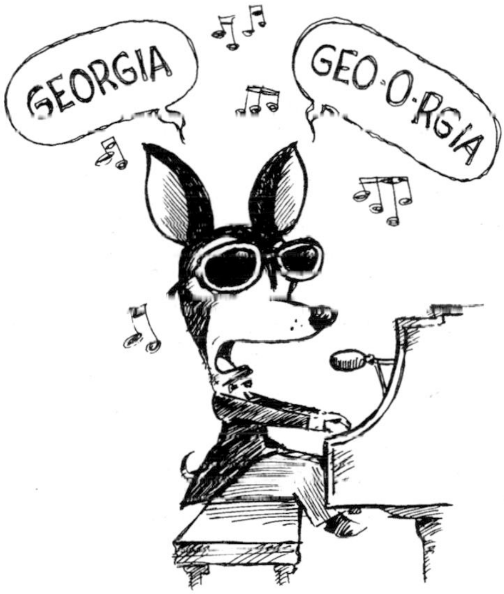
GEORGIA
GEO-O-RGIA

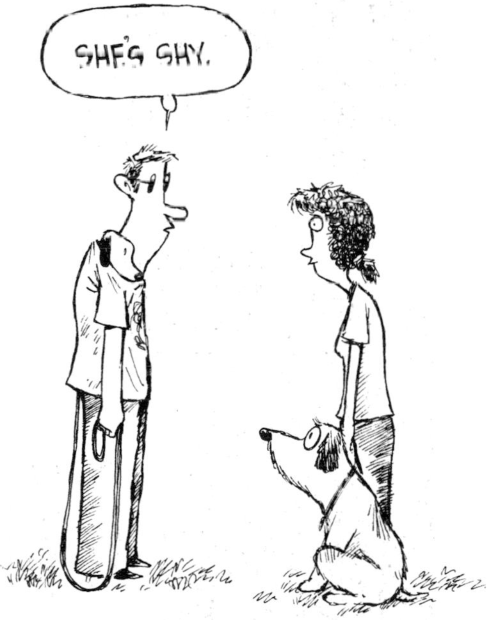
SHE'S SHY.

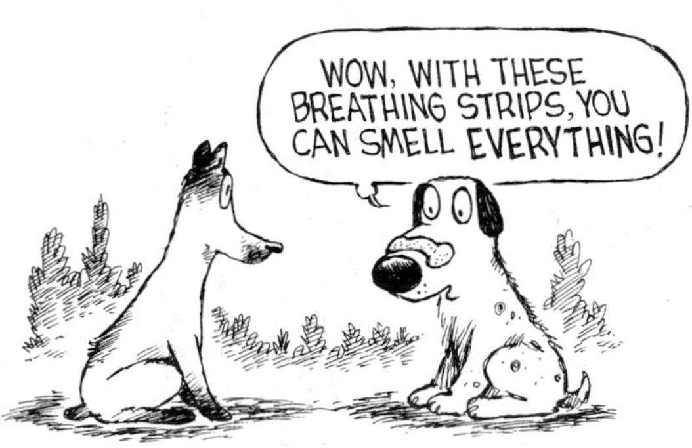
WOW, WITH THESE BREATHING STRIPS, YOU CAN SMELL EVERYTHING!

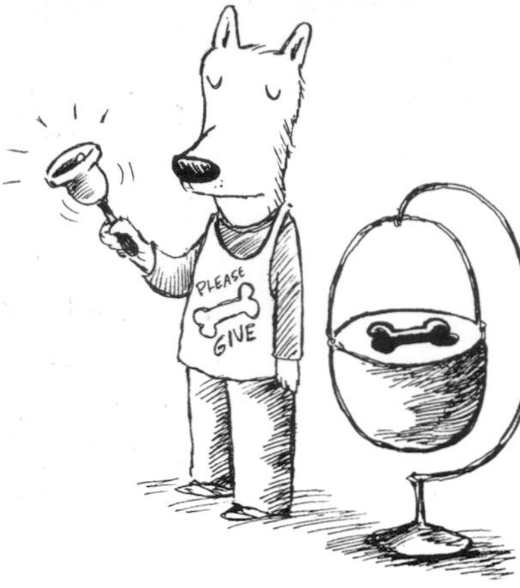
PLEASE
GIVE

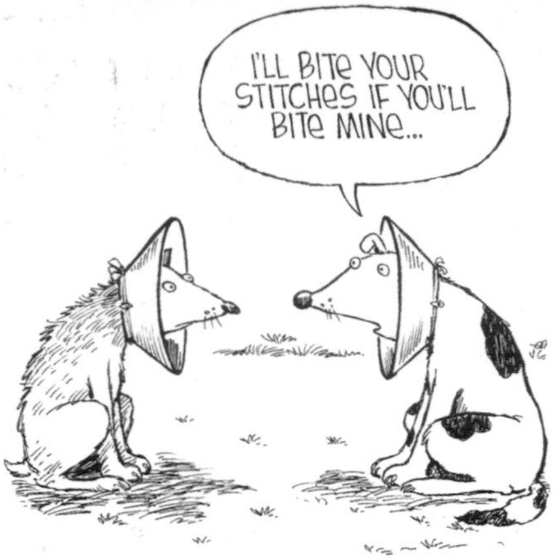
I'LL BITE YOUR STITCHES IF YOU'LL BITE MINE...

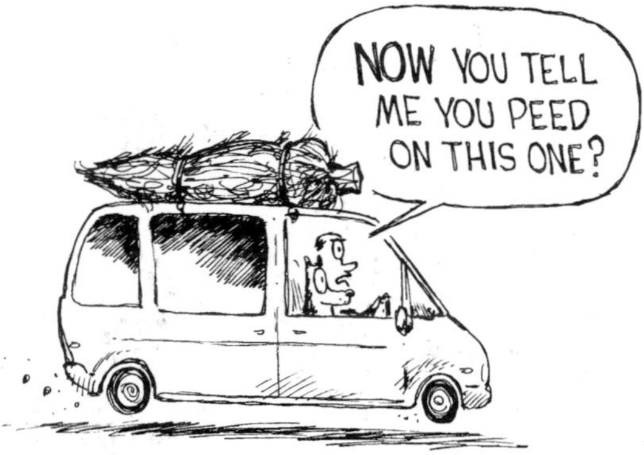
NOW YOU TELL ME YOU PEED ON THIS ONE?

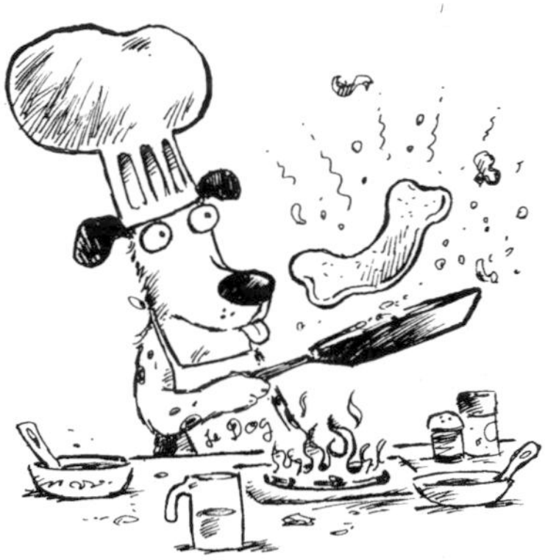

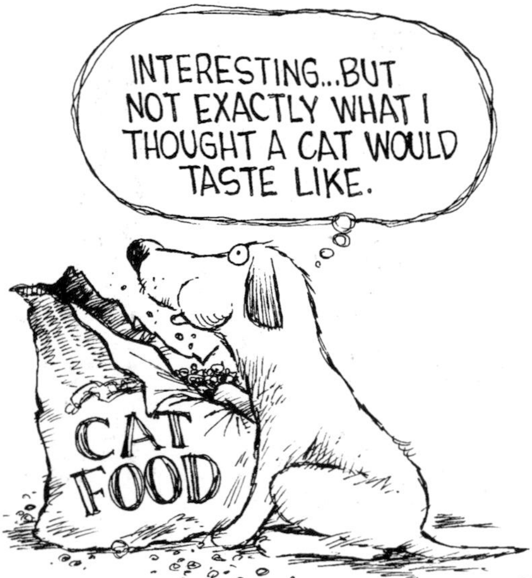
INTERESTING...BUT NOT EXACTLY WHAT I THOUGHT A CAT WOULD TASTE LIKE.
CAT FOOD

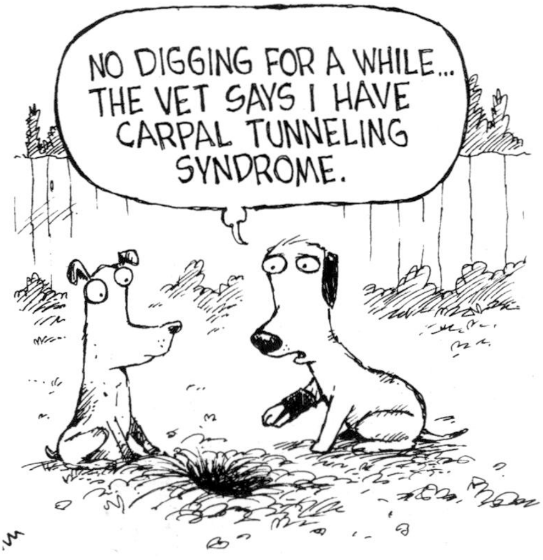
NO DIGGING FOR A WHILE... THE VET SAYS I HAVE CARPAL TUNNELING SYNDROME.

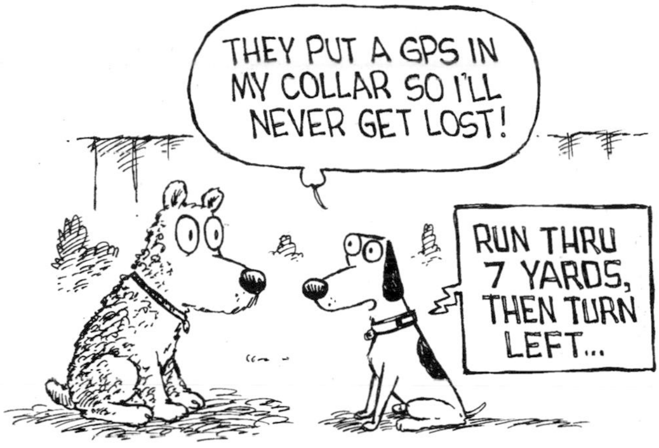
THEY PUT A GPS IN MY COLLAR SO I'LL NEVER GET LOST!
RUN THRU 7 YARDS, THEN TURN LEFT...

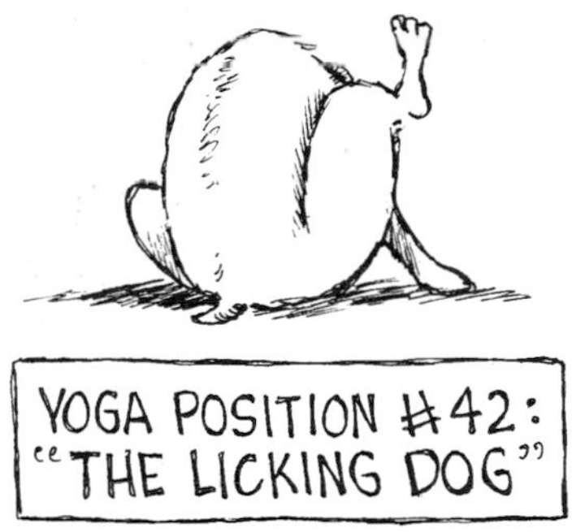
YOGA POSITION #42: "THE LICKING DOG"

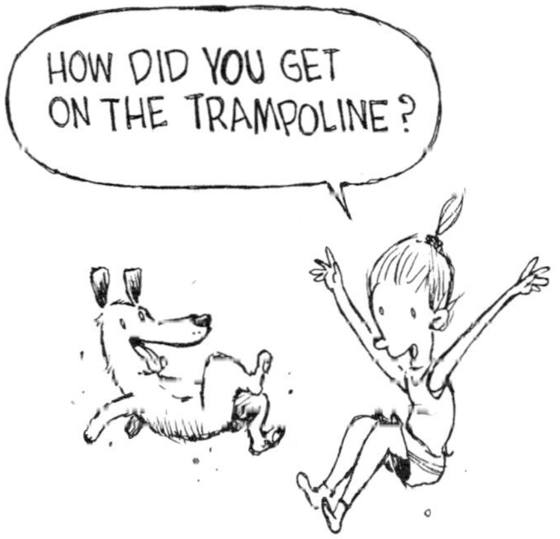
HOW DID YOU GET ON THE TRAMPOLINE?

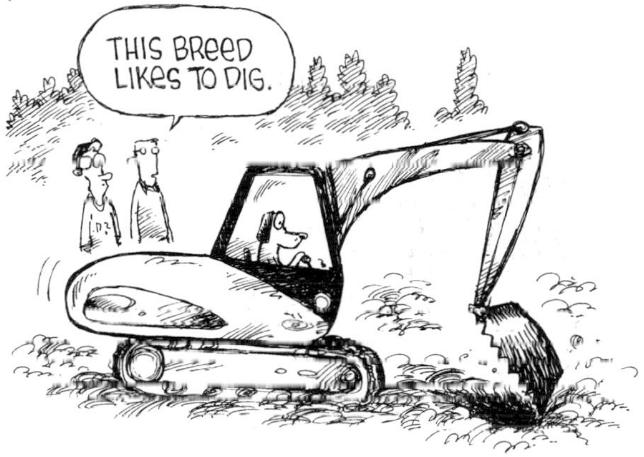
THIS BREED LIKES TO DIG.

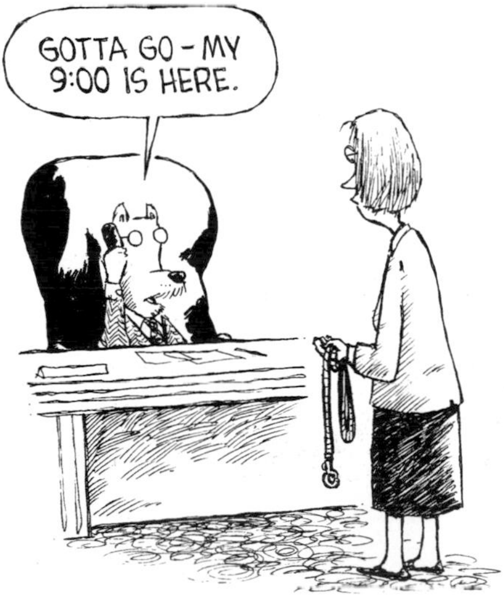
GOTTA GO - MY 9:00 IS HERE.

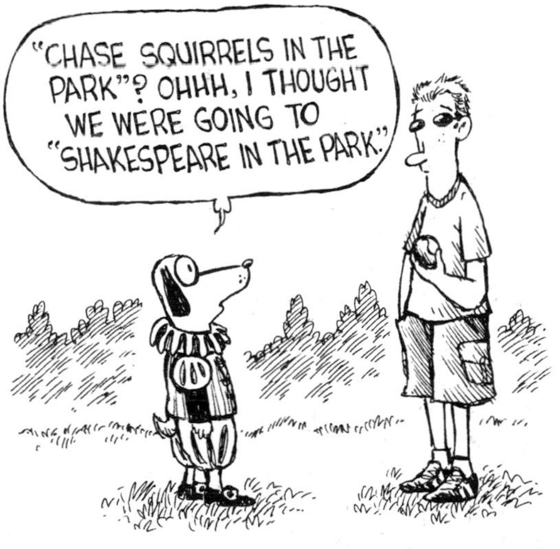
"CHASE SQUIRRELS IN THE PARK"? OHHH, I THOUGHT WE WERE GOING TO "SHAKESPEARE IN THE PARK."

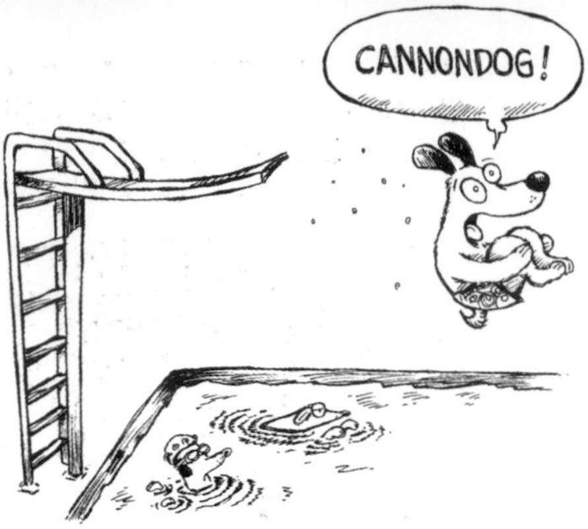
CANNONDOG!

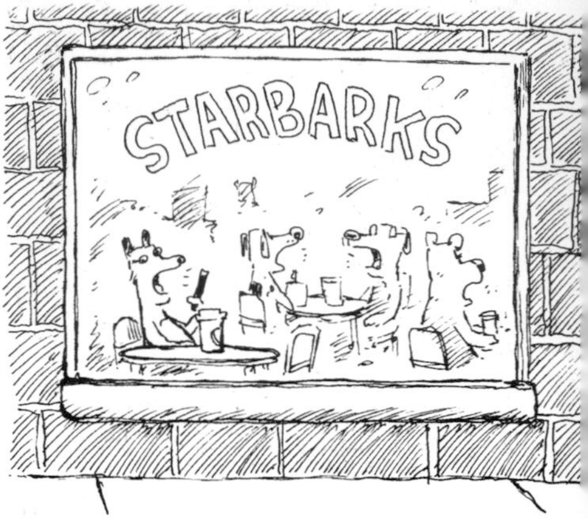
STARBARKS

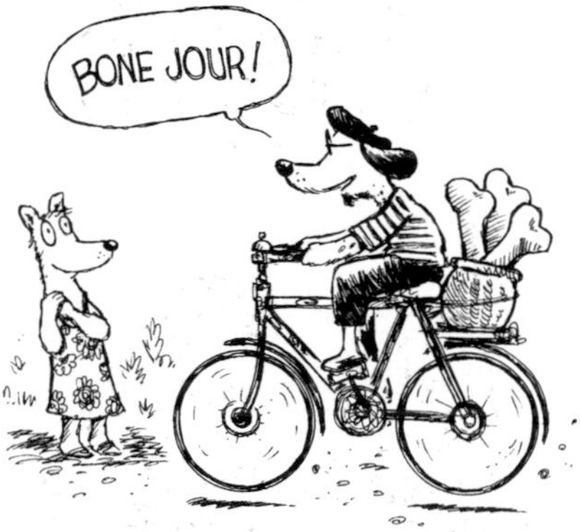
BONE JOUR!

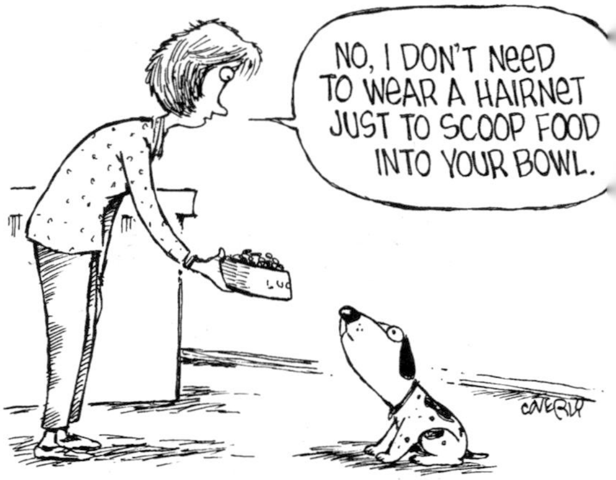
NO, I DON'T NEED TO WEAR A HAIRNET JUST TO SCOOP FOOD INTO YOUR BOWL.

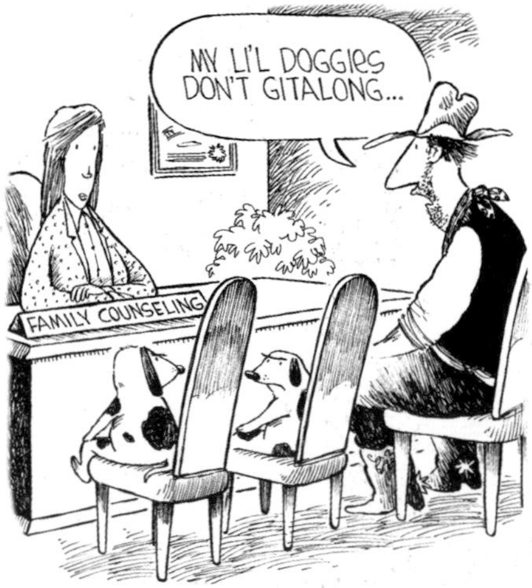
MY LI'L DOGGIES DON'T GITALONG...
FAMILY COUNSELING

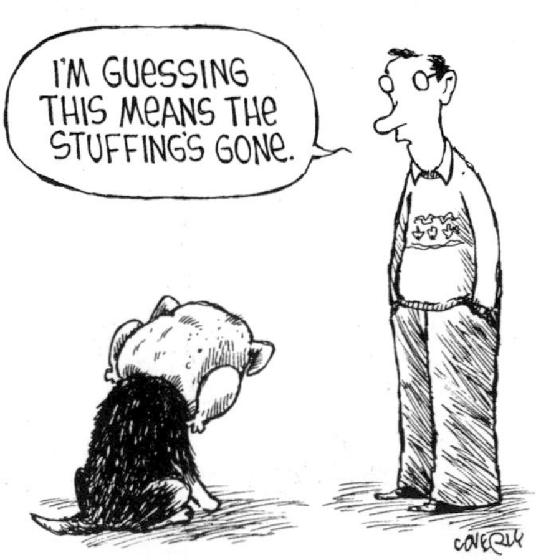
I'M GUESSING THIS MEANS THE STUFFING'S GONE.

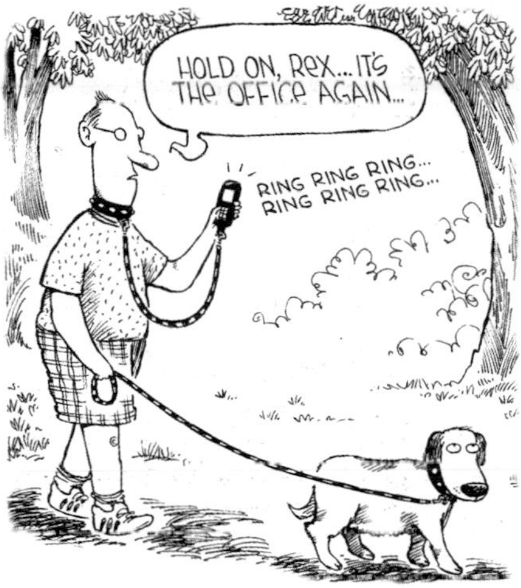
HOLD ON, REX... IT'S THE OFFICE AGAIN...
RING RING RING... RING RING RING...

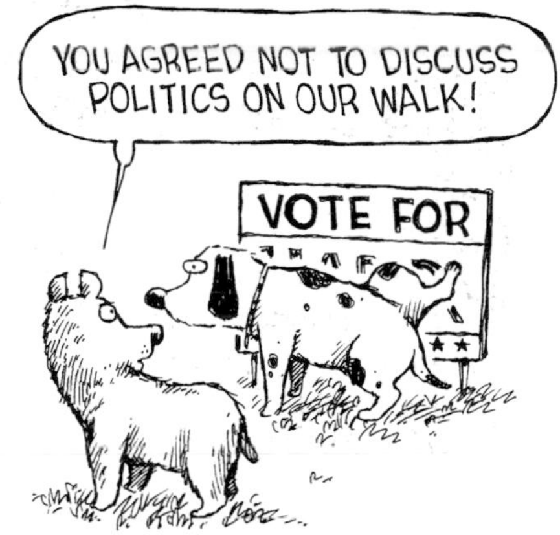
YOU AGREED NOT TO DISCUSS POLITICS ON OUR WALK!
VOTE FOR

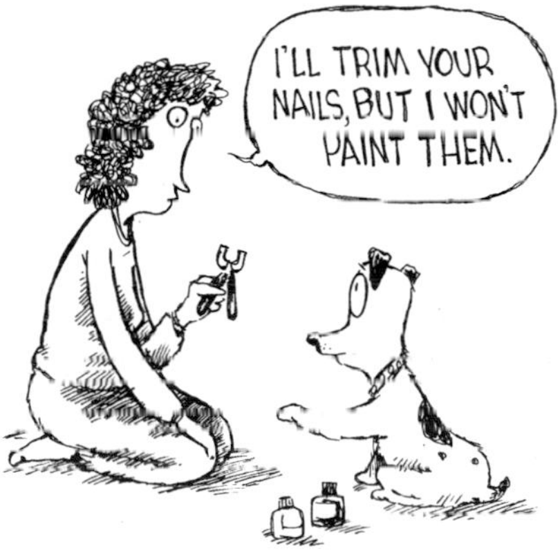
I'LL TRIM YOUR NAILS, BUT I WON'T PAINT THEM.

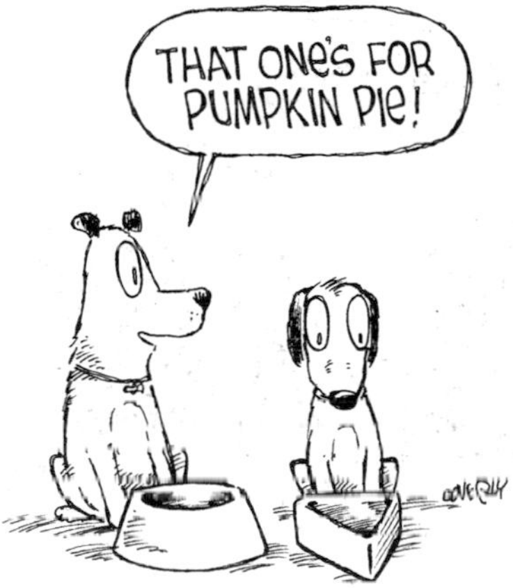
THAT ONE'S FOR PUMPKIN PIE!

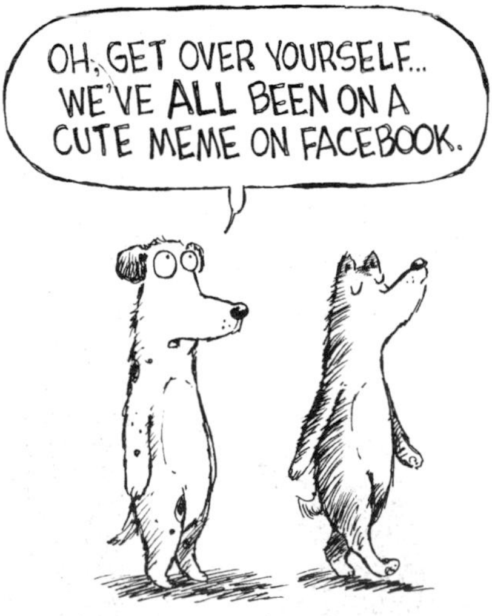
OH, GET OVER YOURSELF... WE'VE ALL BEEN ON A CUTE MEME ON FACEBOOK.

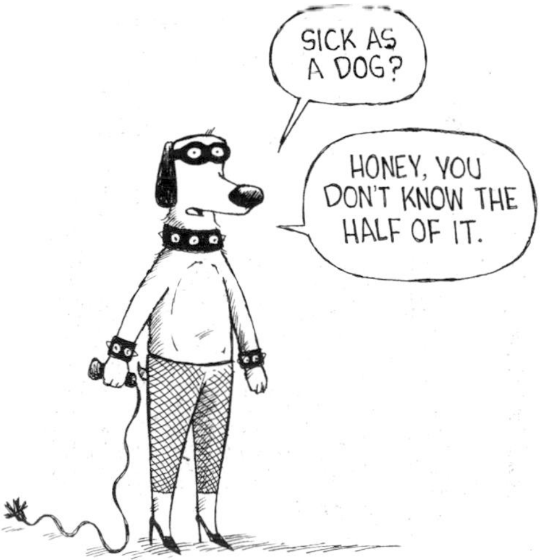
SICK AS A DOG?
HONEY, YOU DON'T KNOW THE HALF OF IT.

Dogs are our link to paradise.
They don't know evil or jealousy or discontent.
To sit with a dog on a hillside on a glorious afternoon is to be back in Eden, where doing nothing was not boring—it was peace.

—MILAN KUNDERA

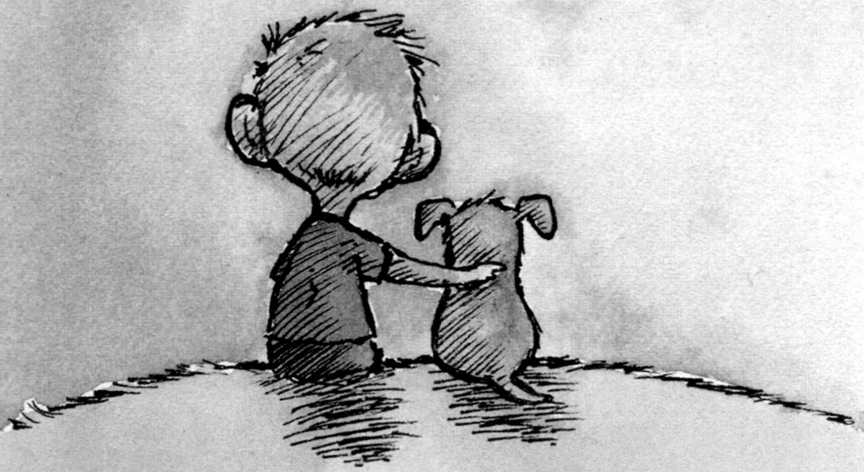